The Developmental State

A volume in the series

Cornell Studies in Political Economy

EDITED BY PETER J. KATZENSTEIN

A full list of titles in the series appears at the end of the book.

Contents

Contents

Contributors

Ha-Joon Chang is Assistant Director of Development Studies, Faculty of Economics and Politics, University of Cambridge.

Bruce Cumings is Norman and Edna Freehling Professor of International History and East Asian Political Economy at the University of Chicago

Ronald J. Herring is John S. Knight Professor of International Relations and Professor of Government, Cornell University.

Chalmers Johnson is President of Japan Policy Research Institute.

Atul Kohli is Professor of Politics and International Affairs at Princeton University.

Michael Loriaux is Associate Professor of Political Science at Northwestern University.

T. J. Pempel is Boeing Professor of International Studies at the Henry M. Jackson School of International Studies, University of Washington.

Ben Ross Schneider is Associate Professor of Political Science, Northwestern University.

Juhana Vartiainen is Senior Research Fellow at Trade Union Institute, Stockholm, Sweden

Meredith Woo-Cumings is Associate Professor of Political Science and Director of The Roundtable on Political Economy (ROPE) at Northwestern University.

Preface

The Owl of Minerva, it is said, takes flight as evening falls. The 1997 financial disaster in East Asia, which started with the collapse of the real estate market in Thailand in the early summer and then spread to Northeast Asia in the autumn, has struck many observers as an omen of the encroaching evening for the Asian model of development, beckoning us to reassess the legacy of industrialization in the region. Indeed, the World Bank recently embarked on a project called "Rethinking the East Asian Miracle," hoping to revise its earlier twists and turns on the "East Asian Miracle" (as the most sustained economic growth of the twentieth century is often called), which finally had convinced some elements in the Bank that East Asia was truly different, especially regarding the role of the state in the economy. After the Asian crisis, however, it is back to the drawing board.

The extraordinary fluctuation of American thinking about East Asia in the past decade—from sharp worries about Japan being hegemonic in the twenty-first century to many contemporary judgments that the market is the only way to go—should give us pause, for a number of reasons. One is philosophical: as the result of some happenstance or sudden new phenomenon (such as the Asian crisis), the entire developmental experience of the last thirty years in East Asia is thrown into question. As the dominant global viewpoint turns and evolves, a mirage replaces a "miracle," and "crony capitalism" comes to signify a region where remarkable growth was once said to go hand in hand with remarkable equity. The World Bank's preferred method of revisiting the East Asian experience now is to go through a developmental checklist of apparent pathologies—opaque regulatory frameworks or ineffective corporate governance—that remained in the shadow of more familiar indicators of development. But why now and not in the past? The problems of corruption and lack of transparency in Southeast Asia and financial instability in the massively leveraged Korean corporate sector have long been understood and well documented. How can one era represent a developmental miracle and the next a mere mirage, when nothing fundamental has changed?

If a particular pattern of industrial development, an intricate relationship between government and business, or a complex of existing policies can be shown in 1998 to be deleterious to the health of a particular economy or even a menace to the good workings of the world economy, that fact does not allow us the pretense that several decades of history can easily be erased. In 1932 the American people decided that the very economic system now presented to the world as the only possible model, namely, the laissez-faire, transparent, price-sensitive free market, was precisely the "Hooverism" that had brought on the crash of 1929, world depression, and catastrophic levels of unemployment. It was half a century before another president could win an election on that same free-market platform. Of course, that does not mean that laissez-faire was necessarily wrong or the cause of the depression, but people *thought* it was the cause—and all the king's horses and all the king's men could not reverse that verdict for two generations.

Now it is fair to say that no other developing country was more frequently praised, lauded, supported, emulated, and showered with all manner of American and global aid than South Korea since it inaugurated its export-led growth in the mid-1960s, a program begun and sustained under close American, International Monetary Fund (IMF), and World Bank tutelage. It cannot be the case that in a few short years or months, this same Republic of Korea (ROK) became a cesspool of crony capitalism. To think so is not simply to read history backward (the fallacy of "presentism") but also to misconstrue completely the very possibilities of reform in our time. Every political economy persists, changes, goes forward or backward, in some deeply complex, intimate, and consequential relationship to its own past. Yet our very human perceptions lead us precisely toward an act of erasure, whereby everything that seemed solid and durable for many decades evaporates overnight in the wake of new phenomena, unintended consequences, or a general reversal of human verdicts and judgments.

There is another sense in which the act of "rethinking" should give us pause: there never was a consensus about the nature and causes of economic development in East Asia (with decades of World Bank studies perhaps proving this point best). Explaining the success of East Asian economies has always been contentious, subject to ideological overtones and shifting judgments and opinions. Even the World Bank's *Miracle* report, so cautious and middle-of-the-road that it seemed to have been written in the best tradition of Harry Truman's proverbial two-handed economist (forever saying "on the one hand" and "on the other hand"), was widely criticized when it was published. Hence it is not clear exactly what it is that we should *re*think; we must wonder what the next iteration will yield. We should expect more than just another chicken scratch on the palimpsest of development.

The contributors to this volume believe that there is less a need to rethink than fundamentally to reexamine the framework of East Asian growth—*and* our own assumptions about that growth. We hope to convey a sense of East Asia in *time* and *place*, thus to understand the historical interplay of forces—historical, political, market, security—that have determined the structure of opportunity in East Asia, which situated and launched the different nations of the area in a path-dependent manner. It is critical that we think historically, not just for the sake of the past but also to delineate the limits of feasible reform in East Asia today, so we can recommend policies that are plausible and effective and not ideologically driven. This is part of the purpose of the book.

What does it mean to think about East Asia in time and place? First, it is to recognize that there is no such thing as the "Asian" crisis, not even an "East Asian" one—even though many analysts still lump free-market Hong Kong together with developmental Korea. East Asia is an enormously heterogeneous and diverse area and cannot be reduced to a single model of trade or political economy. The *Miracle* report recognized this but preferred to place the differences on a continuum, such that Southeast Asia was perceived to be more liberal and open, and Northeast Asia less so—and the twain could meet when Northeast Asia and other developing countries moved closer to the Southeast Asian model. But what if the Northeast Burnham Wood cannot move to the Southeast Dunsinane because Korea has less in common with Thailand than it has with, say, Mexico?

Northeast Asia contains three countries which formed the core of the prewar Japanese empire and whose economic structures were tightly interwoven and articulated: Japan, South Korea and Taiwan. Notwithstanding the great suffering that Japan inflicted on its former colonies, the postwar developmental trajectories of South Korea and Taiwan were heavily influenced by the models and policies that Japan imposed on them before World War II or demonstrated to them in the 1950s and 1960s during Japan's heyday of rapid, export-led growth. Nothing succeeds like success, and thus South Korea and Taiwan learned lessons, absorbed advanced technologies and capital from Japan, and embarked on a similar trajectory of light-industrial exporting under multiyear plans, guided by strong state ministries (if less so in Taiwan than Korea). This gave all three economies a highly neomercantilist, nationalist tendency; in Japan and Korea especially, it meant strong state involvement with and promotion of big economic conglomerates.

We need to be sensitive not just to regional differences in Asia but to very different histories as well. This is another way of saying that we need to be sensitive to "path dependency." South Korea, Japan, and Taiwan are not leopards that can instantly change their spots. We cannot preclude the possibility of Barrington Moore's important point that big changes are often easier than small changes; a radical reform may be possible in East Asia. Of necessity, however, it will be in the direction of an adaptive change, however big, consistent with what went before.

Perhaps the best historical example might be to take the small coterie of foreign IMF and Clinton administration officials who urged and prodded the Korean reform effort in 1997-98 and compare them to the seven-year American occupation of defeated Japan in which the war hero of the Pacific campaigns, General Douglas MacArthur, with the full panoply of extraordinary powers vested in him and his staff at the Supreme Commander of Allied Powers, still could not decisively break the power of the *zaibatsu*—which hunkered down and waited when they could, restructured when they had to, and transmogrified into the post-Occupation *keiretsu*. It was a definite improvement, but not the thorough breakup and reform that MacArthur had planned. We do not expect, just because of the economic difficulties that Japan and South Korea have encountered in the late 1990s, that their political economies will become "more like us," to use James Fallows's phrase. For half a century the United States has sought to make Japan and South Korea "more like us," and yet here they are on the verge of the twenty-first century, still pursuing an economic model more deeply influenced by the historical legacy of nationalism and economic mobilization that has shaped Northeast Asia.

This is not to say that reform is not needed or that the developmental states can continue as before. It would be to everyone's benefit if Japan and South Korea reformed their systems so as to promote more respect for the rule of law (rather than administrative discretion), a concept broadly understood to mean legality, regulation, and transparency throughout the nexus of state, banks, and big business. They need to do this, if for nothing else, to hone the international competitiveness of their industries and come roaring back to prominence. But in this book, we are more concerned with figuring out how things arrived at their current state.

This book grew out of a memorable panel at the annual meeting of the Association of Asian Studies. The intent of the panel was to reexamine the theory of the developmental state, which, for all the criticism that it has weathered over the years, has rarely received full historical and comparative scrutiny. Later on Lawrence Dumas, then dean of Arts and Sciences (and now provost) at Northwestern University, provided the seed money to launch the Roundtable on Political Economy (ROPE), which expanded and carried on the original project, resulting in a major conference at Northwestern. Roger Haydon of Cornell University Press guided this project with unfailing humor, patience, and professionalism, and I thank him for sticking with this book, which is, after all, not entirely uncontroversial in today's academic climate. Peter Katzenstein read the manuscript and offered penetrating criticisms and advice; he is the kind of fair-minded and intelligent reader one can only hope for, and this is a much better book for his input. Kathryn Ibata helped me put together this book at the initial stage, and Erin Chung helped me bring it to fruition.

MEREDITH WOO-CUMINGS

Evanston, Illinois

The Developmental State

CHAPTER ONE

Introduction: Chalmers Johnson and the Politics of Nationalism and Development

Meredith Woo-Cumings

> Capital is wayward and timid in lending itself to new undertakings . . . the State ought to excite the confidence of capitalists.
> —ALEXANDER HAMILTON

This book is about a particular explanation of East Asian industrialization, known as the theory of the developmental state. "Developmental state" is a shorthand for the seamless web of political, bureaucratic, and moneyed influences that structures economic life in capitalist Northeast Asia. This state form originated as the region's idiosyncratic response to a world dominated by the West, and despite many problems associated with it, such as corruption and inefficiency, today state policies continue to be justified by the need to hone the nation's economic competitiveness and by a residual nationalism (even in the contemporary context of globalization).

In this chapter, I want to examine the theory of the developmental state through the prism of Chalmers Johnson's 1982 account: *MITI and the Japanese Miracle.*[1] Johnson, basing his observation on the modal economic planning bureaucracy in Japan, the Ministry of International Trade and Industry (MITI), constructed a Weberian ideal type of an interventionist state that was neither socialist (described as a "plan-

---

1. Chalmers Johnson, *MITI and the Japanese Miracle: The Growth of Industrial Policy, 1925–1975* (Stanford: Stanford University Press, 1982).

irrational" state in which both ownership and management remained in the hands of the state, such as in the former USSR) nor free-market (no plan, and where private control coincided with private ownership) but something different: the plan-rational capitalist developmental state, conjoining private ownership with state guidance. Because this plan-rational Japanese state obtained rapid and sustained industrial growth, as did South Korea with comparable state management of the economy, Johnson's argument about the developmental state came to be seen as a causal argument linking interventionism with rapid economic growth—anywhere in the world.

Johnson's book was not an analytic account in search of causal arrows, however, as anyone familiar with his earlier writings would have realized; rather, it was a historical account in search of meaning—or the intelligible and empathetic "understanding" (*Verstehen*) of heterodox meaning that Max Weber thought essential in the study of different cultures[2]—behind the actions of Japan's policymakers: what circumstances and world views compelled those men to mold institutions that created Japan's famed industrial policy? A different impulse served as the undertow of Northeast Asian development for Johnson, however: nationalism—the exigencies and requirements of national survival and mobilization in a twentieth century dominated by bigger powers in Europe and America. It is often forgotten that Johnson was a prominent scholar of Chinese communism before he wrote about Japan. Much to the consternation of the China field he placed nationalism at the root of Chinese peasant communism; later he would do the same for Japan, setting Japan's industrial policy in the context of Japan's scramble for wealth and power in the world. The centrality to his scholarship of nationalism and social mobilization—and their various manifestations in Northeast Asia in different times and places—has often been poorly understood by scholars working on East Asia and on industrial development.

One big reason for this was the social science and policy orientation of many studies of Japan and Northeast Asia. Because the dependent variable to be explained was "economic growth," research into the political economy of Northeast Asia tended to privilege causal explanations (however spurious) at the expense of the history of economic growth and the context in which such growth occurred. The presentism of social science accounts and the prescriptive, future-oriented nature of policy studies meant that research tended to peak when Japan and other East Asian economies did well, and then to fall when they were perceived to have slid into the doldrums—as in the early 1990s or in the aftermath of the

2. Edward Giddens, introduction to *The Protestant Ethic and the Spirit of Capitalism*, by Max Weber (New York: Charles Scribner's Sons, 1958), pp. 1–2.

"financial crisis" of 1997–98. In other words, a nasty case of attention deficit disorder has plagued a coherent account that would link past with present, yielding a lamentable misunderstanding of what the whole enterprise of the "developmental state" was about.

This volume is concerned less with causality and predictability than with the totality of the Northeast Asian experience, reconsidered and recast against the backdrop of new theorizing about the state and the economy and against the evidence from areas with developmental propinquity to Northeast Asia. The boundaries of the general and the particular and of the predictable and the contingent are far from clear, and the interaction among them is so profoundly complex that we cannot, in the end, apportion the totality of a historical experience into neat causal categories. We seek instead what Hegel meant by the metaphor of the Owl of Minerva: a full understanding of where we have been.

This book has four parts. The first part takes a critical look at the developmental state argument; this introduction is an overview of the many aspects of this argument, seeking to position Johnson's work not only within the context of late developments but also in the context of the twin influences of social mobilization and economic nationalism. Johnson's own article comes next, discussing his argument and its reception. Bruce Cumings then dissects the epistemological basis of the developmental state thesis as exemplified in works by Johnson, Karel van Wolferen, James Fallows, and others. These first three chapters, taken together, present an explication of the developmental state thesis and the archaeology and epistemological underpinning of the original concept.

The second section consists of two historical chapters. Atul Kohli examines the deep colonial background of the developmental state in Korea. T. J. Pempel assesses the historical evolution of the Northeast Asian economies, finding Johnson's arguments about the developmental state wanting in their inward orientation, the implicitly international context of economic nationalism notwithstanding. Pempel also finds the treatment of the popular sector unsatisfactory in the broader literature on the developmental state; when the popular sector is mentioned at all, it is to assert—and not to understand or contest—its acquiescence to the state. Together, these two chapters supply the context for East Asian development—the Japanese imperium for Kohli and postwar American hegemony for Pempel. They cast a wide net capturing concerns that had escaped the more essentialist discourse on the developmental state: the position of labor, the role of land reform in providing stability and support for the developmental state, and the nature of domestic social coalitions.

The third section of the book looks at the "modern" economics of the developmental state. The developmental state paradigm is often thought to be at loggerheads with both neoclassical economics and its cross-dressed version in political science, rational choice theory. The two chapters by economists working in England and Sweden show that this need not be so. Both Ha-Joon Chang and Juhana Vartiainen explain how some of the more recent ideas in economics—for example, the new institutional economics, evolutionary economics, the economics of increasing returns, and transactions theory—can be used to explain the rationality and efficiency of industrial policy.

The concluding section places the developmental state thesis in comparative perspective, overcoming the region-specific tendencies inherent in its original formulation. Michael Loriaux explicitly decouples the developmental state and economic performance, through the example of France (Europe's most unabashedly developmental state): this example illustrates that the developmental state does not necessarily develop. Instead, the developmental state is the stuff of ambition—what Loriaux calls the moral ambition to develop—which is really another way of invoking Johnson's nationalist incitement to development, Cumings's popular acceptance of hegemonic ideology, or simply Albert Hirschman's elusive "will to develop." Ben Ross Schneider follows with an agenda contrapuntal to that of Loriaux: in Latin America, too, there was the moral ambition to develop, but countries there chose a very different (bureaucratic) way to express this ambition than did either their French or Japanese counterparts. Ronald Herring then examines the very different experience of India: that of the failed developmental state.

LINEAGES OF MERCANTILISM AND NATIONALISM IN EAST ASIA

"There is no new thing under the sun," says the Preacher in Ecclesiastes, for "the thing that hath been, it is that which shall be." Perhaps this is also true of the controversy generated by the developmental state idea. Commenting on the sociology of economic analysis in the nineteenth century, Joseph Schumpeter noted that the mercantilist ideas of some German scholars (back to which the notion of the "developmental state" may be traced) were spurned by the large majority of economists: "[The liberal economists] could see nothing but error in them . . . and developed a practice according to which it was all but sufficient for putting a work out of court to attach to it the slightest tinge of mercantilism."[3]

The economists that Schumpeter criticized came from the Anglo-Saxon, Adam Smith tradition and found much to criticize in mercantilist analysis. But mercantilism was a pragmatic adaptation, a theory of eco-

3. Ecclesiastes 1:8 Authorized (King James) Version; Joseph Schumpeter, *History of Economic Analysis* (New York: Oxford University Press, 1954), p. 336.

nomic practice, and not a theory of how economies are supposed to operate. As Perry Anderson put it, "Mercantilism was precisely a theory of the coherent intervention of the political state into the workings of the economy, in the joint interests of the prosperity of the one and the power of the other."[4] Or, to quote Alexander Hamilton, "Capital is wayward and timid in lending itself to new undertakings, and the State ought to excite the confidence of capitalists, who are ever cautious and sagacious, by aiding them overcome the obstacles that lie in the way of all experiments."[5] These practices constituted, at the end of the day, adequate means to obtain rationally defensible ends, such as state building, national autonomy, and the augmentation of national power. But this was also economic heresy: anyone refusing to believe in free trade (the "absolute and eternal wisdom for all times and places") could be labeled "a fool or a crook or both."[6]

Like the earlier mercantilist arguments, the developmental state thesis derives from observations about actual economic practice—first in Japan and later in South Korea and Taiwan. The idea that coherent state intervention into the workings of the market might have something to do with Japanese growth has a long, scholarly pedigree. The works of E. H. Norman on the role of the Japanese state and those of William Lockwood on Japanese economic history are perhaps the best examples of this tradition in the English language.[7] But as Ha-Joon Chang points out in his essay for this volume, the idea that the state can be developmental was at the heart of the writings of early development economists, such as Gunnar Myrdal, Paul Baran, P. N. Rosenstein-Rodan, and Simon Kuznets: in other words, the developmental state is not something new under the sun.

Johnson's account of Japan became influential not because of its original theoretical or analytic power but because it spoke the truth about a Japanese predicament that was instantly recognizable to anyone who has lived it, or who can imagine it by being familiar with similar circumstances. *MITI and the Japanese Miracle* is not a deductive political science study that uses Japan as a "country case" in comparative politics. Rather, it is an account of how the Japanese, faced with the harsh reality of a world dominated by the Western powers, devised a system of political economy

4. Perry Anderson, *Lineages of the Absolutist State* (New York: New Left Books, 1974), p. 36.

5. Alexander Hamilton, quoted in Chalmers Johnson, *The Industrial Policy Debate* (San Francisco: Institute for Contemporary Studies, 1984).

6. Schumpeter, *History of Economic Analysis*, p. 397. For his argument contra Adam Smith's "unintelligent" criticism of "the commercial or mercantile system" in book 4 of *Wealth of Nations*, see chap. 7, "The 'Mercantilist' Literature."

7. E. H. Norman, *Origins of the Modern Japanese State: Selected Writings of E. H. Norman*, ed. John Dower (1941; New York: Pantheon, 1975), and William Lockwood, *The Economic Development of Japan* (Princeton: Princeton University Press, 1968).

that was both admirable and dangerous. Johnson's scholarly task was to make the Japanese experience, wisdom and folly included, explicable. One way to understand the relationship between nationalism in Japan (or South Korea or Taiwan) and economic growth is to invoke José Ortega y Gasset's discussion of the word "incitement."

> The expression most fragrant with the scent of life, and one of the prettiest in the dictionary, is to my mind the word "incitement." It has no meaning except in the disciplines of life. Physics does not know of it. In physics one thing does not incite another; it causes it and the cause produces an effect in proportion to itself. . . . But when the spur's point ever so lightly touches its flank, the thoroughbred breaks into a gallop, generously out of proportion to the impulse of the spur. The reaction of the horse, rather than a response to an outer impulse, is a release of exuberant inner energies. Indeed, a skittish horse, with its nervous head and fiery eye, is a splendid image of stirring life. Thus we imagine the magnificent stallion whom Caligula called Incitus and made a member of the Roman Senate.[8]

How nationalist impulses incited Chinese peasants or MITI bureaucrats to correct "status inconsistency" vis-à-vis the United States is not well understood.[9] But it is central to Johnson's career scholarship and to Liah Greenfeld's powerful analysis of nationalism. Johnson conveyed the truth that the Japanese state was, like the Korean or the Chinese states, a hard-bitten one that chose economic development as the means to combat Western imperialism and ensure national survival: for most of the twentieth century, economic development was a recipe for "overcoming depression, war preparations, war fighting, postwar reconstruction, and independence from U.S. aid," as Johnson notes in Chapter 2. This is in the end what Weber thought comparative politics was all about: the ability to apprehend the essential quality of one country (or group of countries) so as to figure out the politics of another.

The legitimacy of the East Asian state's economic interventions and the developmental determination shown by its population present a vexing phenomenon, a true problem of comparative understanding. To Hirschman, this was the most important puzzle to reckon with. In *The Strategy of Economic Development*, he wrote:

> If we were to think in terms of a "binding agent" for development are we simply not saying that development depends on the ability and determination of

8. José Ortega y Gasset, "The Sportive Origin of the State," in *History as a System* (New York: W. W. Norton, 1961), p. 22.

9. Liah Greenfeld, *Nationalism: Five Roads to Modernity* (Cambridge: Harvard University Press, 1992).

a nation and its citizens to organize themselves for development? Perhaps this is not as tautological and vague as it sounds. By focusing on determination, for instance, we are taking hold of one of the specific characteristics of the development process in today's underdeveloped countries, namely the fact that they are latecomers. This condition is bound to make their development into a less spontaneous and more deliberate process than was the case in the countries where the process first occurred.[10]

Like Hirschman, Johnson places the "binding agent" of East Asian development in both the context of "late development" and the East Asian setting of revolutionary nationalism—not a garden variety nationalism but one that grew from war and imperialism and manifested itself variously: communism in China and North Korea, and the capitalist developmental state in Japan, South Korea, and Taiwan. This is also why the East Asian developmental states have more in common with the late-developing European nations of the past and less with contemporary developing societies in Latin America and elsewhere. Indeed, Hirschman argued that these different security contexts explained why Latin America could not evolve along the "late development" model, adopting instead the "late late development" pattern, relying on import substitution and overvalued exchange rates.[11]

To understand Johnson's insistence that the successful capitalist developmental states have been quasi-revolutionary regimes, carrying out social projects their societies endorsed, one has to go back to his first book, *Peasant Nationalism and Communist Power* (1962). It was in this book that Johnson first articulated his ideas about the nature of nationalism in modern East Asia, the importance of war in establishing institutions of social mobilization (the Communist Party in China, MITI in Japan), and the role of ideology in revolutionary social transformation.

Johnson argued that the Communist rise to power in China should be understood as a species of nationalist movement and that Chinese peasants became unified and politicized as a result of the drastic restructuring of Chinese life that came on the heels of the Japanese conquest of north and east China. The Communist Party was seen as the leader of a war-energized, radical nationalist movement; its ideology an adjunct to Chinese nationalism. It was an argument deeply discomfiting both for the right and the left in scholarship on China, but it did recognize, by giving credit where credit was due, the agency and purpose to Chinese Communist action (at a time when its leaders were assumed to be undeviating creatures of Moscow).

---

10. Albert O. Hirschman, *The Strategy of Economic Development* (New Haven: Yale University Press, 1958), p. 8.
11. Albert O. Hirschman, "The Political Economy of Import Substitution Industrialization in Latin America," *Quarterly Journal of Economics* 82 (1968): 1–32.

Nationalism was not an abstract ideal but a reality born of struggle with the enemy: hence Johnson dates the rise of Chinese nationalism to the 1937–45 period of mass mobilization against the Japanese and not to the 1920s or the Kiangsi period of the early 1930s. As for the nationalism of the prewar period (to which so much China scholarship was devoted), it was "a nationalist movement with a head and no body." It was only when the peasants in the occupied areas in China were socially mobilized by war and resistance organizations that "they became a national population."[12] We might call this the Chinese equivalent of "Peasants into Frenchmen." Elsewhere in his works on comparative communism, Johnson advanced the argument about the "goal culture" of communism, where a key priority was the maintenance of institutions necessary for achieving national goals (such as a classless society, the defeat of imperialism, socialist construction, and so on).[13]

This theoretical scaffolding—the analysis of nationalism, wartime social mobilization, and goal culture in communist society—became the formula for understanding Japan as well. For Johnson, Japan is a case of "an economy mobilized for war but never demobilized during peacetime," and his examination of Japan through the Chinese looking glass led him to think that "the Japanese capitalist developmental state seemed to have squared the socialist circle; it involved very high levels of social goal setting without the known consequences of communism."[14]

This transfer of Chinese experience to Japan has had curious consequences. *MITI and the Japanese Miracle* is a country-specific study without much reference to the external world, as T. J. Pempel correctly notes in Chapter 5 of this volume, but it became more than an account of idiosyncratic practices, analyzed in isolated splendor. It is an *implicitly* comparative account, containing within it a truth about East Asian developmental regimes and their outlook. This is why a whole generation of scholars in comparative politics can deploy any number of country cases (the larger the *N* the better) and still not grasp the basic truth about the political economy of any single country, and why a single case study by an astute analyst of politics can generate insights that are instantly recognizable as true for many different societies.

The wartime period, so important to Johnson for giving rise to both Japanese (economic) nationalism and Chinese (communist) nationalism,

12. Chalmers Johnson, *Peasant Nationalism and Communist Power* (Stanford: Stanford University Press, 1962), pp. 24, 26; see also Chalmers Johnson, "Peasant Nationalism Revisited: The Biography of a Book," *China Quarterly* (December 1977): 766–85.

13. Chalmers Johnson, *Revolution and the Social System* (Stanford: Hoover Institution, 1964), p. 25.

14. Chalmers Johnson, *Japan, Who Governs? The Rise of the Developmental State* (New York: W. W. Norton, 1995), p. 10.

may in fact be the most critical period for understanding the rise of the developmental state elsewhere in East Asia. For Korea, it was Japanese colonialism in this wartime period that bequeathed what Hirschman might call a "growth perspective," comprising not only the developmental determination but also the perception of the essential nature of the road leading toward the developmental goal.

War and colonialism as the deep background for the Korean developmental state was an idea first advanced by Bruce Cumings in *The Origins of the Korean War*. In that book he argued that the Japanese created a kind of developmentalism in Korea that was profoundly predatory but one that also achieved rapid industrial growth; in other words, the early 1960s was not the first time for such growth in South Korea. He also argued that massive social mobilization and dislocation caused by the Pacific War (1931–45) and war-related industrialization led to popular rebellion and civil war after 1945.[15] In my book *Race to the Swift* I also argued for the critical importance to colonial Korea of the wartime period. Korea, as an entrepôt between Manchuria and Japan and as a natural supplier of an abundant variety of mineral resources, cheap labor, and hydroelectricity, was a logical location for a forced industrialization program of the most brutal kind. Its ruling coalition was based on an alliance of the repressive state and "the new zaibatsu" (as the prototype *chaebol*, the Korean transliteration of *zaibatsu*),[16] using the same system of credit-based industrial financing that came to characterize postwar Korea.[17] In Chapter 4 of this volume, Atul Kohli provides an overview of the legacy of Japanese colonialism, which, for all the pain and suffering that it inflicted on the colonized people, seems to have provided Korea with an institutional template for later development.

War in Asia, Johnson thought, was the critical experience that defined the world view of the men who dominated MITI through 1975, "men born in the middle to late Meiji era who virtually all survived the war and continued to work for the government as if they were uniformed military officers." I have argued the same for South Korea's economic policymakers who came into their adulthood toward the end of the war, either in the Japanese military or in its colonial bureaucracy. And one might say the same for octogenarian leaders of China who belatedly seem to find in the East Asian developmental state a better model for continuing growth

15. Bruce Cumings, *The Origins of the Korean War*, vol. 1 (Princeton: Princeton University Press, 1979); see also Bruce Cumings, "The Origins and Development of the Northeast Asian Political Economy," *International Organization* 38, no. 1 (Winter 1984): 1–40.

16. A "chaebol" is a family-owned and managed group of companies that exercise monopolistic or oligopolistic control in product lines and industries, isomorphic to the Japanese *shinko zaibatsu* of the prewar era.

17. Jung-en Woo [Meredith Woo-Cumings], *Race to the Swift: State and Finance in Korean Industrialization* (New York: Columbia University Press, 1991).

and a transition to a planned market economy than have the former Soviet bloc countries. It is in this sense that "the developmental state," as Johnson claims, in Chapter 2 "actually exists in time and space in East Asia and also exists as an abstract generalization about the essence of the East Asian examples. It is both particular and generalizable."

In the postwar period, a nationalism that so incessantly demanded of the populace economic sacrifices and compliance was based, in the case of South Korea and Taiwan, on the military standoff with their quondam compatriot states. Curiously, this insight has long eluded American social science work on South Korea and Taiwan, two places born of civil wars that have not ended; the cold war against their respective enemies continues to define the parameters of state action in these countries, subsuming the development of social and economic institutions to exigencies of national survival. Carl Schmitt, a leading thinker in Weimar Germany, theorized that political actions and motives could be reduced to merely this: that between friend and enemy. "War is neither the aim nor the purpose nor even the very content of politics. But as an ever present possibility it is the leading presupposition which determines in a characteristic way human action and thinking and thereby creates a specifically political behavior. . . . The political does not reside in the battle itself, which possesses its own technical, psychological, and military laws, but in the mode of behavior which is determined by this possibility, by clearly evaluating the concrete situation and thereby being able to distinguish correctly the real friend and the real enemy."[18]

The existence for Taiwan and South Korea of enemies, as well as the ever present possibility of war, has continued to define the relationship of state to society. For Japan, economic nationalism is an attempt to correct status inconsistency with the United States and the European countries. In fact, the pull of nationalism—catching up and getting even—is such an important motivating force behind state action that Johnson wonders if economic development might not have been a mere side effect of the pursuit of economic nationalism.[19]

FINANCE: THE NERVES OF THE DEVELOPMENTAL STATE

Finance is the tie that binds the state to the industrialists in the developmental state. The sixteenth-century French jurist Jean Bodin called finance "the nerves of the state." Theda Skocpol makes the same argu-

18. Carl Schmitt, *The Concept of the Political* (New Brunswick: Rutgers University Press [1976]), pp. 34, 37.

19. Chalmers Johnson, remark at Northwestern University, May 30, 1994.

ment: "The answers to [questions about financial resources] provide the best possible general insight into the direct or indirect leverage a state is likely to have for realizing any sort of goal it may pursue. For a state's means of raising and deploying financial resources tell us more than could any other single factor about its existing (and its immediately potential) capacities to create or strengthen state organizations, to employ personnel, to co-opt political support, to subsidize economic enterprises, and to fund social programs."[20]

Much of the analysis of the developmental state in East Asia and Europe has thus centered on the national structure of finance. In an essay on economic policies in Japan, South Korea, and Taiwan, Johnson argues that state control of finance was the most important, if not the defining, aspect of the developmental state, followed by other aspects such as labor relations, autonomy of the economic bureaucracy, the combination of incentives and command structures, and the existence of the zaibatsu (or the *keiretsu*, the chaebol, or the Chinese business groups).[21] John Zysman, his occasional collaborator from the University of California at Berkeley, elaborating on the insights of Alexander Gerschenkron, also made the argument that credit-based financial structures in France and Japan were effective conduits of industrial policy. The advantage of the credit-based system is that the state can exert influence over the economy's investment pattern and guide sectoral mobility, because in such a structure, firms rely on bank credit for raising finance beyond retained earnings and respond quickly to the state's policy, as expressed in interest rate and other financial policies.[22]

Three of the contributors to this volume wrote their first books on the politics of finance. Loriaux has written extensively about the financial policies of the French "developmental state" and the many problems associated with it, leading eventually to the dismantling of the financial regulatory structure in the 1980s. The Finnish economist Vartiainen has written on the political economy of the credit-rationing system in Finland, which was operative from the early 1940s to the early 1980s. Finland's system bore a stunning resemblance to those in Japan and South Korea and was characterized by state control of interest rates and the prevalence of bank loans as sources of industrial finance (and not equity capital). Foreign capital flows were strictly controlled, and credit was in excess demand for much of the forty-year period. My own work on the fi-

20. Theda Skocpol, "Bringing the State Back In," *Items* 36, nos. 1–2 (June 1982): 6.

21. Chalmers Johnson, "Political Institutions and Economic Performance: The Government-Business Relationship in Japan, South Korea, and Taiwan," in Frederic C. Deyo, ed., *The Political Economy of the New Asian Industrialism* (Ithaca: Cornell University Press, 1987).

22. John Zysman, *Governments, Markets, and Growth: Financial Systems and the Politics of Industrial Change* (Ithaca: Cornell University Press, 1983).

nancial structure of South Korea also showed how the developmental state, operating in an economically munificent realm of cold war politics and security, channeled capital (subsidized though foreign loans or low interest rates) to Korea's big business (the chaebol) and in the process buttressed its own power by creating political interest groups that could be molded into a developmental coalition.[23]

Such a financial structure was also inherently fragile and unstable, for three reasons. First, the incentive of a virtual interest subsidy was so attractive that those firms with access to the loan window tended to resist going public, preferring to remain highly leveraged. But, then, bankruptcy was a perennial threat because highly leveraged firms were vulnerable to declines in current earnings to below the levels required by debt repayment—a fixed cost, compared with payments on equity, as a share of profits. Banks often ended up carrying a huge amount of "nonperforming" loans, and if these were incurred by mammoth firms (the chaebol), the state often had no choice but to bail them out.

Second, because this system is continually in a situation of what Theodore Lowi calls the "state of permanent receivership," whereby any institution large enough to be a significant factor in the community has its stability underwritten (the system promotes bankruptcy but the state cannot let big firms go bankrupt), it is in the interest of the firms to expand in size, to become large enough that the possibility of bankruptcy would pose a social threat.[24] While the state is chary of the expansion mania of firms, once credit is allocated it is difficult to track down the actual use of the funds because various bookkeeping devices can hide it. Thus, the excessive concern of the chaebol with expansion rather than with the soundness of their financial base bred instability for the Korean financial system.

The third point is that since Korea has a small domestic market and thus relies excessively on export (even more so than Japan), Korean firms are tested in the fires of international competition and are more vulnerable to external shocks. A slowdown in the global economy can shake the economy from the roots, and firms can collapse like a house of cards. In the late 1990s when the price of Korea's exports nose-dived, in part because of the devaluation of the Chinese yuan and the Japanese yen and in part because of excessive Korean investment in those industries suffering

23. Michael Loriaux, *France after Hegemony: International Change and Financial Reform* (Ithaca: Cornell University Press, 1991); Juhana Vartiainen, "Finnish Monetary Policy in the Credit Rationing Era," *Finnish Economic Papers* 7, no. 1 (Spring 1984): 42–55; and Woo, *Race to the Swift*.

24. Theodore Lowi, *The End of Liberalism: The Second Republic of the United States* (New York: W. W. Norton, 1979).

from a global glut (such as semiconductors, electronics, and automobiles), the profitability of Korean firms crashed through the floor, helping to set the stage for the massive financial panic that swept through East Asia.

Thus, state interventionism in the market is necessarily Janus-faced. The state can achieve its goal by manipulating the financial structure, but once it does so, it has to socialize risk, either through inflationary refinancing (monetary means) of the nonperforming loans to bail the firms out, or through expansion of the state equity share of the banks (essentially fiscal means) so as to write off the bad loans. The former is indirect taxation on the populace, and the latter, direct.

This sort of financial system was what enabled industrial policy in South Korea and in Japan; the downside was the problem of moral hazard (that is, bailing out firms in trouble) and socialization of the risk. Such dilemmas of the developmental state were dramatically illustrated in 1997–98.

BUREAUCRACY

In his contribution to this volume, Ben Ross Schneider argues that the main distinction between the developmental states in East Asia and Latin America is the structure of the bureaucracy. Schneider characterizes the Latin American "developmental state" (or the desarrollista state) in four aspects. The first is what he calls "political capitalism," where profits and investment depend on decisions made in the state. The second is "developmentalism": the existence of "a dominant developmental discourse on the necessity of industrialization and of state intervention to promote it." The third feature is the political exclusion of the popular sector, and the last is the tradition of a fluid, weakly institutionalized bureaucracy in which political appointments structure power and representation: in other words, "appointive bureaucracy" in which tens of thousands of government officials are affected by regime change (as in Brazil), rather than the professional, meritocratic bureaucracy one finds in Japan or South Korea. The first three attributes of the desarrollo state are evident in the late-developing economies in East Asia, but the fourth constitutes a radical departure. In appointive bureaucracies, Schneider argues, the power of the bureaucrats is highly unstable, and their interests cannot be read off the organizational chart. These officials hold administrative positions but rarely administer in the Weberian fashion. They are also major political players (to the extent that they have wide discretionary power) but lack independent power bases. Consequently the bureaucrats in

Latin American *desarrollo* states do not constitute a powerful social group with predictable and coherent interests; rather, they are brokers, deal makers, and idea peddlers. In Japan, by contrast, the answer to the question, Who governs? is precisely the bureaucracy. In his latest collection of essays Johnson writes:

> Who governs Japan is Japan's elite state bureaucracy. It is recruited from the top ranks of the best law schools in the country; appointment is made on the basis of legally binding national examinations—the prime minister can appoint only about twenty ministers and agency chiefs—and is unaffected by election results. The bureaucracy drafts virtually all laws, ordinances, orders, regulations, and licenses that govern society. It also has extensive extra-legal powers of "administrative guidance" and is comparatively unrestrained in any way, both in theory and in practice, by the judicial system. To find a comparable official elite in the United States, one would have to turn to those who staffed the E-Ring of the Pentagon or the Central Intelligence Agency at the height of the Cold War.[25]

The duties of this bureaucracy are to formulate broad industrial policy, identify the means for implementing it, and ensure (highly regulated) competition in designated strategic sectors.

Ronald Herring, in Chapter 10 of this book, does not doubt that the East Asian developmental states have been effective, but what he wants to know is how and why they got to be so effective, when the same developmental bureaucracy in India, boasting of a long civil service tradition and the deployment of India's best and brightest in its ranks, failed to achieve the same end. Herring's account of the Indian failure is both general and particular, explained by the nature of the state, the business class, and their relationship; domestic politics; and the circumstances of India's absorption into the world system. In the end he boils the Indian difference down to the terrific obstacles India has faced in "managing a continental political economy, more an empire than nation . . . with one arm tied behind its back by commitment to liberal democracy." This account of India also has much to say about China—another continental political economy, more an empire than a nation, but hamstrung not by commitment to liberal democracy but by its residual socialism. Herring invokes Charles Lindblom's analogy about the strong thumb and nimble fingers to suggest that "the successful developmental state is one that knows when to quit." This is another way of putting Johnson's insight that the task of the developmental state in Japan (or South Korea or Taiwan) is a planned transition from a producer-oriented, high-growth economy to a

25. Johnson, *Japan*, p. 13.

consumer-oriented one, which may mean phasing itself out. The point here is not whether it uses the strong thumb or nimble fingers but whether it has the capacity to decide and enact which fingers to use and how, and when to quit. The relationship between the bureaucracy and business has been learned and perfected over time, through a long process of institutional adaptation, sometimes giving more room to the private sector to regulate itself (as in the 1930s) and sometimes taking it away (as in the 1940s), and building on that experience, eventually devising a mode of public-private cooperation that meets the demands of the time. Another way of saying this is that the developmental state is a diachronic phenomenon, occurring over a long period of time in various incarnations and poised to adapt itself to still newer realities.

A scholar of Latin America was quick to note this point. In *Embedded Autonomy*, Peter Evans argued that the bureaucracy, to be called "developmental," had to be effectively "embedded" in society, through "a concrete set of connections that link the state intimately and aggressively to particular social groups with whom the state shares a joint project of transformation." The archetypal developmental state was, for Evans, that rare beast with its tentacles reaching deep into the society while managing to keep its corporate integrity intact.[26] In Chapter 2 of this volume, Johnson put the same point like this: "I invoked the concept of 'developmental state' to characterize the role the Japanese state played in Japan's extraordinary and unexpected postwar enrichment. *I never said or implied that the state was solely responsible for Japan's economic achievements or that it behaved like the state in command economies in assigning tasks and duties to the Japanese people*" (italics mine).

BIG BUSINESS AND THE STATE

The pattern of articulation between the state and business has varied over time in East Asian capitalist states, in response to changing circumstances in the world. The state's relationship to society in Northeast Asia has been variously described, for different times and places, as "embedded" (Evans), "governed interdependence" (Linda Weiss), "governing the market" (Robert Wade), and "dependent development" (Thomas Gold). It has also been analyzed through the prism of bureaucratic structure (T. J. Pempel and Bernard Silberman) or through the ties that force the state to socialize risks with the business sector, namely, the mechanism of industrial fi-

---

26. Peter Evans, *Embedded Autonomy: States and Industrial Transformation* (Princeton: Princeton University Press, 1995), p. 59.

nancing, which was for Korea both munificent and perilous (Woo).[27] The common thread linking these arguments is that the developmental state is not an imperious entity lording it over society but a partner with the business sector in a historical compact of industrial transformation. As Johnson notes in Chapter 2: "The concept of the developmental state means that each side uses the other in a mutually beneficial relationship to achieve development goals and enterprise viability. The state is a catalytic agency in Michael Lind's sense of the term . . . and the managers are responding to incentives and disincentives that the state establishes." In Chapter 3 of this volume, Bruce Cumings discusses the notion of *Staatswissenschaften,*or the German conception of "state science" as the political theory of late development, and sets it apart from the early industrializers' obsession with questions of popular will, democratic representation, the public versus the private, or state versus civil society. To understand this "fused state," or the developmental state, one has to go beyond the bureaucracy and include the zaibatsu or the chaebol, but that immediately gets us to the question of, in the parlance of the late 1990s, "crony capitalism."

The Japanese model led to profound structural corruption, with cash flowing from state to business and from business to politician in truly flood-tide dimensions in Japan and South Korea. "There is a powerful argument that can be made against industrial policy," Johnson writes in Chapter 2: "not that it is a displacement of market forces but that it is more commonly used to protect vested interests than to achieve national development. The state *can* structure market incentives to achieve developmental goals . . . but it can also structure them to enrich itself and friends at the expense of consumers, good jobs, and development." Or as Evans puts it, "For developmental states, connections with society are connections to industrial capital" (and to hardly anything else).[28] The Stanford economist Masahiko Aoki argues in game-theoretic terms that the bureaucracy is both a "delineator of public interests and an agent representing the interests of its constituents vis-à-vis the other interests in the bureaucratic coordinating processes."[29]

The Japanese—or, for that matter, the South Korean—style of state rep-

27. Evans, *Embedded Autonomy;* Linda Weiss and John Hobson, *State and Economic Development* (Cambridge: Policy Press, 1995); Robert Wade, *Governing the Market: Economic Theory and the Role of Government in East Asian Industrialization* (Princeton: Princeton University Press, 1990); Thomas Gold, *State and Society in the Taiwan Miracle* (Armonk, N.Y.: M. E. Sharpe, 1986); T. J. Pempel, introduction to H.-K. Kim, M. Muramatsu, T. J. Pempel, and K. Yamamura, eds., *Japanese Civil Service and Economic Development: Catalysts of Change* (New York: Oxford University Press, 1995); Bernard S. Silberman, *Cages of Reason: The Rise of the Rational State in France, Japan, the United States, and Great Britain* (Chicago: University of Chicago Press, 1993); and Woo, *Race to the Swift.*

28. Evans, *Embedded Autonomy,* p. 234.

29. Masahiko Aoki, *Information, Incentives, and Bargaining in the Japanese Economy* (New York: Cambridge University Press, 1988).

resentation of "particular" interests stands in stunning contrast to world-class Weberian bureaucracies. Recent corruption scandals in Japan and South Korea show politicians with astronomical sums of money contributed by industrial capital, stashed away in "slush funds" ($900 million for one former president and $650 million for another, in the recent Korean cases). One reason is simply that the size of economies in Japan and Korea is larger than in most developing countries; another may be the oligopolistic nature of the industrial groups like the keiretsu or the chaebol: it is easier to coordinate contributions from a few large contributors. All of this is to say that the developmental state is, in some ways, a paradise for big industrialists.

In that sense the greatest difficulty faced by democratic regimes in East Asia today—in particular South Korea—may be the reform of big business. President Franklin Roosevelt, in his message to Congress in 1938 calling for an investigation of concentrated economic power in the United States, said, "The liberty of a democracy is not safe if the people tolerate the growth of private power to a point where it becomes stronger than their democratic state itself."[30] In South Korea the problem of private power is as President Roosevelt described it, but much more so: the chaebol groups have been the private agency of public purpose, having been created by the state through "financial repression," as well as labor repression—in other words, over the dead bodies of both savers and workers.

Since these big firms formed under strong state prodding in the 1960s, it has been hard to delineate a meaningful line between the public and the private in Korea. In many ways the chaebol have been quasi-state organizations, and in others they have been immense private domains, "company towns" writ large that employ, house, feed, clothe, educate, and provide credit to millions of ordinary Koreans. The depth of the problem can perhaps be appreciated by remembering the result of the antitrust law in the American experience, where the dissolution of Standard Oil benefited from the existence of forty-eight states often under separate or different regulatory regimes, so that we got Standard Oil of Indiana, California, or New York. Korea is highly centralized, with no such federal structure.

The modal big business in East Asia is the prewar zaibatsu or the postwar Korean chaebol. The economist Eleanor Hadley, who was on General Douglas MacArthur's staff and later America's leading chronicler of the antitrust experiment in Japan during the Occupation, said the zaibatsu were a "political expression referring to the estate of wealth, and by extension, to the source of this wealth, the combines."[31] In the work of

---

30. Franklin D. Roosevelt, in his message to the Congress, April 29, 1938, calling for an investigation of concentrated economic power in the United States, quoted in Eleanor Hadley, *Antitrust in Japan* (Princeton: Princeton University Press, 1970), pp. 455–56.

31. Ibid., p. 21.

many Japanese historians, the term refers to family-dominated combines that developed following World War I and expanded rapidly in the heavy industrialization drives and wartime conditions of the 1930s and 1940s. The Korean chaebol today is an atavism of the prewar zaibatsu.

The goal of the zaibatsu was not high-market occupancy of one, two, or a few more related markets but an oligopolistic position running the gamut of the modern sector of the economy. The largest, Mitsui, carried on far-flung operations in coals and metals mining, shipbuilding, ordnance, aircraft, heavy and light electrical equipment, and various other fields of manufacturing, not to mention commercial banking, insurance, and trading—that is, not just one oligopoly but a series of oligopolistic positions that provided the foundation for an exceptional combination of business power and wealth. The zaibatsu also favored family exclusivity, adding a personalistic basis of mutual trust to corporate power.[32] Finally, the zaibatsu worked much more for market share rather than solely for their own profit, typically operating at a loss (and during the war, of course, they produced everything under government dictate). Their activity, in short, was rarely driven by ordinary market concerns of price and of supply and demand.

With Korea's big firms we find strong counterparts to the prewar zaibatsu in terms again of their purpose, goals, market positions, size, and organization. The Korean chaebol have oligopolistic positions running the gamut of the modern sector of the economy. Their mammoth and extraordinarily diversified structure, combined with an open call on state-mediated loans, was essential to Korea's success in gaining market share around the world, because losses in one subsidiary could be made up by gains in another.

To return to Eleanor Hadley's phrase "the estate of wealth": the chaebols are also estates akin to that long maintained by the DuPont Corporation in the small state of Delaware, namely, provisioners of their employees' needs in every way. The typical Hyundai worker drives a Hyundai car, lives in a Hyundai apartment, gets his mortgage from Hyundai credit, receives health care at Hyundai hospital, sends his kids to school on Hyundai loans or scholarships, and eats his meals at Hyundai cafeterias. If his son graduates out of the blue-collar workforce and into the ranks of well-educated technocratic professionals (which is every Korean parent's goal), he may well work for Hyundai research and development. The extreme form is seen in the masses of construction teams that Hyundai has long sent to the Middle East; every worker would depart in Hyundai T-shirts and caps carrying Hyundai bags, would live and eat in Hyundai dor-

32. Ibid., pp. 23–25.

mitories, and would use Hyundai tools and equipment to build Hyundai cities in the desert. In the same way that Kim Il Sung built a Confucian-influenced, hereditary family-state in North Korea and called it communism, the Korean chaebol have built large family-run, hereditary corporate estates in South Korea and called it capitalism.

All this is to underscore the point that the case of the Korean chaebol—or the Japanese zaibatsu—is not like what one finds in the Southeast Asian countries: it is not a case of indiscriminate "crony capitalism." What one had in Southeast Asia was not a nationalist mobilization for export-led growth, as in Japan and Korea, but a kind of "protection ring." Indonesia is the worst case, a classic one of sultanlike dictatorship and political monopoly—a sort of capitalism in one family, with Suharto and his relatives and children constituting by far the biggest conglomerate—and with the truly entrepreneurial element, the ethnic Chinese business class, always at the risk of getting prostrated before the rifle butt or the ethnic pogrom (or both, as in the 1965 bloodletting). A state like this is ultimately interested in economic development to the extent that the state gets its payoffs, but it otherwise is not interested in development, in part because the ethnically alien group is synonymous with entrepreneurial business. In Southeast Asia, furthermore, relationships between state and business were *not* forged through industrial policy but through an ethnic division of labor in managing politics and economy. There, the widely discussed lack of transparency and accountability in corporate governance is a result of the elaborate ethnic give-and-take and even protection/racketeering in the worst of circumstances that prevails in Indonesia.

The developmental states of Japan and South Korea have been a paradise for big business, but they did succeed in honing a globe-ranging competitiveness for Japanese and Korean firms, in spite of the "crony capitalism" and "moral hazards" to which the International Monetary Fund (IMF) refers. Chaebol may have emerged in the last thirty years, but the model goes back seventy years. This is another way of saying that we need to be sensitive to "path dependency" in thinking through the issue of reforming big business in East Asia.

Authoritarianism and Development

The developmental state can be "good," that is, effective, especially in terms of the "comparative institutional economics" that Chang and Vartiainen write about. It can be "bad," as we have seen through the kind of corruption that is structural in a system based on state-business collusion, with the intent to hone the competitiveness of national business in the international system. It can also be ugly—undemocratic and authoritarian, explicitly or implicitly. If the developmental state provides grist for the mill of new thinking in economics and political science and much ammunition for those who wish to demonize Japan ("crony capitalism"), the ugly reality of authoritarianism in several East Asian states (past or present) may be the lesson that the rulers of other developing countries find most compelling.

Johnson has argued that while there is no necessary connection between authoritarianism (or, more cumbersome, "soft authoritarianism") and development,[33] there is a sort of elective affinity between the two, in much the same way that Guillermo O'Donnell analyzed the connection between bureaucratic authoritarianism and heavy industrialization in Latin America.[34] Johnson writes in Chapter 2: "Authoritarianism can sometimes inadvertently solve the main political problem of economic development using market forces—namely, how to mobilize the overwhelming majority of the population to work and sacrifice for developmental projects. . . . In the true developmental state, . . . the bureaucratic rulers possess a particular kind of legitimacy that allows them to be much more experimental and undoctrinaire than in the typical authoritarian regime. *This is the legitimacy that comes from devotion to a widely believed-in revolutionary project*" (italics mine).

Western observers have had a hard time understanding the legitimacy of the developmental regime in East Asia, often confusing it with a cultural (or "Confucian") penchant for political acquiescence. Something called "Asian values" must account for weak civil societies, if not their legitimacy (which remains a puzzle). But the power of the developmental state grows both out of the barrel of the gun and its ability to convince the population of its political, economic, and moral mandate. In Chapter 3, Bruce Cumings writes that "power is all of us conducting our daily life as if we are good capitalists, when hardly any of us truly are or can be. The power that van Wolferen cannot find and grasp hold of is precisely the power that derives from Japanese capitalism and its attendant politics being hegemonic—that is, legitimate, accepted without question at a psychological level well below normal consciousness." Frank authoritarianism in interwar Japan, postwar Korea (until 1987), and postwar Taiwan (again, until 1987, when four decades of martial law ended), combined with Western humiliation and strong nationalism, proved a powerful forge on which legitimate political power could finally rise.

33. Johnson, "Political Institutions and Economic Performance."
34. Guillermo O'Donnell, *Modernization and Bureaucratic-Authoritarianism: Studies in South American Politics* (Berkeley: Institute of International Studies, University of California, 1973).

THE DEVELOPMENTAL STATE IN INTERNATIONAL AND COMPARATIVE PERSPECTIVE

T. J. Pempel reminds us in Chapter 5, "The Developmental Regime in a Changing World Economy," that the state is a Janus-faced entity, mediating between the outside world and the domestic society. This is an insight, he argues, that is buried by Johnson's depiction of the developmental state as an isolated world of bureaucrats who, along with politicians and business leaders, pursue "national interests." Furthermore, Pempel contends that "national interests" in Johnson's account are merely assumed as given, existing in a realm devoid of world politics, the strategic goals of superpowers, the actions of multinational corporations, foreign aid, and so on. But the developmental state is unthinkable apart from its relationship to the external world, in particular to the hegemonic power, which opened its market. Pempel, as does Cumings, argues that it is only in this relational context that one comes to appreciate the structural weakness of the developmental state in the world system.

In his earlier work, Johnson saw the importance of the cold war primarily in terms of Japan's extraction of economic gains through market access and through free riding on national defense. Johnson downplayed the role of the cold war in Japanese development because Japan, he thought, would have developed anyway, with or without the cold war. But the cold war was critically important for a number of reasons: not just because the Korean War gave Japan an economic windfall comparable to the Marshall Plan and made South Korea and Taiwan into economic wards of the United States all through the 1950s and 1960s but also because it provided a critical context for the rise of the deviant form of capitalism, at least from the perspective of the prevailing Anglo-Saxon, laissez-faire ideology.

The cold war saw the emergence in Northeast Asia of "semisovereign states," as the result of security dependence *and* market dependence. Pempel sees vulnerabilities attendant in the dependence of East Asian economies, on the single dominant export market provided by the United States. Nearly fifty years ago, Hirschman argued that inordinate export dependency of a given country on a single large market imparted political vulnerability to the exporting country. In the interwar period, Germany constructed a relationship with its economic partners in eastern Europe in such a way as to make the latter depend on the (single) German market, allowing it to exert political and economic pressures on its periphery.[35] Pempel argues in this volume that the type of market dependence one

---

35. Albert O. Hirschman, *National Power and the Structure of Foreign Trade* (Berkeley: University of California Press, 1945).

finds between East Asian countries (Japan, South Korea, Taiwan, and, one might add, China) and the United States is comparable with the one that existed between the former Soviet Union and its satellite states, thus to underscore the vast asymmetry in power between the two regions.

This focus on the cold war sheds light on the difference between what Ronald P. Dore called the "drifter states" in Latin America and the "purposeful states" in East Asia: the difference is in the "will to develop."[36] The cold war and the complex legacies of the Pacific War begot in East Asia divided nations in Korea and China, providing compelling motives for intensive economic mobilization that was unthinkable in the Latin American context. The absence in Latin America of the kind of the vulnerability and urgency one finds in East Asia has to do with Latin America having entered modernity much earlier than did Korea or Taiwan, not to mention attaining political independence a century earlier; it also began industrialization much earlier, in the context of protected enclaves. By and large, this process was guided not by state action but by individual entrepreneurial initiatives, much as it was elsewhere in the pioneer industrial countries. In other words, Latin America was never a "late developer" in the classic Gerschenkronian sense, and thus its states never took a commanding role in crash industrialization programs.

The early insertion of the Latin American economies into the world system, combined with a pattern of industrialization that resembles, on the face of it, the experience of the United States, has resulted in a developmental Gestalt characterized by the economist Fernando Fajnzylber as "showcase modernity," aimed not at self-sustaining development but at reaching a set of elite consumption patterns appropriate for developed countries. This leads to the following mutually reinforcing aspects: a consistent pattern of exuberant consumption, heavily skewed in favor of urban elite groups at the expense of the rural and lower-income majorities; industrial sectors oriented primarily toward the domestic market; the insertion of national economies into the international system via trade in natural resources; and the dubious leadership role played by either the state or national industry.[37]

The timing and manner of Latin America's involvement with the modern world economy, the long-standing penetration of the state by powerful economic interests, and the region's encounter with a peculiar modernity and a peculiar imperial impact (its idiosyncratic internalization of the experience of the United States, in the context of American hegemony in much of the

---

36. Ronald P. Dore, "Reflections on Culture and Social Change," in Gary Gereffi and Donald Wyman, eds., *Manufacturing Miracles: Paths of Industrialization in Latin America and East Asia* (Princeton: Princeton University Press, 1990).

37. Fajnzylber, "The United States and Japan as Models of Industrialization," in Gereffi and Wyman, eds., *Manufacturing Miracles.*

region) seem to point to the weakness of the Latin American state as overde-termined. It was always a state embedded in, penetrated by, or beholden to "the interests," even if the interests changed over the decades.

A better reference point for the East Asian developmental state is northern Europe. In Chapter 7, Vartiainen argues that Austria, Finland, South Korea, and Taiwan (the four countries he examines) shared four attributes of successful state intervention, two of which were related to their external positions in the world system. First, old bureaucratic tradi-tions existed that were capable of providing competent administration (this is unquestionably true of all four). Second, again in all four, the out-come of the wars they suffered shook up the prewar power blocs and re-arranged the previous distribution of power among domestic elites, paving the way toward a more developmental "embeddedness." In that sense, the history of South Korea and Taiwan might not be as unique as one might think. Third, the external position of each of the four coun-tries in the international system was a precarious one, posing security threats of a kind possibly leading to their annihilation—which very nearly happened to South Korea and Taiwan in 1950. Lastly, in spite of their po-sitioning between two major international power blocs, all four main-tained a basic commitment to the bourgeois legal order and respected private property. In the end, all four adopted major policy tools that were remarkably similar: investment subsidies, price controls, credit rationing, and maintenance of interest rates at artificially low levels.

What, then, are the lessons for development in light of the foregoing discussion of political economy in these so-called security states? The ge-nius of South Korea, Taiwan, Finland, and Austria was in harnessing very real fears of war and instability toward a remarkable developmental en-ergy, which in turn could become a binding agent for growth. The pur-suit of power and plenty, in the context either of the security state or of catching up with the rest of the world (more often both), is vastly more effective in generating developmental energy than a general appeal to in-creased welfare, à la Latin American "populism."

The cold war imparted urgency to the developmental projects in Northeast Asia, but in other ways it was not a sine qua non for the rise of the developmental state. What was critical was, as we have seen, the role of nationalism—or what Loriaux calls the "solidaristic vision" for the na-tion. Following the chapter by Vartiainen, Loriaux brings us the experi-ence of France, long hailed as the archetypal developmental state in Eu-rope. He finds many similarities between the political economies of France and the East Asian states, both in their bureaucratic structures and the mechanism of state intervention—most notably allocation of credit by banks and other financial institutions. If, however, the develop-mental state were judged by its outcome, Loriaux is not altogether sure if

France deserves to be called a "developmental state." He contends that the French industrial power antedates both interventionism and the rise to power of its civil service elite, and that economic development after World War II is better seen as an emanation of new international regimes in money and trade rather than through some essential structural or institutional feature of the French domestic political economy: the French developmental state did not develop. Instead, Loriaux argues that the "developmental state" should be seen as a "moral ambition," the expression of which is affected by "environmental conditions: structures, institutions, and norms that regulate society at both the domestic and the international level." The developmental state for him is an embodiment of a normative or moral ambition to use the interventionist power of the state to guide investment in a way that promotes a certain solidaristic vision of the national economy.

Johnson perhaps would agree. He showed in "La Serenissima of the East," an indubitably great pedagogical piece that illustrates the follies of Orientalism, that the same imperative which fueled the Japanese developmental state also fueled medieval Venice, culminating in the fusion, in an ad hoc manner, of the effectiveness of the absolutist state with the efficiency of the bourgeois market, while placing nationalistic goals ahead of spiritual ones. The Japanese case, in other words, is "neither unique, exceptional, purely culturally based, irrational, nor inherently unstable."[38] What Johnson achieves with this kind of comparison (typically one that confounds our expectations) is to show that if Japan poses problems for Western theory, then so much the worse for Western theory. After all, if Venice is not at the core of the Western heritage, what is? "La Serenissima of the East," like the essays by Loriaux and Vartiainen, shows how a comparative study of industrial policy can be illustrative, confounding, and artful—and even pleasant.

LEGACY OF THE IDEA

In the broader arena beyond scholarship, in the 1980s Johnson's argument that the Japanese state was inextricably implicated in managing the economy of America's most formidable industrial rival became hugely controversial—in part because of much hand-wringing about Japan's skyrocketing trade surplus and the loss of American competitiveness and in part because of Johnson's companion argument about the United States, namely, that industrial policy might work well here too. For all the controversy and all the intellectual pummeling that Johnson took, however,

38. Chalmers Johnson, "La Serenissima of the East," in *Japan*, p. 25.

the developmental state argument rarely received thoughtful scrutiny. It was an argument that one thought one knew and therefore assumed away: the bureaucracy as a monolithic social engineer or a benevolent and omniscient chaperon of national interest—we have heard this before; it is not important.

MITI and the Japanese Miracle spawned a veritable cottage industry of books on the role of the state in the economy, and it framed both popular and scholarly debate. Johnson was simultaneously the visionary who unearthed the occult secrets of Japan's industrial mastery and a reviled "Japan-basher," the earnest writer laboring in the East Asian vineyards and the unorthodox zealot, the much quoted scholar and notorious "revisionist." In short, he must have been saying something rather important. Johnson soon had a school named after his fashion—predictably, "the revisionists." This school became enormously popular and influential in the late 1980s, but its adherents took his arguments far beyond his starting point. The main trouble with the Japanese system, said Karel van Wolferen, was that it was so different and culturally distinct as to pose a threat to the Western way itself.[39] The more one probed into van Wolferen's *Enigma of Japanese Power*, the more one became convinced of the virtue of being "more like us" (in James Fallows's words) and not like them: the mysterious Other.[40] In Chapter 3, Cumings subjects this revisionist genre to critical examination and wonders whether all this handwringing about the Japanese threat constitutes the eternal recurrence of the yellow peril.

Johnson's *MITI and the Japanese Miracle*, judged by historian John Dower to be "a landmark publication, sometimes described as the most influential political science study of Japan ever published in English," is not a deductive political science study, using Japan as a "country case" in comparative politics.[11] Rather, it is an account of how the Japanese, faced with the harsh reality of a world dominated by the Western powers, devised a system of political economy that was both admirable and dangerous, and Johnson's scholarly task was to make the Japanese experience, wisdom and folly included, explicable.

How did Johnson's argument produce such different interpretations and conclusions about Japan? For all the affinity between "revisionist" work and Johnson's own, Johnson has never been a culturalist, rigorously staying away from arguments that attributed the development in East Asia

39. This is a point made by John Dower in "Sizing Up (and Breaking Down) Japan," a paper prepared for publication in the Japanese periodical *Shiso*.

40. Two of the best known "revisionist" works are Karel van Wolferen's *The Enigma of Japanese Power* (New York: Alfred A. Knopf, 1989), and James Fallows's *More Like Us: Making America Great Again* (Boston: Houghton Mifflin, 1989).

41. Dower, "Sizing Up (and Breaking Down) Japan."

to the differential Confucian influences in China, Korea, and Japan. This is a sensitive and important issue, in part because culture is a difficult variable to incorporate in social scientific analyses and in part because of the inevitable charge of "Orientalism" that taints attempts to understand East Asia as a unique culture. Even the very best study of East Asia in cultural terms, Weber's *Religion of China*, revealed his Occidental bias in seeing little developmental virtue and potential in Confucianism, and Karl Wittfogel's *Oriental Despotism* found in East Asian "hydraulic culture" a natural propensity to totalitarianism.[42] Indeed, one of the important contributions of Johnson's work (like that of Dore) is to place the analysis of ideology and culture in the historical context of late development and economic nationalism, thus deftly bypassing culturalist landmines in the study of East Asia.

Johnson's own vision of Japan, complex and often mercurial, is also responsible for the diverse and often contradictory interpretations and conclusions. His work is a swinging pendulum, sometimes arguing that America also needs to be a developmental state, with a planned industrial strategy to compete against East Asian states, and sometimes sharing the revisionists' deep anxiety about the alien system of political economy he did so much to explain. The developmental state in Johnson's mind is sometimes a hero and sometimes an antihero; it is at once a role model and a negative example, an object of admiration and criticism. There is, in other words, enough in his work to give comfort to both admirers *and* detractors of East Asian industrialization.

Of the admirers of the developmental state at its benign best, one of the best known is Alice Amsden, who in *Asia's Next Giant* illustrated the way that the state in South Korea facilitated the process of technological learning and presided over industrial transformation. Robert Wade showed how the state in Taiwan (the least statist of the three Northeast Asian developmental countries) managed to dictate successfully the terms of economic growth. More has been written about the role of the Japanese state in aiding the technological development of strategic industries, of course; Laura D'Andrea Tyson's *Who's Bashing Whom* is a particularly good example of this economic genre.[13] Taken together, these works represent a new perspective, arguing for the economic rationality of industrial policy in terms of efficiency, albeit much more broadly defined

42. Max Weber, *The Religion of China*, ed. Hans H. Gerth (New York: Macmillan, 1964); Karl Wittfogel, *Oriental Despotism: A Comparative Study of Total Power* (New Haven: Yale University Press, 1957).

43. Alice H. Amsden, *Asia's Next Giant: South Korea and Late Industrialization* (New York: Oxford University Press, 1989); Wade, *Governing the Market*; Laura D'Andrea Tyson, *Who's Bashing Whom? Trade Conflict in High-Tech Industries* (Washington, D.C.: Institute for International Economics, 1992).

than in conventional economics. According to this line of argument, industrial policy is an efficient way to improve on market coordination, reduce transaction costs, and promote dynamic efficiency. One of the most succinct summaries of such economic logic is *The Political Economy of Industrial Policy*, by Cambridge University economist Ha-Joon Chang. He applied the insights of the "new institutional economics" (and its insistence that nonmarket institutions are effective means of transmitting information and organizing economic life) to analyze industrial policies in Japan and South Korea.[44] In his contribution to this volume, Chang defines the developmental state in political, ideological, and institutional terms as "a state which can create and regulate the economic and political relationships that can support sustained industrialization" and which "takes the goals of long-term growth and structural change seriously, 'politically' manages the economy to ease the conflicts inevitable during the process of such change (but with a firm eye on the long-term goals), and engages in institutional adaptation and innovation to achieve those goals."

Such economic and political relationships often imply a corporatist framework, involving large economic groupings (like the keiretsu or the chaebol) with which the state can coordinate and negotiate investment decisions. The commitment to collective goals may be manifested through promotion of national ideologies and sentiment (often demanding sacrifices in immediate economic welfare) and ironclad guarantee of the capitalist regime of property rights. By institutional adaptation and innovation, Chang means the ability of the state sector both to accommodate itself to the changing requirements for remaining competitive in the global market place and to provide support for educational infrastructure and for research and development.

Detractors of Johnson's work were many, as the next chapter makes clear; *MITI and the Japanese Miracle* provoked the entire field of modern Japanese studies. This was perhaps Johnson's major contribution, to sharpen debate and generate new arguments about how the system worked in Japan. In doctoral dissertations on East Asian political economy, it became de rigueur to set up Johnson's argument at one end of the theoretical spectrum (stretching from pluralism to statism). The developmental state thesis thus became a target for the field of East Asian political economy, in much the same way that the 1970s arguments about dependency and world-systems theory had been for sociology and comparative politics. It is always as important to know what scholars argue against as it is to know what they argue for; that a new generation of

44. Ha-Joon Chang, *The Political Economy of Industrial Policy* (New York: St. Martin's Press, 1994).

Ph.D.'s made their careers in opposition to Johnson is nonetheless a tribute to his influence.

The recent wave in political science, rational choice theory, came forth not merely to dispute Johnson's account but to bury it. According to J. Mark Ramseyer and Frances Rosenbluth, for example, the bureaucracy was not at the center of Japanese political life; instead, it was but one of several clusters of interest. In place of the plan-rational state was the rational, well-informed, and strategically thinking Japanese voter. The state was the mere "agent" of this "principle," this active and aware voter. Thus, for example, the powerful Ministry of Finance took its cues not from the career bureaucrats but from policies set in the Japanese Diet (legislature). Although this rational-choice account of Japan had many targets (virtually the entire field of Japan politics), perhaps the key one was Johnson's developmental state thesis.[45]

Of course, there were also those who thought the developmental state paradigm was the old wave, a period piece, a historical artifact describing the Japan of twenty years ago or even the South Korea of ten years past but no longer relevant in the 1990s. In this view, both Japan and South Korea were said to have entered a phase of postdevelopmentalism, with the bureaucracy now relinquishing many of its prerogatives to a powerful private sector it can no longer control.

Kent Calder suggested, on the other hand, that the obsolescence of this paradigm was the least of Johnson's problems; far worse, Johnson's analysis never captured the reality for any period in postwar Japanese history. Even in the sphere of financial policy, widely considered as the best tool the Japanese state possessed to influence industrial outcomes, Calder argued that private sector strategic moves and calculations made the big difference, not administrative guidance by the state.[46] There were other attempts to offset the statist bias in Johnson's account of Japan by emphasizing the role of the private sector. Richard Samuels advanced the theory of the "politics of reciprocal consent," conceiving of the Japanese state and society as occupying overlapping arenas of mutual appropriation; Daniel Okimoto's preferred description of the Japanese state was the "societal state," whereas Ellis Krauss and Michio Muramatsu split the difference between pluralism and the developmental state argument and called it "patterned pluralism."[47]

45. J. Mark Ramseyer and Frances McCall Rosenbluth, *Japan's Political Marketplace* (Cambridge: Harvard University Press, 1993), pp. 182–84; see also the many index references to Johnson in Ramseyer and Rosenbluth.

46. Kent E. Calder, *Strategic Capitalism: Private Business and Public Purpose in Japanese Industrial Finance* (Princeton: Princeton University Press, 1993).

47. Richard J. Samuels, *The Business of the Japanese State: Energy Markets in Comparative and Historical Perspective* (Ithaca: Cornell University Press, 1987); Daniel Okimoto, "Japan: The Societal State," and Ellis Krauss and Michio Muramatsu, "Japanese Political Economy Today:

The biggest legacy of the developmental state thesis probably lies outside the university. The lure of the developmental state for other nations, especially China and Southeast Asia, prompted the World Bank to produce its *Miracle* report, hoping to stifle the siren song of state-led industrialization. No doubt the best epitaph for a new idea is when the objects of that idea finally have no choice but to grant its legitimacy and do their best to emulate it. In its widely publicized book *The East Asian Miracle*, the World Bank suggested that Johnson's account of state interventionism, and others like it, was not merely heretical as theory but misleading on empirical grounds as well. It argued that industrial policy, defined as an attempt to achieve more rapid productivity growth by altering industrial structure, was generally unsuccessful. Instead, industrial growth in Northeast Asia was market conforming, and productivity growth was not significantly higher in promoted sectors. The bank further noted that the industrializing states in Northeast Asia held little relevance for developing economies and that the real role model which they should emulate could be found in the more open economies of Southeast Asia that pursued comparative advantage based on factor intensity.[48]

The 1980s–90s debate in the United States on industrial policy also owed much to the arguments Johnson made about Japan. Some now think the time for industrial policy has come and gone. This is odd, given that the practical effects of the developmental state paradigm have been profound in the 1990s, giving unprecedented force to American trade strategy. Indeed, the debate about the Japanese developmental state has done more than almost any other economic idea to change American foreign economic policy. Industrial policy in the East Asian context meant government policy to develop or retrench industries in order to achieve and maintain global competitiveness. In the American context, the term may be less goal-specific, referring to sensible public policy to improve general economic welfare, such as creating educated and skilled workforces, supporting promising industries, developing better infrastructure, and promoting effective regional policies. In either case, the concept of industrial policy looked like voodoo to the majority of professional economists, but that did not prevent the idea from making its way into the zeitgeist in the 1990s.

Shortly after its inauguration in 1993, the Clinton administration moved toward a "results-oriented" or managed trade policy. Laura Tyson headed the new Economic Security Council; she had been a collaborator

---

The Patterned Pluralist Model," both in Daniel I. Okimoto and Thomas P. Rohlen, eds., *Inside the Japanese System: Readings On Contemporary Society and Political Economy* (Stanford: Stanford University Press, 1988).

48. World Bank, *The East Asian Miracle: Economic Growth and Public Policy* (New York: Oxford University Press, 1993).

of Johnson's at Berkeley, and her work on competitiveness policy is deeply informed by the Japanese case. In her *Who's Bashing Whom?* she advocated a strategic industrial policy focused on high-technology industries, and in many ways that is what Clinton has emphasized as well. Others followed suit, namely, Robert Rubin, Charlene Barshefsky, Robert Reich, and many less well known officials, who remained "hawkish" where trade was concerned, especially with regard to East Asia. Paul Krugman, a critic of the developmental state paradigm who has spilled much ink lately in arguing that Johnson is passé, nonetheless showed his indebtedness to Johnson's scholarship. As Krugman wrote in *The Age of Diminished Expectations*, "My own proposal is that we adopt an explicit, but limited, U.S. industrial policy, that is, the U.S. government should make a decision to frankly subsidize a few sectors, especially in the high technology area, that may plausibly be described as 'strategic,' where there is a perceived threat from Japanese competition."[49]

It may be that, for all the triumphalist talk about the Anglo-Americanization of the global economy at the end of the 1990s, the United States is coming to resemble Japan rather more than less. The developmental state in East Asia has always been a paradise for big business, and unlike the northern European "welfare states," the protective gaze in Northeast Asia has never been downward, toward the downtrodden, but rather upward, toward the privileged, to help big business compete more vigorously in the global marketplace—with its legitimacy resting in the eternal invocation of nationalism. The developmental state has provided a far greater trickle-down effect than any Reaganite ever imagined, yielding an egalitarian payoff at the end of the developmental tunnel.

The state in service of oligopoly also characterizes the new American political economy in the late 1990s, as antitrust legislation gives way to government-sanctioned merger of large manufacturing firms to expand America's global market share (as in the merger of McDonnell-Douglas and Boeing, to become the mega–aircraft manufacturer); government-brokered international cartels in semiconductor chips agreed to in August 1996, to regulate the supply of semiconductor chips and to moderate the cycles of shortage and glut afflicting the industry, thus to replace the cumbersome "managed trade"; and the rise of "universal banking" in the United States, as in Europe and Japan, which has eroded the Glass-Steagall prohibitions against mixing commercial and investment banking.

The prevailing academic wisdom in the late 1990s views the developmental state as inefficient and obsolete, and it has proven less capable

49. Paul Krugman, *The Age of Diminished Expectations* (Cambridge: MIT Press, 1994), p. 153.

than before of providing anchors that moor societies against the deleterious effects of globalism and the American model of efficient market capitalism. But I would suggest that it is much more resilient and efficacious than the Western observers give it credit for—with or without the East Asian economic crisis of the late 1990s. This is because the amalgam of powerful interests in Northeast Asian countries cannot be easily dismantled because of the existence of entrenched interests.

The main question today is whether the denizens of this paradise can successfully curtail their bureaucratic excesses to boost the international competitiveness of their industrial producers. Trimming some bureaucratic fat off the "developmental state" does not mean the end of the developmental state; rather, it is a requirement for survival. Whether it can be done hangs in the balance today, but those who have confidently dismissed the model may wake up one day to find the East Asian states roaring back to prominence. Johnson, of course, believes that his model is hardly passé because of the fluid nature of industrial policy: it will continue to be both a practical strategy for East Asian nations and something from which the United States needs to learn. He argued in his *Industrial Policy Debate* that industrial policy is contingent, rather than set in stone or a strategy of just one type; quoting Ueno Hiroya, "Unlike traditional fiscal and monetary policies, industrial policy demonstrates no clear relationship between its objectives and the means of attaining them. Its conception, content, and forms differ, reflecting the stage of development of an economy, its natural and historical circumstances, international conditions, and its political and economic situation, resulting in considerable differences from nation to nation and from era to era."[50]

Thus Japanese industrial policy could be protectionist in the 1950s and 1960s but oriented toward free trade and the internationalization of the Japanese economy today. In other words, Johnson thinks that Japan's industrial policy is not declining but changing, because industrial policy is first of all an attitude, an orientation, and only after that a matter of technique, shifting with the changing needs of the time. The future will tell us whether he is right.

50. Chalmers Johnson, "Introduction: The Idea of Industrial Policy," in *Industrial Policy Debate* (San Francisco: Institute for Contemporary Studies, 1984), p. 6.

CHAPTER TWO

The Developmental State:
Odyssey of a Concept

Chalmers Johnson

One of my main purposes in introducing the idea of the "capitalist developmental state" into a history of modern Japanese industrial policy was to go beyond the contrast between the American and Soviet economies. The American-Soviet comparison had become a feature of virtually all the canonical works of the American side during the cold war—such as Samuelson's *Economics* textbook. I wanted, instead, to call attention to the differences, not the similarities, between the capitalist economies of the United States and Britain, on the one hand, and Japan and its emulators elsewhere in East Asia, on the other. During the 1970s, when I was doing the research for *MITI and the Japanese Miracle* (1982), these differences were beginning to show, even though there was, and is today, enormous ideological resistance in the English-speaking countries to any attempt to take them seriously.[1]

Looking back on the era of the 1970s, Ronald Dore, in *Flexible Rigidities: Industrial Policy and Structural Adjustment in the Japanese Economy, 1970–1980*, noted in the second paragraph of his introduction that "they [the Japanese] don't *believe* in the invisible hand." "Why on earth, then," Dore asks, "should Japan, an economy which almost flaunts its rigidities as a matter of principle, be the most successful among the OECD [Organization for Economic Cooperation and Development] countries at dy-

1. Compare David Williams, "Beyond Political Economy: A Critique of Issues Raised in Chalmers Johnson's *MITI and the Japanese Miracle*," in *East Asia: International Review of Economic, Political, and Social Development* (Frankfurt: Campus, 1985), 3:231–47. See also David Williams, *Japan: Beyond the End of History* (London: Routledge, 1994). Chalmers Johnson, *MITI and the Japanese Miracle: The Growth of Industrial Policy, 1925–1975* (Stanford: Stanford University Press, 1982); page references will be given parenthetically in the text.

namically adjusting to these challenges—absorbing the oil-price rises, controlling inflation at a low figure, and shifting the weight of its industrial structure away from declining to competitive industries?"[2]

Japan's "flagrantly flouting all received principles of capitalist rationality," to use Dore's words (p. 18), was turning it into one of the world's richest big nations and the model for all the other countries of East Asia, including China. The cases of the so-called East Asian NICs (newly industrialized countries) were also calling into question the lectures of scores of American "dependency theorists" and World Bank officials who droned on about why Latin America was doomed to underdevelopment. At the same time, the Americans and the British, the exemplars of the "principles of capitalist rationality," were being repaid for their orthodoxy with stagflation, high rates of unemployment, and a hollowed-out manufacturing base. Their decline was checked only marginally during the succeeding decade by Ronald Reagan's credit card binge, which left the United States as the world's largest debtor, and Margaret Thatcher's determination to let the market rule, which only made Britain surly.

During the 1990s, as a result of overconfidence and arrogance, Japan allowed a speculative bubble to develop in its domestic economy. The spiral upward in prices was based primarily on overinvestment in productive capacity and unrestricted bank lending using inflated real estate prices as collateral. When the inevitable collapse came, instead of reforming its banking practices and holding its companies responsible for bad investment decisions, Japan exported the bubble to South Korea and Southeast Asia, thereby precipitating the East Asian economic crisis that started in 1997. Many writers in the United States concluded from these events that the Asian "miracle" was a flash in the pan and that the "end of history," that is, the elimination of all alternatives to the American way of life, had finally and definitively arrived. Unfortunately for them, these American writers have seen only those aspects of the Asian economic crisis that neoclassical economics illuminates for them. They have refused to notice the cold war context in which the Asian economies flourished or how overextended they themselves are as the economic and military guarantors of the Asian system. In any case, my history of the Ministry of International Trade and Industry (MITI) was devoted to an explicit period of twentieth-century history, as its subtitle indicates: *The Growth of Industrial Policy, 1925–1975.*

I invoked the concept of "developmental state" to characterize the role the Japanese state played in Japan's extraordinary and unexpected post-

2. Ronald Dore, *Flexible Rigidities: Industrial Policy and Structural Adjustment in the Japanese Economy, 1970–1980* (Stanford: Stanford University Press, 1986), pp. 1, 6.

war enrichment. I never said or implied that the state was *solely* responsible for Japan's economic achievements or that it behaved like the state in command economies in assigning tasks and duties to the Japanese people. Nonetheless, many reviewers, usually self-identified as "economists," allege that I did. Thus began one major stream of response to the concept: it was heretical. Anglo-American "theory" taught that there were only two possible explanations for Japan's wealth—it must be an extreme instance of "getting the prices right," or Japan was toying with socialism and would soon begin to show signs of Soviet-type misallocation of resources and structural rigidities. It could not exemplify the role of the state in a market economy, because even what Adam Smith had to say on that subject was no longer credited in the extreme, "rational choice" version of Western economic individualism.[3]

This line of attack on the concept "developmental state" came as a surprise to me. When I wrote the history of MITI, I did not realize the extent to which economics had become the doctrinaire orthodoxy of the "West" during the cold war and economists the censors of social science deviancy within the English-speaking university establishment. My book was not even consciously directed at the world of academic economics but rather at such issues as the uses of the state in the setting and achievement of social goals, the failures of Soviet-type socialist displacement of the market, comparative state bureaucracies, and public-private cooperation. Thus, I tended at first not to pay too much attention to reviewers who noted that "economists . . . will quibble with some of Johnson's formulations" (*Journal of Asian Studies*) and "I am afraid that Johnson has unnecessarily alienated many economists" (*Journal of Japanese Studies*).[4] I came to realize, however, that my book was an ideological red flag to the bull of Anglo-American cold war orthodoxy about economic correctness. That is to say, MITI, industrial policy, Japan's economic growth, and above all the idea of a "developmental state" continue to threaten people on both sides of the Pacific with deep vested interests in the cold war relationships.

Thus, without ever contradicting or even confronting the historical evidence I had presented from both prewar and postwar Japan, critics developed several standard ploys for dealing with my book. These and variations on them have been repeated over and over again. One, suggested, for example, by Kuroda Makoto, MITI's chief negotiator with the United States over trade in semiconductors, is that my history is accurate enough

3. See Chalmers Johnson and E. B. Keehn, "A Disaster in the Making: Rational Choice and Asian Studies," *The National Interest* 36 (Summer 1994): 14–22.
4. Leon Hollerman, review of *MITI and the Japanese Miracle*, by Chalmers Johnson, *Journal of Asian Studies* 42, no. 2 (February 1983): 414–15; Kozo Yamamura, review of *MITI and the Japanese Miracle*, by C. Johnson, *Journal of Japanese Studies* 9, no. 2 (1983): 211. Henceforth, untitled reviews of my book will be given as "review."

but no longer relevant because Japan has changed and no longer does industrial policy in the old way. Another (compare Karl Zinsmeister for the Heritage Foundation) invites readers to imagine how mind-blowingly rich the Japanese would be if the state had *not* intervened. Or I am taxed with "understat[ing] the economic activities of the private sector" (Nakamura Takafusa), without ever specifying what "private" might mean in Japan as opposed to the United States or how and by whom the incentives the Japanese private actors faced were changed over time.[5]

Since my book was published in the early 1980s, several other writers have taken up the same broad subject—the role of the state in the Asian market economies—and analyzed it in contexts different from the Japanese and with attention to other aspects of Japan's activities than industrial policy. The most important of these works are Alice Amsden, *Asia's Next Giant*, on the fundamentally different microeconomics of the Korean developmental state from those recommended by the English-language economics textbooks; Robert Wade, *Governing the Market*, on many aspects of Taiwan's economic growth but particularly on the corporatist politics that sustain the developmental state; and Jung-en Woo (Meredith Woo-Cumings), *Race to the Swift*, on how the single most important tool of industrial policy in the growth of South Korea was control of finance. Another critically important work that theoretically distinguishes the capitalist developmental state from the Soviet-type command economy, market socialism, and laissez-faire is Yu-Shan Wu, *Comparative Economic Transformations: Mainland China, Hungary, the Soviet Union, and Taiwan.*[6]

In a sense, these works led to the World Bank's unintended paean to economic success: *The East Asian Miracle: Economic Growth and Public Policy* (1993). The Japanese aid-giving authorities forced the ideological conservatives of the bank to write this study as a condition for further Japanese funding. The study does not actually say anything new and is intentionally misleading on fundamentals, but in the foreword the president of the World Bank, Lewis T. Preston, writes, "This diversity of experience

5. Kuroda Makoto, "Myths about MITI," *Tokyo Business Today* (April 1988): 64; Karl Zinsmeister, "MITI Mouse: Japan's Industrial Policy Doesn't Work," *Policy Review* (Spring 1993): 28–35; Nakamura Takafusa, review, *Japan Quarterly* (October–December 1982): 484–86. Compare James Fallows et al., "Up against the *Wall Street Journal,*" *The American Prospect* (Summer 1993): 21–27.

6. Alice H. Amsden, *Asia's Next Giant: South Korea and Late Industrialization* (New York: Oxford University Press, 1989); Robert Wade, *Governing the Market: Economic Theory and the Role of Government in East Asian Industrialization* (Princeton: Princeton University Press, 1990); Jung-en Woo, *Race to the Swift: State and Finance in Korean Industrialization* (New York: Columbia University Press, 1991); Yu-Shan Wu, *Comparative Economic Transformations: Mainland China, Hungary, the Soviet Union, and Taiwan* (Stanford: Stanford University Press, 1994).

[in East Asia] reinforces the view that economic policies and policy-advice must be country-specific, if they are to be effective."[7] If Jeffrey Sachs and similar advisers in Russia and Eastern Europe had taken this stricture seriously when they were asked to help restructure the command economies there, the outcomes might be much less vexed and politically volatile.

I do not here feel the need to review the theory of the developmental state. That has already been done quite brilliantly in the works cited above, as well as in the articles collected in this volume. Before leaving the subject, however, I would like to mention two articles that in my view make major contributions to synthesizing the different aspects of the developmental state and solving noteworthy East Asian puzzles (for example, was Hong Kong before its return to China an example of laissez-faire? Answer: no). These are Ziya Onis, "The Logic of the Developmental State," and Manuel Castells, "Four Asian Tigers with a Dragon Head: A Comparative Analysis of the State, Economy, and Society in the Asian Pacific Rim."[8] These works deserve to be better known. For my own thoughts on the developmental state after *MITI and the Japanese Miracle*, see the collection of my essays entitled *Japan, Who Governs? The Rise of the Developmental State.*[9]

The developmental state exists and is in the process of altering the world balance of power, whether or not the Anglo-American academic and journalistic establishments recognize it.[10] My purpose here is not to restate what has already been well said but to undertake three lesser tasks: first, to summarize what *MITI and the Japanese Miracle* actually said, which has often gotten lost in the ideological disputation about its possible implications: second, to reveal for the first time the editorial debate that preceded publication of the book over whether the Japanese case constituted a model; and, third, to consider the reviews under four broad headings: (1) What was more important, the market or industrial policy? (2) Is Japan a democracy, and is the capitalist developmental state compatible with democracy? (3) Did Japan's success depend on the period in which it occurred? and (4) What is the nature of bureaucratic-civilian relations (these terms are preferable to public-private) in the capitalist develop-

7. World Bank, *The East Asian Miracle: Economic Growth and Public Policy* (New York: Oxford University Press, 1993), p. vi.

8. Ziya Onis, "The Logic of the Developmental State," *Comparative Politics* 24, no. 1 (October 1991): 109–26, and Manuel Castells, "Four Asian Tigers with a Dragon Head: a Comparative Analysis of the State, Economy, and Society in the Asian Pacific Rim," in Richard P. Appelbaum and Jeffrey Henderson, eds., *States and Development in the Asian Pacific Rim* (Newbury Park, Calif.: Sage, 1992), pp. 33–70.

9. Chalmers Johnson, *Japan, Who Governs? The Rise of the Developmental State* (New York: Norton, 1995).

10. Chalmers Johnson, "The Empowerment of Asia," *Australian Quarterly* 67, no. 2 (Winter 1995): 11–27.

mental state? These four areas cover all the serious controversies surrounding *MITI and the Japanese Miracle.*

THE THESIS

In the immediate paragraphs below, I quote extensively from *MITI and the Japanese Miracle* in order to provide a synopsis of the argument it contains. The essence of the argument is that credit for the postwar Japanese economic "miracle" should go primarily to conscious and consistent governmental policies dating from at least the 1920s:

[A] state's first priority will define its essence. . . . For more than 50 years the Japanese state has given its first priority to economic development. Some of the Japanese state's priorities for economic development, such as the imperialism of the Pacific War, were disastrous, but that does not alter the fact that its priorities have been consistent. (Pp. 305–6)

Overcoming the depression required economic development, war preparation and war fighting required economic development, postwar reconstruction required economic development, and independence from U.S. aid required economic development. The means to achieve development for one cause ultimately proved to be equally good for the other causes. There are striking continuities among the state's various policy tools over the prewar and postwar years. (P. 308)

The issue is not one of state intervention in the economy. All states intervene in their economies for various reasons. . . . The United States is a good example of a state in which the regulatory orientation predominates, whereas Japan is a good example of a state in which the developmental orientation predominates. A regulatory, or market-rational, state concerns itself with the forms and procedures—the rules, if you will—of economic competition, but it does not concern itself with substantive matters. (Pp. 17, 19)

A state attempting to match the economic achievements of Japan must adopt the same priorities as Japan. It must first of all be a developmental state—and only then a regulatory state, a welfare state, an equality state, or whatever other kind of functional state a society may wish to adopt. (P. 306)

The fundamental problem of the state-guided, high-growth system is that of the relationship between the state bureaucracy and privately owned business. This problem erupted at the very outset of industrial policy. . . . Over the past 50 years Japan developed and attempted to implement three different solutions to this problem—namely, self-control, state control, and cooperation. None of them is perfect, but each is preferable to either pure laissez faire or state socialism as long as forced development remains the top priority of the state. (Pp. 309–10)

The Supreme Commander for the Allied Powers (SCAP) never singled out the civilian bureaucracy as needing basic reform. However, SCAP eliminated completely from political life one major rival of the economic bureaucracy, the military; and it transformed and severely weakened another, the zaibatsu. . . . The purge had little effect on the economic ministries. . . . Even more important was SCAP's insistence that the economic functions previously shared between the government and the zaibatsu should now be placed exclusively in governmental hands. (Pp. 41, 44)

The Enterprises Bureau's next big initiative was the enactment of the Foreign Capital Law (1950). The Foreign Exchange and Foreign Trade Control Law of 1949 had already given the government power to concentrate all foreign exchange earned from exports (by law such foreign exchange had to be sold to a foreign exchange bank within 10 days of its acquisition), and this power made possible the control of imports through the use of a foreign exchange budget. MITI made every effort to suppress imports of finished goods, particularly those that competed with domestic products, but it urgently sought imports of modern technology and machinery. The problem was to keep the price down and to "untie the package" in which such foreign technology normally came wrapped—to separate the foreign technology from its foreign ownership, patent rights, know-how agreements, proposals for joint ventures, capital participation, voting rights, and foreign managers on boards of directors. The Foreign Capital Law dealt with this problem. It established a Foreign Investment Committee and stipulated that foreign investors wanting to license technology, acquire stock, share patents, or enter into any kind of contract that provided them with assets in Japan had first to be licensed by the committee. (P. 217)

Specialists on modern Japan will differ as to the precise elements and the weight to be attached to each element in such a model, but the following, based on the history of MITI, is my own estimation of the essential features of the Japanese developmental state. . . . The first element of the model is the existence of a small, inexpensive, but elite state bureaucracy staffed by the best managerial talent available in the system. . . . The duties of this bureaucracy would be first, to identify and choose the industries to be developed (industrial structure policy); second, to identify and choose the best means of rapidly developing the chosen industries (industrial rationalization policy); and third, to supervise competition in the designated strategic sectors in order to guarantee their economic health and effectiveness. These duties would be performed using market-conforming methods of state intervention. (Pp. 314–15)

The second element . . . is a political system in which the bureaucracy is given sufficient scope to take initiative and operate effectively. This means . . . that the legislative and judicial branches of government must be restricted to "safety valve" functions. . . . A non-Japanese example would be something like the American legislative branch's relationship to the wartime Manhattan Project or to the postwar nuclear submarine development program. (Pp. 315–16)

The third element of the model is the perfection of market-conforming methods of state intervention in the economy. . . . [Japanese methods include] creation of governmental financial institutions, whose influence is as much indicative as it is monetary; the extensive use, narrow targeting, and timely revision of tax incentives; the use of indicative plans to set goals and guidelines for the entire economy; the creation of numerous, formal, and continuously operating forums for exchanging views, revising policies, obtaining feedback, and resolving differences; the assignment of some governmental functions to various private and semiprivate associations (JETRO [Japan External Trade Organization], Keidanren); an extensive reliance on public corporations, particularly the mixed public-private variety, to implement policy in high-risk or otherwise refractory areas; the creation and use by the government of an unconsolidated "investment budget" separate from and not funded by the general account budget; the orientation of antitrust policy to developmental and international competitive goals rather than strictly to the maintenance of domestic competition; government-conducted and government-sponsored research and development (the computer industry); and the use of the government's licensing and approval authority to achieve developmental goals. Perhaps the most important market-conforming method of intervention is administrative guidance. . . . It is necessary to avoid overly detailed laws that . . . put a strait jacket on creative administration. . . . Highly detailed statutes serve the interests primarily of lawyers, not of development. . . . At its best Japanese administrative guidance is comparable to the discretionary authority entrusted to a diplomat negotiating an international agreement. Success depends upon his skill, good sense, and integrity, and not on a set of legal requirements that no matter how well crafted can never truly tell a negotiator what to do. (Pp. 317–19)

The fourth and final element of the model is a pilot organization like MITI. . . . MITI's experience suggests that the agency that controls industrial policy needs to combine at least planning, energy, domestic production, international trade, and a share of finance (particularly capital supply and tax policy). . . . The key characteristics of MITI are its small size . . . , its indirect control of government funds (thereby freeing it of subservience to the Finance Ministry's Bureau of the Budget), its "think tank" functions, its vertical bureaus for the implementation of industrial policy at the micro level, and its internal democracy. It has no precise equivalent in any other advanced industrial democracy. (Pp. 319–20)

THE TAKE-HOME MESSAGE

Many of these quotations, particularly the four-part model, come from the final chapter of *MITI and the Japanese Miracle*, titled "A Japanese Model?" This chapter did not exist in the original manuscript but was added at the insistence of the chief editor of Stanford University Press. Although usually such editorial decisions are of no great importance, except perhaps to the author, in this instance they relate to what is perhaps the single most important question concerning the *Japanese* developmental state. Is it duplicable? Is there really a Japanese model? What are the general, culture-free lessons to be learned from the Japanese case?

There is no longer any question that the Japanese use of market mechanisms for developmental purposes has been successfully emulated in other countries. The most important examples, in descending order of their distance from the Japanese precedent, are South Korea, Taiwan, Singapore, and Hong Kong. The growth of these five capitalist developmental states has also tended to promote growth in the surrounding areas—through trade, investment, emulation, and other influences. During the 1990s, the People's Republic of China also began to adapt the institutions of Japan's developmental state to its own Leninist heritage, a command economy it was attempting to dismantle. Beyond Japan and the NICs, this growth has often occurred without an explicit pilot agency such as MITI and has produced severe economic and environmental dislocations together with high levels of structural corruption. These were the primary reasons why Thailand and Indonesia were the countries first affected by the economic crisis that began in 1997. None of the Asian cases is a clone of the Japanese experience. Some followers improved on the Japanese model (for example, state control of *chaebol*—that is, *zaibatsu*—banks in Korea), and others ignored Japanese-type controls on unchecked growth and paid the consequences (for example, repeated bouts of inflation in mainland China). Nonetheless, as is made clear below and in other papers in this volume, all the East Asian cases reflect particular forms of state guidance that were first demonstrated to be effective by Japan.

That was not, however, the take-home message I had in mind when I was writing the history of MITI. I never doubted that Japan was a better model for both the second and third worlds than Anglo-American capitalism, but I was trying to signal by way of a broader conclusion a different point—namely, that the "learn-from-Japan" craze then sweeping the United States was dangerously ahistorical and simple-minded. I conceived the book in terms of eight chapters: an introduction to the Japanese developmental state, an analysis of the functions and status of the Japanese state bureaucracy, and six chapters on the history of Japanese industrial policy from 1925 to 1975. My primary focus was the prewar and postwar continuities, both institutionally and in terms of personnel, that my research had revealed. To the extent that I had a didactic purpose at all, it was to stress that Japan's case would be hard to emulate. If nothing more, it depended to a large extent on losing a big war to the right people at the right time.

The only reviewer who ever divined this message from the published book was Walter Goldfrank. He accepted that "the structures and practices of MITI (Ministry of International Trade and Industry) and its predecessor ministries particularly, bear primary causal responsibility for the growth and diversification of postoccupation Japanese industry."[11] He then asked, Is this history generalizable? His answer (and mine) is, Yes, but only if a nation is similarly committed to the mobilization of industry. → *mainly because of Cold War*

The Japanese case is actually one of an economy mobilized for war but never demobilized during peacetime. The political costs of running an economy in this fashion were not ones that Americans under Ronald Reagan were about to pay. "Although he does not put it so baldly," wrote Goldfrank, "Johnson argues that the Japanese model is not transferable: its economic bureaucrats enjoy a scope and initiative unthinkable in U.S. politics, while its planning and control mechanisms have evolved through a sequence of conjunctures and state interventions that together have amounted to a long and nonrepeatable learning process." That is certainly one of the conclusions that I drew from my research while I was in the process of doing it. I had no doubt that other Asian, African, and Latin American nations would try to emulate Japan, but I did not recommend that the United States try it. I instead stressed that the United States would have to match Japan—just as it had matched, not copied, the USSR—when Japan's enrichment started to turn to empowerment. In doing so, the Americans would have to draw on and perhaps reform their own particular national heritage, not copy that of a country fifteen hundred years older than they were.

I wrote my history of MITI during the summer and autumn of 1980, after some eight years of research on the subject. I then submitted it to Stanford University Press, which had already published three earlier books of mine. Its chief editor, J. G. Bell, was one of the most talented academic publishers of the time. He had extraordinary knowledge of trends in scholarly publishing about Asia and an almost perfect ear as an editor. I trusted his advice about the structure of my manuscript. On December 29, 1980, Bell wrote to me, in part:

A strong last chapter seems to me absolutely necessary. Such a chapter might go over some of the same ground as Chapter 1, and would surely make the same basic point that you make in Chapter 1, but would be very different from Chapter 1 by reason of its references to specifics now known to the reader. Without such a chapter the reader is baffled. Which of the various elements of MITI's success are to be considered central, and how do they relate to the others? The fact that they get the brightest guys from Todai? The fact that so many high-level bureaucrats go on from MITI to become high executives in industry? The fact that MITI operates in some terrain between state socialism and *laissez-faire* capitalism that is free of the major drawbacks

11. Walter Goldfrank, review, *Contemporary Sociology* 12, no. 6 (November 1983): 722–23.

of both extremes? The fact that MITI somehow has a mandate to anticipate difficulties, plan accordingly, and get its plans embodied in legislation? What does MITI's 50-year experience add up to? What is the take-home message?

On January 3, 1981, I replied:

In the case of MITI, I tried to write a narrative history about how the Japanese state economic apparatus grew (something that I believe is quite original since histories of bureaucracies are rare), combined with two chapters on, respectively, the Japanese economy and the Japanese bureaucratic polity. Your comment that the "effect [of the narrative history] is one of accident, expediency, chance" leads me to think that I have succeeded, even though you don't like it, since that is precisely the message I wanted to convey to any country thinking of setting up its own MITI. The narrative *is* what's original about this book—it is really hidden history. Most books on Japan do not even *mention* MITI, let alone the Ministry of Munitions. All books that do mention MITI do nothing more than that—because nobody knows anything about it, and the ministry—like all bureaucracies—prefers to remain confidential. What I consider original about the book is not chapter one but (a) the time frame, and why the external observer must take this larger time frame into consideration; (b) the identification of some key political actors in Japan who are normally overlooked—*because they are bureaucrats* (i.e., Yoshino, Shiina, Kishi, Sahashi, etc.); and (c) the detailed analysis of the ways in which an effective state bureaucracy works. . . . I certainly could write a last chapter, but some of my conclusions would be distinctly downbeat and perhaps unnecessarily harsh on the Japanese. I do not think, for example, it would be nice to say that fascism may be good for a nation, or to call the final chapter—as at one time I was thinking of doing—"From the Wonderful Folks Who Brought You Pearl Harbor."

Bell's reply of January 7 was unyielding:

Now, then, whether argument or narrative, there can be no serious doubt that the book needs a Conclusion. . . . You should set forth your conclusions without regard to whether some readers might regard them as downbeat, pro-fascist, unnecessarily hard on the Japanese, mean to Eldridge Cleaver, etc., so only that you say as courteously as possible exactly what you think the facts warrant saying. . . . You should let all us chickens in on the take-home message, whether this be that "accident, expediency, chance" is the name of the game as opposed to the various forms of economic, racial, and historical determinism, . . . or whatever. Because us chickens can read what you *wrote*, but us can't read what you *think* about what you wrote unless you *write* it. Dig? OK if it's not socko, better if it is.

There it was. I had asked his advice and he had given it. He once commented that the original manuscript ended the way bagpipe music usually ends: it sounded like the piper had walked off a cliff. The book needed a chapter that set forth a Japanese model, regardless of whether I thought creating such a model was a good idea. When Gary Allinson later wrote in a review for the *American Political Science Review* that chapter 9 was "a tour de force, an exemplary model in its own right," Bell never let me forget that it was written at his insistence and that such advice is what good editing is all about.[12]

Today I agree with him. But, analytically speaking, the issue still remains that it is hard to abstract a "model" from historical reality. This is one of the errors of both the Marxists and the neoclassical economists: they overgeneralize the histories of Germany and France, on the one hand, and of England and the United States, on the other. These kinds of errors are not new in what are called the social sciences—Bentham believed he could draft a system of laws for any country from China to Peru, and Rousseau actually drafted a constitution for Poland without ever going there.[13] But any social science worthy of the name, it seems to me, must deal with both the generalizable and the particular without ruling one or the other out of court. The current fad for "rational-choice theory" and other forms of extreme economic reductionism are simply the latest examples of attempts at social science that fail this elementary test. They are combinations of sterility and hubris that resemble Scholasticism. I believe that the "developmental state" actually exists in time and space in East Asia and also exists as an abstract generalization about the essence of the East Asian examples. It is both particular and generalizable.

THE TRANSLATION

Even before *MITI and the Japanese Miracle* was published, officials of MITI had heard about my research and approached me for permission to do a translation. The JETRO officer in San Francisco, who reported to Tokyo on activities at the University of California, Berkeley, where I was then teaching, had written back to his ministry about what I was doing. Nonetheless, the ministry did not know much about me; I had not spent a lot of time interviewing at MITI, and most of my research was documentary, except for a major interview with former vice-minister Sahashi Shigeru. Each of us should probably have been more cautious about the other before agreeing to work together.

12. Gary Allinson, review, *American Political Science Review* 77 (March 1983): 242–43.
13. My thanks to Professor Leslie Lipson for reminding me of these early examples of misplaced universalism, in a letter dated September 8, 1994.

A Senior MITI officer, Yamada Katsuhisa, the former secretary of Miyazawa Kiichi when he was MITI minister and in 1980 head of the Planning Office in the Ministerial Secretariat, flew to California to say that the ministry itself wanted to translate my book as a way of instructing new officers about the difficulties of Japan's postwar high-speed growth. I agreed, and he arranged for a group of bright, young MITI officials, each partly educated in an English or an American university, to do the translation. They were unpaid and did the work after hours. I met with them on several occasions in Tokyo to resolve problems. They did a good job, and the terms *hatten-shiko-kata kokka* (developmental state) and *kisei-shiko-kata kokka* (regulatory state) became better known in Japan than their English equivalents did in the United States.[14]

MITI also used the translation to promote the political career of Yano Toshihiko, who retired in 1981 as vice minister and the following year ran successfully for the upper house of the Diet. He is the listed "supervising translator" (*kanyakusha*), even though he did not actually participate in the work, and with each copy of the book the ministry included a long dialogue between me and Yano in which he repeatedly says that I got the history right but did not pay enough attention to the ways Japan and the ministry were opening up to the outside world. My book thus helped both Yano's political campaign and MITI's public relations effort to convince the outside world that MITI had changed. Yamada suggested to me that if I would write a sequel about MITI after 1975, stressing Japan's commitment to "internationalization" (*kokusaika*), he would arrange interviews with all the then living ministers and vice ministers. I declined on grounds that it is impossible to have perspective on a governmental agency while it is actually making and implementing policy. But it also occurred to me that I was being set up to become the ministry's captive propagandist. There is no doubt in retrospect that it would probably have been better if I had entrusted the translation to a scholar (as I did with the Korean and Chinese translations). But having the book published with MITI's blessing ensured extensive reviews in Japanese—it was briefly on the business books best-seller list in September 1982—and that it would be widely read.[15]

Looking back on it, MITI may have more regrets about translating my book than I do about not ensuring a scholarly translation. The ministry has always been ambivalent about its own history and industrial policy, depending on whether it was writing in Japanese or in English. In Japanese, MITI officers reviewed the book lavishly. In the official house organ of

14. Chalmers Johnson, *Tsusansho to Nihon no kiseki*, trans. Yano Toshihiko (Tokyo: TBS Britannica, 1982), pp. 20–25.

15. *Nikkei Business*, September 20, 1982, p. 211.

the ministry, Iwatake Teruhiko (MITI, 1934–59) wrote, "The value of this book lies in showing the great contributions of MITI officials to high-speed growth," which was of course precisely why the ministry translated it.[16] In a rather hostile interview with Bernard Krisher, the then MITI minister, Abe Shintaro, used my book to defend the ministry. "At one point in the interview," wrote Krisher, "Abe came close to boasting about this protectionism. He rose from his desk to fetch a copy of Chalmers Johnson's new book, *MITI and the Japanese Miracle*, which describes the origins and operations of the system." This system was "the MITI way, a quiet protectionism that never acknowledges its name."[17]

In English, on the other hand, the ministry has consistently argued that its role and that of industrial policy have been overstated by foreign observers. In the early 1980s, Japanese propaganda organs emphasized the "special circumstances surrounding the 1950s–1960s" when MITI was hyperactive, and they listed "ways in which Americans exaggerate Japan's industrial policy."[18] A decade later, they were still at it: "There are even those who argue that Japan is fundamentally different with a set of rules that are [*sic*] incompatible with those generally accepted elsewhere. . . . In Japan, we use the term 'industrial policy' to mean those government strategies that are put in place to supplement the market mechanism only when and where necessary."[19]

The point is obvious. MITI is emphatically not an academic research organ. It has always taken shelter in secrecy and likes to confuse its competitors with disinformation. In 1973, when the ministry changed the name of the Enterprises Bureau to the Industrial Policy Bureau, some officers complained that it was not a good idea to say too publicly exactly what that key bureau actually does. In Kozo Yamamura's review of *MITI and the Japanese Miracle*, he goes out of his way to reassure an unknown MITI official who, he says, wanted to issue a denial that the ministry was as powerful as I had described it. Not to worry, writes Yamamura, "There are many of us outside Japan who do not believe MITI in effect 'runs' the Japanese economy or that MITI has 'perfected' the art of industrial poli-

16. Iwatake Teruhiko, in *Tsusan Jyanaru*, September 1982, pp. 148–49.
17. Bernard Krisher, interview of Abe Shintaro, *Fortune*, October 4, 1982, pp. 91–92, 96.
18. Japan Economic Institute (JEI) of America, *Japan's Industrial Policies* (Washington, D.C.: JEI, 1984). The JEI is "registered under the Foreign Agents Registration Act as an agent of the Japanese Government." See also *Japan's Postwar Industrial Policy* (Tokyo: JETRO, January 1985), which acknowledges that "industrial policies have made a considerable contribution to the rapid expansion of the Japanese economy," in combination with favorable international factors and high levels of education, Japanese-style employment practices, and weak shareholder control of companies.
19. Japan Economic Foundation (JEF), *Japan: A Perspective on Industrial Policy* (Tokyo: Acorn, June 1994), pp. 1, 2. The JEF is a MITI-created foundation.

cymaking."[20] I think Yamamura misunderstood his informant, who was merely trying to prevent foreigners from finding out too much. Much the same worry was expressed by Kuroda Makoto, MITI's best-known hardline negotiator, after Sony's Morita Akio wrote about how Japanese capitalism differs from Anglo-American capitalism: "We must not provide a dangerous basis for the argument that says Japan conducts itself by a different set of rules and must be treated differently. . . . For some time I have repeatedly stated that we should avoid expressions such as 'Japanese-style practices.' "[21] Just a few years after his review, even Yamamura was asking, "Will Japan's economic structure change? Confessions of a former optimist."[22]

MITI is not interested in abstract analysis of the Japanese economic system, and while its translation of my book may have served its interests at one time, it no longer did so a few years later. Nonetheless, because of its prompt translation, my book was widely read and reviewed in Japan as well as the United States. Hiraiwa Gaishi, then head of Tokyo Electric Power and later president of Keidanren, concluded his review by saying that Japan needed a "new MITI" for the period after 1975. A leading automotive journal castigated MITI as industry's "overprotective mama" and as a bureaucratic *sokaiya* ("corporate extortionist"). Takemura Ken'ichi, a journalist of the pulp magazines, used his review to tell Ronald Reagan to provide some real incentives for people in the United States to save, to stop protecting declining industries and the lawyers who represent them, and to create modern trading companies that can compete anywhere in the world.[23]

In this varied context, I received my most comprehensive review in any language. A doctoral candidate at Keio University, Oyama Kosuke, writing in the obscure *Kikan Gyosei Kanri Kenkyu* (Administrative management research quarterly), presented the book's argument, reviewed major foreign reviews, and concluded that my book raised four fundamental issues of continuing controversy.[24] I agree with him. In the pages that follow I want to analyze each of Oyama's four categories, laying out what is at issue, what is often misunderstood or obscured, and where the controversies stand nearly two decades after the book was published. It goes without saying that this categorization is somewhat artificial and that some is-

20. Yamamura, review, p. 215.

21. *Bungei shunju*, April 1992, pp. 176–93. Kuroda Makoto quoted in Chalmers Johnson, "Comparative Capitalism: The Japanese Difference," *California Management Review*, Summer 1993, p. 59.

22. Kozo Yamamura, ed., *Japan's Economic Structure: Should It Change?* (Seattle: Society for Japanese Studies, 1990), p. 13.

23. Hiraiwa Gaishi, review, *Zaikai*, September 21, 1982, p. 100; *Jidosha Hambai*, October 1982, p. 58; Takemura Ken'ichi, review, *Shukan Post*, September 10, 1982.

24. Oyama Kosuke, review, *Kikan Gyosei Kanri Kenkyu*, no. 29 (March 1985): 68–72.

sues, such as the compatibility of the developmental state with democracy and relations among bureaucrats and civilians, clearly overlap. Nonetheless, Oyama's framework is useful so long as it is not pushed too far.

INDUSTRIAL POLICY VERSUS THE MARKET

Oyama's first point concerns the question of how influential the Japanese state's industrial policy was and how much of Japan's high-speed economic growth was actually the result of market forces. He cites as specific representatives of the market forces school Kozo Yamamura in his review of *MITI and the Japanese Miracle* in the *Journal of Japanese Studies* and Komiya Ryutaro, who during the 1980s was Japan's best-known exponent of Anglo-American economics and a critic of MITI but who subsequently retired as a professor and went to work for MITI as head of its research institute. Yamamura indeed poses the question directly in his review: "To what extent has the postwar economic performance been due to the policies of a 'developmental state' and to what extent to 'market forces?'"[25]

Yamamura's alternative explanation to the developmental state is that "Japan was still 'catching up' with the West and was 'lucky' in many ways." He also throws in the old canard about how Japan was about to undergo fundamental structural change that would reveal MITI's accomplishments to be meaningless: "I have the distinct feeling that Johnson will come to regret all this discussion concerning MITI's 'effectiveness' and some of the other laudatory remarks he made about MITI. Because when Japan too begins to have its economic woes, as it clearly has begun to have, MITI's batting average is going to decline awfully quickly. In this sense, I think Johnson's book came out ten years too late."[26]

I do not know whether Yamamura came to regret his prediction, but Japan went on in the decade after he wrote these words to extract a cool trillion dollars from the rest of the world while racking up the greatest trade surpluses ever recorded. Even when the Japanese economy fell into a self-induced recession in the 1990s, its households continued to save close to a fifth of their income, it became the creditor nation to the rest of the world, including the United States, and each year the government invested several hundred billion dollars in infrastructure. Are these the "economic woes" Yamamura had in mind?

As for Yamamura's own explanation for Japan's high-speed economic growth, it boils down to good luck. Yamamura believes that industrial policy was not important in Japan's catching up with and overtaking external

25. Yamamura, review, pp. 212–13.
26. Ibid., pp. 214.

47

reference economies because "the 'winners' had been in effect 'pre-selected' by the Western nations."[27] All Japan had to do was emulate them. He does not go into why, among all the nations allied with the United States, Japan was the only one that carried this catch-up strategy to the point of altering the world balance of power. As far as he is concerned, Japan was just lucky.

I would argue that the very contrast between industrial policy and market forces is false and probably ideological. Industrial policy is not an alternative to the market but what the state does when it intentionally alters incentives within markets in order to influence the behavior of civilian producers, consumers, and investors. Americans are perfectly familiar with the state's structuring the domestic real estate market to favor family ownership of houses. American industrial policy allows its citizens to deduct mortgage interest payments in calculating their taxable income, and they respond by obtaining and carrying large mortgages. As Richard E. Caves concludes from the same evidence that Yamamura dealt with, the analytical issue is "the overall pattern of business incentives created by MITI's policies. . . . MITI has enough instruments to create substantial positive inducements for many types of conforming decisions by the private sector; it can also make life thoroughly miserable for any company that defies its wishes. . . . MITI has been able to guarantee a fat price-cost margin and easy access to needed inputs for any sector it chose to encourage."[28] Altering market incentives, reducing risks, offering entrepreneurial visions, and managing conflict are some of the functions of the developmental state, as I have demonstrated historically and as some economists have started to demonstrate theoretically.[29]

There *is* a powerful argument that can be made against industrial policy, but Yamamura does not make it. The real objection is not to its use as an alternative to or a displacement of market forces but that it is more commonly used to protect vested interests than to achieve national development. The state *can* structure market incentives to achieve developmental goals, as the Japanese case clearly illustrates, but it can also structure them to enrich itself and its friends at the expense of consumers, good jobs, and development. Several reviewers of *MITI and the Japanese Miracle* made this point. Robert Reich, for example, stressed that Japan's private business strategies depended on its public industrial policies—"Neither could exist without the other." But because the United States has an easily lobbied government, its industrial policies serve primarily

27. Ibid., p. 213.

28. Richard E. Caves, review, *Journal of Economic Literature* 21 (March 1983): 102–4.

29. See, for example, Ha-Joon Chang, *The Political Economy of Industrial Policy* (New York:St. Martin's Press, 1994).

the interests of politically well-connected, declining industries, not the goal of high value-added jobs for Americans. "Rapid industrial change," writes Reich, "is relatively easy to achieve when the leaders who plan it have no serious worries about politics. . . . [This was] Herbert Hoover's dream of an associationist state—a dream which came to brief fruition in Franklin Delano Roosevelt's National Recovery Association. Neither provides for direct review by, or accountability to, the people in the factories, towns, or regions that will be affected."[30] This was even more true in the case of contemporary Japan from 1925 to 1975, a point to which I will return in the next section.

Before leaving the issue of the economists and their views on industrial policy, I would like to raise the question of why arguments like those of Yamamura, although logically flawed, recur so often and with such vehemence in English-language discourse. I believe it is because they are ideological. Although there is a contemporary impulse in academic social science to overlook or discount ideology, Martin Malia reminds us of the costs of doing so in the case of the former USSR. One of the most embarrassing failures of "revisionist" Sovietologists was their inability to see the strains within the USSR that led to its collapse. The key variable that they consistently discounted or misconstrued during the last three decades of the Soviet Union's existence was ideology.[31]

In dealing with Japan, Western ideologists want to defend Western laissez-faire capitalism against Soviet-style displacement of the market. A central ideological dimension of the cold war was to posit a "free" market system in which the state served only as referee over and against the socialist displacement of the market for state ends. The achievements of the Japanese developmental state were inconvenient for both sides in this debate. They illustrated to the West what the state could do to improve the outcomes of market forces, and they illustrated to the Leninists that their big mistake was the displacement of the market rather than using it for developmental purposes.

Western ideologists sensitive to these issues are quick to intervene in discussions of Japanese capitalism. David Williams has noticed an interesting instance in the book edited by Ezra Vogel, *Modern Japanese Organization and Decision-Making* (1975). Williams observes:

[Peter] Drucker, the dean of American business experts, wrote an article for the volume titled "Economic Realities and Enterprise Strategy." A unique case in Vogel's collection, Drucker's article is immediately followed by a set of dissenting comments by Hugh Patrick. Why, we must ask, should the argu-

30. Robert B. Reich, review, *New York Review of Books*, June 24, 1982.
31. Martin Malia, *The Soviet Tragedy: A History of Socialism in Russia, 1917–1991* (New York: Free Press, 1994).

ments of one of the most influential students of world business trends require immediate correction by an economist? The reason is actually quite bold: Drucker's conclusion, that Japanese firms pursue financial ends other than short term profits, denies one of the key tenets of mainstream economic analysis. The universal reach of classical political economy requires stiff rejection of the very idea that Japanese economic practice could differ in any substantial way from Anglo-American economic practice by definition. It was because the issue was so fundamental to all theoretically aware economic discussion that Patrick was forced to attack Drucker's conclusions, as it were, on the spot.[32]

Given these ideological considerations, the subject of Japan as a "developmental state" arouses resistance to its dispassionate study that has grown only more intense since my history of industrial policy was published.

DEMOCRACY AND THE DEVELOPMENTAL STATE

In his review, Oyama stresses and agrees with my contention that in the Japanese developmental state "the politicians reign and the bureaucrats rule" (*seijika wa kunrin-shi, kanryo ga tochi-suru*).[33] He also notes, however, that even though Japan is ruled by bureaucrats, it is more "democratic" than the military and/or bureaucratic authoritarianism that prevailed in all East Asia and many regimes in Latin America at the time. Yet, he is also concerned that MITI's policies have strengthened the abstract entity called Japan but have not done much to enrich the lives of Japanese consumers and city dwellers. The Japanese people's standard of living did not change anywhere near as much as the change in the Japanese gross national product. Furthermore, because I stressed that after MITI officials failed in the 1960s to enact specific new legislation authorizing their orders to industry, they continued their oversight anyway under the cover of "administrative guidance," the question naturally arises: Is Japan a democracy under the rule of law, or is it merely administered through law when convenient?

These critically important questions lie at the heart of the study of the Japanese polity and, by extension, of the developmental state. In addressing this subject, American political science has squandered at least a decade trying to force Japan into various versions of American pluralist, constitutional, and rational choice theory, while avoiding empirical re-

---

32. Williams, "Beyond Political Economy," p. 245.
33. Johnson, *Tsusansho to Nihon no kiseki*, p. 356.

search on the Japanese state itself. Many political scientists in Japan contributed to this obfuscation by agreeing that Japan was really just a late-blooming version of American democracy and a proper place to apply the usual voting studies, game-theoretic electoral rules, and principal-agent theories of bureaucracy. Even to suggest otherwise was "revisionism" and "Japan-bashing."

The result is that there is still not even an elementary mapping of the Japanese government in English. There is no history of the prewar Ministry of Home Affairs (Naimusho), the pinnacle of the developmental state until it was dismembered into many other agencies by the American occupation. There are also no histories of the Ministries of Finance, Justice, Construction, Transportation, and so forth; no analysis of the thousands of nonprofit foundations (*zaidan hojin* and *shadan hojin*) created in the 1980s and 1990s for bureaucratic purposes; and no understanding of what, if anything, changed when during 1993–94 Japan changed parties and prime ministers four times. Writing in 1994 in the newsletter of the Institute of Social Science of the University of Tokyo, Professor Hiwatari Nobuhiro confesses, "Political studies of Japan have not yet fully addressed either the symbiotic relationship between the bureaucracy and politicians or the role of political parties. We still need an understanding of the Japanese state."[34]

One persistent theme in the reviews of *MITI and the Japanese Miracle* is that the book came dangerously close to a defense of fascism. For example, in an insightful review of the book, Christopher Howe says: "One may question whether in his [Johnson's] comparisons with systems such as that in the U.S., he has adequately weighed the political implications of the existence of such a powerful, semi-autonomous group in society. For as the author shows, from 1936 the same group that devised the post-war 'miracle' worked hard for one of the most despicable political regimes experienced in the twentieth century." Murray Sayle echoes this point: "In his magisterial *MITI and the Japanese Miracle*, Chalmers Johnson credits the capitalist developmental state with being 'a genuine Japanese invention.' With respect I believe that Mussolini holds the patent, although he never got his model to fly." Richard Nielson adds: "There are severe political difficulties in a democracy to effectively implement an industrial policy. . . . [Johnson treats] the political issue as a constraint. . . . Industrial policy was an important component of fascist ideology." And even the distinguished theorist of technology policy Kodama Fumio worries many Japanese and foreigners (notably E. O. Reischauer, former Ameri-

---

34. Hiwatari Nobuhiro, "After the Earthquake Election: Rethinking the Role of the Bureaucracy," *Social Science Japan*, July 1994, p. 14.

can ambassador to Japan) when he praises MITI for its commitment to "social engineering."[35]

My position on this controversy is to deny any necessary connection between authoritarianism and the developmental state but to acknowledge that authoritarianism can sometimes inadvertently solve the main political problem of economic development using market forces—namely, how to mobilize the overwhelming majority of the population to work and sacrifice for developmental projects. An authoritarian government can achieve this mobilization artificially and temporarily, but it is also likely to misuse such mobilization, thereby making it harder to achieve in the future. In the true developmental state, on the other hand, the bureaucratic rulers possess a particular kind of legitimacy that allows them to be much more experimental and undoctrinaire than in the typical authoritarian regime. This is the legitimacy that comes from devotion to a widely believed-in revolutionary project.[36] Korean public anger at the rules the International Monetary Fund tried to impose on South Korea in 1997 is a good example of public support for a developmental state. The leaders of a developmental state do not enjoy legitimacy in the sense of a mandate bestowed on them by civil society. The concept of civil society (or its absence) has, in any case, been invoked much too facilely by foreign "experts" trying to explain the failure of such revolutionary regimes after the fact.[37] The legitimacy of developmental states cannot be explained using the usual state-society categories of Anglo-American civics.

The successful capitalist developmental states have been quasi-revolutionary regimes, in which whatever legitimacy their rulers possessed did not come from external sanctification or some formal rules whereby they gained office but from the overarching social projects their societies endorsed and they carried out. As Ha-Joon Chang and Robert Rowthorn note, "Even central planning works better than the market for situations where there is one overriding objective, as in wartime or in a space program."[38] This one overriding objective—economic development—was present among the Japanese people after the war, among the Korean people after Syngman Rhee, among the Chinese exiles and the Taiwanese

35. Christopher Howe, review, *Bulletin of the School of Oriental and African Studies* 47, no. 1 (1984); Murray Sayle, "Japan Victorious," *New York Review of Books*, March 28, 1985, p. 40 n. 3; Richard Nielson, review, *Sloan Management Review* (Winter 1983): 84; and Kodama Fumio, "Tsusansho ni yoru kiseki wa futatabi kano ka" (Is the MITI-produced miracle possible a second time?), *Chuo Koron*, March 1983, pp. 139–47.

36. On this point, see Castells, "Four Asian Tigers with a Dragon Head."

37. See, in particular, X. L. Ding, "Institutional Amphibiousness and the Transition from Communism: The Case of China," *British Journal of Political Science* 24, no. 3 (July 1994): 293–318.

38. Ha-Joon Chang and Robert Rowthorn, "Introduction," in Chang and Rowthorn, eds., *Role of the State in Economic Change* (Oxford: Oxford University Press, 1995), p. 18.

after Chiang Kai-shek acknowledged that he was not going home again, among the Singaporeans after the Malayan Emergency and their expulsion from Malaysia, among the residents of Hong Kong after they fled communism, and among Chinese city dwellers after the Cultural Revolution. What distinguishes these revolutionaries from those in the Leninist states is the insight that the market is a better mechanism for achieving their objectives than central planning. The market includes people who want to work for a common goal; central planning excludes them.

Can such revolutionary legitimacy in a developmental state ever be democratic? One must first note, in the words of John Schaar, "Democracy is almost the most prostituted word of our age, and anyone who employs it in reference to any modern state should be suspect of either ignorance or bad motives."[39] With that stricture in mind, if one means by democracy some form of state accountability to the representatives of the majority of citizens combined with respect for the rights of minorities, the answer is probably no. At the same time, the leaders of the developmental state do enjoy legitimacy in the sense that their claim to political power is based on some source of authority above and beyond themselves. They differ in this sense from authoritarian rulers whose continued rule depends on their monopoly of force remaining a genuine monopoly. The source of authority in the developmental state is not one of Weber's "holy trinity" of traditional, rational-legal, and charismatic sources of authority. It is, rather, revolutionary authority: the authority of a people committed to the transformation of their social, political, or economic order. Legitimation occurs from the state's achievements, not from the way it came to power.

Such legitimacy based on projects or goals is, of course, fragile in that it normally cannot withstand failure. Equally serious, it cannot adjust to victory and the loss of mission. The legitimacy of the leaders of a developmental state is like that of field commanders in a major military engagement. It comes from people working together, and it probably cannot long survive either defeat or victory. This problem is an abiding source of instability in such regimes, one that often leads to severe crises, such as after Japan's defeat in World War II or the Korean revolution of 1987.[40]

To the extent that a developmental state possesses legitimacy and is not just a dictatorship of development, its leaders are somewhat akin to those of revolutionary mass movements. It goes without saying that they manip-

---

39. John Schaar, *Legitimacy in the Modern State* (New Brunswick, N.J.: Transaction Books, 1981), p. 23.

40. For further discussion of this issue, see Chalmers Johnson, "What Is the Best System of National Economic Management for Korea?" in Lee-Jay Cho and Yoon Hyung Kim, eds., *Korea's Political Economy: An Institutional Perspective* (Boulder, Colo.: Westview, 1994), pp. 63–85.

ulate their followers through propaganda, have enormous difficulty in being held responsible for failures, and often misuse the state for private purposes. But they can also alter the balance of power. The postwar bureaucratically led movement to enrich Japan was a revolutionary project, one that enjoyed legitimacy among the Japanese people for what it promised rather than for how its leaders got there. To think of such a regime as authoritarian is to both miss the point and fail to recognize real authoritarianism when it occurs.

THE TIME FRAME

Oyama's strictures on the time frame of my study—1925 to 1975—can be dealt with speedily. He makes two points, with both of which I agree. The issue here is not a difference but a clarification of views. Oyama's first point is that 1925 to 1975 is an arbitrary time frame and that there are several other ways of periodizing modern Japanese history. He specifically mentions Bernard Silberman's division of Japan's modern century into a period of bureaucratic absolutism, 1868–1900, and a period of limited pluralism, 1900–1936.[41] Although I believe Silberman's division mislocates the periods of absolutism and does not deal with the prewar and postwar continuities surrounding World War II, I accept Oyama's basic point that there are other possibilities.

Hidaka Rokuro's three cycles of democracy and bureaucracy seem to me more accurate in identifying periods of relative absolutism. His cycles—each of which has two parts, democratization followed by bureaucratization—are cycle one, Meiji Restoration to the constitution, followed by 1890 to the end of Meiji (1912); cycle two, Taisho democracy, 1912 to 1931, followed by militarism, 1931 to 1945; and cycle three, postwar democratization, 1945 to 1960, followed by high-speed growth and single-party rule, 1960 to 1989.[42] This schema is obviously quite different from that of Silberman. But not evident in either of them is the fact that Japan's preoccupation with industrial policy coincides with the greatest periods of both militarism and democracy. The high tide of state influence over the economy occurred during the war and the occupation. One of my purposes in stressing the era 1925 to 1975—from the founding of the Ministry of Commerce and Industry to the aftermath of the "oil

41. Bernard S. Silberman, "The Bureaucratic State in Japan: The Problem of Authority and Legitimacy," in Tetsuo Najita and J. Victor Koschmann, eds., *Conflict in Modern Japanese History* (Princeton: Princeton University Press, 1982), pp. 226–57.

42. For Hidaka's periodization, see Chalmers Johnson, "The People Who Invented the Mechanical Nightingale," in Carol Gluck and Stephen R. Graubard, eds., *Showa: The Japan of Hirohito* (New York: Norton, 1992), pp. 71–90.

shock"—was precisely to see Japan in a different light than that shed by the usual "victor's history."

Japan was working on and implementing industrial policy before 1925, of course, and I agree with Arthur Tiedemann in his review for the *American Historical Review.* "Many of the concerns, attitudes, practices and policies that he [Johnson] believes originated as responses to the 'situational imperatives' of the post-1925 period really are rooted more deeply in Japan's past."[43] But the period 1925 to 1975 is still a distinct unity in my opinion because it was dominated by men born in the middle to late Meiji era who virtually all survived the war and continued to work for the government if they were not uniformed military officers, and because it was a period of global, not just Japanese, concern for economic policy. Japan's use of industrial policy to transform its economy coincided with Stalin's First Five-Year Plan, Hitler's New Order, Roosevelt's New Deal, Keynesianism, the German Wirtschaft Wunder, the Chinese Great Leap Forward, the "welfare state," and many other ideologies and formulations of the proper role of the state in economic affairs. Japan made a critically important contribution to this era and to the modes of thought and political lessons that grew out it. The period of my history also virtually coincides, in Japanese terms, with the Showa era, and while I agree that there is nothing sacrosanct about 1925 to 1975, that is also true about the Showa period, the twentieth century, or the "postwar" era.

Oyama's second point is more important. He asks why I ended my study in 1975. What started to change then? More precisely, did the success of the Japanese developmental state in the postwar era depend on unusually favorable international conditions? If the postwar conditions were unusually favorable, is the developmental state possible under different international conditions? These questions are in line with Goldfrank's criticism that "Johnson's book consistently understates the contributions of world-systemic factors (e.g., Japanese and U.S. imperialism, the opportunities in the Asian regimes)."[44] Although I would not put it in Goldfrank's terms, I accept his point.

The cold war both promoted and camouflaged the enrichment of Japan and the rest of capitalist Asia. In *MITI and the Japanese Miracle,* I described the Korean War as the virtual equivalent of the Marshall Plan for Japan. There is no question about the importance of the environment in which Japan's high-speed economic growth occurred. But two points at least need to be made as guides to future research. First, the policies, attitudes, and delusions of the United States need to be studied, as do those who responded to them. Second, Japan was not the only country allied

43. Arthur Tiedemann, review, *American Historical Review* 88, no. 1 (February 1983).
44. Goldfrank, review, pp. 722–23.

with the United States or prepared to manipulate the Americans' preoccupation with the USSR to its own advantage. But it was Japan that gave a virtuoso performance of how to extract the most from the United States while paying the least to support its global strategies. That cannot be explained by "world-system factors." In a more general sense, the gains from a developmental state strategy may never again be as great as they were from 1945 to 1975, but other things being equal, a developmental state will always extract more of what gains are possible within a particular international environment than will a state with different priorities.

Japan's commitment to industrial policy did not end in 1975. If anything it became more intense. The new roles for industrial policy that began after 1975 were the nurturing of high-tech industries not already developed in reference economies, promoting Japan's national interests while pretending to support its competitors' rules for so-called "free trade" and "borderless economies," and achieving national security through technonationalism.[45] This agenda was very different from that of 1925 to 1975. The mid-1970s saw the end of the era of Japan's catching up and the beginning of its uneasy tenure as an economic superpower, which is why my book ends there.

GOVERNMENT-BUSINESS RELATIONSHIPS

Oyama's last point of controversy is his most important. It concerns the patterns of interaction within the developmental state between the official state bureaucracy and "privately" owned and managed business enterprises. This area was and remains controversial because scholars cannot agree on how to incorporate and weigh cultural differences as they manifest themselves in economic organizations and labor-management relations. It is the area where scholars have most often trapped themselves by projecting onto Japan the norms of the American private sector. David Friedman, Kent Calder, Daniel Okimoto, and Richard Samuels have all sought to improve on my picture of the developmental state by decreasing the weight of the state in economic affairs and increasing the influence of private managers allegedly responding to private incentives. I believe that they have all erroneously (perhaps also ideologically, because they are all Americans writing during the last decade of the cold war) conceived the relationship between the government and private actors as dichotomous and zero-sum and that Calder, in particular, has failed to

45. On technonationalism, see Richard J. Samuels, *"Rich Nation, Strong Army": National Security and the Technological Transformation of Japan* (Ithaca: Cornell University Press, 1994), and Jeff Shear, *The Keys to the Kingdom: The FS-X Deal and the Selling of America's Future to Japan* (New York: Doubleday, 1994).

grasp that "private" may mean something different in Japan's ethical system than it does in his own.[46]

Oyama accurately notes that I claim to have found three different patterns of public-private interaction during the fifty years of Japan's industrial policies that I cover. These are self-control, state control, and public-private cooperation. By self- or private control I meant that the state delegated control to private cartels for each industry and that each industrial sector was run by the members of the cartels in response to state incentives. This pattern prevailed from approximately 1931 to 1940, and it resulted in almost total control of Japanese manufacturing by zaibatsu organizations.

This pattern was followed by state control, meaning the direct imposition of state institutions onto the private economy, displacing private cartels, private ownership, private labor organizations, and private management with so-called control associations (*toseikai*) during the war and public corporations (*kodan, jigyodan,* and so on) during the occupation and after the restoration of sovereignty down to the present time.[47] Just as private control was never complete during the first period—steel, communications, and the most important portion of rail transport were state enterprises—state control was never complete during the second period. This was particularly true of the *toseikai*, which were covertly dominated by the zaibatsu. The most complete achievement of state control actually occurred during the Allied Occupation. This second period lasted from approximately 1940 to 1952.

Neither self-control nor state control worked very well. The first led to extremes of concentration and oligopoly that elicited violent protests against "monopoly capitalism" from workers and particularly from the military and other groups committed to national unity and a national singleness of purpose. The second led to the bureaucratism and misallocation of resources everywhere associated with state socialism. These conditions contributed directly to Japan's defeat in World War II, in which it was not so much outfought as it was outproduced. After 1952, the Japanese public and private sectors reconciled with each other and perfected cooperative management schemes. These schemes avoided an emphasis

---

46. See David Friedman, *The Misunderstood Miracle: Industrial Development and Political Change in Japan* (Ithaca: Cornell University Press, 1988); Kent E. Calder, *Strategic Capitalism: Private Business and Public Purpose in Japanese Industrial Finance* (Princeton: Princeton University Press, 1993); Daniel Okimoto, *Between MITI and the Market: Japanese Industrial Policy for High Technology* (Stanford: Stanford University Press, 1989); and Richard J. Samuels, *The Business of the Japanese State: Energy Markets in Comparative and Historical Perspective* (Ithaca: Cornell University Press, 1987).

47. Although long out of date, still the only study of postwar public corporations is Chalmers Johnson, *Japan's Public Policy Companies* (Washington, D.C.: American Enterprise Institute, 1978).

on either private profit or the state's socialization of wealth. They were made possible by the elimination of the military from public life, the reform of the zaibatsu replacing owners with managers, and the offering of career job security to male heads of households in strategic, exporting industries. This new approach worked phenomenally well and captured the attention of industrial sociologists around the world. They launched what amounts to virtually a new discipline under the rubric of the "principles of Japanese management."[48]

Oyama, however, perceptively argues that the differences between these three modes are more apparent than real. He believes that each of them boils down to Murakami Yasusuke's "compartmentalized competition" (*shikirareta kyoso*).[49] In all three periods there is a single pattern in which the state cartelizes or compartmentalizes each industry, restricting new entrants. It does so by promoting and protecting so-called *keiretsu* (industrial groups) from any form of legal or financial challenge by outsiders and protecting the domestic economy from international competition. Each individual industry thus enjoys a stable, cooperative environment in which it can divide up the domestic market and export to the American market, given the Americans' postwar willingness to trade access to their market for the right to have U.S. military bases on Japanese soil and other passive forms of support for their foreign policies.

The cartels of the 1930s, the wartime control associations, and the postwar keiretsu all had a similar structure. It consisted of a state "mother" agency or bureau (*genkyoku*) that maintained a "vertical relationship" with its clients, an officially recognized trade association for each industry, and individual enterprises managing their affairs through ad hoc, nonlegal, *Gemeinschaft*-type relationships. In Oyama's perspective, the government-business relationship in Japan has always been "informal and covert" (*hikoshiki-sei ammoku-sei*). State control was never fully achieved before or during the war, and it has never been fully surrendered to the present day.

I believe these are stimulating propositions that deserve further research. The chief evidence for my alleging a dialectical progression toward public-private cooperation is that in the third period Japan perfected new forms of management, enlisted extraordinary labor commit-

48. See, inter alia, Uchihashi Katsuto, Okumura Hiroshi, and Sataka Makoto, eds., *Nihon kaisha genron* (Principles of Japanese companies) (Tokyo: Iwanami Shoten, 1994), 6 vols., and Matsumoto Koji, *The Rise of the Japanese Corporate System*, trans. Thomas I. Elliott (London: Kegan Paul International, 1991). By foreign writers, the seminal works are Rodney Clark, *The Japanese Company* (New Haven: Yale University Press, 1979), and W. Mark Fruin, *The Japanese Enterprise System* (Oxford: Clarendon Press, 1992).

49. Murakami Yasusuke, *Shinchukan taishu no jidai* (The age of the new middle mass) (Tokyo: Chuo Koron Sha, 1984).

ment, and got rich, whereas in the earlier periods it faltered badly. The Japanese have not always been the masters of creative industrial management, to say the least. But the favorable postwar outcome may be due to factors other than improved state-civilian relationships. The exact nature and terms of the internal organization of "Japan, Inc." remain obscure, and the ideological attempts of the Americans during the cold war to redefine Japan as an appropriate ally did not help in clarifying them.

Rather than attempting this sort of research, Calder reformulates Japan's modern economic history. He asserts that the state's schemes for defensive modernization during the Meiji era were "mainly in support of private-sector objectives" and that "institutionally speaking, the role of the private sector in the Japanese economy was thus prior to that of the state."[50] His evidence for these propositions is drawn from a history of the Industrial Bank of Japan (IBJ), which he only obliquely acknowledges was from 1902 to 1952 a government organ and was "privatized" by order of the Allied Occupation. I also believe he has failed to do elementary area studies research on the different meanings of *ko* and *shi* in Japan and "public" and "private" in the United States.[51] He fails to understand that even his "private" managers in the post-Occupation IBJ are not American-style, short-term profit maximizers but engaged in a nationally sanctioned cooperative enterprise. The Japanese manager, as Rodney Clark classically put it, has "a view of management as a bureaucratic and cooperative venture: the government of a company rather than the imposition of an entrepreneurial will on a market place and a work force by superior skill, courage, or judgment."[52]

Calder's error, like that of the writers mentioned earlier who overstate or misinterpret the role of the private sector in Japan, comes from a combination of parochialism and ideology. Given the history of federalism and the separation of powers in the United States, it is a particularly inappropriate venue from which to study the East Asian state. This source of error was then compounded by the imperial pretensions of the United States during the Occupation and the cold war. These writers, in my opinion, are trying to force Japan to fit the paradigms of government that they were taught in American political science courses. The best of them learn from their failed attempts and go on to become mature, serious comparativists. They then begin to confront what X. L. Ding is getting at when he writes,

50. Calder, *Strategic Capitalism*, p. 25.
51. See Patricia Boling, "Private Interest and the Public Good in Japan," *Pacific Review* 3, no. 2 (1990): 138–50.
52. Clark, *Japanese Company*, pp. 36–37, quoted in Johnson, *MITI and the Japanese Miracle*, p. 62.

In East Asia, the pattern of state-society relations historically differs notably from the modern Western pattern, and the distinctive features of the East Asian pattern do not simply disappear after industrialization or democratization. In East Asia, the states are organizationally pervasive, without clear-cut boundaries. Their powers and functions are diffuse, and they pay little respect to due process. Consequently, the lines between public and private, political and personal, formal and informal, official and nonofficial, governmental and market, legal and customary, and between procedural and substantial, are all blurred. This is the case in precommunist China, in semi-authoritarian Taiwan, as well as in democratic Japan.[53]

I believe Hiwatari is right when he advises that "Calder should consider who created and protected the special kind of bank (long-term credit bank) that he asserts is the headquarters of 'corporate-led strategic capitalism.' "[54] However, it is equally important to stress, as I did in the earlier discussion of industrial policy versus the market, that regardless of the cultural or nationalistic norms that may prevail in either the state or civilian enterprises, both entities need each other. That is what I think the Japanese discovered as a result of their disastrous midcentury experiences and what American political scientists have yet to discover. The concept "developmental state" means that each side *uses* the other in a mutually beneficial relationship to achieve developmental goals and enterprise viability. When the developmental state is working well, neither the state officials nor the civilian enterprise managers prevail over the other. The state is a "catalytic" agency, in Michael Lind's sense of the term, and the managers are responding to incentives and disincentives that the state establishes.[55] This is not an easy combination to put together, but when it is done properly, it can produce miracles of economic development. Whether, in the current climate of economic "globalization" and Anglo-American triumphalism, it can mange to maintain its equilibrium is something that remains to be seen. But I am quite certain that if the developmental state goes under, the U.S. regulatory state will not be far behind.

53. Ding, "Institutional Amphibiousness," p. 317.
54. Hiwatari, "After the Earthquake Election," p. 12.
55. Michael Lind, "The Catalytic State," *National Interest* (Spring 1992): 3–12.

CHAPTER THREE

Webs with No Spiders, Spiders with No Webs: The Genealogy of the Developmental State

Bruce Cumings

In his book on Japan, James Fallows begins one chapter with a story about finding an English translation of Friedrich List's *The Natural System of Political Economy* in a bookshop in Japan. He writes that it had taken him five years to find an English version of List's work, and on doing so he exhales his version of eureka: *"Friedrich List!!!"*[1] He goes on to argue that List, not Adam Smith, was the economic theorist behind Japan's industrial growth.

Now compare E. H. Norman, writing in 1941, who began a passage about Prussian influence on post-Restoration Japan by saying, "It is a commonplace that Itō [Hirobumi] modelled the Japanese constitution [and much else] very closely upon the Prussian."[2] Or compare Karl Marx, who in 1857 noted that the only original American economist was Henry Carey, a Listian thinker who saw the United States as a late-developing industrial power, needing strong protection of its market and its nascent industries.[3] Since Carey's *Principles of Social Science* was widely read in Japan in the 1880s,[4] perhaps Fallows ought also to exclaim, *"Henry Carey!!!"* In a mere few sentences we have uncovered not a truth about civilizational

1. James Fallows, *Looking at the Sun: The Rise of the New East Asian Economic and Political System* (New York: Pantheon, 1994), p. 179.
2. E. H. Norman, *Origins of the Modern Japanese State: Selected Writings of E. H. Norman*, ed. John W. Dower (1941; New York: Pantheon, 1975), p. 451.
3. Karl Marx, "Bastiat and Carey," in *Grundrisse: Foundations for the Critique of Political Economy*, trans. Martin Nicolaus (New York: Vintage Books, 1973).
4. Robert Schwantes, "America and Japan," in Ernest R. May and James C. Thomson Jr., eds., *American–East Asian Relations: A Survey* (Cambridge: Harvard University Press, 1972), p. 122.

"difference" but a circular argument that ignores capitalist similarity and the influences of temporal stages and international competitition on industrial policy: thus to reinvent the wheel.

So, my first point is that whatever we might say about Japan's state-directed development, it is or ought to be understood as a variant of the European continental tradition and not something sui generis. Now let me say a few things about state theory in general.

Recent work in state theory has sensitized some sectors of American social science to the following ideas: (1) there is something called the state; (2) it sometimes has its own interests but in any case does not merely reflect interests external to it, either class (Marx) or political (Weber), but is a force in its own right; (3) states differ from one another according to their "capacities," for example, no agency in the American state performs "the MITI function" of administrative guidance; (4) states sometimes have a realm of autonomy, although it is not easy to specify that realm (thus "relative autonomy"); (5) ergo both the American pluralists (David Truman, Robert Dahl) and the vulgar Marxists (the "instrumental" theory of the state) are wrong.

In spite of a fine recent literature on "bringing the state back in" and any number of research projects spawned by it, however, it still seems to me that Americans continue to reinvent ideas that had their theoretical origin and a much fuller praxis in nineteenth-century Europe.[5] In ways similar to what Alasdair MacIntyre writes about our moral discourse, state theory comes to us not whole but in fragments and shards from the past, ripped from time and context.[6] If a Lockean liberalism with a seemingly natural "fit" had a multiple and fissured genealogy in America,[7] how much more so for non-Lockean formulations? Because these ideas suffuse the literature on Northeast Asian states, we have a double remove and therefore the rather large problem of comprehending states such as

5. This is not surprising, because late-twentieth-century capitalism presents many of the same problems of comprehension as did the mid-nineteenth-century version, and one good definition of intelligence is the recombination of existing ideas. But all readers need to do to see my point is to pick up Hegel, Marx, or Weber—or such lesser lights as Otto Hintze, Joseph Schumpeter, Friedrich List, V. I. Lenin, or, for that matter, Alexander Hamilton—and begin reading. For an exhaustive compendium of more-recent social science theory on the state, see Bob Jessop, *State Theory: Putting the Capitalist State in Its Place* (University Park: Pennsylvania State University Press, 1991). This book has many welcome suggestions, such as "bringing in" discursive theory to help us think about the state, but Jessop ends up not quite knowing what to think about his subject (see especially pp. 360–63).

6. See especially Alasdair MacIntyre, *After Virtue* (Notre Dame: University of Notre Dame Press, 1979).

7. Ruminating about this genealogy was the lifework of Louis Hartz. See his *Liberal Tradition in an Interpretation of American Political Thought since the Revolution* (New York: Harcourt, Brace, 1991) and *The Founding of New Societies* (New York: Harcourt Brace Jovanovich, 1969).

those in Japan and Korea—themselves at a different but closely studied remove from European state practice.

THE "DEVELOPMENTAL STATE"

It is fair to say that in the American context, the label "developmental state" identifies the most formidable theory of the East Asian state and is a breath of fresh air compared with the liberal constructions of the modernization literature or the successive "pluralist" conceptions of postwar Japan.[8] Chalmers Johnson is widely credited with coining the term "developmental state" and establishing it as a third category alongside liberal and Stalinist conceptions.[9] This was a key breakthrough in the American literature on Northeast Asia.

The fresh air comes in swooshes with *MITI and the Japanese Miracle*, which eschews various explanations of Japanese success that occupy the public mind, namely, that the market drives it, that collectivism drives it, or that national character is the explanation or a diffuse notion of "culture" which tells us that if we give a few teenage miscreants a good caning, we will have no more crime in the streets. Johnson rightly thinks that much Japanese "difference" can be explained situationally, in terms of "late development, lack of resources, the need to trade . . . and so forth."[10]The argument takes truly original and controversial form in the postulation of a genealogy of bureaucratic departments and careers (an "economic general staff") spanning the presumed 1945 watershed, preeminently the interwar forerunners of MITI and the dark knight of industrial policy, Kishi Nobosuke—who, like Itō Hirobumi before him, had a formative period of German learning. Manchukuo is resituated not as a failed puppet state run by a restive Kwantung Army but as the birthplace of the Japanese "miracle."[11]

8. "Patterned pluralism," "bureaucratic inclusionary pluralism," "network state"—all such terms seek to graft an American pluralist conception onto an unyielding Japan. See Ellis S. Krauss and Michio Muramatsu, "Japanese Political Economy Today: The Patterned Pluralist Model," in Daniel I. Okimoto and Thomas P. Rohlem, eds., *Inside the Japanese System: Readings on Contemporary Society and Political Economy* (Stanford: Stanford University Press, 1988); Inoguchi Takashi, *Gendai Nihon Keizai no Kōzu* (The structure of the Japanese political economy) (Tokyo: Tòyò Keizai, 1983); and Daniel Okimoto, *Between MITI and the Market: Japanese Industrial Policy for High Technology* (Stanford: Stanford University Press, 1989).

9. Chalmers Johnson, *MITI and the Japanese Miracle: The Growth of Industrial Policy, 1925–1975* (Stanford: Stanford University Press, 1982).

10. Ibid., pp. 6–11.

11. Ibid., pp. 124–44. Kishi spent seven months in Germany in 1930 and determined that German industrial rationalization "was devoted to technological innovation in industries . . . and to generally increasing efficiency . . . [with] emphasis on government-sponsored trusts and cartels as the main means of implementing reforms" (p. 108).

Johnson takes the importance of technology to Japanese growth seriously, but mainly in the context of how MITI rode herd on the acquisition of new technologies and how at critical turning points MITI directed advanced technologies and cheap finance to new industrial sectors—especially the shift to heavy and chemical industries in the 1950s.[12] He rightly traces a German lineage in Japan's success, but only to *Handlespolitik* or neomercantilism in the first instance and with more emphasis on Japanese learning from Germany in the 1930s than in the 1880s.[13] Like nearly everyone else, Johnson takes "Japan" as his unit of analysis. Mostly missed, therefore, is the shaping and constraining influence of American hegemony in the postwar period, or the collapse of the world system in the interwar period.

The book is perhaps best known for the trichotomy of states that are "plan rational" (Japan), "plan ideological" (Stalinist states), and "regulatory" (the New Deal American state). The virtue of this analysis is to suggest that planning can be as "rational" as market allocation, or more so. The vice is, once again, the aura of reification and righteousness surrounding the term "rational." But that is not surprising, because the real German lineage that Johnson asserts is from Max Weber to MITI. Modern bureaucracy for Weber is "the most rational and impersonal form of state administration," Johnson writes, and he finds no problem locating the angel of rationality: it is a technocratic elite of bureaucrats, signified above all by MITI, but embodied in the servants of the Japanese state more generally: the "way of the bureaucrat" (*kanryōdō*) is Japan's modern substitution for the "way of the warrior" (*bushidō*).[11] But as many critics have pointed out, Johnson is at a loss to show how and why the angel of rationality got things right in Japan.

Another example of thinking about the East Asian state is Richard Samuels's approach that seeks to split the difference between the "pluralist" and "developmental state" perspectives. By examining several case studies in Japan's energy regime, Samuels argues that his cases give forth "no evidence to support the prevailing view of a Japanese bureaucracy that purposefully chooses policies to anticipate and conform to the demands of the market." Instead, the state "negotiates rather than leads," in part because of "limits to state capacity," in part because of "the politics of reciprocal consent" in which business firms and the state negotiate and mutually limit each other. At the same time, Samuels acknowledges that Japan still has "an undeniably pervasive, developmental state."[15]

12. Ibid., p. 31.
13. Ibid., pp. 17, 36, 103–8.
14. Ibid., pp. 22–23, 36–37, 39–42.
15. Richard J. Samuels, *The Business of the Japanese State: Energy Markets in Comparative and Historical Perspective* (Ithaca: Cornell University Press, 1987), pp. x, 2, 261.

Samuels rightly points out that "identifying state structures" is not always easy; it is not clear where "state structures" leave off and "social structures" begin. Nor is it easy to judge the "relative autonomy" of states. Samuels prefers to examine "state capacities," which, he thinks, can be identified.[16]

This analysis captures rather than transcends the general confusion in state/society distinctions: it is true that there is "a fundamental theoretical problem" in identifying and separating "state and social structures" or in specifying "the extent to which and the conditions under which state preferences are autonomous." It therefore follows that "states and markets belong to businessmen and bureaucrats alike" and that "state power and private power frequently enhance each other." It does not follow, however, that these distinctions make "the politics of reciprocal consent comprehensible," nor does it follow that this web is "a web with no spider."[17]

Samuels substitutes a murky lens for the specious clarity of the state-society literature; "the politics of" is a phrase with no meaning, and "reciprocal consent" merely acknowledges what sharp state/society distinctions try to hide, namely, that states appropriate the market and firms appropriate the state, in a political range from conflict of interest to consensus. Nor can Samuels possibly identify "state capacities" by peering inwardly at Japan alone, when, for example, Japan was locked into a world energy regime that shaped government departments just as it stifled national and private oil firms.[18]

Whether consciously or unconsciously, Samuels draws on recent state theory that seeks to establish the state as "a social relation." Bob Jessop, a prominent theorist of the state, attributes the genesis of this concept to Nicos Poulantzas; in any case it is not a useful concept but merely a truism. After you have said that the state is also "a social relation," where do you go next? Jessop goes here, specifying "the relational character" of the state as follows: "The relation between state structures and . . . specific strategies pursued by specific forces to advance specific interests over a given time horizon in terms of a specific set of other forces each advancing their own interests through specific strategies. Particular forms of state privilege some strategies over others."[19] What does this say? Merely that some forces have ways of advancing their interests within the state and that they have to account for others doing the same.

The last example is a book that parodies my discussion of the state, moving one step beyond Johnson and Samuels to argue that Japan is

16. Ibid., pp. 3–5, 286.
17. Ibid., pp. 286–88.
18. Yul Sohn, a former student of mine, has a book forthcoming on the auto and oil sectors in the 1930s.
19. Jessop, *State Theory*, p. 10. See also pp. 149–50.

"stateless," so seamless is the web-with-no-spider. Karel van Wolferen's *Enigma of Japanese Power* would merit no more than a footnote were it not so influential in American liberal circles, helping to "make Japan strange" once again.[20] Nor is it just liberals who liked the book: at one point in late 1993, van Wolferen performed the feat of having articles published simultaneously in *New Left Review, Foreign Affairs,* and the *National Interest,* thereby blanketing the spectrum of intellectual opinion. The editors of the *New York Times* not only have opened their op-ed page to him several times but have also written editorials based on his work—which they think located a "third system" after capitalism and communism, namely, the Japanese System.

This book resuscitates an essentialist treatment not just of Japan but of "the West" as well. We get it on the very first page: "In the late 1980s the West is beginning to harbor doubts about Japan as a responsible partner in politics and trade." As in nineteenth-century accounts of "the Orient" Japan is an enigma, opaque, led by a mysterious "System," and "single-mindedly pursuing some obscure aim of its own." Indeed, what "drives" the Japanese people has become "something of an international conundrum." The System "systematically suppresses individualism," a predictable trope, but one distended to absorb all-that-we-hold-dear: the Japanese do not accept Western logic or metaphysics, going all the way back to "the Greeks": there are "logically reasoning Westerners," and then there are the Japanese. The "crucial factor" in all this is "the near absence [in Japan] of any idea that there can be truths, rules, principles or morals that always apply, no matter what the circumstances." For van Wolferen "the West" connotes a site of "independent, universal truths or immutable religious beliefs, transcending the worldly reality of social dictates and the decrees of power-holders"; "Japan" is where people adjust their beliefs to situations, in "a political culture that does not recognize the possibility of transcendental truths." Much like Allan Bloom's *Closing of the American Mind,* he retreats to classical theory to buttress his exaltation of the West—only to get Plato flat-out backward.[21]

The truths that the Japanese dishonor seem to connote, for van Wolferen, a medieval European metaphysics that the Enlightenment struck down; in any case the only "transcendent truth" he can put his fin-

20. Karel van Wolferen, *The Enigma of Japanese Power: People and Politics in a Stateless Nation* (New York: Alfred A. Knopf, 1989).

21. Ibid., pp. 1–10, 23–24. "Plato . . . was fully aware of the corrupting potential of power. His magnificently rational and poetic mind first saw the need for liberation from myths, from tradition and from brute power as the fundamental justification for political action" (p. 24). Presumably that is why in *The Republic* Plato saw in power the architectonic force for creating the just society, one that could be maintained only by inculcating soothing myths in the minds of its "guardians," controlling the content of music and poetry from on high, and the like.

ger on, as with many nineteenth-century accounts, is "Western individual-ism." In Japan there are individuals; van Wolferen has even met some of them. But the Japanese, he opines, "are less free than they should be." The stunning presumptuousness of this judgment recalls Nietzsche's point: "A man as he *ought* to be: that sounds to us as insipid as 'a tree as it ought to be.' "[22]

The Japanese state is also peculiar to van Wolferen: "Statecraft in Japan is quite different from in Europe, the Americas and most of contem-porary Asia. For centuries it has entailed a balance between semi-autonomous groups that share in power." Today these groups tend to be officials of certain ministries, "political cliques and clusters of bureaucrat-businessmen"; all are components of "the System," for which "no one is ultimately in charge." Thus figuring out the Japanese state is like "grop-ing in the proverbial bucket of eels"; so much about the System is "mad-deningly elusive" or "unaccounted for in the categories of accepted polit-ical theory."[23] Furthermore Japan is not alone (in spite of van Wolferen just having said it was); the list of the inscrutable expands: "The Japanese, Korean and Taiwanese experiences show that a third category of politi-cal economy can exist, beside the Western and communist types." He now brings up Chalmers Johnson's developmental state, "a variant that tradi-tional political and economic theory has overlooked" (a falsehood, as Johnson himself indicates), thus to argue that "Japan [and Korea and Tai-wan] represents a largely uncharted economic and social-political cate-gory."[24]

Van Wolferen is the most explicit of a group of analysts who decided, some time in the 1980s (but only in the 1980s), that Japan was not a democracy. Since 1945 the dictum of the Japan field was that the Ameri-can Occupation had bequeathed not only a pluralist democracy but also the only one in East Asia and almost the only one in the "developing" world—Japan became the glorious exception proving an inglorious rule. From this standpoint the 1930s had to become a parenthesis, an unfortu-

22. Ibid.; Friedrich Nietzsche, *The Will to Power*, trans. Walter Kaufmann (New York: Ran-dom House, 1987), p. 181. Compare Michael Adas: over several centuries, "European judgements about the level of development attained by non-Western peoples were grounded in the presuppositions that there are transcendent truths . . . which exist inde-pendent of humans, and that [they] are equally valid for all peoples . . . [and] that Euro-peans better understood these truths." Adas notes that usually these were Christian truths, that is, beliefs. He also argues, quite rightly in my view, that attitudes like van Wolferen's ought not to be called racist: racism was "ideologically subordinate to a more fundamental set of European convictions that arose out of their material accomplishments," namely, "that Europeans were technologically and scientifically superior to all other peoples" (*Ma-chines as the Measure of Men*: Science, Technology, and Ideologies of Western Domination [Ithaca: Cornell University Press, 1990] pp. 6–7, 274; see also pp. 338–42).
23. Van Wolferen, *Enigma*.
24. Van Wolferen, *Enigma*, pp. 5–8, 23–24; Johnson, *MITI*, p. 36.

nate aberration in the long march of Japanese democracy. The argument is that in spite of five decades of Japan's parliamentary system and the constitution we wrote for it, "one should not be misled" by "familiar labels" into thinking Japan is a democracy. The logical corollary is that the 1930s now become the distant point of origin, instead of an unfortunate hallucination.[25] Presumably Japan was doing in the 1980s what it had been doing since the 1940s, because no one argues for fundamental change in its "system." One could hardly have a better example of Nietzsche's teaching on the endless reinterpretation of the origin or Foucault's transformations of the discursive, changing black to white and white to black while the real Japan stays the same.

The virtue of discursive revision is to open new fields of inquiry, however, and both van Wolferen and Johnson therefore shine their light on the new point of "origin," the 1930s: Johnson does it responsibly, emphasizing pre-1933 German programs of industrial rationalization that impressed the likes of Kishi, whereas van Wolferen floods his portrait with the black ink of Nazism; indeed, for him "German" is a sign saying "Nazi." But there was no Japanese Hitler: no one was in charge then, either; fascist Japan was a "headless chicken." Then as now, "Japan" connoted "the System," which is "neither 'state' nor 'society,' [but] nevertheless determines how Japanese life is lived and who obeys whom." If we read on, we find that van Wolferen also has conflated the state with the grandest category, culture: "State, society and culture, in one grand amalgam, affect most Japanese as an enveloping natural phenomenon, an inescapable force."[26] A web with no spider.

Web with no spider, or spider with no web? Leaving no stone unturned, van Wolferen speculates on whether there might be some "master plan" behind Japan's activities—"the Protocols of Nippon," we can call it. Good Western empiricist that he is, he finds "no convincing concrete evidence for a master-plan." But then again, evidence does not really matter: even if he has not located Japan's scheme for "industrial domination of the world," "what they are doing has the same effect as if there were such a plan." Given that there is a plan (in effect), "the [Japanese] phoenix appears stuck on a collision course."[27]

Our intrepid guide to occult Japan, resident there for somewhere between seventeen and twenty-five years according to the publisher's no-

---

25. Van Wolferen, *Enigma*, p. 25; also p. 22, where he argues that World War II was not a watershed so much as the point when the "bureaucratic power system" was consolidated. He is also explicit on the continuities: the System refers to "a consolidation of pre-1945 bureaucratic institutions" (p. 348).

26. Ibid., pp. 36–39, 272.

27. Ibid., pp. 403–7; earlier (p. 10), van Wolferen warned that if Japan is pushed too hard, it might "reawaken irrational xenophobic sentiments."

tices, closes his book by recommending that to avoid the collision, the Phoenician must become, well, more like The West: "the System" can be changed by adopting the rule of law, fostering "individual political awareness and a sense of individual responsibility," the emergence of independent political parties "truly representing the interests of the middle class and the factory workers," and parliamentary checks and balances. Alas, this path will be tortuous: "The wonderful alternative of turning the System into a genuine constitutionalist state, and Japanese subjects into citizens, would require realignments of power akin to those of a genuine revolution."[28]

DEVELOPMENTAL POWER AND AUTHORITARIANISM

Van Wolferen's assumption that the Japanese state is authoritarian, whether in the 1930s or the 1980s, is merely a provincial and undigested view. A more important question about Northeast Asia is whether there a relationship between "the developmental state" and authoritarianism. Historically speaking there unquestionably is: Japan was highly authoritarian at the 1930s point when, according to Johnson, its developmental aspect was born and when it moved deeply into heavy industry; South Korea was highly authoritarian during the entire postwar period down to 1993 but was more so in the 1970s and 1980s when it moved from light to heavy industries and became a major world economic power; meanwhile, wunderkind Taiwan was under martial law from 1947 to 1989. All had remarkably large militaries compared with other, similar states, and these militaries intervened in politics in 1930s Japan and in South Korea from 1961 to 1993.

Theoretically speaking, however, there is no reason why this had to be. The whole problem of coercive force, military power and military organizations, and authoritarianism is deeply vexed and confused in the literature on the state. First, authoritarian dictators and military authorities cannot supply or account for the "rationality" of industrializing states; they must do somebody else's bidding. Second, in the industrial epoch military power has always been less important than other forms of power (a world-historical example is the collapse of the Soviet Union). Third, "weak" states may be highly authoritarian, just as some states are so "strong" that one barely knows they exist.[29] Recourse to brute force, for

---

28. This is the last statement in the text of *Enigma* (see p. 433).

29. Immanuel Wallerstein is one of the few who understand this point, and his discussions of it are subject to endless misreading. Here is his definition of the modern world's array of "strong" and "weak" states: "States have been located in a hierarchy of effective

example, is a far less effective method of influencing students than is teaching them political science (for example, convincing them that Japan is a web with no spider or, as in recent "rational-choice" literature, that it is really the Japanese people and the politicians they elect who guide economic strategy, rather than MITI or the Ministry of Finance). Fourth, international coercive force (usually military force) comes relatively late in the tenure of the most powerful of the industrial nations, that is, the hegemon, and is only a superficially effective method for rising and declining industrial states (as Japan learned after Pearl Harbor and as the United States is learning after the cold war).

So, here I would briefly conclude that for historical reasons still to be surveyed, the East Asian "developmental" states have usually been authoritarian; they have preferred to jail laborers, students, and intellectuals because they lacked more effective ways of dealing with them. But I would rather name them "bureaucratic-authoritarian industrializing regimes," or BAIRs, to signal (for the Northeast Asian region) the greater weight of the state (as opposed to the market), the typical kind of coercion they deploy (that is, not fully legitimated), and the nature of the task for which they are cut out: industrialization, late in world time. I also would argue that if you cannot find the prewar Japanese *BAIR* in the postwar period, you should look for it not in the mysterious inner sanctum where Liberal Democratic Party (LDP) bigwigs open their pockets to business bribes and bureaucratic missives but in the external region where South Korea and Taiwan *completed* the Japanese state with overgrown, security-conscious military, police, and intelligence bureaucracies, thus to keep the region's anticapitalists at bay and to leave no rationale for Japan to remilitarize.

FLY IN THE OINTMENT: SOCIETIES MAKE STATES, STATES MAKE SOCIETY

It is one thing to inform a history text with the liberal notion that the rise of the middle class is the explanation for modernity and "civic culture" and therefore the answer to everyone's problems, or to argue that the proletariat is the class of universal salvation; it is quite another to

---

power which can be measured neither by the size and coherence of their bureaucracies and armies nor by their ideological formulations about themselves but by their effective capacities over time to further the concentration of accumulated capital within their frontiers as against those rival states." Nor were these states fully "sovereign": "The very existence of this hierarchy provided the major limitation." Wallerstein, *Historical Capitalism* (London: Verso, 1983), pp. 56–57.

bring these classes into real historical existence as a matter of state policy and "late development." Yet artificial class making, as part and parcel of full-blown industrialization, has been the project of all the Northeast Asian states, founded precisely on mid-nineteenth-century theory. That theory was best reflected in debates "between" Hegel and Marx, which I will now survey—knowing full well that to cite Karl Marx in the 1990s is, for most Americans, like asking Nero for a lesson in fiddling and kindling. But then Francis Fukuyama disinterred Hegel at the end of the cold war, so . . .

The first modern representative state also just happened to be found in the hegemonic power of the 19th century, England. Its primary industrial rival, Germany, could produce only some unavailing, pale reflection of the liberal state. But at the level of theory it could work an elegant and sublime substitution: namely, Hegel—who towered over any English thinker in his time. Marx took Hegel to be the exemplary theorist of the representative state and instantly took his measure: however dazzling he was, Hegel merely recapitulated Germany's position vis-à-vis the advanced economies:

> The German *status quo* is the *undisguised consummation of the ancien régime* and the *ancien régime* is the *hidden defect of the modern state*. The struggle against the German political present is the struggle against the past of modern nations . . . the present German regime . . . [is] an anachronism, a flagrant contradiction of universally accepted axioms. . . .
>
> In Germany, therefore, we are about to begin at the point where France and England are about to conclude. . . . This is a good example of the *German* form of modern problems, an example of how our history, like some raw recruit, has up to now been restricted to repeating hackneyed routines that belong to the past of other nations.

As for Hegel, he supplied the ideality for which there was no reality:

> We Germans have lived our future history in thought, in *philosophy*. We are the *philosophical* contemporaries of the present without being its *historical* contemporaries. . . . What for advanced nations is a *practical* quarrel with modern political conditions is for Germany, where such conditions do not yet exist, a *critical* quarrel with their reflection in philosophy.[30]

I have elided Marx's most important statement, carrying a prescience founded in genius and requiring no emphasis: in England and France "it

---

30. Karl Marx, *Critique of Hegel's Philosophy of Right* (1844), in *Karl Marx: Early Writings*, intro. Lucio Colletti, trans. Rodney Livingstone and Gregor Benton (New York: Vintage Books, 1975), pp. 247–49.

is a question of the solution; here it is only a question of the collision." Why a collision? Because a middle class brought into being in hothouse conditions could never establish its hegemony short of a bloody reckoning with its reactionary enemies ("clod-hopping squires and philistines"),[31] classes forged in the long run of "real" history. Germany thus combined the "civilized defects" of the modern world with the "barbaric defects" of the old regime. How can such a country, "in one *salto mortale*," overcome "not only its own limitations but those also of the modern nations"?[32]

History's answer was that it could not, and those who enjoy pointing out the progressive teleology in Marx's thought need also to reckon with Germany's trajectory (Bismarck to Weimar to Hitler to catastrophe, and then and only then to liberalism) and the diabolical unfolding of barbarism within "civility," foregrounded by Marx in 1844. Both Marx and Hegel could hardly have been more explicit about Germany's predicament: for Marx, it was that Germany "did not pass through the intermediate stages of political emancipation at the same time as modern nations";[33] for Hegel, far more the optimist of course, it was the task of the state to overcome Germany's debilities: "It is a prime concern of the state that a middle class should be developed, but this can be done only if the state is an organic unity . . . i.e., it can be done only by giving authority to spheres of particular interests, which are relatively independent, and by appointing an *army of officials* whose personal arbitrariness is broken against such authorized bodies."[34]

Marx places the German domestic configuration in the time and space of the world system and declares the task hopeless, whereas Hegel conjures it in the thin air of an ideal type and then foists the problem off on the bureaucrats. This is a theory of "late" state formation and of "late" democratization: in Marx you get the kernel idea for two of the best American accounts of democracy, those by Barrington Moore Jr. and Louis Hartz. But in Hegel you get the answer to Japan's dilemma after the Meiji Restoration: the Hegelian conception is the perfect one, the ideal one, a neo-Confucianism of the modern state. Copy the perfect Hegelian conception, and copy it perfectly, but first construct the civil service that will construct the modern economy and the modern parliamentary democracy, and finally the modern society: in short, foist the problem off on the bureaucrats.

What can be concluded so far about the state? First, there is truth in the idea that state "actors" sometimes have their own interests, giving the state "apparatus" a sometime autonomy; it is also true that states differ in

31. Located, of course, in Prussia and Austria (ibid., p. 252).
32. Ibid., pp. 248, 252.
33. Ibid., p. 252.
34. Hegel, quoted in Marx, *Critique of Hegel's Doctrine of the State*, in *Karl Marx*, p. 116.

their "capacities" (Costa Rica does not have national police, Spain and South Korea do). But the state is also an arena as well as a resultant of class and interest group conflict, not just bureaucratic conflict,[35] and it occasionally (especially in determinate crises) acts with little discernible autonomy—a spider without need of a web. Furthermore, we have historical examples of what seems to be capitalism with no state, as we will see, especially in America. So, here we have only a partial truth.

Second, Hegel is right, states can make classes (an insight that political scientist Steven Krasner has explored). Third, Americans generally cannot think dialectically and therefore do not understand that states and external interests constantly interact and are made and remade in daily strife;[36] if "state" or "society" does not dominate in a clear either/or fashion, there must therefore be a web or an aspic in which both get stuck. Fourth, the external interests that interact with and shape the state are often external to the nation, that is, they are "international." Fifth, Americans have woefully inadequate conceptions of power. Because states traffic in power, this is no small liability. Finally, no one anywhere has an adequate conception of the executive arm of government or the politics of the executive; these remain cloaked and mysterious. Yet the executive is the paradise where the angel of rationality takes wing.

To take the last of these points, right after quoting Hegel on the middle class, Marx refers to *the executive:* "Of all the various powers the executive is the hardest to analyse. To a much greater degree than the legislature it is the property of the whole people."[37] A maximum leader (Roosevelt or Reagan here; Kim Il Sung, Mao, or Itō there) somehow reaches outside the state and across the classes to "the whole people," thus to stir them, awe them, or stupefy them, and how it is done remains a mystery.[38]

The modern conundrum for all the Japan experts, and particularly the

---

35. For a similar conclusion, see Jessop, *State Theory*, p. 9. (In his rhetoric, "state actions . . . should be understood as the emergent, unintended [?; he must mean intended and unintended] and complex resultant of what rival 'states within the state' have done and are doing on a complex strategic terrain." Unfortunately, Jessop nearly always defines that terrain as internal to the nation-state, which is wrong.)

36. Although some Americans do understand: see Herbert Franz Schurmann, *The Logic of World Power: An Inquiry into the Origins, Currents, and Contradictions of World Politics* (New York: Pantheon, 1974), and my exuberant discovery of his ideas in "Reflections on Schurmann's Theory of the State," *Bulletin of Concerned Asian Scholars* (November–December 1976): 55–64.

37. Marx, *Critique of Hegel's Doctrine of the State*, p. 116.

38. In an old and forgotten book, Robert MacIver has a stimulating discussion of the cloak of authority, from a president's demeanor to a Supreme Court justice's gown and cloistered secrecy. See *The Web of Government* (New York: Macmillan, 1947), pp. 39–47.

best,[39] of course, is the majesty and mystery of the emperor. Beginning with World War II potboilers, people have sought to pin Japanese aggression on Hirohito: their opponents have said no, he only studied spiders, he was not the spider you are looking for. But they usually offer no alternative spiders, save the beleaguered and inadequate Tōjō. Why? Because, Japan has no spiders. This was not Samuels's dictum, let alone van Wolferen's; it was the dictum of a great Japan specialist, William W. Lockwood, from whom all the others have learned: "A web it may be, but a web with no spider."[40]

This metaphor seems to sweep away all too many Japan specialists (and others locate no spiders in contemporary South Korea or Taiwan, either). It is possible that they have just not found the spider yet. In North Korea and China, to the contrary, the spider prowls the realm in gigantic hypertrophied form, as if in a science fiction movie; in much American literature Mao Zedong, or Kim Il Sung were metaphors for an omniscient and omnipresent being. Yet it is possible that *in* China and North Korea we merely see the external form of the spider. Thinking about the executive as Marx and Hegel do is one way to find the spider.

It seems that power itself disappears in Japan or is hard to locate: you cannot say "take me to your leader," van Wolferen jokes, because "Japan does not have one." And elsewhere, "Japanese power . . . is highly diffuse; and while this makes it particularly pervasive, it is not so immediately noticeable."[11] In this rendering, power presumably discloses itself if we locate a contemporary analogue of Hideki Tōjō burning films of the Nanjing massacre, shouting at MITI to get its next plan ready, or scheming to "grow" the trade surplus.

One of Michel Foucault's lasting contributions was to show us that power resides in daily life, in eddies and rivulets coming from a central source, itself unknown, just as the daily rivulets of this power are called something else. Power is in the spontaneous tears that clouded my eyes the first time I laid eyes on an American president at close range, when I was less than twenty. Power is in the rush that comes to the head of a political scientist who found himself on Air Force One and thereupon called as many friends as he could from the presidential airplane. Power

39. For example, Maruyama Masao, *Thought and Behavior in Modern Japanese Politics*, ed. Ivan Morris (New York: Oxford University Press, 1963); See also Andrew Barshay's well-done discussion in *State and Intellectual in Imperial Japan: The Public Man in Crisis* (Berkeley: University of California Press, 1988), pp. 4–10.

40. William W. Lockwood, "Japan's 'New Capitalism,' " in William W. Lockwood, ed., *The State and Economic Enterprise in Japan* (Princeton: Princeton University Press, 1965), p. 503.

41. Van Wolferen, *Enigma*, pp. 20, 43. Or perhaps the problem is that Japan's leaders do not listen to the voters (as ours always do): "Japanese power-holders systematically use power in ways and for ends over which the voter has ultimately no control whatsoever" (p. 22). That is, until the summer of 1993 and the fall of the LDP old guard.

is Robert S. MacNamara giving over his Martha's Vineyard home for President Clinton's first summer vacation. Power is C. Martin Wilbur telling his students not to read William Hinton, Marius Jansen telling his seminar not to read E. H. Norman as rendered by John Dower,[42] or Park Chung Hee throwing protesting students into military boot camp. Power is Lenin writing in *State and Revolution* that the dictatorship of the proletariat cannot end until people change their habits and their ethos and come to live their daily lives as good communists. Power is all of us conducting our daily life as if we are good capitalists, when hardly any of us truly are or can be. The power that van Wolferen cannot find and grasp hold of is precisely the power that derives from Japanese capitalism and its attendant politics being hegemonic—that is, legitimate, accepted without question at a psychological level well below normal consciousness. The web is there, and so is the spider, but no one has the lenses to see: "The logic is perfectly clear, the aims decipherable, and yet it is often the case that no one is there to have invented them, and few can be said to have formulated them."[43]

NATIONAL ECONOMY

In quoting Marx I elided the implicit theory of world economy that he placed alongside the summed-up failings of the German ancien régime, where he gave equal weight to each as shapers of the German state: "The relationship of industry and the world of wealth in general to the political world is one of the main problems of the modern age. In which form does this problem begin to preoccupy the Germans? In the form of *protective tariffs*, or a *system of prohibitions of national economy [Nationalökonomie]* . . . one fine morning our cotton barons and iron heroes woke to find themselves transformed into patriots." With this and a pun on the German word for cunning (*listig*),[44] Marx moves from Hegel to List— *"Friedrich List!!!"*—and immediately suggests to historians the genealogy since then from List to the American protectionist Henry Carey, from List to Lenin,[45] or from List—and von Stein and von Gneist—to Itō Hirobumi (none with tender mercies for democracy, all with every bias toward *Nationalökonomie*). Had Hegel spoken so explicitly about how to construct

42. I witnessed Professor Wilbur saying this in a class in 1969; the anecdote from a Princeton seminar was related to me by Mark Peattie.

43. Michel Foucault, *History of Sexuality*, vol. 1, *Will to Know* (London: Penguin Books, 1976), p. 95.

44. Marx, *Critique of Hegel's Philosophy of Right*, p. 248.

45. Lloyd C. Gardner pointed out a certain affinity between List's and Lenin's views on national economy and late development in *Architects of Illusion: Men and Ideas in American Foreign Policy, 1941–1949* (Chicago: Quadrangle Books, 1970), p. 120.

the national economy instead of the civil bureaucracy, Japan would have had another perfect model to copy. But then, of course, real German history from the 1840s to the 1880s gave Japan a model with no ideality, and one that clearly worked: late industrialization, fashioned by the state in the hothouse of the world economy.

If we pause for a moment and ask, what our theory would predict so far for the United States—what was the nature of the state, what classes would need to be made, what collisions could be expected, what position in the world economy would the United States occupy—the simple answers tumble forth instantly: the bourgeois revolution was "history," first carried abroad from England and then realized in the American Revolution, coterminous with the French; by the 1780s American democracy was already the modern state form Hegel craved and Marx wished to overcome. The collision, too, was "history," for it had happened in Europe: no Prussian "clod-hopping squires and philistines" existed in the New World, let alone peasantries groaning under their rule, thus American democracy would always be innocent of a truly conservative social formation (except for landowners in the slaveholding South) and therefore innocent of the past. Likewise, it would be innocent of the European future: socialism; as a result, its Left Wing would be similarly anemic.[46]

Instantly, too, the exception crops to mind: the Civil War, which for Barrington Moore was the most European of American collisions, but still a peculiar one: a northern middle class and industrial elite colliding with an "export-led" capitalist, landed class shipping cotton to "the empire of free trade," as well as a curiously "late" slave formation.[47] The proletariat was not much in evidence either, but it could be "made" by importing masses of European peasants or southern sharecroppers—albeit with the necessary revisions of the Yankee moral order and the virtues of hard work.[48]

What about the American state? It could not make a pretense of itself, just as Hegel's state was all pretension (Prussians again). When the United States began its heavy industries, Washington barely had paved streets, with pigs and goats wandering hither and yon, feeding on the street garbage and slurping from fetid streams; President Harrison was once observed walking these streets, pants with torn cuffs and lunchtime dribble speckling his shirt. The idea of a stiff-necked civil service, let alone the bureaucrat as a stock national character, let alone a mysterious

46. Louis Hartz's theory again, in *The Liberal Tradition in America*.

47. Barrington Moore Jr., *Social Origins of Dictatorship and Democracy: Lord and Peasant in the Making of the Modern World* (Boston: Beacon, 1966).

48. See Daniel T. Rodgers's brilliant interpretive history *The Work Ethic in Industrial America, 1850–1920* (Chicago: University of Chicago Press, 1980).

executive with a "master plan" for "industrial domination of the world" (even though such domination would come soon enough "in effect")—all this was as far from American practice as a Confucian scholar-official wielding his calligrapher's brush to lay another tax on the peasants. Or perhaps Washington was the wrong place to look.

The nineteenth-century American state might instead be exemplified by Los Angeles in the 1890s–1920s, where a few rich individuals owned the water, owned the power, owned the new oil wells, built the homes, laid the streets and the railways, not to mention founding Hollywood and endowing the colleges and the great libraries: entrepreneurship, capital, "social overhead," "cultural capital" and legitimation, all provisioned with no need of "the state." When in 1913 one of these individualists, a county bureaucrat named William Mulholland, watered a rapidly growing city with a long, high-technology aqueduct snaking in from the high Sierra and stood there as the first gush came out saying, "There it is, take it!" was he a laissez-faire entrepreneur, a state bureaucrat, or an Asian satrap mobilizing great waterworks to irrigate the stupefied masses of the desert, thus to enrich himself and his cronies?[49]

To carry the analogy further, was this a "strong" or a "weak" state? Did it have "relative autonomy"? What were its "capacities"? Where did the buck stop—with the Los Angeles Police Department and the granite-faced Hall of Justice, or with William Chandler, who used anarchist Ortie McGanical's bombing of the *Los Angeles Times* building to keep an open shop from 1911 to 1941? At any rate, there seem to have been classes in Los Angeles that no state had to construct, rather a state constructed by the ruling class, through a seamless web of Anglo-Saxon power that dominated the City of Angels until World War II (again with an imported proletariat, this time from Mexico, China, and Oklahoma).

This is not an idle matter, because Los Angeles at the turn of the century was capitalism at its most *advanced*, occupying the horizon of world capitalism; Anglo-Saxons may have been hydraulic despots, but they were not atavisms of an obsolescent Asiatic Mode of Production. Instead, they were avatars of the Pacific Rim. We may think of them metaphorically as the multicultural, transnational executives of their day, because many were intermarried with Mexicans and Spaniards or descendants of such hacienda families and were typically transfrontier (born in Ohio, rich in Pasadena), thereby beginning the completion of the American national market. Today, multinational executives deploy a power that leads many to question the future existence of the nation-state or even international

49. I would say all of the above. Be that as it may, this history is collapsed but not violated in the great Roman Polanski film *Chinatown* (1972); for an excellent account, see Mike Davis, *City of Quartz: Excavating the Future in Los Angeles* (New York: Vintage, 1992).

relations as we ordinarily conceive them;[50] southern California showed all that a century ago.

But this was not truly *industrial* California. That did not come until World War II, and then there was no problem finding the state. Indeed, a form of state-business relationship previously unknown in the United States but rather familiar to us now from the East Asian cases suddenly mushroomed out from the New Deal, with state/business cartels forging dams, steel mills, shipbuilding plants, and aircraft factories and "making" a full-blown working class in southern California that went from a few tens of thousands to two million strong in the decade of the 1940s.

What should we call it: industrial policy? America, Inc.? The System? Enough of this; it suffices again to quote Marx. America, he thought in 1857, was

> a country where bourgeois society did not develop on the foundation of the feudal system, but developed rather from itself [Hartz]; where this society appears not as the surviving result of a centuries-old movement, but rather as the starting-point of a new movement [no Prussia]; where the state, in contrast to all earlier national formations, was from the beginning subordinate to bourgeois society, to its production, and never could make the pretence of being an end-in-itself [no Hegel]; where, finally, bourgeois society itself, linking up the productive forces of an old world with the enormous natural terrain of a new one, has developed to hitherto unheard-of dimensions and with unheard-of freedom of movement, has far outstripped all previous work in the conquest of the forces of nature, and where, finally, even the antitheses of bourgeois society itself appear as vanishing moments [old lefts and new lefts].[51]

And what of America in the world economy? Its industry got started late, as did its thrust to global hegemony, so we would expect a period of *Nationalökonomie* to incubate industry and hold the British off, followed by a victory for British economic thought—List giving way to Smith. If that seems a bit pat, Marx had it down by 1857; lo and behold, the quotation above begins with Henry Carey: "Carey is the only original economist among the North Americans. Belongs to a country where bourgeois society. . . ." Except that Carey thought that this political economy which Marx found so exceptional, creating itself de novo before his eyes, was the natural economy: Carey happily regarded it "as the eternal, normal

50. On the last point, Susan Strange is quite brilliant in "Supranationals and the State," in John Hall, ed., *States in History* (New York: Cambridge University Press, 1987), pp. 289–305.

51. Marx, "Bastiat and Carey," p. 884. Marx also wrote that the United States was "the most modern form of existence of bourgeois society" (*Grundrisse*, p. 104).

relations of social production"—that is, "Carey's generality is Yankee universality."[52]

The unnatural and the abnormal to Carey was the British doctrine of free trade, which he saw as a form of highway robbery: "Carey sees the contradictions in the economic relations as soon as they appear as *English* relations."[53] And further:

> Originally [for Carey], the English relations were distorted by the false theories of her economists, internally. Now, externally, as the commanding power of the world market, England distorts the harmony of economic relations in all the countries of the world. . . . Having dissolved this fundamental harmony in its own interior, England, by its competition, proceeds to destroy it throughout the world market. . . . The only defence lies in protective tariffs— the forcible, national barricade against the destructive power of large-scale English industry. Hence, the state, which was at first branded the sole disturber of these *"harmonies économiques,"* is now these harmonies' last refuge. . . . [W]ith Carey the harmony of the bourgeois relations of production ends with the most complete disharmony of these relations on the grandest terrain where they appear, the world market, and in their grandest development, as the relations of producing nations.[54]

It would demean Marx's argument to cast it in our contemporary terms of "free trade" versus "protection," Japan's "agents of influence" versus the "Japan-bashers," and so on. It is a humbling argument, for it places our debates exactly where they belong: in the self-interest of our corporations, the myopia of our economists, the fatuity of our politicians, and the provincialism of our academic theory.

The more important thing is to extrude the implicit theory of the state. First, the state under conditions of national competition becomes the "national barricade"—Nationalökonomie again. But elsewhere Carey had branded it the disturber of the domestic economy. Therefore, he must think the state is good for some things (protection) but not good for others (intervention in the "free market"). Exactly so: historically this is nothing more than Republican Party praxis (Smoot-Hawley plus J. Edgar Hoover plus laissez-faire), but analytically it means the state is not simply a domestic expression but is also formed from without by something else: national competition ("the grandest development") in the world market ("the grandest terrain"). Nationalökonomie is not just for Germans but for everyone; the state should regulate competition by opening and clos-

52. Marx, "Bastiat and Carey," p. 884, 888.
53. Ibid., p. 887.
54. Ibid., p. 886.

ing within the grand terrain of the world market—in other words, Karl Polanyi's theory of the state.[55] The state in the milieu of the world becomes a guarantor of Polanyi's "principle of social protection" against the backwash and the ravages of world market competition.

The state's "autonomy," for Marx, consisted of it separating itself from society and becoming a power over and above it, much as Polanyi saw in the rise of the world market the extrusion of economic relations from social relations and the subordination of society by economic imperatives (the unregulated market separating itself and becoming a power over and above society and, perhaps, the state). Thus for Marx the modern state means "the separation of the state from the body of society, or (as Marx writes), 'The abstraction of the *state as such* . . . was not created until modern times. The abstraction of the *political state* is a modern product."[56]

For Hegel, however, modern society establishes the distinction between public and private, and because individuals are atomized by the market (Marx says of Hegel's theory), the state itself must therefore provide a new form of unity—in Hegel's thought, an abstracted unity that substitutes for a lost organic community. It then follows that the state may become a conservator of past "protections" threatened by market relations or international competition: "It is precisely *because* Hegel's vision of the contradictory and self-destructive character of modern society is so lively that he tried so hard to resuscitate and adapt to modern conditions certain aspects of the "organic" feudal order which still survived in the Prussia of his day. Hegel sees these more organic institutions as an elementary way of compensating for the newly unleashed individualism of bourgeois society. . . . The task of a modern state, in this sense, must be to restore the ethic and the organic wholeness of the antique *polis* . . . and to do this without sacrificing the principle of subjective freedom."[57] Whereas John Locke presents the state (or "civil government") as the separated "impartial judge" of private conflicts, for Hegel this separation of state and civil society was a contradiction of his deepest understanding of human society, and so he hypothesizes a state that will restore the lost organic wholeness for which he yearned, yielding a fusion of what we call state and society.[58]

55. Karl Polanyi, *The Great Transformation: The Political and Economic Origins of Our Time* (Boston: Beacon, 1944); see also Fred Block and Margaret Sommers, "Karl Polanyi," in Theda Skocpol, ed., *Vision and Method in Historical Sociology* (New York: Cambridge University Press, 1984). On state-sponsored industrialization as a way to insulate Latin American countries during the depression, see Guillermo A. O'Donnell, *Modernization and Bureaucratic-Authoritarianism: Studies in South American Politics* (Berkeley: Institute of International Studies, University of California, 1973), pp. 54–55.

56. Colletti, introduction to *Karl Marx*, p. 33.

57. Ibid., pp. 30–31.

58. Ibid., pp. 31–32.

In Yankee America, to the contrary, any conception of medieval organicism had been so completely lost or obliterated that Locke's theses seemed like the essence of sweet reason. But in East Asia *all* the modern states, including the Communist ones, have responded in some fashion to Hegel's passion for conserving a threatened organic heritage—leading to what Meiji thinkers called the "family state" or what became in North Korea a state/society modeled on the ruling family.

The state is not only a historic and domestic product, differing according to time and place. It is also a residuum of international competition; it has a *lateral* dimension that also may be strong or weak (penetrated or autonomous, to make it simple). If this is so, then state formation will again differ according to world time and position within the world system. Another German, Otto Hintze, had a similar idea: that states are determined "first, [by] the structure of social classes, and second, [by] the external ordering of the states—their position relative to each other, and their over-all position in the world."[59]

This is a good beginning toward thinking this thorny problem through—why it should be that we cannot think of the state as just a domestic product. As Meredith Woo-Cumings has argued, American social science can be grouped into *regional* theories of the state (the dependent state in Latin America, the developmental state in East Asia, the pluralist state in North America).[60] That could not happen if nations did not differ according to their placement in the larger world. Strong states are those whose citizens are habituated to the existing forms at home, and those capable of imposing their will abroad; the latter, in its hegemonic form, will mean everything from consuming the strong state's products to consuming its exported culture. Ultimately, as Robert Cox has pointed out, it will mean replicating the forms of the indigenous revolution that made the strong state possible in the first place.[61]

Perhaps some rising states will get a bit lathered up and overdo all this, to the point where in their haste to succeed, they appear as mere copiers, a mimicry that dishonors both self and other. That is Japan, for van Wolferen. So now listen to Marx on Carey: "As a genuine Yankee, Carey absorbs from all directions the massive material furnished him by the old world, not so as to recognize the inherent soul of this material, and thus to concede to it the right to its peculiar life, but rather so as to work it up

59. Otto Hintze, quoted in Theda Skocpol, *States and Social Revolutions: A Comparative Analysis of France, Russia, and China* (New York: Cambridge University Press, 1979), pp. 29–31.

60. Jung-en Woo [Meredith Woo-Cumings], *Race to the Swift: State and Finance in Korean Industrialization* (New York: Columbia University Press, 1991).

61. Robert W. Cox, *Approaches to World Order* (New York: Cambridge University Press, 1996).

for his purposes, as indifferent raw material, as inanimate documentation for theses, abstracted from his Yankee standpoint. Hence his strayings and wanderings through all countries . . . a catalogue-like erudition."[62]

America's Lockean experience makes it very hard even to define the state such that students can understand the concept. A benign "civil government" in the mid–nineteenth century, ranging from town meetings to local constables to weak governors to the spots on President Harrison's shirt, will not seem to stand "over and above" an atomized society. Such was hardly the case by the end of that same century, when city police, strike-breaking irregulars, Pinkerton gendarmes,[63] the national guard, and bunkered, blank brick armories stood against the unwashed mass in burgeoning industrial cities. But then that apparatus was made *for* the immigrant, unwashed mass; it still had little to do with proper Yankees.[64]

With the New Deal came the possibility of an American theory of the state, whether an interventionist socialist-cum-fascist state as the Republican right wing had it, or the new federal bureaucracies that regulated the economy and accommodated and provided upward mobility for a new Democratic Party constituency. Today, most Americans, when required to define the state, will stumble toward an intuited Weberian conception of bureaucracy ("the federal government"), just as some social scientists now find in that same bureaucracy the collection of interests affording "relative autonomy."

THE BUREAUCRATIC WEB

How, then, should we think about bureaucracy as part of our thinking about the state? Should we be Weberians? In preparing this study, I once again picked up Max Weber, particularly the astute and definitive interpretations of Guenther Roth, as well as other standard texts.[65] I came away marveling again at what a great comparativist Weber was. But in contrast to earlier readings, I found him less the exemplar than the captive of European rationality (which he signified always as "the West" or "the Occident") and thereby blinded in his judgments and understanding of non-Western societies. Furthermore, in spite of much protest to the con-

62. Marx, "Bastiat and Carey," p. 888.

63. Nineteenth-century America privatized even the most basic state function: coercion. The minute one thinks of an organization such as the Pinkertons, it causes problems for Weber's famous definition of the state as a collectivity "that (successfully) claims the *monopoly of the legitimate use of physical force* within a given territory." In *From Max Weber: Essays in Sociology*, trans. Hans Gerth and C. Wright Mills (New York: Oxford University Press, 1946), p. 78.

64. Rodgers, *Work Ethic.*

65. Max Weber, *Economy and Society: An Outline of Interpretive Sociology*, ed. Guenther Roth, trans. Ephraim Fischoff, 2 vols. (Berkeley: University of California Press, 1978).

trary by Weberians, in spite of Weber's own statements that belief in rationality is just that (belief) and bureaucracy is the modern form of domination, he remains a glorifier, and a provincial (that is, German) one at
that, of bureaucracy as such.

We can sample this in one pregnant passage of his *General Economic History*, where he equates Western capitalism with modern civilization and
sums its causes up as "a rational organization of labor"; "the entry of the
commercial principle into the internal [domestic] economy," with con-
comitant lifting of national and ethical barriers to commerce; and the
disintegration of "primitive economic fixity" in the wake of "the entrepreneur organization of labor." All this, he says, happened only in "the western world." If this just seems to paraphrase Marx, he goes on: "Only the
occident knows the state in the modern sense, with a professional administration, specialized officialdom, and law based on the concept of citizen-
ship. . . . Only the occident knows rational law. . . . Furthermore, only the
occident possesses science. . . . Finally, western civilization is further distinguished from every other by the presence of men with a rational ethic
for the conduct of life."[66]

Weber goes on to contrast "the west" not simply with "the Hindu and
the Chinese," as was his wont, but with the three civilizations under study
here. The "mandarin" was, according to Weber, "a humanistically educated literatus . . . but not in the least trained for administration"; furthermore, in China the mandarins were merely "a thin stratum of so-
called officials," existing above "the unbroken power of the clans and
commercial and industrial guilds."[67] In Japan, "the feudal organization"
led to a "complete exclusiveness as regards the outer world"; Korea, too,
had an "exclusive policy," which was "determined" there on "ritualistic
grounds."[68]

66. Max Weber, *General Economic History*, trans. Frank H. Knight, intro. Ira J. Cohen (New
Brunswick, N.J.: Transaction Books, 1981), pp. 312–14.

67. Ibid., p. 338.

68. Ibid., pp. 338, 344. The difference between Weber and Schumpeter, manifested in
Weber's incomprehension of East Asia and Schumpeter's empathy (especially his love for
the thoroughly non-Western Japan), resides in Schumpeter's ability to distance himself from
conceptions hallowed in "the West"—as evidenced in Karl Jaspers's anecdote about their encounter in a Vienna coffeehouse just after World War I: "Schumpeter remarked how
pleased he was with the Russian Revolution. Socialism was no longer a discussion on paper,
but had to prove its viability. Max Weber responded in great agitation: Communism, at this
stage in Russian development, was virtually a crime, the road would lead to unparalleled
human misery and end in a terrible catastrophe. 'Quite likely,' Schumpeter answered, 'but
what a fine laboratory filled with mounds of corpses,' Weber answered heat-
edly. 'The same can be said of every dissecting room,' Schumpeter replied. Every attempt to
divert them failed. Weber became increasingly violent and loud, Schumpeter increasingly
sarcastic and muted. The other guests listened with curiosity, until Weber jumped up, shouting 'I can't stand any more of this,' and rushed out. . . . Schumpeter, left behind, said with a
smile, 'How can a man shout like that in a coffeehouse?' " Quoted in Richard Swedberg,

Of Weber's judgments here on China, Korea, and Japan, it need only be said that he was wrong on all counts. Mandarins were trained, not to mention highly skillful, in administration; Japan was more feudal before the Tokugawa isolation than after; Korea's isolation in the same period was "determined" by a devastating international war in the 1590s, just as was Japan's, and had no precedent before that for a "Hermit Kingdom."

More important is Weber's life-theme, *rationality*. In the passage above, the term functions in three ways: First, it completes the circle of his argument, that is, by defining the Western (really, central European) state as "rational," such that all its characteristics (many of which were absent in England and America) also become "rational." Second, rationality is meant to substitute for Hegel's ideality of the Spirit—that is, for Weber "rationality" becomes the source of the state's knowledge and simultaneously of its legitimacy (or "rationale"). Third, the conflation of rationality in general with the (again, central European) West in particular, to the exclusion of all non-Western civilizations, yields the formulation West = rational, East = something else.

It would be banal to trace this provincial subjectivism through the modernization literature of the early postwar period, for which Weber enunciated nearly every theme; instead let Weber draw the modernizers' conclusion for them: the rational state existed only in the West, and it is "the rational state in which alone modern capitalism can flourish."[69] The tautology is less interesting than the flat-out falsehood of the statement, read in the reality of the 1990s when even Communist China grows at double-digit rates, a reality against which all the incantations of Western rationality now beat helplessly. To pile heresy upon heresy, let me now say that Marx was better than Weber: *on bureaucracy*.

Hegel had provided for Marx and the rest of us a conception of civil service that seems oddly Chinese: let the civil service be chosen through civil exams, from the best classes to be sure, but with room for all who have talent. But Hegel's conception of the state, as we have seen, began with the distinctly un-Chinese observation that the modern era is the era of public and private, or "state" and "civil society."

Hegel seeks to overcome this division through representative government, whereby delegates are chosen and entrusted to "superintend the state's interests" in civil society. Marx points out that this hardly solves the problem of the state's alienation from civil society: it is the civil service in

---

"Introduction: The Man and His Work," in Joseph Schumpeter, *The Economics and Sociology of Capitalism* (Princeton: Princeton University Press, 1991), p. 90 (a reference for which I am indebted to Meredith Woo-Cumings).

69. Weber, *General Economic History*, p. 339.

the form of administration, judiciary, or police that in turn represents the state in civil society (or in Germany, the monarch), and often with force majeure. Hegel gets around this objection by arguing that the civil servant is not loyal to the monarch but chosen on the basis of his specialized knowledge; if every citizen has the opportunity to join "the class of civil servants" and there are specified procedures for deciding who joins (civil service examinations), then we need not worry about the arbitrary exercise of state power.[70] The reader will note that Hegel's reasoning is quite compatible with contemporary doctrine.

Marx rejects such arguments, of course. He finds in the examination system a *"bureaucratic baptism of knowledge,"* not a Weberian test of modern, rational-legal competence.[71] Both Hegel and Weber, Marx would have said if he had heard of the latter, understand that the direction of the bureaucracy must come from without, that is, from the realm of politics, but they proceed to "rationalize" that fact by equating the occult and shrouded raison d'état with objective knowledge, examined objectively, in tests open to all. In this manner, the direction *appears* to come not from above but from below—from society as a whole.

Hegel introduces a confusion, however, by saying that not just anybody ought to be a bureaucrat; guarantees against arbitrary power are also lodged in the official—in, for example, the civil servant's "dispassionate, upright and polite demeanor." Where do we find such people? Generally speaking, Hegel says, in the middle class—"pillar" of the state. Likewise, the bureaucrats are part of the definition of what it means to be middle class. Marx then intrudes Hegel's idea, discussed above, that the state should also develop the middle class.[72] And with that, Hegel's argument reveals its circularity and its bourgeois presuppositions, a dog biting its own tail: a government of the middle class, by the middle class—and *for* the middle class?

As for the Weberian position that bureaucratic rationality connotes a belief in bureaucratic rationality, Marx chocked even that belief up to superstition: "The 'bureaucracy' is a network of *practical* illusions of the 'illusion of the state.' The bureaucratic mind is a Jesuitic, theological mind through and through. The bureaucrats are the Jesuits and theologians of the state. The bureaucracy is the religious republic." The practiced autonomy and public-spiritedness of the bureaucracy, cherished by the German civil servant also as a matter of faith, was merely another illusion:

70. Marx, *Critique of Hegel's Doctrine of the State*, pp. 111–12.

71. He also says in a typical flourish: "It is not recorded that Greek and Roman statesmen ever took examinations. But what is a Roman statesman compared to a Prussian civil servant!" (ibid., p. 113).

72. Ibid., pp. 115–16.

The bureaucracy appears to itself as the ultimate purpose of the state. As the bureaucracy converts its 'formal' purposes into its content, it comes into conflict with 'real' purposes at every point. It is therefore compelled to pass off form as content and content as form. The purposes of the state are transformed into purposes of offices and vice-versa. The bureaucracy is a magic circle from which no one can escape. Its hierarchy is a hierarchy of knowledge. The apex entrusts insight into particulars to the lower echelons while the lower echelons credit the apex with insight into the universal, and so each deceives the other.

The bureaucracy is the imaginary state alongside the real state; it is the spiritualism of the state. . . . Within itself, however, *spiritualism* degenerates into *crass materialism*, the materialism of passive obedience, the worship of authority, the *mechanism* of fixed, formal action, of rigid principles, views and traditions. As for the individual bureaucrat, the purpose of the state becomes his private purpose, *a hunt for promotion, careerism.*[73]

In due time the bureaucracy takes the last, breathtaking leap of identifying its interests as those of the state, thereby transforming "those of the state" once again back into mere private interests.

A magic circle arrayed in a hierarchy of (claimed) superior knowledge, out for itself in the name of the commonweal, is a species of Marxism that any American can understand; it might be Ronald Reagan talking about the federal government (with the aid of a good speechwriter). In America there is no civil service tradition worthy of the name, and if the Washington of today is not the colorful one of President Harrison, we can blame that on the horde of gray-on-gray bureaucrats who now live and work on its clean and paved streets, perceived to be pointy-headed pencil pushers slurping at the public trough.

To give movement to this catatonic horde, this "series of fixed bureaucratic minds held together by passive obedience and their subordinate position in a hierarchy," Marx says, requires an external animus, a spark from above or without, which will take the dead weight of bureaucratic routine and set it in motion, give it a direction (the bureaucracy "receives its content from outside itself"). Yet this animus is far from some reductionist "executive committee" animated by the bourgeoisie: it is the "real state" that does this, that body toward which the bureaucrats are properly Jesuitical.[74]

But what, then, is the "real state" in the direction of which the bureaucrats genuflect, from their position in the "imaginary state"? It is again the "executive," which for Hegel is the monarch, which for the Catholic Church is the Vatican, which for North Korea is "the Great Leader," but which for Marx remains a thing dark and mysterious, "vexed." We might

73. Ibid., pp. 107–8.
74. Ibid., pp. 108, 111.

call it the locus of real rationality to which the bureaucrats devote themselves, in the web of their careers and conflicting interests: the spider in the web.

From whence comes that "executive" rationality, that impetus from without? Because we are dealing with "developmental states" that (irrationally) get their prices wrong and therefore (rationally) get late industrialization right, let us leave the answer to this question to a later paper. Until then, The reader can think about Marx's allusion to the state as something that can be sprinkled, perhaps like salt in a shaker. This comes in a commentary on Hegel's idea that the monarch "entrusts" to the bureaucrats "particular public functions." Marx writes: "Thus the monarchy . . . distributes the state among the bureaucrats, just as the Holy Roman Church ordains its priests. The monarch is a system of emanations."[75] Immediately the image comes to mind of the Japanese emperor bowing before the assembled multitude on his birthday, or Kim Il Sung or his rotund son hailing the masses from atop the P'yôngyang plaza.

In East Asia, Korean, Japanese, and Chinese society had long experience with "civil government" in the form of Confucian statecraft and bureaucracies full of scholar-officials and their assorted underlings. If Americans were asked to make neither the state nor the classes of modern industry, East Asian societies lacked both. But with a long background in bureaucracy, it is scarcely surprising that the most promising route was to remake the state as prelude to making the classes. Their attraction to Hegel and their disdain for Locke was thus quite overdetermined; nor could they read Weber without intuiting that his teleology could never be theirs.

STAATSWISSENSCHAFTEN: STATE SCIENCE OF LATE INDUSTRIALIZATION

Our discussion thus far has indulged in a kind of science unknown in America: what nineteenth-century Germans called *Staatswissenschaften*, or "state science" (as distinct from, say, social science). When Itō Hirobumi came back from Germany and quipped, "I understand the secret of the state, now I can die a happy man,"[76] it was first of all because he had met

75. Ibid., p. 113. Jessop gropes toward Marx's point in *State Theory*, p. 9; see also pp. 366–67, where he offers the heresy (for state theorists) that "the state does not exercise power," rather power comes from without and actuates elements of the state apparatus.

76. Itō's statement is in Jon Halliday, *A Political History of Japanese Capitalism* (New York: Pantheon, 1975). In 1872 the Japanese government directed its chargé d'affaires in Berlin, Aoki Shūzō, to draft a constitution for Meiji Japan. He sought the aid of Rudolf von Gneist, then a professor at the University of Berlin and a famous constitutional scholar. Aoki submitted his draft in 1873, titled "Governmental Principles of Great Japan." Other provisional

Lorenz von Stein, author of the classic text *Der Begriff der Gesellschaft und die soziale Geschichte der Französischen Revolution bis zum Jahre 1830*. As Immanuel Wallerstein argues, von Stein understood "society" to be a concept of Staatswissenschaft because it has meaning primarily "in the antimony, society/state."[77] For von Stein, society and state were not simply linked inextricably in meaning but also fused in a number of senses: for example, states decide who constitutes the citizenry ("civil society"). If for Hegel the monarch embodied the state and vice versa (a different fusion), the novelty of the French Revolution was that after it was over, the state embodied the popular will (or should have). The question then becomes, who embodies (or creates or knows) the popular will?[78]

Fortunately, this last question is not one we have to solve. The point instead is that in German "state science" the conception of the *fused state* is born or, rather, first noticed in the aftermath of the French Revolution, as a point of definitional anxiety and political reality. It is then a short step to observe the disorders of that same revolution, to relate them to novel ideas about "popular will," and to conclude, well, who needs that?

To put the point baldly, of what value is civil society in a race for industrialization? For the Germans invented the field of state science (as opposed to "political science") not to solve the problems of liberty, equality, and fraternity at the dawn of the industrial epoch but to solve the mid-nineteenth-century problems of the second industrial revolution and, more important, catching up with England. Here, in short, is a political theory of late development that put off to a distant future the magnificent obsession of the early industrializers with questions of popular will, democratic representation, public versus private, or state versus civil society.

Think of the difference with our social science, where these questions still predominate and where "the state" either is not taken serious as a category for analysis or is criticized as something wont to be reified, a hypothetical construct in comparison with a society that we know well: made up of individuals, roles, clusters of interest, pressure groups, classes (defined by income), and the like. But looked at from von Stein's perspec-

---

drafts followed in 1876, 1878, and 1880, guided by the constitutions of Prussia, Austria, and Denmark. Itō Hirobumi visited later, meeting principally with von Gneist and Lorenz von Stein. Itō later asked his chief aid, Inoue Kowashi, to draft a constitution, and the latter was guided in turn by Herman Roesler, a German political scientist in Tokyo. See Helen Hardacre, *Shintō and the State, 1968–1988* (Princeton: Princeton University Press, 1989), pp. 115–18.

77. Von Stein's title is rendered in the English version as *The History of the Social Movement in France, 1789–1850*. Immanuel Wallerstein aptly points out that the English title omits "the *concept* of society" (*Unthinking Social Science: The Limits of Nineteenth-Century Paradigms* [New York: Blackwell Publishers, 1991], pp. 65–66).

78. Wallerstein, *Unthinking Social Science*, pp. 66–67.

tive, "society" is also a hypothetical or mere rhetorical construct, endlessly reified and morally valenced as "civil society," "democratic society," "pluralist society," "found only in the West," and so on. I can understand him: when I gaze southward from the window of my university office past the broad vista of the Midway Plaisance, past the "demilitarized zone" of vacant, hollow buildings, to the Woodlawn "community"—the site of sixty years of social activism by everyone from Saul Alinsky to Hillary Clinton, decades of social science research, urban renewal, and other intersections of "state" and "society," all of it for naught or so it would appear from the bombed-out buildings and blasted lives of the citizens today—I ask myself if all this talk about civil society is merely rhetoric, masking a criminal intent to deceive our students. It is probably the same feeling Marx had, in first reading Hegel and then getting a load of the Prussian king and his entourage.

In any case, our rhetoric is not the rhetoric of mid-nineteenth-century Germany or twentieth-century Japan, Korea, or China. They were drawn inexorably toward state science, whether of the von Stein or the Leninist variety. Sooner or later all the Northeast Asian nations fashioned states worthy to the battle of late industrialization, and all of them did so in conditions ranging from the complete absence to the overwhelming presence of hegemonic American ideology (1930s Japan versus 1960s Japan, North Korea versus South Korea, post-1949 China versus post-1949 Taiwan). This is why I cannot accept Wallerstein's distinction that state science is for semiperipheral states outside the cultural domain of the hegemon, or Theda Skocpol's point that "state building" is the business of revolutionaries after a conjunctural cataclysm.[79] The meaning of "state building" in Northeast Asia's fused state/societies is that recourse to the state comes first, followed by conscious or unconscious attempts to create industry, big business (the Korean *chaebol*, for example, all have a state-blessed birthright), and then and only then "society," that is, the groups requisite for and appropriate to contemporary imaginings of "modernity." The *space* may have been semiperipheral or, more accurate, in heaven-sent or carved-out breathing spaces of the world (uncolonized Northeast Asia circa 1850–1910; indulgent America's part of Northeast Asia circa 1945–70; revolutionary-nationalist East Asia circa 1945–75), but the *time* was "late," with imperial and industrial antagonists breathing hotly on the neck. Nothing concentrates the mind more than grand opportunity combined with overwhelming danger.

It is not the case that "in the beginning was the word." In the beginning, as with the human being, was the *conception*, something residing in a prediscursive groping for its own name—Itō searching for the answer

---

79. Ibid., p. 66; Skocpol, *States and Social Revolutions*.

to the state.[80] In Northeast Asia that name turned out to be Staatswissenschaften. American analysts have not seen this because they have not been looking for it; they have been preoccupied with the creation of a different *space*, that space between the rational intellect and theology in the first place, that space between the citizen (read "intellectual" most of the time) and the state later on—or what is now apotheosized by Jürgen Habermas as "the public sphere" and what is now anathematized for all East Asia: no "civil society." In some ways, East Asia has meant industrialization without Enlightenment, a crude adoption that strikes at the heart of Western civilization: behold, they took the baby and not the bathwater.[81]

A state science of late industrialization is not hegemonic ideology. It cannot take the world as its oyster and reckon for the whole. It takes the world as its octopus and reckons for the parts. To put it another way, Northeast Asia, beginning with Japan, has not exported universals. It has consumed Western universals only to pass that which it did not want—the supreme and unforgivable insult. Our universals have been British universals, artifacts of England's preeminence after Waterloo.[82] The mid–nineteenth century was not merely England as the workshop of the world but England as the ventriloquist for the world (especially the American world). Germany was the bête noire of this world, shamelessly copying the inventive wizardry of the English and then dumping the shabby results in British markets. If we were to specify one German thinker with the most influence on Americans from this period, the one *they* sought to copy perfectly, it would not be Hegel, Marx, or von Stein but Leopold von Ranke, father of empirical historiography, tutoring a classically ahistorical people calling themselves Americans and who were preternaturally disposed toward empiricism (and, of course, American idealism would seek shelter amid the swamp gas of Koenigsberg, provided by Immanuel Kant).

As Wallerstein rightly points out, Ranke was the father of a second form of universal thought, the *ideographic* as opposed to the *nomothetic*: "it was

80. Or as Schumpeter put it in discussing his notion of "vision," it is a "preanalytic cognitive act that supplies the raw material for analytic effort." Quoted in Richard Swedberg, *Schumpeter: A Biography* (Princeton: Princeton University Press, 1991), p. 181.

81. Schumpeter would have said, Bravo! The individual, social, and class conflict of contemporary "civil society," he thought, represented "a profound error": "In the normal group or society, these conflicting elements are integrated with the cooperative elements harmoniously in the framework of a common culture and faith. . . . As soon as the members of any group, a family for example, lose sight of the framework of individual values and beliefs and see among them only conflicts of interest we witness a social disintegration, that is, a pathological phenomenon . . . namely, our society is falling apart" (Schumpeter, "The Future of Private Enterprise," in *Economics and Sociology*, p. 403).

82. Wallerstein, *Unthinking Social Science*, p. 191.

'universalizing' in the sense that all particulars were equal."[83] But Rankean thought was also a form of replication; he and his disciples assumed that the historian could be trained to the objective standard of a camera lens, achieving results identical to the popular notion of the innocent eye of the camera: the historian's "eye" is merely there to record "the facts." The perfect history is that which perfectly replicates "the past." Walter Benjamin inveighed against the idea that history could be apprehended *wie es eigentlich gewesen ist* (as it really was), but his was a postmodern consciousness.[84] The German and Japanese consciousness was the mirrored reflection of hegemonic thought: a replicative consciousness in search of an elusive perfection, through which the particulars could become not hegemonic, not dominant, but merely equal.

The difference between the American and the East Asian experience is quite breathtaking: here, replication of the British model thus to supersede; there, selective replication of Continental experience thus to pass muster. The first, being hegemonic in intent, was holistic; the second, being egalitarian in intent, was particular.[85] Inevitably the latter would fasten on *technique* stripped away from Weltanschauung and give you *kokutai*, *Juche*, and the insoluble *t'i-yung* problem.[86] As we saw in our brief discussion of Weber, hegemonic thought eliminated Japan by definition, just as British free-trade ideology would be unavailing to Germany: yet more reason for state science. If internally the state would create "the modern," externally it would defend the terrain against the hegemonic power, its products, and its world view.

Wallerstein asserts that after World War II, Staatswissenschaften disappeared as a school of thought in Germany and elsewhere, but that is far from the case.[87] In Japan and South Korea, the United States fashioned liberal constitutions (albeit with the requisite loopholes in the precarious Republic of Korea), but the interwar bureaucrats continued apace as if

83. Ibid.

84. Walter Benjamin, "Theses on the Philosophy of History," in *Illuminations*, ed. and intro. Hannah Arendt, trans. Harry Zohn (New York: Schocken, 1985), p. 255.

85. That is, the point of late industrialization is to achieve equality and thereby protect one's own national space within the world system, not to become hegemonic throughout the globe. Obviously this is a controversial contention, but it seems to me a better description of Japan and Germany since the 1850s than the typical recourse to their pathological and failed attempts at hegemony in the 1930s–40s.

86. The earlier discussion of Henry Carey's selective borrowing is no contradiction, for he represented the minority lineage in the United States, the majority being American followers of Adam Smith, who first colonized Harvard and then spread everywhere. The terms in the text all share the character pronounced *tai* in Japanese, *ch'e* in Korean, and *t'i* in Chinese, meaning something similar to "base" or "main principle." In the postwar period the Japanese obsession has not been with *kokutai* but with *shutai*, which is *chuch'e* in Korean, that is, "the Great Juche Idea of the Great Leader Kim Il Sung."

87. Wallerstein, *Unthinking Social Science*, p. 195.

nothing had happened. In North Korea, China, and Taiwan the constitutions were Leninist; if each may well greet the twenty-first century without Lenin, the central bureaucrats have perdured and no doubt will perdure.

Still, the central experience of Northeast Asia in this century has not been a realm of independence where autonomy and equality reigned, but with enmeshment in another web: the hegemonic web. This web had a spider: first England/America, then America/England, then war and defeat, then unilateral America, then and down to the present, hegemonic America. Japan, South Korea, and Taiwan industrialized mostly within this web. North Korea and China defined themselves as outside the web, thereby endowing the web with overriding significance—and so they structured their states to resist enmeshment. Japan, South Korea, and Taiwan have thus had states "strong" for the struggle to industrialize but "weak" because of the web of enmeshment: they are semisovereign states. North Korea and China had states "strong" for industrialization and "total" for hegemonic resistance. But as the century ends, both are being drawn into the web. This suggests that the nearest thing to a new truth about the state since Hegel, Hintze, and Marx is that state machineries are embedded in the world system, that their autonomy within it is quite limited, and that the specific institutional forms states may take around the world cannot be understood apart from the workings of the whole. That whole is the one Marx called "the grandest terrain," the world market.

To return once again to *MITI and the Japanese Miracle*, we can now appreciate its significance: Chalmers Johnson uncovered a truth about Japanese state science that had eluded a generation of analysts, thereby revaluing the entire field of modern Japanese politics. If this book did not exist, it would have had to have been invented: but who would have had the intelligence, the learning, the iconoclasm, and the courage to do so, had it not been for him?

CHAPTER FOUR

Where Do High-Growth Political Economies Come From? The Japanese Lineage of Korea's "Developmental State"

Atul Kohli

Three decades of sustained, high economic growth has made South Korea a "model of development." Performance of other developing countries is now often judged against that of "East Asian newly industrialized countries (NICs)," including South Korea. Scholars and policymakers around the world have become curious: How did South Korea do it? Can others learn from the experience? A large body of literature has developed—some of it of rather high quality—attempting to interpret the Korean political economy.[1] A central debate in this literature concerns the relative roles of the state and of the market in explaining South Korea's economic success. While hardly any sensible observer continues to deny the state's extensive role in Korean economic development, the current debate bogs down over the interpretation of this role—over the

1. The literature here is rather large; the bibliographies in any of the following sources (especially Amsden and Woo) offer a more complete list of references. An incomplete list (given alphabetically) of some of the major works with a political economy focus would include Alice H. Amsden, *Asia's Next Giant: South Korea and Late Industrialization* (New York: Oxford University Press, 1989); Bruce Cumings, "The Origins and Development of the Northeast Asian Political Economy: Industrial Sectors, Product Cycles, and Political Consequences," *International Organization* 38, no. 1 (Winter 1984): 1–40; Frederic C. Deyo, ed., *The Political Economy of New Asian Industrialism* (Ithaca: Cornell University Press, 1987); Stephan Haggard, *Pathways from the Periphery: The Politics of Growth in the Newly Industrializing Countries* (Ithaca: Cornell University Press, 1991), especially the chapter on South Korea and some of his other work cited therein; Leroy P. Jones and Il Sakong, *Government, Business, and Entrepreneurship in Economic Development: The Korean Case* (Cambridge: Harvard University Press, 1980); Edward Mason et al., *The Economic and Social Modernization of the Republic of Korea* (Cambridge: Harvard University Press, 1980); Larry E. Westphal, "Industrial Policy in an Export-Propelled Economy: Lessons from South Korea's Experience," *Journal of Economic Perspectives* 4, no. 3 (Summer 1990): 412–59; and Jung-en Woo, *Race to the Swift: State and Finance in Korean Industrialization* (New York: Columbia University Press, 1991).

extent to which state intervention was "market conforming" versus "market distorting" or, to use a related set of concepts, the extent to which the state "led" rather than "followed" the market.[2]

Interesting and significant as this debate is, it is also incomplete. Much of it revolves around unraveling the economic role of the South Korean state and, in turn, tracing the impact of this role on economic outcomes. The prior question of *why* the South Korean state was able to do what it did and the related genetic issue of the historical roots of the Korean political economy thus tend to get underemphasized. Because there is much to be learned about the Korean "model of development" by adopting a longer historical perspective, especially tracing its origins back to its Japanese colonial lineage, this neglect is unfortunate.

Few economists working on Korea ascribe much significance to the continuities that link colonial and postcolonial Korea.[3] This problem also characterizes the works of several institutionally sensitive scholars of South Korea; among these, some discuss the colonial period but quickly conclude that the impact was not of lasting significance,[4] others deny the contributions of this past altogether,[5] and yet others virtually ignore it, presumably because of a view that significant changes in the South Korean economy began only after the adoption of an "export-led model of development" in the early 1960s.[6] Korean scholarship on Korea has its

2. The conceptual distinction between government's leading or following the market is made in Robert Wade, *Governing the Market: Economic Theory and the Role of Government in East Asian Industrialization* (Princeton: Princeton University Press, 1990), esp. p. 28 and chap. 10. The scholar who has probably gone the furthest in suggesting that Korean government "distorted" prices to get growth up is Alice Amsden; see *Asia's Next Giant*, esp. chap. 6. For the argument that South Korean and other East Asian economic successes resulted from "free-market" conditions, see Bela Balassa's essays in his own edited volume, *The Newly Industrializing Countries in the World Economy* (New York: Pergamon, 1981), and Anne O. Krueger, "Trade Policy as an Input to Development," *American Economic Review* 70, no. 2 (1980): 228–92.

3. See, for example, Charles R. Frank Jr., Kwang Suk Kim, and Larry E. Westphal, *Foreign Trade Regimes and Economic Development: South Korea* (New York: Columbia University Press, 1975); Parvez Hasan, *Korea: Problems and Issues in a Rapidly Growing Economy* (Baltimore: Johns Hopkins University Press, 1976); and Anne O. Krueger, *Studies in the Modernization of Korea: The Developmental Role of the Foreign Sector and Aid* (Cambridge: Harvard University Press, 1979). For an early exception, see Paul Kuznets, *Economic Growth and Structure in the Republic of Korea* (New Haven: Yale University Press, 1977).

4. See, for example, Jones and Sakong, *Government, Business, and Entrepreneurship*, pp. 22–37.

5. See, for example, Amsden, *Asia's Next Giant*, where in five pages (pp. 31–35) the author quickly concludes that the "inheritance" left by the Japanese colonialists to Koreans was "useless" for their future developmental struggles.

6. Stephan Haggard, for example, has made valuable contributions to unraveling the "why" and "how" of South Korean industrialization. The bulk of his analytic energy, however, is devoted to the onset of the export-led model under Park Chung Hee. See, for example, Haggard, *Pathways from the Periphery*, the chapter on South Korea, where only about two paragraphs are devoted to the colonial period.

own, albeit understandable, blind spots; the nationalist impulse often leads to a denial of any continuity between colonial and postcolonial periods, lest the contemporary achievements be viewed as a product of a much disliked colonial rule.[7] Only a handful of Korean specialists, especially those with a strong historical bent, have understood and emphasized the Japanese colonial roots of the more recent, high-growth Korean political economy.[8] Building on the insights of this last group of Korean specialists, most importantly Bruce Cumings, I attempt in this essay to reinterpret some specific historical materials with the hope of deriving general lessons of interest to scholars of comparative and international development.

The argument below is that Japanese colonialism, as brutal as it was, left an imprint on a political economy that later evolved into the high-growth, South Korean path to development. As Cumings has argued, Japanese colonialism differed in important respects from the colonialism of European powers. As late colonizers, the Japanese made ruthless use of state power to pry open and transform Korea in a relatively short period.[9] Japanese colonial impact was more intense, more brutal, and deeply architectonic; it also left Korea with three and a half decades of economic growth (the average, annual growth rate in production was more than 3 percent) and a relatively advanced level of industrialization (nearly 35 percent of Korea's "national production" in 1940 originated in mining and manufacturing).[10] While there were important discontinuities in the

7. I have examined only the English-language publications of Korean scholars. One good example of the nationalist bias in what is otherwise an excellent study is Sang-Chul Suh, *Growth and Structural Changes in the Korean Economy, 1910–1940* (Cambridge: Council on East Asian Studies, Harvard University, 1978). My confidence in extrapolating the broader assertion from limited materials was enhanced when another scholar, who had examined many of the Korean-language sources, reached the same conclusion. See Woo, *Race to the Swift*, pp. 19–20.

8. Most significant here are the contributions of Bruce Cumings. He states his basic thesis in a summary form in "Origins and Development of the Northeast Asian Political Economy." Scattered but brilliant insights on this topic can also be gleaned from his other writings: *The Origins of the Korean War: Liberation and the Emergence of Separate Regimes, 1945–1947,* vol. 1 (Princeton: Princeton University Press, 1981); *The Origins of the Korean War: The Roaring of the Cataract, 1947–1950,* vol. 2 (Princeton: Princeton University Press, 1990); and "The Legacy of Japanese Colonialism in Korea," in Ramon H. Myers and Mark R. Peattie, eds., *The Japanese Colonial Empire, 1895–1945* (Princeton: Princeton University Press, 1984), pp. 478–96. Another very important book that helps trace historical continuities is Carter J. Eckert, *Offspring of Empire: The Koch'ang Kims and the Colonial Origins of Korean Capitalism, 1876–1945* (Seattle: University of Washington Press, 1991). See also Woo, *Race to the Swift*, and Dennis L. McNamara, *The Colonial Origins of Korean Enterprise, 1910–45* (New York: Cambridge University Press, 1990).

9. Cumings, *Origins of the Korean War,* vol. 1.

10. Although these issues will be discussed in greater detail below, the economic data here is taken from Suh, *Growth and Structural Changes,* tables 11 and 17. Note that the "national production" data do not include construction, trade, services, and public utilities that

postcolonial period, the grooves that Japanese colonialism carved on the Korean social soil cut deep. South Korea under Park Chung Hee can be argued to have fallen back into the grooves of an earlier origin and traversed along them, well into the 1980s. Of course, this was not inevitable; historical continuities seldom are. Korea had competing historical legacies: for example, there was the distant legacy of Chosŏn (that is, of Korea under the rule of Yi dynasty) with its agrarian bureaucratic tradition; then there were indigenous revolutionary tendencies that found expression in North Korea; and there was the possibility of considerable American influence. Moreover, completely new paths could have been charted. Subsequent decisions were thus critical in putting South Korea on a path that reestablished historical continuities. Nevertheless, it is difficult to imagine South Korea adopting a growth path that it did without a deeply influential Japanese colonial past.

I trace below the colonial origins of three patterns that many scholars now readily associate as elements of the South Korean "model." First, I discuss how the Korean state under the Japanese influence was transformed from a traditional agrarian bureaucracy into a highly authoritarian, penetrating organization. This is followed by an analysis of a second pattern, namely, the new state's production-oriented alliances with the dominant classes, an alliance that buttressed the state's capacity to both control and transform. Relatedly, it is also important to take note of the structural changes in the economy; not only did the colonial economy experience growth and industrialization, but it was heavily export-oriented, including exports of manufactured products. And lastly, there was the third pattern of brutal repression and systematic control of the lower classes in both the cities and the countryside. The cumulative impact of these state-class configurations was to help create a framework for the evolution of a political economy that is both repressive and high growth. Toward the end of this discussion I will also briefly suggest—though not develop, leaving that for another essay—how these patterns continued into subsequent periods.

The main task of this paper is not to set the historical record straight. That is for historians of Korea; they are already busy doing so, and I am only building on some of their work. Given the importance of the South Korean case in the contemporary discourse on development, I hope to reinterpret and synthesize some specific materials with general implications. Three sets of general ideas will be debated via the historical materials. First, there are Korea-related comparative questions. For example, how much choice does a developing country really have when adopting a

---

are generally included in the more conventional "national income" data; the latter for pre–Second World War Korea are not readily available.

specific development strategy—that is, to what extent was South Korea a beneficiary of its historical inheritance, as distinct from creating anew a high-growth, export-oriented "model of development?" Closely related is the issue of transferability of the Korean "model" across national boundaries: if the roots of contemporary South Korean political economy are indeed as deep as a relatively unique colonial experience, can others really emulate the experience? Second, at a higher level of generality, there are theoretical issues revolving around the concept of "developmental states": what characterizes them and where do they come from? And lastly, at the most general level, there is at least an implication in this essay that some of the variations we notice today among the more or less dynamic Third World political economies may have some of their roots in a variable colonial past. If so, a further investigation of this analytic claim would require reopening the issue of the colonial roots of the contemporary Third World that has unfortunately been lost in the postdependency scholarship on development.

THE CONSTRUCTION OF A COLONIAL STATE

The Agrarian Bureaucratic State in Traditional Korea

By the time the Japanese gained decisive influence over Korea—say around 1905, after the Japanese victory in the Russo-Japanese War of 1904—the old state within Chosŏn was already in an advanced stage of disintegration. While it is not necessary to recall historical details, a brief understanding of the state-society links in late Chosŏn are essential to appreciate changes wrought by Japanese colonial power.[11] The Yi dynasty had provided continuous and, for the most part, stable rule to Korea for nearly five hundred years. The same intricate state and class alliances that were responsible for this stability, however, also became major constraints on successful adaptation to changing external pressures, especially in the second half of the nineteenth century. For example, the clearest manifestation of the powerlessness of a centralized monarchial state was the continued inability to collect taxes owed to the state on agrarian incomes, es-

11. The best book on the late Chosŏn continues to be James B. Palais, *Politics and Policy in Traditional Korea* (Cambridge: Harvard University Press, 1975). For a differing account, see Ching Young Choe, *The Rule of the Taewongun, 1864–1873: Restoration in Yi Korea* (Cambridge: East Asian Research Center, Harvard University, 1972). A good "overview" account is provided by Ki-baik Lee, in Carter J. Eckert et al., *Korea Old and New: A History* (Seoul: Ilchokak Publishers, 1990). For another useful but abbreviated account that helps put traditional Korea in a comparative perspective vis-à-vis China and Japan, see John K. Fairbank, Edwin O. Reischauer, and Albert M. Craig, *East Asia: Tradition and Transformation* (Boston: Houghton Mifflin, 1978), chaps. 12 and 20.

pecially from the powerful Yangban elite, the landowning-official class of Korea.[12] This recurring inability, in turn, came to be associated with several problematic political trends. First, the state resorted to squeezing the peasantry via "taxation" (for example, corvée labor and military service), contributing to brigandage and a restive peasant population. Second, the state's limited resources exacerbated the competition and tensions in what was already a personalized and factionalized elite at the apex of the political pyramid. Finally, financial limitations made it difficult to mobilize any serious military response to growing external pressures.

How does one explain immobilism in a centralized polity? The leading historian of late Yi Korea, James Palais, traces the roots of this conundrum back to the manner in which the monarchy and the Korean officials-cum-aristocrats, the Yangban, mutually checked each other's powers. The power of the Yangban class rested in part on access to hereditary land wealth but also on a close identification with the centralized bureaucracy, which both helped secure socioeconomic privileges and was a further source of wealth and power. Also, the recruitment of the aristocracy to the bureaucracy via the examination system enabled landed power to be deeply embedded all through the Korean state, checking the scope of royal authority vis-à-vis the Yangban.[13] While this balance of power was a source of stability for several centuries, as external pressures grew—and along with them the state's need for taxes and other socioeconomic resources—it also became a major constraint on monarchial power to initiate reforms. The monarchial state, according to Palais, "could not solve the problem of creating adequate political authority for the achievement of national goals." The Yi state was thus simultaneously "centralized and weak."[14]

In addition to the limiting balance of power between the monarchy and the Yangban, there were other factors at work that contributed to the Yi state's immobilism. First, it was not merely the presence of a powerful land-controlling stratum in society that limited the state's capacity; it was also that landed groups exercised direct control on state offices.[15] Second, the Korean monarchy remained to the end a highly personalistic, patrimo-

12. Palais, *Politics and Policy in Traditional Korea*.

13. For a discussion of how "open" or "closed" Korea's examination system may have been to non-Seoul-based landed elite, see Edward Wagner, "The Ladder of Success in Yi Dynasty Korea," *Occasional Papers on Korea* 1 (April 1974):1–8. Prolonged study of Chinese classics that was necessary to succeed in the exams appears to have been a major impediment for those without an independent source of wealth. Nevertheless, below the highest levels, there is evidence to indicate that some merit-based recruitment did occur.

14. Palais, *Politics and Policy in Traditional Korea*, esp. chaps. 1–4 and 14. The direct quotes are from p. 5. Palais subsequently modified some of these views. See James B. Palais, *Confucian Statecraft and Korean Institutions* (Seattle: University of Washington Press, 1996).

15. Fairbank, Reischauer, and Craig, *East Asia*, p. 307.

nial institution, incapable of acting along "the modern distinction be-tween public and private realms" and thus incapable of designing state-led national goals of economic development.[16] Third, the ruling strata below the monarch was highly factionalized.[17] Such strife in the ruling strata made it difficult to design cohesive responses to growing challenges. Fi-nally, it is important to note that the reach of the Yi state from the center to the periphery was rather limited. Although provincial and county offi-cials were directly appointed from Seoul, each county magistrate was re-sponsible for governing nearly 40,000 people (there being some 330 mag-istrates for about 12 million Koreans).[18] Because these magistrates were rotated frequently, they often depended on the well-entrenched Yangban elite for local governance. Moreover, the lower-level officials—below the magistrate—were not salaried employees. Rather, they made up a heredi-tary group that was allowed to collect and keep some local taxes as com-pensation for its services. These petty functionaries operated virtually as local czars, not easily influenced from above and responsible for the "ve-nality and exploitation of the peasant population."[19]

How was Korea's traditional agrarian state transformed into what some may describe as a "developmental" state?[20] The impact of Japanese colo-

16. Cumings, *Origins of the Korean War*, 1:10.

17. As I read the historical evidence, James Palais is probably correct in denying intraelite factionalism the central place in his analysis of the political problems of Yi Korea. See Palais, *Politics and Policy in Traditional Korea*, esp. the introduction. Nevertheless, most historical treat-ments document a deeply factionalized elite in Yi Korea. See, for example, Lee, in Eckert et al., *Korea Old and New*, where he concludes that "intra-bureaucratic strife" rendered "the deci-sion making process dilatory and ineffective" (p. 110). Fairbank, Reischauer, and Craig, *East Asia*, also note that factional struggles were "hereditary" and "endemic" in Yi Korea (p. 313). I see no analytic conflict, therefore, in suggesting factionalism as an additional debilitating trait.

18. See Palais, *Politics and Policy in Traditional Korea*, chap. 2. Palais cites the figure of 10 million for Korean population in the mid–nineteenth century. Later research has revised this estimate upward. See Tony Mitchell, "Fact and Hypothesis in Yi Dynasty Economic His-tory: The Demographic Dimension," *Korean Studies Forum* 6 (Winter–Spring 1978–80): 65–93. I owe this reference to James Palais.

19. Lee in Eckert et al., *Korea Old and New*, p. 111.

20. I use quotations around the evocative concepts of "predatory" and "developmental" states to indicate my considerable discomfort in describing these states as such. "Predatory" is mislead-ing because it creates a state versus society image; in reality, where "predation" prevails, political and economic elites often collude to squeeze and misuse a society's resources. "Developmental" is also misleading because the states so described are often not strictly developmental. For exam-ple, both the Japanese colonial state and the subsequent South Korean state under Park Chung Hee, while successful agents of economic transformation, were also, to varying degrees, rather brutal states. The normative calculus, in turn, of evaluating a state that is simultaneously brutal and helps promote economic growth is clearly complex. In any case, two useful essays that dis-cuss the concept of developmental states are Chalmers Johnson, "Political Institutions and Eco-nomic Performance: The Government-Business Relationship in Japan, South Korea, and Tai-wan," in Deyo, ed., *Political Economy of the New Asian Industrialism*, pp. 136–64, and Peter Evans, "Predatory, Developmental, and Other Apparatuses: A Comparative Political Economy Perspec-tive on the Third World State," *Sociological Forum* 4, no. 4 (Fall 1989): 561–87.

nial power was decisive in altering both the nature of the Korean state and the relationship of this state to various social classes. The transformation of the state is discussed immediately below and the changing relationship of the state to social classes in subsequent sections.

Toward a "Developmental" State

The Japanese military victory over the Russians in 1904 marked the emergence of Japan as the major regional power, a power that had been rising steadily since the Meiji restoration in the 1860s. Subsequently, Japan, with the acquiescence of Western powers, had a relatively free hand in dominating and molding Korea. Japanese motives in Korea, like the motives of all imperial powers, were mixed; they sought to control it politically and to exploit it for their own economic advantage. Security concerns were dominant because Korea had been an object of regional power competition for quite some time, but the Meiji oligarchs of Japan readily associated national power with national wealth and national wealth with overseas economic opportunities.[21]

Certain aspects of Japanese imperialism are essential to note for a full understanding of the colonial impact on Korea.[22] First, the Japanese had themselves barely escaped being imperialized. As both a late developer and a late imperialist, Japan colonized neighboring states with which it shared racial and cultural traits. Proximity meant that many more Japanese ended up playing a direct role in colonial rule, including a much larger role as military and police, than was ever the case in European overseas colonies. The near geographical contiguity and shared cultural and racial traits also implied that the Japanese could realistically consider their rule to be permanent, leading eventually to a full integration of colonies into an expanded Japan. As I will discuss below, this possibility, in turn, influenced both the economic and the political strategies of Japan in Korea, especially the Japanese-initiated industrialization of Korea.

Furthermore, Japanese colonial strategy was deeply informed by their own successful domestic reform efforts following the Meiji restoration. Of all the colonizing nations, Japan stands out as nearly the only one with a successful record of deliberate, state-led political and economic transformation. By trial and error the Meiji oligarchs had designed a political economy that was well suited for the task of "catching up" with advanced Western powers. The essential elements of this political economy are well

21. Hilary Conroy, *The Japanese Seizure of Korea, 1868–1910* (Philadelphia: University of Pennsylvania Press, 1960); Peter Duus, "Economic Dimensions of Meiji Imperialism: The Case of Korea, 1895–1910," in Myers and Peattie, eds., *Japanese Colonial Empire*, pp. 132–33.

22. Mark Peattie, introduction to *Japanese Colonial Empire*, ed., Myers and Peattie, pp. 3–60.

known and can be briefly reiterated: the creation of an effective centralized state capable of both controlling and transforming Japanese society;
deliberate state intervention aimed, first, at agricultural development
and, second, at rapid industrial growth; and production of a disciplined,
obedient, and educated workforce. It was this model of deliberate development, with its emphasis on state building and on the use of state power
to facilitate socioeconomic change—in contrast, say, to the British, who
having created a private property regime waited in vain for Bengali za-
mindars in India to turn into a sheep-farming gentry—that moved the
Japanese colonizers.[23] And, in Mark Peattie's words, much of what Japan
undertook in its colonies "was based upon Meiji experience in domestic
reform."[24]

It is not surprising that the earliest Japanese efforts in Korea were focused on destroying the old Chosŏn state and replacing it with a modern
colonial state; both political control and economic exploitation depended on it. A fair number of political measures had thus been put into
place during 1905–10, especially 1907–9, even prior to the formal annexation of Korea in 1910. Subsequently, the decade of 1910–20 was again
critical, when, under very harsh authoritarian circumstances, a highly
modern and repressive state was constructed.

A key architect of the new colonial state was the Meiji oligarch and the
former Meiji era premier of Japan, Ito Hirobumi. As a young man Ito had
been one of the handful of leaders who had led the Meiji "revolution"
and who had subsequently participated in the reform efforts that followed the destruction of the Tokugawa shogunate. Ito had traveled extensively in Europe and had been fascinated with Prussian bureaucracy as a
model for Japan. The Prussian "model" offered him a route to Western
rationality and modernity without "succumbing" to Anglo-American liberalism.[25] Within Japan, Ito in 1878 had "led the campaign to make the
bureaucracy the absolutely unassailable base and center of political
power in the state system." Subsequently, Ito helped reorganize Tokyo
University in 1881 as a "school for government bureaucrats," and by 1887
"a basic civil service and entrance apprenticeship based on the Prussian

23. Hyman Kublin, "The Evolution of Japanese Colonialism," *Comparative Studies in Society and History* 2, no. 1 (October 1959): 67–84, has argued that Japanese "colonial doctrine"
evolved in Formosa (later Taiwan) and was subsequently implemented in Korea. This is true
insofar as Formosa was colonized in 1895 and Korea in 1910. However, it is important to
note that Kabo reforms in Korea (tried around 1895) and early experimentation in Formosa were simultaneous efforts, both probably a product of a single "colonial official mind-
set" in Japan—a product of Meiji Japan—with simultaneous political learning going on in
both Korea and Formosa.

24. Peattie, introduction, p. 29.

25. Jon Halliday, *A Political History of Japanese Capitalism* (New York: Pantheon, 1975), p.
37.

model [had been] installed."[26] With this experience behind him, when Ito was appointed in the early 1900s to run the Korean protectorate, where his powers as resident-general were near absolute—"The uncrowned King of Korea"—he was quite self-conscious of his task: "Korea can hardly be called an organized state in the modern sense; I am trying to make it such."[27]

Ito and his successors set out deliberately to construct a new colony. The first task was to gain central control. With superior military power behind them, the Japanese in 1907 dismantled the Korean army, repressed those who "mutinied," incorporated other army officers into a Japanese-controlled gendarmery, and forced the Korean monarch to abdicate. Having captured the heart of the state, the colonial rulers sought to create systematically a depersonalized "public arena," to spread their power both wide and deep, and to co-opt or repress native Korean political forces. For example, the patrimonial elements of the monarchial state were destroyed rather early and replaced by a cabinet-style government run by Japanese bureaucrats.[28] Because the appointments of these and other lower-level bureaucrats were governed by "elaborate rules and regulations which, in the main follow[ed] the lines of the Imperial Japanese services," the new Korean state quickly acquired a "rational" character.[29] Scholarly observers have in retrospect characterized the Japanese colonial civil service as "outstanding," composed of "hard working and trusted cadres" who deserve "high marks as a group."[30] Elements of the meritocratic Japanese style of bureaucratic government were thus transferred to Korea. Unlike in Japan, however, the colonial government displayed a great deal of brutality and violence toward its subjects.

26. Ibid., pp. 35–36. For a discussion of the development of the Prussian bureaucracy, especially concerning how some such traits as an espirit de corps, an ethos of public service, a degree of insulation from aristocratic interests, tight internal authority structure, and a relative absence of corruption developed, see Hans Rosenberg, *Bureaucracy, Aristocracy, and Autocracy: The Prussian Experience, 1660–1815* (Cambridge: Harvard University Press, 1958). For evolution of this bureaucracy in nineteenth-century Germany, see Gary Bonham, *Ideology and Interests in the German State* (New York: Garland Publishers, 1991), esp. chaps. 2, 7, and 8.

27. George Trumball Ladd, *In Korea with Marquis Ito* (New York: Charles Scribner's Sons, 1908), pp. 435, 174.

28. For details, see His Imperial Japanese Majesty's HIJM's Residency General, *Annual Report for 1907 on Reforms and Progress in Korea* (Seoul, 1908).

29. Alleyne Ireland, *The New Korea* (New York: E. P. Dutton, 1926), p. 104, and HIJM's Residency General, *The Second Annual Report on Reforms and Progress in Korea (1908–9)* (Seoul, 1909), p. 45.

30. Peattie, introduction, p. 26.

The new civil service. While other colonial powers also created a competent civil service (for example, the British in India), the Japanese colonial project was distinct in both the extent and the intensity of bureaucratic penetration. There were some 10,000 officials in the Japanese-Korean government in 1910; by 1937, this number was up to 87,552. More than half of these government officials in 1937, 52,270 to be exact, were Japanese. Contrast this with the French in Vietnam (where the presence of the French was already more significant than, say, that of the British in Africa), who ruled a nearly similar-size colony with some three thousand Frenchmen; in other words, there were nearly fifteen Japanese officials in Korea for every French administrator in Vietnam.[31] The presence of Korean bureaucrats, trained and employed by the Japanese, was also sizable: nearly forty thousand Koreans qualified as government officials just before the Second World War. While most of the Koreans did not occupy senior positions in the colonial government, there can be little doubt that, over the four decades of colonial rule, they became an integral part of a highly bureaucratic form of government. Moreover, during the Second World War, as the demand for Japanese officials grew elsewhere, many Koreans moved higher up in the bureaucratic hierarchy. I will return below to the issue of continuity: this sizable cadre of Japanese-trained Korean bureaucrats virtually took over the day-to-day running of a truncated South Korea, first under American military government and eventually when a sovereign state was formed.

Another characteristic of the colonial government that needs to be underlined is the successful links that the Japanese created between a highly concentrated power center in Seoul and a densely bureaucratized periphery. All bureaucracies face the problem of how to ensure that the officials at the bottom rung faithfully implement central commands. This, in turn, requires ensuring that lower-level officials respond mainly to those above them in the bureaucratic hierarchy, rather than to personal interests or to the interests of societal actors with whom they interact. Of course, certain circumstances were helpful in establishing authority links between the center and the periphery: ruling arrangements in Seoul were highly authoritarian—the power of the Japanese governor-generals in both policymaking and implementation was absolute, and nearly all of them were senior military men—and Korea was not a very large country (again, for example, note the contrast with the role of the British in India).

31. Michael E. Robinson, in Eckert et al., *Korea Old and New*, p. 257.

The police force. In addition to the civil bureaucracy, the Japanese developed a well-organized police force. Once again, there is nothing unique about colonial powers developing a police force. What is noteworthy here are both the extensive and the intensive natures of police supervision in colonial Korea. The colonial police force was designed on the lines of the Meiji police insofar as it was highly centralized and well disciplined and played an extensive role in social and economic control.[32] The police force in colonial Korea grew rapidly, from some 6,222 gendarmes and police in 1910 to 20,777 in 1922 and again to over 60,000 in 1941.[33] One scholar suggests that at the height of the colonial rule, there were enough police so that the lowest-level police officer knew "every man in the village."[34] While senior police officers were typically Japanese, over half the police force was made up of Koreans, often lower-class Koreans. These Koreans were trained by the Japanese in police academies, especially established within Korea for the purpose. Records indicate that for every Korean police position there were ten to twenty applicants, suggesting a high level of collaboration between Koreans and Japanese (this was to become an explosive issue in postindependence Korea).[35] Beyond formal training, the Japanese maintained very close supervision over their police force; for example, during 1915–20, about two thousand policemen—or nearly one out of every ten available officers—were sternly disciplined every year for transgression of police rules.[36]

This extensive and closely supervised police force, which penetrated every Korean village, performed numerous functions other than "normal" police duties of law and order maintenance. Powers granted to police included surveillance and control over "politics, education, religion, morals, health and public welfare, and tax collection."[37] The police, in military uniforms and replete with swords, also had summary powers to judge and punish minor offenders, including the punishment of whip-

32. One scholar of Meiji Japan thus notes: "The police . . . had operational responsibility for a bewildering variety of government programs and policies in addition to public safety, traffic control, and criminal investigation and apprehension. They enforced economic controls, discouraged unionism, inspected factories, censored publications, licensed commercial enterprises, arranged for public welfare aid, supervised druggists and publications, controlled public gatherings, managed flood control and fire prevention, maintained surveillance of people suspected of 'dangerous thoughts,' and did countless other things that brought government close to the daily life of every Japanese." See Robert M. Spaulding Jr., "The Bureaucracy as a Political Force, 1920–45," in James William Morley, ed., *Dilemmas of Growth in Prewar Japan* (Princeton: Princeton University Press, 1971), pp. 36–37.

33. Robinson, in Eckert et al., *Korea Old and New*, p. 259.

34. Ching-Chih Chen, "Police and Community Control Systems in the Empire," in Myers and Peattie, eds., *Japanese Colonial Empire*, p. 225.

35. Ibid., p. 236.

36. Ibid., pp. 236–39.

37. Robinson, in Eckert et al., *Korea Old and New*, p. 259.

ping. Even in production, local police were known to have "compelled villages to switch from existing food crops" to cash crops and to adopt "new techniques" in rice production so as to facilitate exports to Japan. Moreover, during land surveys (conducted during 1910–18; more on this below), as a result of which tenancy and conflicts over land increased, local police "always intervened in favor of landlords."[38] It is thus not surprising that even a Japanese observer was led to conclude that Terauchi (the first Japanese governor-general of Korea, following Ito and formal annexation) and his successors had transformed the "entire Korean peninsula into a military camp."[39]

One final aspect of the police role concerns the links between the police and local society via local elites. The police successfully utilized the proverbial carrot and stick to incorporate "village elders" and others into a ruling "alliance." The police thus buttressed their already extensive powers by co-opting indigenous authority structures. So armed, the police used the knowledge and influence of the local elites to mold the behavior of average citizens in such diverse matters as "birth control, types of crops grown, count and movement of people, prevention of spread of diseases, mobilization of forced labor and to report on transgressions."[40] The police and many local elites thus came to be viewed and despised by Koreans at large as "collaborationists"; unfortunately for Koreans, while many of the landed elite were indeed eventually eliminated as a political force (that is, via land reforms following the Korean War), much of the colonial police was incorporated directly into the new state structure of South Korea.

In sum, the old agrarian state which had proved capable of meeting the challenge of modernity came to be replaced by a colonial state with considerable capacity to penetrate and control the society; this state was simultaneously oppressive and efficacious. A highly centralized apex with near absolute powers of legislation and execution—and thus of setting and implementing "national" goals—and pervasive, disciplined civil and police bureaucracies constituted the core of the new state.

The politics of the new state. For the most part, the political practices of the Japanese colonial state in Korea were brutally authoritarian. For exam-

38. Chen, "Police and Community Control Systems," pp. 228–31. It is important to note that the extensive role of the police remained intact throughout the colonial period. For example, when Americans finally arrived in Korea after the Japanese surrender, they found (for instance, in South Cholla province) that police departments were the biggest within the local bureaucracy, and within the police departments, "economic sections" of the police were important. See Grant E. Meade, *American Military Government in Korea* (New York: King's Crown Press, Columbia University, 1951), esp. p. 31.

39. The quote is from Shakuo Shunjo and is cited in Chen, "Police and Community Control Systems," p. 222 n. 26.

40. Ibid., p. 226.

ple, Korean newspapers were either suspended or heavily censored, political protest was met with swift retribution, and political organizations and public gatherings were generally banned. Those professing Korean nationalist sentiments were thus either exiled or remained fragmented; while there was latent and scattered sympathy for nationalists and for communists all through the colonial period, a coherent nationalist movement was never allowed to develop within Korea.[11] The Japanese also used "thought police" to detect and eliminate political dissidence, and also developed a "spy system" to buttress the civil and police bureaucracy that was "probably better developed in Korea than anywhere in the world."[12]

The colonial authorities were deliberate in their use of repression as a means to instill fear in the minds of Koreans and thus to minimize dissidence and reinforce bureaucratic control: to avoid "restlessness" in the "popular mind," note government reports of the period, it was "essential" to "maintain unshakable the dignity of the government" and "to impress the people with the weight of the new regime."[13] When Koreans still resisted, Governor-General Terauchi Masatake supposedly responded, "I will whip you with scorpions,"[14] and when eventually the Koreans succumbed, the gloating satisfaction is also obvious in official documents: "They have gradually yielded their obstinate prejudices and their disdainful attitude."[15]

In spite of the ubiquitous state that the Japanese created, it would be a mistake to believe that a thorough bureaucratic penetration and politics of fear were the only ruling instruments in the hands of the colonialists. There is no doubt that bureaucratic growth enabled the new state to undertake many more economic activities which contributed to economic growth (more on this below) and that repression enabled the establishment of order, freeing the state elite to focus on other economic matters. For this, the Japanese needed to solicit cooperation from the native population; hence they resorted to the politics of "divide and conquer," as well as a massive effort at resocialization.

First, a segment of the Korean political elite in the precolonial period was co-opted.[16] These Koreans from the political class were both officially

---

41. See Chong-Sik Lee, *The Politics of Korean Nationalism* (Berkeley: University of California Press, 1963), passim. For a discussion of the brief, more liberal interlude, see Michael E. Robinson, *Cultural Nationalism in Colonial Korea, 1920–1925* (Seattle: University of Washington Press, 1989).

42. Andrew J. Grajdanzev, *Modern Korea* (New York: John Day, 1944), p. 55.

43. Government-General of Chosen, *Results of Three Years' Administration of Chosen since Annexation* (Seoul, 1914), pp. 2–3.

44. Quoted in Peattie, introduction, p. 18.

45. Government-General of Chosen, *Thriving Chosen: A Survey of Twenty-Five Years' Administration* (Seoul, 1935), p. 81.

46. For example, when confronted with the fact of being left behind in the race to modernity, many Koreans had looked to Meiji Japan as a model for their own advancement;

and unofficially incorporated into the new system of colonial rule. Second, and relatedly, the colonial state forged numerous implicit and explicit "alliances" with Korean propertied classes. The nature of these turned out to be of critical long-term significance. While I return to a detailed discussion of this issue below, it should be noted here that, on the whole, Korean money groups—in both the city and the countryside—were in no position to oppose colonial rule. Many got along by tolerating, if not cooperating with, the colonial project, and some even benefited from the colonial rule. Third, the Japanese undertook considerable expansion of education, facilitating propaganda and political resocialization. Whereas in 1910 nearly 10,000 students attended some sort of school, by 1941 this number was up to 1.7 million, and the rate of literacy by 1945 was nearly 50 percent. The focus was on primary education, and the curriculum was designed with the "object" of raising "practical men able to meet the requirements of the state."[47]

To conclude, the Japanese colonialists in Korea replaced the decrepit Yi state with a centralized, illiberal state. Central decision making was highly concentrated in the office of the governor-general. The governor-general's will, reflecting the imperial design and goals, was translated into implemented policies via the use of an extensive, well-designed, and disciplined bureaucracy. The new state also achieved considerable downward penetration: both the civil and police bureaucracies reached into the nooks and crannies of the society, while continuing to respond to central directives; Korean elites in the localities were co-opted into the ruling "alliance," in the context of pervasive intelligence and surveillance by the police and the state.

The Colonial State, Propertied Classes, and Economic Change

To pursue the imperial interests of Japan, the colonial government developed a full policy agenda to transform the economy of Korea. The

---

for better or for worse, therefore, "modernity" to many Koreans came to be represented by Japan. See Gregory Henderson, *Korea: The Politics of Vortex* (Cambridge: Harvard University Press, 1968), esp. p. 67. Moreover, some Korean elites, enamored with Japan, had participated in the Japanese-supported Kabo reforms of 1895. Later, the pro-Japanese Korean organization Ilchin-hoe (Advancement Society) enjoyed considerable support between 1905 and 1910; at its least popular phase in 1910, the Ilchin-hoe still enjoyed a membership of nearly 140,000 and had some 100 subsidiary organizations. See, for example, Vipin Chandra, "An Outline Study of the *Ilchin hoe* (Advancement Society) of Korea," *Occasional Papers on Korea* 2 (March 1974): 43–72.

47. The quote is from official documents of the Government-General and taken from Ireland, *New Korea*, p. 190.

broad strategy of transformation was two-pronged: the state utilized its bureaucratic capacities to undertake quite a few economic tasks, and, more important, the state involved propertied groups—both in the countryside and in the cities and both Japanese and Koreans—in production-oriented alliances leading up to sustained economic change. The results measured by the criteria of growth and industrialization were a considerable success. But they were accompanied by growing misery and exploitation, as much of the fruit of growth was taken out of Korea.

Two general observations ought to be noted at the outset. First, the governor-general in Korea was an agent of the Japanese imperial government, which exercised absolute powers in Korea. The colonial state in Korea thus pursued Japanese needs and interests that changed over time.[48] In broad brush strokes, during the early phase, say, the first decade of the colonial rule, Japan treated Korea mainly as a strategic gain that could also be exploited in a fairly classic fashion: exchange of agricultural products for manufactured goods. Subsequently, as Japanese demand for food outpaced its own supply, the colonial state aggressively undertook measures to increase food production in Korea. Manufacturing was discouraged in this early phase, again in a fairly classic fashion, to protect Japanese exports to Korea. Following the First World War, however, with swollen company profits, Japan sought opportunities for export of capital and thus relaxed restrictions against production of manufactured products in Korea. As the same time, following the need to co-opt nationalistic pressures within Korea, the colonial state also involved selected and prominent Korean businessmen in the growth of manufacturing. Aggressive industrialization of Korea occurred only in the 1930s. This was in part a result of Japan's strategy to cope with the depression—that is, to create a protected, high-growth economy on an empirewide scale—and in part a result of Japan's aggressive industrialization, again on an empirewide scale, that reflected national power considerations.[49] It is important to notice that Japan was able to switch its imperial policies in Korea frequently and decisively; this, in turn, underlined the highly centralized nature of authority within the Japanese-controlled Korean state.

The second related observation concerns the pressures on the governor-general in Korea to reduce the budget deficit by enhancing revenues within Korea and reducing expenditures, much of it caused by the need to maintain terrific repression throughout the society. Reading through

48. For one review of Japanese colonial economic policies, see Samuel Pao-San Ho, "Colonialism and Development: Korea, Taiwan, and Kwantung," in Myers and Peattie, eds., *Japanese Colonial Empire*, pp. 347–86.

49. See, for example, E. B. Schumpeter, *The Industrialization of Japan and Manchukuo, 1930–1940* (New York: Macmillan, 1940), esp. chaps. 9–11, 21, and 22, as well as the conclusion.

historical documents of the time, especially the annual reports of the governor-general in Korea, it becomes clear that the colonial authorities in Korea were concerned with the continual net revenue inflow from Japan to Korea, used to cover the shortfall in the budget. This was in marked contrast to Taiwan, where the colonial subjects were relatively acquiescent and thus the cost associated with maintaining political order was greatly less than it was in Korea. The general point, then, is that, unlike many other governments, the colonial state in Korea did not operate with a "soft budget constraint." On the contrary, there was consistent pressure to economize, "hardening" the budget constraint, with significant effort to deploy the state's coercive power to extract tax revenues.

Increased State Capacity

The increased capacity of the new colonial state in Korea to undertake economic tasks directly is evident fairly early in the historical record. For example, there was the issue of state capacity to collect taxes. The old Yi state had shown deterioration in its capacity to extract taxes from society, especially from landowners. The contrasting performance of the colonial state is notable. Land revenue in 1905, the year the Japanese influence in Korea started to grow, was some 4.9 million yen; by 1908, this had jumped to 6.5 million yen, or a real increase of some 30 percent in three years.[50] Subsequently, numerous other sources of revenue were added to that obtained from land—for example, railways, post office, and customs; receipts from the ginseng monopoly and from such public undertakings as salt manufacture, coal mines, timber work and printing bureaus—and the jump in revenue intake was phenomenal: whereas the total revenue in 1905 (land and other revenues) was 7.3 million yen, by 1911, one year after formal annexation, the total revenue intake was 24 million yen, or an increase of more than 300 percent.[51] The factors that help explain this increased state capacity were twofold. First, the colonial state, backed by superior coercive power, snapped the stranglehold landowning groups had on the Yi state, pensioning off the Yangban elite and replacing them with Japanese career bureaucrats. I will return to this issue below. Second,

50. The figures are from HIJM's Residency General, *Annual Report for 1907* and *Second Annual Report on Reforms and Progress in Korea (1908–9)*. The real increase was probably somewhat less because this simple calculation does not take account of increase in production, which, in any case, we know to have been relatively small in those years.

51. The 1905 figure is from HIJM's Residency General, *Annual Report for 1907*, and the 1911 figure is from Government-General of Chosen, *Annual Report on Reforms and Progress in Chosen (Korea), (1910–11)* (Seoul: Keiji, 1911). While reliable data on inflation for these years is not readily available, there is no indication in government documents of huge price increases.

the colonial elite utilized the newly created civil and police bureaucracy to collect taxes. More specifically, as early as 1906, thirty-six revenue collection officers, again replete with uniforms and swords, were posted all over Korea to identify cultivated land, owners of the land, and the revenue due from the land.[52] Although the rate of taxation on land was not increased, it was regularized. Additionally, uniformed revenue officers worked in conjunction with local police officers in the process of tax collection, lest any one forget this newly established separation of state and society, or the willful presence of the new state in society.

The successful land survey that the Japanese conducted in Korea between 1910 and 1918 similarly highlighted the resolve of the new state to impose the capitalist order in Korea. The colonial state made an exhaustive land survey a priority. Over a period of eight years the Japanese invested some 30 million yen in the project (compared, say, with the total revenue intake of the Government-General in 1911 of 24 million yen). The survey "mapped all plots of land, classified it according to type, graded its productivity and established ownership."[53] As a result of the survey, the colonial state secured a revenue base and enhanced its control over the Korean agrarian sector by dispossessing some landlords (who could not on paper prove their ownership rights) and replacing them with new immigrants from Japan, mostly from Kyushu. The survey was a massive assertion of the colonial will, altering permanently the regime of property rights that had undergirded the Korean political economy for half a millennium.

Over time, the colonial state in Korea undertook numerous other infrastructural projects. This is no place for a comprehensive discussion; I simply wish to flag some of the main areas.[54] First, Korea was the gateway to imperial expansion into China, and therefore the Government-General invested heavily in infrastructure. The result was that Korea's roads and railways were among the finest that a developing country inherited from their colonial past. Second, as mentioned above, the Japanese made significant investments in Korea in primary education. Given the long gestation period, however, the returns on this investment were probably reaped less by colonial Korea than by the two sovereign Koreas, which inherited a relatively literate labor force. Third, the colonial government ran a number of economic enterprises directly: for example, railways, communications, opium, salt, and tobacco. Judged by the regular financial contribution that these public undertakings made to public revenues,

52. HIJM's Residency General, *Annual Report for 1907*, chap. 5.

53. See Robinson, in Eckert et al., *Korea Old and New*, p. 265. There is apparently also a good doctoral thesis on the subject of this land survey by Edward Gragert at Columbia University. Unfortunately, I was unable to locate this unpublished manuscript.

54. For a full discussion, see Ho, "Colonialism and Development."

they were run relatively efficiently. And finally, the Government-General played an important role in the overall process of capital accumulation. Although I will return to this issue again below and the direct role of the new colonial state in extracting taxes has already been noted, a few other points also deserve attention. The currency and banking reforms that the new colonial state undertook rather early led to a significant jump in private, institutional savings: for instance, deposits in the Bank of Chosen (Korea) doubled from some 18 million yen in 1911 to 37 million yen in 1913, and the number of depositors in the postal savings bank went up from about 20,000 in 1909 to 420,000 in 1913 (the corresponding sums of deposits being 120,000 yen in 1909 and 981,000 yen in 1913).[55] Later during the colonial rule, the Government-General required Koreans to buy government bonds that helped finance the industrialization drive of the 1930s. While capital inflows from Japan remained the dominant source, local capital accumulation also increased considerably. Facts and figures aside, the general point again is this: the colonial state in Korea, even more than the Japanese Meiji state on which it was modeled, became heavily and directly involved in economic tasks and, judged strictly by economic criteria, performed these tasks with ruthless effectiveness.

More significant than the state's direct economic role was the indirect role that led up to the involvement of wealthy groups in productive activities. The mechanics of how these state–private sector alliances were created are important because similar arrangements were later central to South Korea's phenomenal economic success. The dynamics of change in both the agrarian and industrial sectors thus deserve our attention.

The State and the Agrarian Sector

The colonial state restructured its relationship with the Korean landed classes. The highest Yangban elite who held offices in the Yi state were pensioned off.[56] As career bureaucrats took over official functions, the direct control by landed classes of the state weakened. The successful land survey further confirmed the supremacy of the new state because, as a result of it, the capacity of the landed classes to evade the reach of the state shrunk. In return, however, the state offered the landowners legal protection of their property, as well as political protection against peasant unrest. For example, the Japanese introduced a new legal code—based on the Meiji legal code—that created Western-style legal private property, thus se-

55. Government-General of Chosen, *Results of Three Years' Administration of Chosen* (1914), p. 19.

56. Government-General of Chosen, *Annual Report on Reforms and Progress in Chosen (Korea)*, (1910–11), pp. 18–19.

curing the control of Korean landed groups over land in perpetuity. The Japanese in the process ended up owning a significant amount of agricultural land in Korea. Most Koreans who controlled land before the arrival of the Japanese, however, were allowed to maintain and, in some cases, even expand their land ownership.[57] Moreover, as mentioned above, many among the landed elite were incorporated into local governance, cooperating with and helping local agents of the state maintain control over villages. Students of colonialism often distinguish direct and indirect colonial rule, but the Japanese political arrangements in Korea utilized both forms: direct bureaucratic penetration was buttressed by the authority of local influentials. This arrangement also suggests that, contrary to some more recent arguments, the presence of a landowning class does not necessarily inhibit the formation of a powerful "developmental" state; much depends on the specific relationship between the state and landowners.[58]

The Japanese colonial government periodically made significant efforts to boost agricultural production, especially Korea's main product, rice. The underlying motivation was changing Japanese economic needs: for example, before 1919, the efforts to boost production were minimal. Following rice shortage and related riots in Japan in 1918, a major plan to expand rice production in Korea was implemented. The success on this front contributed to "overproduction," and after a glut and pressures from Japanese rice producers, all plans to increase rice production were canceled in 1933. Again, however, the war with China in 1938–39 created food shortages in Japan, and Korea was "resuscitated as a granary of the Empire."[59]

During the early phase the Japanese focused their efforts on land improvement, especially on irrigation, drainage, and reclamation of arable land. The resulting increase in production was not huge and resulted from both extensive and intensive efforts; increase in rice production between 1910 and 1924 averaged around 1.5 percent per annum, and land productivity in the same period improved at about 0.8 percent per annum.[60] Subse-

---

57. The colonial government's own assessment is interesting. While lamenting the political opposition from educated Koreans, government documents of the period note: "People of the upper class having personally experienced imperial favor and being in a position to feel directly or indirectly the benefit of the new regime, seem to be contented with it." See Government-General of Chosen, *Results of Three Years' Administration of Chosen* (1914), p. 64. See also Robinson, in Eckert et al., *Korea Old and New*, pp. 266–67.

58. Joel S. Migdal, *Strong Societies and Weak States: State-Society Relations and State Capabilities in the Third World* (Princeton: Princeton University Press, 1988), for example, tends to view state capacity in agrarian societies as inversely related to the power of landowning and other traditional elites. Peter Evans, "Class, State, and Dependence in East Asia: Lessons for Latin Americanists," in Deyo, ed., *Political Economy of the New Asian Industrialism*, pp. 203–26, makes a similar argument.

59. For these policy swings and for the direct quote, see Grajdanzev, *Modern Korea*, pp. 92–94.

60. Suh, *Growth and Structural Changes*, p. 73, table 33.

quently, when the rapid increase in rice production became a goal, Korea's Japanese rulers utilized the knowledge acquired during the Meiji transformation and concentrated their efforts on spreading the use of improved seeds, fertilizer, and irrigation. The gains were significant: the percentage of paddy land using improved seed doubled between 1915 and 1940, reaching 85 percent; fertilizer input expanded ten times during the same period; and between 1919 and 1938 land under irrigation increased annually by nearly 10 percent.[61] As a result, rice production between 1920 and 1935 grew at nearly 3 percent per annum, and nearly two-thirds of this growth resulted from improvements in land productivity.[62] The overall rate of increase in rice production per unit of land for the colonial period (1910–40) averaged a respectable 2 percent per annum (compare this, for example, with India's post–green revolution—say, 1970 to present— rates of productivity increase in cereal production, which have been only a little higher than 2 percent per annum). While some of these improvements may have been a "spontaneous" response to food shortages and higher prices in Japan, it is nevertheless difficult to imagine a relatively quick increase in supply without significant public efforts, especially in providing new seeds and in facilitating the spread of fertilizer.

It is a sad fact that increases in production in Korea did not lead to improvement in food consumption. The bulk of the increased production ended up in the export market, and imported goods did not become consumption items for the vast majority. As a well-documented study concludes, "per capita use of food grains as a whole declined substantially after the early years of the colonial period." The same author points out that this disjuncture between production and consumption was a result of several causes but mainly due to a combination of population growth and few nonagricultural opportunities that increased the burden on tenants and on small farmers.[63] If there was steady growth in production but the consumption for the majority of the population declined, given the considerable inequality in land ownership, it is likely that the incomes of landowning groups, many of them Japanese, mushroomed. Other available evidence is consistent with this proposition: the rates of return on agricultural investment were very high for most of the period; income inequalities widened; and, as noted above, there was rapid growth of small depositors in saving institutions. The general point is that Korean landowning groups did rather well under colonial

61. Ibid., p. 77, table 34, and p. 73, table 33; Shigeru Ishikawa, *Economic Development in Asian Perspective* (Tokyo: Kinokuniya Bookstore, 1967), pp. 84–109.

62. Suh, *Growth and Structural Changes*, p. 73, table 33. See also Ishikawa, *Economic Development*, pp. 84–109.

63. Suh, *Growth and Structural Changes*, pp. 86–87.

government; they became part of an implicit but comfortable colonial alliance.

Three other characteristics of the changing agrarian sector are noteworthy. First, Japanese corporations and entrepreneurs ended up owning large tracts of Korean agricultural land—anywhere from one-quarter to one-third of all the arable land. This was a result of a conscious government policy that began with the hope of attracting Japanese immigrants to Korea, but when that goal met with only limited success, Japanese corporations became heavily involved. Especially significant as a landowner was the infamous Oriental Development Company, which, like most other Japanese landowners, leased lands to tenants, collected rents in kind, most often rice, and sold the rice in the export market back to Japan.[64] The rate of return on such activities was high, higher than in Japan, and many a fortunes were made.[65] From my standpoint, the direct involvement of the Japanese in Korean agriculture helps explicate two points: the mechanics of how the more advanced techniques of agricultural production may have been transferred from Japan to Korea, and the mechanics underlying "forced exports," whereby Japanese landowners sold rice grown in Korea back to Japan directly.

A second characteristic of the changing agrarian sector was its heavy export orientation. For instance, while total Korean rice production during the colonial period nearly doubled, rice exports to Japan during the same period increased six times.[66] Additionally, although the overall economy of the Japanese empire was protected, trading within the empire was relatively free of tariffs and other restrictions. Rapid growth of exports to the metropole with a more advanced agriculture thus points to an additional source—the quintessential source of competition—that must have also contributed to sustained improvements in agricultural productivity. Lastly, the geography of the changing agrarian scene is worthy of attention. Rice production and Japanese ownership of Korean land were both more concentrated in the southern half of Korea. The bulk of rice exports also originated in the south, keeping it more rural than the north.

To conclude this discussion on the changes in the agrarian sector, two developments of long-term consequence need to be underlined. The nearly obvious point is that a productive agriculture was a necessary component of rapid economic growth, first during colonial Korea and later, even more prominently, in sovereign South Korea. While many developing countries, such as in Africa, are still attempting their agricultural rev-

---

64. For example, see Karl Moskowitz, "The Creation of the Oriental Development Company: Japanese Illusions Meet Korean Reality," *Occasional Papers on Korea* 2 (March 1974).

65. Suh, *Growth and Structural Changes*, p. 85, table 39.

66. Ibid., p. 92, table 43.

olution, and others, such as India and the Philippines, hailed their green revolution from the mid-1960s onward, Korea was already undergoing a biological revolution in agriculture in the first half of this century. Just before the Second World War, rice yields in Korea were approaching Japanese yields, which were then among the highest in the world (for example, if the U.S. yields in 1938 were 100, Japan's were 154, and Korea's, 111).[67] Rapid increase in agriculture production, in turn, provided both food and inputs to sustain an industrial drive, on the one hand, and yielded high incomes and savings that found their way back into a growing economy, on the other hand. A decade hence, after land reforms were implemented in South Korea, the productive agricultural base and related incomes also contributed to the emergence of a domestic market for manufactured goods.

The other, less obvious legacy concerns the "model of development" that undergirded the agrarian transformation. As in Meiji Japan, but even more so, the colonial state in Korea established its superiority as the key actor that would direct economic change. The state then employed various carrots and sticks to incorporate the propertied groups in a production-oriented alliance. A key focus of the state's efforts was improving the technology of production, namely, better seeds, fertilizer, and irrigation. Even after decolonization, these efforts left behind a bureaucratic infrastructure that was adept at facilitating technology-intensive agricultural development. Moreover, public subsidies from the colonial state helped improve the profitability of private producers, as well as productivity and production. This pattern of state and propertied class alliance for production, centered around technology and other public subsidies, would repeat itself in subsequent periods and in numerous other economic activities, especially in industry, to which I now turn.

The State and Industrialization

The extent of Korea's industrialization during the colonial phase was both considerable and nearly unique in the comparative history of colonialism; the average, annual rate of growth in industry (including mining and manufacturing) during 1910–40 was nearly 10 percent, and by 1940, nearly 35 percent of the total commodity production originated in the industrial sector.[68] Although I analyze the why and how of this experience below, as well as its long-term significance, my main point is not that South Korea somehow inherited a relatively industrialized economy. It did not! A fair amount of the heavy industry was located in the north, and

67. Grajdanzev, *Modern Korea*, p. 87, and Ishikawa, *Economic Development*, p. 95, charts 2–5.
68. Suh, *Growth and Structural Changes*, p. 48, table 11, and p. 46, tables 17 and 18.

significant industrial concentrations were destroyed during the Korean War. Nevertheless, a war-destroyed economy, with an experience of rapid industrialization behind it, is quite different from a tradition-bound, nearly stagnant, agrarian economy.[69] I will return below to the issue of the creation of a trained and disciplined working class. At the apex of the social pyramid and from the standpoint of the colonial legacy, several issues of long-term significance deserve our attention here: the style of development, especially a state-dominated, state-private sector alliance for production and profit that emerged under Japanese rule; the emergence of a significant entrepreneurial strata among Koreans; and a growing economy whose structure was already heavily export oriented.

The Japanese approach to Korea's industrialization went through three more or less distinct phases. During the first decade of colonial rule, Japan sought to protect the Korean market as an outlet for Japanese manufactured goods. Rules and regulations were thus created to inhibit the start-up of new factories in Korea by both Japanese and Korean entrepreneurs. The fact that annual growth rates in the manufacturing sector during this decade still averaged a respectable 7 percent reflected the very low starting base. This growth had several components. There were the new public sector investments in power, railways, and other infrastructure. The private sector growth originated mainly in food-processing industries—especially rice mills—that were initiated by Japanese migrants with the hope of selling rice back to Japan. Exchanging Japanese manufactured goods for Korean rice and other primary products was, of course, the initial colonial policy. The Government-General thus helped Japanese entrepreneurs start up these mills by providing both financial and infrastructural support. Finally, some of this early growth also involved the participation of Koreans. Small-scale manufacturing did not require the permission of the Government-General. Moreover, incomes of landowning Koreans had started to rise, and not all their demand could be met by Japanese imports. Emulating the Japanese migrants, Koreans set up small industries (often called household industries in Japanese colonial documents; they employed ten to twenty workers) in such areas as metals, dyeing, papermaking, ceramics, rubber shoes, knitted

69. This distinction can be sharpened by using the concepts of "idea gaps" and "object gaps" proposed in the "new" economic growth theory. Whereas the "object gap" refers to lack of concrete objects as factories, that direct attention to savings and investment bottlenecks in development, the "idea gap" refers to the knowledge base on which development rests. The "new" growth theory emphasizes (as did several previous growth theories) the role of knowledge and technology in economic growth. See, for example, Paul Romer, "Idea Gaps and Object Gaps in Economic Development," paper presented at the World Bank Conference, "How Do National Policies Affect Long-Run Growth?" Washington, D.C., February 7–8, 1993. One may thus argue that in Korean colonial economic history, even if "objects" were destroyed during decolonization, the legacy of "ideas" was substantial.

cotton socks, and sake and soy sauce. The number of small factories thus increased from 151 in 1910 to 1,900 in 1919; 971 of these 1,900 factories were owned by Koreans.[70]

The First World War transformed Japan from a debtor to a creditor country. With swollen company profits, the Japanese imperial government sought opportunities for Japanese capital overseas, including in Korea. Restrictions on manufacturing in Korea were abolished, and thus began a second phase in Korean industrialization. Japanese investors did not rush in. The competitive pressure from Japanese manufactured goods was considerable, and the Government-General wanted to encourage complementarities rather than competition between Japanese exporters to and Japanese investors in Korea. The colonial state supported a select few Japanese investors by helping them choose areas of investment, providing cheap land, raising capital for investment, guaranteeing initial profits via subsidies, and moving workers to out-of-the-way locations. As a result, major business groups such as Mitsui and Mitsubishi moved into Korea; others followed. The average annual rate of growth in industry during the 1920s was over 8 percent. A significant component of this was Japanese private investment in textiles, some in processing of raw materials and some rather large-scale investments in mining, iron, steel, hydroelectric power, and even shipbuilding. The number of factories employing more than fifty workers went up from 89 in 1922 to 230 in 1930.[71]

Korean participation in this second phase, while a distant second to the role of Japanese capital, was not insignificant. Relatively small-scale Korean "household industries" continued to mushroom. Their growth reflected several underlying trends: rising demand resulting from growing incomes of wealthy Koreans and Japanese in Korea, as well as economic growth in Japan; the role of Japanese factories as "Schumpeterian innovators" that were followed by a "cluster" of Korean imitators; and forward and backward linkages created by Japanese investments.[72] Moreover, after the Korean nationalist uprising in 1919, the colonial government liberalized its ruling strategy for several years and sought to co-opt some wealthy Korean businessmen. Enterprising Koreans with initial capital—often with roots in land wealth—were thus allowed to enter medium-to large-scale trade and manufacturing. Those willing to cooperate with the Government-General were also rewarded with credit, subsidies, and other public supports. Of the 230 factories that employed more than fifty work-

---

70. Soon Won Park, "The Emergence of a Factory Labor Force in Colonial Korea: A Case Study of the Onoda Cement Factory," Ph.D. diss., Harvard University, 1985, pp. 16–18.

71. Ibid., p. 42.

72. Young-Iob Chung, "Japanese Investment in Korea, 1904–45," in Andrew Nahm, ed., *Korea under Japanese Colonial Rule* (Center for Korean Studies, Western Michigan University, 1973), p. 93.

ers in 1930, 49 thus came to be Korean-owned.[73] Major Korean chaebols, such as Kyŏngbang—the Korean group which was most prominent during the colonial period and which began in textiles—Kongsin Hosiery, Paeksan Trading Company, Hwasin Department Store, and Mokpo Rubber Company, therefore got started during this time period.[74]

During the 1930s and well into the Second World War, Korea underwent very rapid industrialization. The rate of industrialization hastened and the process acquired considerable depth during this phase. The annual average rate of growth of industry was nearly 15 percent, and a significant component of new growth originated in heavy industries, especially the chemical industry. The moving force behind these developments was, once again, government policies. As the Western world went into a depression and protected economies sprouted, Japan aggressively sought growth by creating an import-substituting economy of sorts on an empirewide scale.[75] After annexing Manchuria in 1931, moreover, Korea became an advanced military supply base for the Japanese war efforts in China. The Korean economy was thus developed by the colonial government as part and parcel of an empirewide strategy to promote rapid growth, with a potential war always in mind.

The development of hydroelectric power in northern Korea during the 1920s and early 1930s had brought down costs of electricity and thus barriers to starting new factories. Raw materials such as coal and iron ore were also concentrated in the same part of Korea, reducing transportation costs. With wages for workers nearly half that in Japan and with absolutely no labor protection laws (more on this below), "market conditions" for investment in Korea, especially in northern Korea, were far from adverse during the 1930s. A "push" factor was also at work: the Japanese imperial government had tightened control on Japanese industry within Japan, while giving business a freer hand elsewhere in the empire. Nevertheless, the direct role of the Government-General in encouraging business into Korea was essential. The colonial state periodically laid out its industrial policy, indicating the preferred direction of economic change, especially, given war planning, where the government expected demand to grow. Moreover, government and business cooperated to an extent that contours of corporate policy were "indirectly fixed" by the government's economic plans.[76] Another analyst notes that "adaptability

73. Park, "Emergence of a Factory Labor Force in Colonial Korea," p. 42.

74. The point here is not that these same groups subsequently facilitated Korea's export-led growth. Some contributed to this process, others failed, and yet other new ones also emerged. The point here is that a "system" was being created. I am indebted to Chung-in Moon's criticisms that forced me to clarify this point.

75. Schumpeter, *Industrialization of Japan and Manchukuo*, chap. 21.3 and 22.8, by G. C. Allen.

76. Eckert, *Offspring of Empire*, p. 73.

to state economic priorities was a prerequisite for successful large-scale enterprise" in colonial Korea.[77]

The Government-General utilized several economic and noneconomic instruments to ensure compliance with its preferred economic direction. First, the colonial state kept a "tight control on the colony's financial structure."[78] The Chosen Industrial Bank, which helped finance new investments and which had controlling interests in a number of diverse industries, was under the jurisdiction of the Government-General. This issue was critical for Korean investors who had no other independent source of credit. Even for Japanese *zaibatsu*, who could raise some of their finances from corporate sources in Japan, cooperation with the state was important; for example, the Government-General floated compulsory savings bonds within Korea as a way of helping Japanese companies finance some of the gigantic investment projects (hydroelectric power and fertilizer plants) in northern Korea. Second, there were the perennial subsidies; one analyst estimates that these were of the order of 1 percent of "gross national product" per year.[79] These were used selectively to promote the government's priorities. For example, the highest subsidy for a time was provided to Mitsubishi to encourage gold mining; the Japanese imperial government needed the gold to pay for such strategic imports from the United States as scrap iron, copper, and zinc.[80] The next largest subsidy was provided to producers of zinc and magnesium, products necessary for manufacturing airplanes.[81] Tax exemptions were similarly used discriminately to both encourage and direct economic activity.

Although it is difficult to assess the significance of noneconomic factors in this state-directed, state-business alliance, they are nevertheless worth noting. The governor-general would periodically exhort businessmen to eschew narrow "capitalistic profits and commercial self-interest" and to consider the economic "mission" of Korea from the standpoint of the "national economy." The direction of influence between the state and business is also nicely captured by the fact that both Japanese and Korean businesspeople referred to the governor-general as *jifu* (a loving father), highlighting the benevolent upper hand of the state. In the words of Carter Eckert, businessmen were intricately incorporated into the policy-

77. McNamara, *Colonial Origins of Korean Enterprise*, p. 9.

78. Eckert, *Offspring of Empire*, p. 73.

79. Chung, "Japanese Investment in Korea," p. 91.

80. There is a great self-congratulatory discussion of how Governor-General Ugaki Kazushige thought of this scheme to provide subsidies for gold mining. See his speech in Government-General of Chosen, *Thriving Chosen* (1935), pp. 85–87.

81. Grajdanzev, *Modern Korea*, pp. 138–40.

making process, and what they lost in "autonomy," they made up for "magnificently" by way of "corporate profits."[82]

A few specific examples of government-business cooperation will further help flush out the nature of this mutually convenient alliance. The example of government subsidies for Mitsubishi to encourage gold mining has already been noted. Mitsui was similarly granted the ginseng monopoly by the Government-General in exchange for a healthy share of the sprawling profits as taxes on the monopoly. The case of the smaller Onoda cement factory has been studied in detail and is interesting.[83] The Government-General discovered large limestone deposits in Korea during its surveys. This information was provided to cement manufacturers in Japan. The Government-General also indicated its needs for cement within Korea, thus encouraging Onoda to invest in Korea. Most important, the Government-General laid the groundwork for Onoda's expansion by ordering provincial governors to buy cement from Onoda factories for all government construction projects during the agricultural expansion phase in the 1920s, regularly setting aside nearly 10 percent of the annual budget intended for agricultural production projects for purchase of this cement.

The level of cooperation between the Government-General and colonial Korea's largest Japanese business group, Nihon Chisso, was so intricate that it is difficult to tell where the public efforts ended and private efforts began. For example, the preliminary work for the construction of hydroelectric power plants—such as the necessary surveys, choice of location, soil tests—was conducted by the Government-General. Private energies of Nihon Chisso were then tapped, but again, the Government-General played a critical role in capital accumulation by putting at the company's disposal the service of the government-controlled Industrial Bank and by floating savings bonds. The government further helped move workers from the south to the labor-scarce northern region, where power generators were to be located, and subsequently remained deeply involved in the pricing and distribution of electrical power. What the government got out of all this collaboration was a ready supply of cheap electricity in Korea, which, in turn, became the basis for rapid industrialization. From Nihon Chisso's point of view, hydroelectric power was only one of numerous projects that the company undertook in Korea. What it

82. All the materials in quotations in this paragraph are from Eckert, *Offspring of Empire*, pp. 73–74. Note that the exhortations to businesspeople began rather early with colonial rule. A government report of 1914 notes that the governor-general called business leaders to a party, explained the government's policies, and urged them to be concerned not only with profits but also "to bear in mind the promotion of the interest of the state." See Government-General of Chosen, *Results of Three Years' Administration of Chosen* (1914), p. 13.

83. Park, "Emergence of a Factory Labor Force in Colonial Korea," pp. 83–99.

did buy in the process was the enormous goodwill of the Government-General, which subsequently translated into opportunities for expansion in a number of other lucrative fields, such as nitrogen and fertilizer production.

Several of the larger Korean business groups also benefited from a close cooperation with the Government-General. For example, new research has documented how the largest Korean business group, Kyŏngbang, financed its investments with the help of the Government-General.[84] The subsidies provided by the government between 1924 and 1935 added up to nearly "one fourth of the company's paid-up capital in 1935."[85] Furthermore, the main source of finance was loans from the government-controlled Chosen Industrial Bank. Personal relationships of key actors helped secure the bonds between Kyŏngbang, the Industrial Bank, and the Government-General. The terms of the loans were very favorable, indicating a comfortable and close relationship between the colonial state and a Korean business group. Another research similarly documents the close cooperation between the colonial state and the Min brothers in the field of banking and Pak Hŭng-sik in commerce; these ventures eventually matured into such major Korean chaebols as the Hwasin Department Store.[86]

Within the framework of a war economy, the planned government business cooperation became the basis of the very rapid industrialization of Korea during 1930–45. During some years the rates of growth were especially breathtaking: for example, between 1936 and 1939, industrial production more than doubled. By the early 1940s, agricultural and industrial production was nearly equal (each providing some 40 percent of the national production); by 1943, heavy industry provided nearly half the total industrial production.[87] Some specific patterns within this overall economic transformation also deserve our attention, especially because they proved to be of long-term significance.

First, the colonial state preferred to work with large business groups. Following the Meiji model, but with a vengeance in Korea, the Government-General utilized various means to encourage the formation of large-scale business enterprises: larger groups enjoyed preferred interest rates on credit, lower charges on electricity, direct price supports, and such indirect subsidies as lower transportation costs on government-controlled railways. Nearly two-thirds of the total production in the late 1930s was thus produced by only a handful of Japanese zaibatsu in Korea.

84. Eckert, *Offspring of Empire.*
85. Ibid., p. 84.
86. McNamara, *Colonial Origins of Korean Enterprise.*
87. Park, "Emergence of a Factory Labor Force in Colonial Korea," p. 51, tables 11 and 12.

Since the Korean, family-centered, but gigantic enterprises also came into their own under this regime, herein may lie the origin of chaebols.[88]

It is important to underline a second pattern, namely, that a significant stratum of Korean entrepreneurs emerged under the colonial auspices. If judged mainly by the proportion of total private capital or of large enterprises that Koreans owned, the Korean presence in comparison with that of the Japanese appears minuscule.[89] As has been pointed out by others, however, this approach is misleading. A significant minority of firms (nearly 30 percent) were owned jointly by Koreans and Japanese. More important from the standpoint of the emergence of an entrepreneurial class was the scale of Korean participation by 1937: "There were 2,300 Korean-run factories throughout the industrial spectrum, and about 160 of these establishments employed over 50 workers."[90] These figures are for all Korea, and because it is fair to assume that most of these must have concentrated in the south after the Communists took over the northern half, one may observe with some confidence that colonialism left behind a considerable density of entrepreneurship in South Korea.

A third pattern concerns the geographical distribution of industry. Those wishing to deny continuities with the colonial period again point to the fact that much of the industry was located in the north and was thus not inherited by South Korea. This is partly true, insofar as the largest chemical and other heavy industries were indeed located in the northern provinces. A number of qualifications, however, are also needed. The chemical, metal, and electricity-generating industries, which were concentrated in the north, constituted 30, 8, and 2.2 percent respectively of the total industrial production in 1938.[91] That adds up to some 40 percent, leaving a good chunk for the south. More than half the total industry was probably located in the south. The nature of southern industries was also distinct; they tended to be in such fields as food processing, textiles, machine and tools, and tobacco-related industries. By contrast, the industries in the north were highly capital intensive, high-cost production units that were not well integrated with the local economy. Northern industries were much more likely to evolve into white elephants, requiring continuous protection, rather than into nimble, labor-intensive exporters of consumer products.

The last pattern concerns the deep ties that came to link the colonial

---

88. This theme is well developed in McNamara, *Colonial Origins of Korean Enterprise*, esp. pp. 127–30.

89. This, for example, is the approach adopted in Suh, *Growth and Structural Changes*.

90. Eckert, *Offspring of Empire*, p. 55.

91. These and the subsequent facts concerning geographical distribution of industry are from Grajdanzev, *Modern Korea*, Appendix 3.

Korean and Japanese economies. This pattern is, of course, not unique to Japan and Korea; it tends to characterize many metropoles and their colonies. What is unique, however, is the degree to which Korea was already an exporting economy and the degree to which it was already exporting manufactured products to Japan during the colonial phase. If the average "foreign trade ratio" for a country of the size of Korea in 1938–39 was 0.24, Sang-Chul Suh estimates that Korea's boreign trade ratio in those years was around 0.54, suggesting that Korea was exporting twice as much as any other comparable economy. Moreover, 43 percent of these exports were manufactured goods.[92] How many other developing countries in the world emerged from colonialism with this type of an economic profile? Critical to note here is not only the structure of the economy that was inherited by South Korea but also the psychological legacy: whereas most developing countries emerged from the Second World War with a distrust of open economies—because they either associated openness with stagnation (as in India) or import substitution with successful industrial growth (as in Brazil)—many South Korean elites came to associate, rather early, an export orientation with a high-growth economy.

To sum up this section, the highly authoritarian and bureaucratic state that the Japanese constructed in colonial Korea was effective in promoting growth. The state utilized its bureaucratic capacities to undertake numerous economic tasks directly, anywhere from collecting more taxes to building infrastructure, to promoting production. More important, the state incorporated property-owning classes in production-oriented alliances. The colonial state was a highly purposive state; it put increasing production near the top of its priorities. Propertied classes were offered various rewards—especially, handsome profits—for cooperating with the state in fulfilling this economic agenda. The state, in turn, utilized numerous means—including promotion of technology, control over credit, subsidies, capital accumulation, and even noneconomic exhortations—to ensure compliance from both Korean and Japanese landlords and businesspeople. As a result of this state-business alliance, the economy was successful in exporting manufactured goods. Moreover, as documented by revisionist historians, a substantial stratum of Korean entrepreneurs developed, individuals who either flourished while cooperating with the state or who wished for larger government support so they could also flourish. In either case, a "model" of development—inspired by Meiji Japan but also transformed in a colonial setting—was in the making that would situate a state-directed economy with state-business alliance at the heart of the strategy of transformation.

92. Suh, *Growth and Structural Changes*, pp. 120–21, table 58.

ATUL KOHLI

THE COLONIAL STATE AND THE POPULAR SECTOR

The colonial authorities sought to transform Korea in accordance with Japanese imperial needs. Controlled involvement of the popular sector—peasants and workers—was essential for the success of this project, and both the colonial state and the propertied classes collaborated to ensure their compliance. While English-language studies of popular sector in colonial Korea are meager, the available evidence suggests that both peasants and workers benefited little from the colony's rapid economic transformation. This was part of a deliberate plan that served important political and economic interests. From a political standpoint, the highly repressive and penetrating colonial state succeeded in putting the lid on Korean society and focused its attention on economic growth. Incomes and wages generally lagged behind productivity gains, facilitating higher profitability, savings, and investments. Moreover, because much of the growth was export-oriented, lagging incomes and the limited mass demand did not become a constraint on growth.

Because repression and exclusion of the popular sector was integral to the colonial political economy and because critical components of this "model," especially the harsh political control of the working class, continued well into the future, it is important to analyze the structure and the dynamics of the labor-repressive strategy. First, as far as trends in the colonial countryside were concerned, Yi Korea was hardly a haven for the lowly tenants, peasants, or others at the bottom of the social hierarchy. As late as 1800, Yi Korea was a slave society, and even though the practice of slavery declined sharply through the nineteenth century, it was the Japanese who abolished slavery in Korea. The recurring fiscal crises of the Yi state had also led Korean rulers to squeeze the peasantry, especially via indirect taxation, thus contributing to misery, rebellion, and brigandage. What the Japanese did in this situation was rationalize the strategies of both extraction and control.

While well-organized gendarmes subdued pockets of the openly rebellious peasant population and continued to do so for quite some time, the bulk of the peasantry was systematically brought under state's domination. First, the legalization of private property in the hands of landlords, as well as a regularization of land rents, created a legitimate basis for tenancy as the modal relationship adjoining the tiller and the landowner. Although tenancy had been practiced in Korea for a long time, probably forever, given steady population growth, tenancy increased throughout the colonial period; toward the end of the period, nearly 70 percent of farming households worked under tenancy arrangement of one type or another.[93] And as most students of agrarian societies understand, tenancy

93. Robinson, in Eckert et al., *Korea Old and New*, p. 307.

as the main mode of production makes tenants dependent on landowners, and dependencies tend to be especially severe where tenants are not legally protected, where attempts to forge a tenants organization are met with swift retribution, and where the weight of the state is mainly behind the landowners.

The Japanese strategy for controlling the peasant population was twofold: direct and effective downward penetration of the state, and incorporation of landowning or other influential local groups as ruling allies. While sporadic peasant rebellion never died out, the ruling strategy was effective at establishing a repressive order.[94] In addition to severe economic dependencies, which sap the rebellious energy of any social group, the effectiveness of control rested on a combination of direct and indirect rule. The traditional system of influence within villages, as well as of information flows, was buttressed by a well-organized bureaucracy: local police with uniforms and telephones; tax collectors, also replete with uniforms; and an intelligence service that periodically prepared reports for the provincial and central governments on a wide variety of issues.

The Korean working class originated under Japanese rule. Although Korea was still largely an agrarian country in the 1940s (more than 70 percent of the population still derived its livelihood from agriculture), a considerable working class had also come into being by then. For example, if there were less than ten thousand industrial workers in 1910, the population of industrial workers had reached 1.3 million in 1943.[95] Assuming a minimum family size of four, a good 20 percent of the population must have thus depended on industrial work for their livelihood. Moreover, another 15 percent of Koreans lived outside Korea in the Japanese empire, a significant minority working as unskilled urban labor in Japan and some in Manchuria. Because many of the workers within Korea had been moved from the populated south to factories in the north and because most of the Koreans working in the empire returned to Korea when the empire disintegrated, a significant minority of the population in colonial Korea found itself moved around and uprooted from its traditional social niche.[96]

The colonial state collaborated with both Japanese and Korean capitalists to devise the structures of control for this working class. The state provided the broad framework, which, in its essence, was brutally simple: at-

---

94. For evidence on the nature and extent of lower-class restiveness, especially as expressed through the communist movement, see Robert Scalapino and Chong-Sik Lee, *Communism in Korea*, pt. 1, *The Movement* (Berkeley: University of California Press, 1972), esp. chap. 3.

95. Park, "Emergence of a Factory Labor Force in Colonial Korea," pt. 1.

96. See Cumings, *Origins of the Korean War*, vol. 1, chap. 2, for a moving discussion of the human toll exacted by the large-scale movement of Koreans under Japanese rule.

tempts to create a labor union were prohibited; trespasses were met with severe retribution; and few, if any, laws existed to regulate and protect workers.[97] These restrictions did not fully succeed in eliminating unionization attempts and even strikes—especially in the somewhat more liberal 1920s and again in the late 1930s, when with a war economy, labor demand and thus labor's bargaining power increased—but they do help underline the highly antilabor stance of the colonial state.[98]

Within this broad framework, individual companies had a fairly free hand in setting down labor management practices (at least until the war years, when the state became actively involved in the control and mobilization of labor). Not surprisingly, Japanese companies, such as the Onoda cement factory, adopted a Japanese labor management style.[99] Japanese managers sought to create a skilled, disciplined, and hierarchically organized workforce in exchange for decent wages—wages were often higher than earnings in both Korean-owned factories and in agriculture but lagged way behind the steady productivity gains—and job security. Young Koreans of peasant origins, with only little education, were hired at a rather early age (say, at from eighteen to twenty-two), provided on-the-job training, occasionally sent to Japan for more specialized experience, punished hard for lack of punctuality or diligence, rewarded for loyalty and steady performance, and, for those who survived the various tests and hurdles, given assurances of continuous service pension and retirement fund benefits. The carrots and sticks appear to have been quite successful: in this one specific case, at least, over a few decades, young Korean peasants were transformed into "Onoda men," who, in spite of such social problems as being treated second to Japanese workers, took pride in their skilled industrial work in a Japanese company.

Because there is very little research available that does not depend on company documents, one has to be wary of how "satisfied" and "loyal" Korean workers really were. There was very little real increase in wages throughout this period of high growth. Moreover, when economic opportunities increased during the hypergrowth of the 1930s, workers voted with their feet; for example, the rate of turnover in the Onoda cement factory during the 1930s rose sharply as skilled workers took their skills elsewhere for higher wages.[100] Most important, workers were totally forbidden to form any organizations of their own. Any efforts were met with

97. Grajdanzev, *Modern Korea*, p. 182.

98. Park, "Emergence of a Factory Labor Force in Colonial Korea," pp. 60–80; Asagiri, "Korea: Labour Movement," *Labour Monthly* 11, no. 9 (September 1929): 568–70; and Ta Chen, "The Labor Situation in Korea," *Monthly Labor Review* (November 1930): 26–36.

99. The following account is based on the case study of Onoda cement factory in Park, "Emergence of a Factory Labor Force in Colonial Korea," pt. 2, B, sections 1, 4, 5, and 9.

100. Ibid., p. 142.

dismissal, arrest, and a permanent police record. Industrial relations in colonial Korea were thus "absolutely one sided," favoring the management.[101] Workers were closely supervised. The factories themselves were "very closed, isolated, and protected place(s)." The workplace was "closed to outsiders by a wire fence, the constant patrol of its guards, and the availability of police protection in case of an incident." Finally, closing the state and company cooperation loop, the Japanese management "kept radical elements out by tight inspection and in doing this they were fully supported by government policy and a strong police posture."[102]

Workers' conditions in Korean-owned factories were certainly no better, and may have been worse. One case study of the largest Korean business house that is readily available would certainly support this view.[103] For example, 80 percent of the workers at Kyŏngbang's textile mill were unmarried peasant girls in their late teens, some even recruited from tenant families who worked the lands owned by the mill owners. The factories operated around-the-clock, each girl working a grueling twelve-hour shift, with one forty-minute rest period. Since labor control was deemed essential, work was under "intense labor supervision." Discipline inside the factory was "severe" and extended to personal lives. All the girls lived in dormitories within a factory compound and needed permission both to leave the compound and to receive visitors. The system resembled "a low-security prison." Whenever labor conditions in this and other plants became turbulent, "strikes were repressed with the same energy as was used to repress communism." State "intimidation and force" were thus central to this relatively simple and "crude approach to social control."

During the war years social controls on workers tightened as the state got directly involved in labor management. A *sampo* system was established, whereby, "industrial patriotism clubs," involving employers and employees, were created and aimed at increasing production. Workers' representatives—paid full-time salaries by employers—and employers formed associations that designed programs of "educating the workers, making the production process more efficient and preventing disputes among workers."[104]

In sum, a bureaucratic and penetrating authoritarian state collaborated with property-owning groups in colonial Korea to carve out a rather repressive and exclusionary strategy to control the laboring classes. This

101. Ibid.

102. Ibid., p. 184.

103. See Eckert, *Offspring of Empire*, chap. 7, from where the account in this paragraph is drawn.

104. This quote and the materials in this paragraph are drawn from George E. Ogle, *South Korea: Dissent within the Economic Miracle* (London: Zed Books, 1990), p. 6.

strategy of control, moreover, was necessary for rapid economic transformation. To repeat, with the majority of the lower classes subdued, the colonial state was free to concentrate its architectonic energies on devising and pursuing a strategy of economic transformation. Moreover, the political capacity to hold wages behind productivity gains facilitated high rates of profitability and thus continued investment and growth.

GENERAL INFERENCES

If Korea at the turn of the twentieth century was a mini-China, by mid-century, Japanese colonialism had transformed it into a mini-Japan. While this statement both oversimplifies and distorts, the grain of truth in it is essential for understanding the subsequent high-growth political economy of South Korea. And if this claim is acceptable, a number of general inferences follow. To draw these out, I address three themes below: the implications of the historical materials discussed above for a comparative understanding of Korea; the insights that can be derived from these historical materials for the study of the nature and origins of "developmental states"; and some general thoughts on the importance of reopening the issue of the variable colonial pasts of developing countries, so as to appreciate fully the roots of the divergent paths that these countries are now traversing.

Korea in a Comparative Perspective

It is clear above that Japanese colonialism in Korea helped establish some basic state-society patterns that many now readily associate as integral to the later South Korean "model" of a high-growth political economy. These patterns include a highly bureaucratized, penetrating, and architectonic state; a state-dominated alliance of state and property owners for production and profits; and repressive social control of the working classes. Demonstrating parallels between historical and contemporary situations, however, is clearly not enough to sustain an argument for historical continuity; one also needs to point out the mechanisms whereby continuity was maintained.

It would take a separate essay to demonstrate fully exactly how and why there was a fair amount of institutional continuity between colonial Korea and subsequent South Korea, especially under Park Chung Hee.[105] In any

105. I am currently involved in writing such an essay, but in the context of a larger study from which the present essay is drawn. The larger study is a comparative analysis of the "state and economic development" in four countries, namely, Korea, Brazil, India, and Nigeria.

case, elements of such an argument already exist in the literature, and for our present purposes, a brief outline will suffice.[106] More than a fifteen-year interlude, a traumatic interlude one may add, occurred between the Japanese leaving Korea and when a truncated South Korea settled on a high-growth path under Park Chung Hee. This interlude was marked by an American occupation, a civil war, a division of the country into a Communist and an anti-Communist half, establishment of a government with some nationalist and democratic credentials in the south, and then a degeneration of this government under diverse pressures, leading up to a military coup. In spite of all this social drama, when diverse historical legacies were simultaneously unleashed and when the future was anything but certain, how did South Korea under Park Chung Hee end up resembling colonial Korea in its basic state-society outlines?

The answer revolves in part around the structures that were simply never altered in any fundamental way and in part around conscious choices made by leaders of South Korea. For example, Cumings has demonstrated with great care how and why the American occupying forces in Korea left the colonial state more or less intact; the alternative would have been to unleash a popular revolution of nationalist and radical forces. As a result, the bureaucracy, the police, and the military that sovereign South Korea inherited were essentially colonial creations. In Cumings's own words, in spite of a prolonged American involvement in Korean affairs, "it was Japan's impact that lasted," and "whether it was in the military, the bureaucracy or the polity, Americans during the occupation found themselves playing midwife to a Japanese gestation, rather than bringing forth their own Korean progeny."[107]

Not only were state structures kept intact but the state's capacity and willingness to direct economic change, as well as the economic instruments used by the state—for example, control over credit—continued from the colonial to the postcolonial period.[108] There is little evidence, moreover, that Korean businesspeople in South Korea made much of a fuss over these arrangements. On the contrary, there was a fair amount of continuity in the state-dependent nature of Korean capitalism as well. For example, Carter Eckert has found that "60 percent of the founders of South Korea's top fifty *chaebol*" had participated directly in business under colonial auspices.[109] Because these businessmen had either flour-

---

106. Cumings, "Legacy of Japanese Colonialism"; Eckert, *Offspring of Empire*, and McNamara, *Colonial Origins of Korean Enterprise.*

107. See Cumings, "Legacy of Japanese Colonialism," pp. 479–80. For his detailed analysis of why and how Americans left the colonial state more or less intact in Korea, see Cumings, *Origins of the Korean War*, vol. 1, chap. 5.

108. See Woo, *Race to the Swift*, for the specific issue of state control over credit.

109. Eckert, *Offspring of Empire*, p. 254.

ished with the help of the colonial state or complained and periodically petitioned the colonial state for more support, it is likely that their political preferences strengthened the state-directed, state-business alliance for production and profit. Finally, the corporatist patterns of worker control were also colonial in origin: the employer-employee "clubs" for promoting "patriotism" and production, in the words of a labor analyst, became "one of Japan's permanent contributions to Korea's industrial relations system."[110]

None of these continuities were inevitable. North Korea, a product of the same historical legacy, clearly went on a very different path. In South Korea, the chaos of the Rhee period could have continued indefinitely; alternatively, a new leadership could have undertaken basic changes and put South Korea on a totally different path. However, the postcoup leadership chose continuity with colonial patterns. Complex motivations of national security and of protecting sectional social interests were at work, but it was the nature of the leadership that finally undergird the choice of continuity. Park Chung Hee was a product of the Japanese colonial Korean army, trained in Japanese military academy in Manchuria. Chong-Sik Lee, one of the leading Korea scholars in the United States, describes him as a "Japanophile," fascinated by the "Meiji model," and bent on steering Korea along the Japanese path to modernity.[111] South Korean leaders often covered such proclivities with an anti-Japanese rhetoric here and a nationalist flourish there. Desirous mainly of high economic growth, however, such leaders as Park Chung Hee knew well that the key elements of the "model" left behind by the Japanese were still intact in the early 1960s: a highly pervasive and penetrating state that could be turned authoritarian, purged of corruption, and made to refocus attention on matters economic; a state-dependent business stratum that understood the benefits of cooperating with a purposive state; and a highly controlled working class. Because this "model" had worked in the past, until proven to the contrary or forced to abandon it, there was no reason why it ought not to work for sovereign South Korea as well. Moreover, the extent to which postwar Japan remained a "reference society" for South Korea was itself, in part, a product of considerable colonial contacts that had created links of language and economic structures as well as a shared understanding of how to construct high-growth political economies.

If the case for considerable continuity is thus persuasive—and this does not necessitate denying either some important changes in the subsequent

110. Ogle, *South Korea*, p. 6.

111. Chong-Sik Lee, *Japan and Korea: The Political Dimension* (Stanford: Hoover Institution Press, 1985), pp. 62–63.

political economy, or the credit due to Koreans for their economic achievements, before and after independence—it follows that the roots of the high-growth Korean political economy lie deep in a unique colonial experience. Two further implications follow. First, quite a few development scholars compare South Korea's economic performance to that of other slower-growing developing countries. The underlying assumption often is that all these countries began from more or less the same starting point of very low per capita incomes in the 1950s, but somehow South Korea (and a few other NICs) rushed ahead. The question then becomes, Why South Korea? In light of the discussion above, this manner of posing the question appears inappropriate. The starting point for comparison has to be deeper in history, especially in the formative colonial phase. Even if South Korea's low per capita income in the 1950s was similar to that of an India, a Brazil, or a Nigeria, South Korea's starting point was very different: it had a much more dynamic economy in the half a century preceding the 1950s, and by the 1950s its deeper state-society configurations were relatively unique.

Second, some development scholars pose the puzzle of South Korea's phenomenal economic success in the following terms: Why was South Korea able to switch to an "export-oriented policy" in the early 1960s, whereas many other developing countries continued on the "import substitution" path?[112] Again, this manner of framing the comparative question is somewhat misconceived. South Korea indeed made some important policy changes under Park Chung Hee, but their significance can easily be exaggerated; moreover, the state-society configuration that enabled these policies to succeed had deeper historical roots. In this sense, South Korea under Park Chung Hee did not so much "switch" as it fell back into the grooves of colonial origins or, to be more precise, chose one of the two or three main alternatives that were available to it from its complex historical legacy. Revolutionary communism, a corrupt and wasteful autocracy of the Rhee type and a more American-style open democracy were all realistic possible paths along which South Korea could have traveled. The key elements of the eventual path it adopted, however,—a Japanese-style, state-driven export economy—were deeply etched into the social fabric. More specifically, the Korean economy, especially the southern Korean economy, had already been export oriented, its entrepreneurs had considerable experience in selling abroad, and the state within this economy had learned from its own history that strong support for business and exports, along with tight control over labor, was a route to high economic growth.

112. For example, see Haggard, *Pathways from the Periphery*.

Nature of "Developmental States"

Among scholars who share the view that states have played both a positive and a negative role in economic development, a pressing subsequent question concerns the comparative analysis of "developmental" and "predatory" states.[113] More specifically, what distinguishes patterns of state intervention in the economy, and why do some developing country states end up successfully transforming their economies, whereas others end up as "rent seekers," preying on their own society's scarce resources? While detailed comparative analyses are the best route to develop answers to this complex but important question, the single country materials presented above also speak to the issue, especially because the Korean case is central to any such analysis and because the Korean state was itself, at the turn of the century, transformed from a "predatory" to a "developmental" state.

Peter Evans has described "developmental states" as exhibiting the characteristic of "embedded autonomy"; "autonomy" of bureaucratized states from social entanglements gives them a capacity to direct social change, and social "embeddeness," in turn, especially the links these states forge with business and industrial classes, enable state elites to incorporate these powerful groups in the state's economic project.[114] The historical materials analyzed above are not inconsistent with this account of "developmental states." Nevertheless, the Korean historical materials also suggest some qualifications and further specification.

The first important qualification concerns the issue of where the policy goals of any state-directed economy come from. Arguments about "developmental states," whether in Peter Evans's or in other versions, often focus more on explaining a state's capacity to implement goals and less on where these goals come from in the first place. The latter issue requires an explicit focus on the political process of a society. Policy goals of any society reflect complex processes involving how the highest authorities balance their own preferences against national and international pressures. In the colonial Korean case discussed here, it was clear that the major shifts in policy goals—trade of raw materials for manufactured goods, followed by encouragement of food production in the early phase; encouragement of Japanese investments in manufacturing, along with some Korean participation during the middle phase; and finally, in the last phase, a war economy with rapid industrialization—mainly reflected Japanese priorities, with an occasional concession to Korean pressures. In sovereign polities, this process of policy prioritization is often highly com-

---

113. For one insightful analysis of this question, see Evans, "Predatory, Developmental, and Other Apparatuses."
114. Ibid.

plex and would require a more detailed study than the colonial type of case discussed here. Nevertheless, the general point ought to be clear: since efficacious states can be used by their leaders to accomplish various goals, including nondevelopmental goals, the politics of how developmental goals emerge as a priority must be an important component of any study of "developmental states."

The juxtaposition of the late Chosŏn or Yi state against the colonial state also yields some further insights about "predatory" and "developmental" states. The late Chosŏn state was personalistic and factionalized at the apex, with very little downward reach in the society; it was also deeply penetrated by landowning classes. These characteristics bequeathed political incapacity. The result was that the Yi state was quite incapable of laying out and pursuing an agenda of socioeconomic change. By contrast, the colonial state turned out to be highly efficacious. While this was no developmental state in the sense that it helped develop the whole society—on the contrary, it was a rather brutal, exclusionary state, not to mention colonial—it nevertheless could establish order and facilitate economic growth. How did it achieve this capacity? The changes introduced by the Japanese that helped increase state capacity can be best thought of as changes along three dimensions: changes in the state structures; creation of new economic instruments in the hands of the state; and new patterns of state-class relations. Because all these have been discussed in some detail above, they now require only a brief reiteration.

First, the significant changes in the state structure were three: creation of centralized authority with a clear agenda of change; depersonalization of authority structures, so that public and private interests were first separated and only then reintegrated on a new basis, with public goals mainly in command; and downward penetration of the state's authority in society via the creation of a disciplined bureaucracy.[115] These changes enabled the new political authorities to formulate specific public goals and to implement them in the far reaches of the society.

Second, the state also created a number of economic instruments that did not exist before and that enhanced the state's capacity to direct the economy: a rationalized currency system, banks and other credit institutions that the state controlled, long-and short-term economic plans, production-oriented new technology, and a variety of direct and indirect subsidies. Finally, the state and social classes established a new relationship. In both the countryside and the city, the state and property-owning classes entered an alliance which was set mainly on the state's terms but which was nevertheless mutually beneficial: the state desired and suc-

115. Note that Peter Evans's "autonomy" component of the "embedded autonomy" formulation mainly directs attention to the second of these three structural components. See ibid.

ceeded in securing steady increases in production, whereas the property-owning groups received enough political support to ensure healthy profits. The state and property-owning classes also collaborated to control peasants and workers in what amounted to a successful, labor-repressive strategy.

This last point directs attention to another important modification in Evans's type of formulation of "developmental states," namely, the significance of downward penetration of systematic political control. Far too much analytic attention is being devoted in contemporary attempts to understand "developmental states" to the apex of the political economy. This is unfortunate because the relationship of the state to laboring classes, especially the modalities of participation and control in the process of production, is a central part of the "story" of how and why some states succeed in industrializing their economies. For example, it is clear in the account above that the colonial state and Japanese and Korean businessmen collaborated not only to strictly control any demand-making or dissident actions of workers but also to train them at work, pay a living wage, transmit some pride in their endeavors, and provide job security. This combination of "carrots and sticks" generated considerable control over the lives and behavior of workers. While hardly conducive to the creation of a free and desirable society, this control, in turn, both contributed to productivity gains and, more important, enabled the state to single mindedly pursue economic growth.

A bureaucratized and penetrating authoritarian state with clear, growth-oriented goals, armed with a panoply of economic instruments and allied with propertied but against laboring social classes, is the stuff of which transformative power in the hands of the state is made. Or so, at least, such emerges from the study of this one specific case. Neither the brutal, controlling nature nor the colonial origins of this specific "developmental state" can be recommended to others on normative grounds. And yet, for those who believe that states have an important role to play in facilitating economic development, the question remains: how can power to develop be generated without outside forces remolding state structures or without states that repress and control large majorities of their own citizens? The study of other cases and imaginative rethinking may yield insights into how to approximate "developmental states" without acquiring some of their worst features.

Rethinking Comparative Colonialism

Finally, I wish to conclude with some speculative thoughts concerning future research directions. Developmental success has always ignited intellectual inquiry: Why did "they" succeed? Why not the "others"? Marx and Weber struggled over these questions, trying to understand the early rise of capitalism in northwestern Europe. Ever since, successful industrializers have attracted scholarly attention. It is hardly surprising that in our own times the successful NICs should attract similar attention. The puzzle is especially appealing when, in a group assumed to be more or less similar, some move ahead, while others are left behind. Scholarly imagination then wants an explanation for both the speedy growers and the laggards.

A variety of answers have been proposed in more recent years as to why some developing countries have better-performing economies than do others; these vary from sharply market-oriented answers, through more state-focused analyses, all the way to religion and culture as the real variables. What many of these efforts in the hands of "developmentalists" lack, unfortunately, is historical depth. Large-scale processes of historical transformation often tend to display long historical continuities; when they do not, ruptures, new beginnings, and shifts in path are dramatic. Establishment of sovereignty or, at least, the post–Second World War beginning is often assumed by development scholars as the "new beginning" from where comparative analyses of developing countries must begin. This trend is unfortunate, because it is likely that a significant component of the explanation for why countries traverse different developmental paths lies in their colonial heritage.

An earlier generation of "dependency" scholars was well aware of historical continuities. That body of scholarship lost its intellectual sway for a variety of reasons, however, including the tendency to homogenize the antidevelopmental nature of all colonialism. A central question in the minds of a new generation of scholars became, Why are developing countries traversing such different paths? Any framework that mainly drew attention to a universal constraint (for example, "world capitalism" or "neocolonialism") was thus likely to loose appeal; satisfactory answers would rather have to explain why countries dealt differently with the same set of constraints. Unfortunately, however, in rightly discarding dependency propositions, scholars also threw out the proverbial baby with the bathwater. They threw out the colonial pasts of the developing world. Instead of asking, Could the roots of varying performances be located in a variety of colonial pasts? most developmentalists now focus on the nature of post–Second World War states, social structures, and policy choices as the primary explanations of divergent performances.

If the historical discussion in this essay is persuasive, it suggests that the roots of economic dynamism in the critical case of South Korea are located, at least in part, in the state-society relations created under the auspices of Japanese colonialism. This finding, in turn, directs attention to unique aspects of Japanese colonialism: as a late developer, who had perfected a state-led model for catching up in the world economy, Japan in its colonies constructed a political economy that also turned out to be well suited at catching up. In other historical cases, different colonial powers, in different time periods, pursued a variety of colonial ruling strategies. They thus left behind a variety of political economies: distributive politics and a slow-growing economy in India; incomplete states that readily turned into predatory states in much of Africa; and semisovereign political economies that came to be dominated by foreign investors and agrarian oligarchies before the onset of deliberate, state-led developmental experiments in large parts of Latin America. Is it not possible that the legacy of colonialism, though varying from case to case, especially from region to region, was of long-lasting significance in much of the developing world? If so, it behooves scholars interested in understanding divergent paths of contemporary developing countries to pay attention once again in their comparative analyses to the colonial pasts of these countries.

CHAPTER FIVE

The Developmental Regime in a Changing World Economy

T. J. Pempel

The phenomenal economic performances of Japan, South Korea, and Taiwan have attracted great attention from both policymakers and academic analysts. How, it was asked, were countries such as Japan, South Korea, and Taiwan (as well as, in some analyses, Singapore, Hong Kong, and, sometimes, Malaysia and Thailand) able to achieve their high levels of macroeconomic growth while most other so-called less developed countries have languished in the world's economic backwaters?

For many, interest in Asian success has been largely fear-driven: would Northeast Asian economic success come at the expense of the economic well-being of the West? For others, the response has been a call to "look East" for replicable models.[1] Still others have examined the Asian experience with an eye toward validating preconceived notions about the relative power of "markets" or "the state."[2]

Economic slowdowns in much of Asia abated some of the fears and blind admiration. Then, in the wake of the financial crises of the late 1990s, the world began to look to Asia more as a potential source of an "Asian contagion" that might threaten the world's economic stability than as a model for emulation. But only the most myopic policymakers have returned to past assumptions about East Asian successes as little

1. The phrase "Look East" was advanced by Malaysian prime minister Datuk Seri Mahathir Mohamad. On Latin America, a good example of looking toward East Asia is Jorge Castaneda, *Utopia Unarmed* (New York: Knopf, 1993).

2. A well-known example of the former is the World Bank policy research report entitled *The East Asian Miracle: Economic Growth and Public Policy* (New York: Oxford University Press, 1993).

3. Compare Paul Krugman, "The Myth of Asia's Miracle," *Foreign Affairs* 73, no. 6 (November/December 1994):62–78.

more than temporary fortuities.[3] The Northeast Asian experience in particular promises to be on the political agenda well into the future.

Most fundamentally, Asian growth poses questions about sources, rather than consequences. Not surprisingly, a host of competing explanations have been offered for Asia's economic success.

Such debates have been as much ideological as methodological or epistemological. In reality, Asian economic development has been one of history's most overdetermined outcomes. This is not to say it was "easy"—quite the contrary. If it had been easy, the numbers of successful imitators would be uncountable. But numerous factors combined to spur growth in the region. Attempting to isolate any one "key" cause results in debates over whether "my variable can swallow your variable." Numerous forces triangulated to make the isolation of some single, super cause all but impossible: "Victory finds a hundred fathers but defeat is an orphan." I do not attempt to unravel the interwoven and often mutually reinforcing contributions to Asian economic growth. Rather, I examine several more specific puzzles presented by the East Asian cases, particularly those surrounding the concept of the "developmental state."

The "developmental state," as has been pointed out throughout this book, has been one of the most compelling explanations for the economic success of Northeast Asia. It is my contention that the concept, valuable as it may be, has several important drawbacks, especially in its central focus on the primacy of governmental bureaucracy and in its consequent downplaying of the socioeconomic coalitions and international conditions behind these successes. As a consequence, I also believe the model is unlikely to be easily implanted by other countries seeking to replicate the East Asian experience.

These limitations, it is argued, are to some extent overcome if one examines the East Asian experience more broadly, through a notion I label the "developmental regime." Stressing "regime" over "state," I contend, aids in understanding the role played by both domestic socioeconomic conditions and international relations in Northeast Asian economic performance. Such a broader picture, however, paints an even more pessimistic picture for potential emulators of the Asian experience.

The Developmental State

Asia's sudden emergence as an economic colossus stimulated scholars and policymakers alike to begin a grail-like quest for what Meredith Woo-Cumings has called the "regional solipsism" of an "Asian developmental

theory holding that the self can know nothing but its own modifications and that the self is the only existent thing

model."[4] One of the most powerful and persuasive attempts at a political explanation for East Asian success has been the concept of the "developmental state."[5] The East Asian states, it is argued, have been successful because governments there have acquired control over a variety of things presumed critical to economic success: they can extract capital; generate and implement national economic plans; manipulate private access to scarce resources; coordinate the efforts of individual businesses; target specific industrial projects; resist political pressures from popular forces such as consumers and organized labor; insulate their domestic economies from extensive foreign capital penetration; and, most especially, carry through a sustained project of ever-improving productivity, technological sophistication, and increased world market shares. Initially and most forcefully articulated by Chalmers Johnson with specific reference to Japan (and subsequently to South Korea and Taiwan), the developmental state is seen as one of three ideal types of states, all categorized by the state's relationship to the domestic economy.

The United States and Britain exemplify the "regulatory state." Such states are organized for and define as their principal mission the setting of basic "fair" rules for economic competition and the umpiring of private market disputes. Most economic outcomes are the outgrowth of impersonal and short-term price variations, and specific end products are not taken as the province of the regulatory state. National economic improvement is presumed to arise from the relatively unfettered interaction of freely competing businesses and consumers.

"Developmental states," on the other hand, define their missions primarily in terms of long-term national economic enhancement. They actively and regularly intervene in economic activities with the goal of improving the international competitiveness of their domestic economies. Rather than accepting some predefined place in a world divided on the basis of "comparative advantage," such states seek to create "competitive advantages." In this sense, the developmental state is a logical descendant of the German historical school with its emphasis on economic nationalism and neomercantilism. Central to the activities of such developmental states is a highly competent and autonomous national bureaucracy.

Two distinct types of developmental states exist, however. One, associated with the Leninist states of the former Soviet Union and Eastern Europe, was driven by bureaucrats who were "plan ideological," defining

---

4. Jung-en Woo [Meredith Woo-Cumings], *Race to the Swift: State and Finance in Korean Industrialization* (New York: Columbia University Press, 1991), p. 5.

5. Chalmers Johnson, *MITI and the Japanese Miracle: The Growth of Industrial Policy, 1925–1975* (Stanford: Stanford University Press, 1982).

their mission in terms of Marxian, class, and other objectives divorced from questions of economic efficiency per se. In contrast, the "plan-rational" state (associated with Japan and various other states in East Asia) pursued not blind ideological goals but enhanced economic competitiveness.[6]

The concept of the developmental state contributes several important foci to the debates over politics and economic growth. Four are worthy of particular note. First, analysts of the developmental state stress the primacy of politics, as carried out most particularly by a nation's governmental bureaucrats and technocrats. In this way, they concentrate attention on the ways in which economic development can result from a politically constructed project aimed at improving national economic competitiveness; growth need not be (and perhaps never is) the passively generated consequence of multiple and uncoordinated invisible hands. The developmental state underscores the ways in which political power, if wielded astutely, can contribute positively and effectively to a nation's economic well-being.

Stress is laid on the fact that political representatives, rather than individual, utility-maximizing consumers, can be key shapers of economic transactions. Such representatives frequently define their economic agenda in terms of improving long-term national economic competitiveness rather than enhancing the short-term well-being of that country's individual citizens or consumers. As Michael Mandelbaum puts it: "Governments . . . tend to be less concerned with the total worth of the world's output than with the value of their own country's share of it. They consider the single state, not the community of states, to be the salient economic unit even as it is the basic unit of international politics. Governments are thus often willing to violate the rule of the market, to interfere with economic transactions, to lower the latter's net welfare, if these actions will provide more wealth for their own citizens."[7]

From such a perspective, neoclassical economists who emphasize the ultimate economic benefits of an allegedly "free market" are taken to be not the articulators of some universally valid scientific principle but the

6. The distinction between market rational and plan rational, though utilized quite explicitly by Johnson, was first noted by Ralf Dahrendorf, "Market and Plan: Two Types of Rationality," in Dahrendorf, ed., *Essays in the Theory of Society* (London: Routledge and Kegan Paul, 1968). Bernard S. Silberman also puts forth a convincing case for distinguishing two types of bureaucratic rationality—professional and organizational rationality. See *Cages of Reason: The Rise of the Rational State in France, Japan, the United States, and Great Britain* (Chicago: University of Chicago Press, 1993).

7. Michael Mandelbaum, *The Fate of Nations* (Cambridge: Cambridge University Press, 1988), p. 332.

vocalizers of little more than a talismanic chant. In the suggestion of Jeffrey Henderson and Richard P. Applebaum, such an orientation should really be seen as "market ideological."[8]

A focus on political construction also provides a serious alternative to popular, but intellectually squishy, "explanations" of Asian economic performance based on notions of national culture such as "Confucianism," "the Confucian ideal of rule," "post-Confucianism," "samurai Confucianism," and the like.[9] It also offers a strong counter-argument to the claims of those who see in Asian development a replication of Western style pluralism[10] or game theoretic postulations that government bureaucrats are no more than the slavish "agents" of politicians who are the nation's real "principals."[11]

A second major contribution of studies of the developmental state lies in its attention to the possibility of more than one historical path to economic development. Linked quite explicitly to Gerschenkronian theories of late development, the developmental state challenges a variety of widely accepted but highly simplistic models, from the crudest Marxian version of stages of history with its universalistic treatment of "capitalism,"

8. Jeffrey Henderson and Richard P. Applebaum, "Situating the State in the East Asian Development Process," in Applebaum and Henderson, eds., *States and Development in the Asian Pacific Rim* (Beverley Hills: Sage, 1992), p. 19.

9. Lucian W. Pye, *Asian Power and Politics: The Cultural Dimensions of Authority* (Cambridge: Harvard University Press, 1985); Kent E. Calder and Roy Hofheinz Jr., *The Eastasia Edge* (New York: Basic, 1982); Michio Morishima, *Why Japan Has "Succeeded": Western Technology and the Japanese Ethos* (Cambridge: Cambridge University Press, 1982); Steve Chan, *East Asian Dynamism: Growth, Order, and Security in the Pacific Region* (Boulder, Colo.: Westview, 1990).

10. For example, Michio Muramatsu and Ellis S. Krauss, "The Conservative Policy Line and the Development of Patterned Pluralism," in Kozo Yamamura and Yasukichi Yasuba, eds., *The Political Economy of Japan,* vol. 1, *The Domestic Transformation* (Stanford: Stanford University Press, 1987), pp. 516–54. Other examples would include "bureaucratic-inclusionary pluralism," in Inoguchi Takashi, *Gendai Nihon Seiji Keizai no Kozu: Seifu to Shijo* (The structure of contemporary Japanese political economy: Government and markets) (Tokyo: Toyo Keizai Shinbunsha, 1983); "pluralism from a leftist point of view," in Otake Hideo, *Gendai Nihon no Seiji Kenryoku Keizai Kenryoku* (Political power and economic power in contemporary Japan) (Tokyo: Sanichi Shobo, 1979); the "parapolitical nexus hypothesis" and "interest-oriented, catchall hypothesis," offered in Murakami Yasusuke, "The Japanese Model of Political Economy," in Yamamura and Yasuba, eds., *Political Economy of Japan*; and "canalized pluralism by an LDP (Liberal Democratic Party)–bureaucracy compound," in Sato Seizaburo and Matsuzaki Tetsuhisa, *Jiminto Seiken* (LDP power) (Tokyo: Chuokoronsha, 1986). A good discussion of such viewpoints is found in Mabuchi Masaru, *Okurasho Tosei no Seijikeizaigaku* (The political economy of Ministry of Finance controls) (Tokyo: Chuokoronsha, 1994), pp. 25–31.

11. J. Mark Ramseyer and Frances McCall Rosenbluth, *Japan's Political Marketplace* (Cambridge: Harvard University Press, 1993). Compare Donald P. Green and Ian Shapiro, *Pathologies of Rational Choice Theory* (New Haven: Yale University Press, 1994).

to Western-biased theories of modernization, or to aeronautical metaphors such as "takeoff into self-sustained economic growth."[12] Not all states, the developmental statists contend, advance along comparable historical paths toward similar teleological goals.

Third, in its best formulations, the developmental state concentrates attention on the ways in which long-term economic success requires that bureaucratic directives be compatible with international market forces. With her suggestion that developmental states "deliberately get prices wrong," Alice Amsden seems to offer a direct counter to this argument, but she makes it clear that these prices are "wrong" only when judged by neoclassical economic standards. When state bureaucrats set multiple prices for different economic actors, the results can be "right" in creating profitable long-term investment opportunities within the international marketplace.[13]

Robert Wade is among the most explicit in articulating the links between state and market. For him, East Asian economic success rests on "governed markets" that are outgrowths of more than blind bureaucratic control. Instead, the key is a "synergistic connection between a public system and a mostly market system, the outputs of each becoming inputs for the other."[14] In short, the rule-making power of state bureaucrats in itself is irrelevant to growth unless bureaucrats construct economic rules that advance the long-term capital and technological character of the nation as a whole, rather than simply enhancing the power of government agencies or lining the pockets of predatory rulers.

Finally, by implication if not by explicit design, the concept of the developmental state, as well as the economic successes of Japan, Korea, and Taiwan, suggests that far more options exist for industrializing countries than is implied by the pessimistic predictions of culturally based modernization theory, dependency theory, or world systems theory.[15] The culturalist thread in modernization theory resonates with a strong presumption that most political cultures of the so-called Third World are immutably

12. The latter is most closely associated with W. W. Rostow, *The Stages of Economic Growth* (Cambridge: Cambridge University Press, 1960).

13. Alice H. Amsden, *Asia's Next Giant: South Korea and Late Industrialization* (New York: Oxford University Press, 1989), pp. 13–14.

14. Robert Wade, *Governing the Market: Economic Theory and the Role of Government in East Asian Industrialization* (Princeton: Princeton University Press, 1990), p. 5.

15. It is important to recognize that there have been several waves of dependency theory and world systems theory, including some that are sensitive to various possibilities for improved economic conditions in less-industrialized countries. See, for example, Peter Evans's notion of "dependent development" or Jeffrey Henderson's notions of globalized production (Evans, *Dependent Development: The Alliance of Multinational, State, and Local Capital in Brazil* [Princeton: Princeton University Press, 1979], and Henderson, *The Globalization of High Technology Production: Society, Space and Semiconductors in the Restructuring of the Modern World* [London: Routledge, 1989]).

opposed to state initiatives and economically oriented decision making. As Martin Carnoy has argued, this tradition reaches back at least to Karl Marx's ambiguous treatment of India, a society the latter saw as "typically Asian"—stagnant, immutable, and incapable of change from within.[16] Weber, as does much of the subsequent development and modernization literature, laments the difficulties of overcoming lethargic and nonentrepreneurial cultures.[17] Related criticisms are leveled at the weakness of state institutions in developing countries. Stephen Krasner has concluded that "most developing countries have very weak domestic political institutions," while Samuel Huntington has suggested that in most Third World countries, "governments simply do not govern."[18]

Focusing on the limits of domestic and international power resources rather than on creativity and adaptability risks treating the world as a hierarchically ordered system of dominance that is self-reproducing over time. New states are seen to be incorporated into this relatively fixed hierarchy in ways that permanently inhibit their abilities to engage in self-sustaining growth projects.[19] Moreover, domestic democratization is presumed to be precluded by a coalescence of interests between an authoritarian state, a domestic military and upper class, and rapacious international governments or their agents.[20] Studies of the "developmental state" and the experiences of the Northeast Asian economies demonstrate, in contrast, the unmistakable reality that dependency is less a determinant international structure and more a set of shifting constraints within which individual nation-states have room to maneuver.[21]

16. Carnoy, *The State and Political Theory* (Princeton: Princeton University Press, 1984), pp. 174–76.

17. See, for example, Max Weber, *The Protestant Ethic and the Spirit of Capitalism* (New York: Charles Schribner's Sons, 1958); Gabriel Almond and Sydney Verba, *The Civic Culture* (Boston: Little, Brown, 1963); Sydney Verba, ed., *Political Culture and Political Development* (Princeton: Princeton University Press, 1965).

18. Stephen D. Krasner, *Structural Conflict: The Third World against Global Liberalism* (Berkeley: University of California Press, 1985), p. 28, and Samuel P. Huntington, *Political Order in Changing Societies* (New Haven: Yale University Press, 1968), p. 2, both as cited in Joel S. Migdal, *Strong Societies and Weak States: State-Society Relations and State Capabilities in the Third World* (Princeton: Princeton University Press, 1988), p. 7.

19. See, for example, Andre G. Frank, *Dependent Accumulation and Underdevelopment* (New York: Monthly Review, 1978), and the world systems theorists, most notably Immanuel Wallerstein, *The Modern World System* (New York: Academic Press, 1974), and *The World Capitalist System* (Cambridge: Cambridge University Press, 1980), among others.

20. On this latter see the literature surrounding bureaucratic authoritarianism, including Fernando H. Cardoso and Enzo Faletto, *Dependency and Development in Latin America* (Berkeley: University of California Press, 1979); David Collier, "Overview of the Bureaucratic-Authoritarian Model," in Collier, ed., *The New Authoritarianism in Latin America* (Princeton: Princeton University Press, 1979); and Peter Evans, *Dependent Development*.

21. Stephan Haggard, "The Newly Industrializing Countries in the International System," *World Politics* 38, no. 2 (January 1986): 346.

Weighed against such very positive contributions, however, most formulations of the developmental state also contain certain shortcomings. Three demand serious attention. First, the developmental state privileges the political and economic role played by state bureaucrats. To assert a dirigiste form of control over the private economic actors requires an elaborate economic bureaucracy that not only commands a wide array of policy instruments and has extensive control over production resources but also possesses substantial informational resources, has a high degree of analytic competency to formulate and implement decisions, and is organized around a centralist chain of command.[22]

Because of its theoretical targets—neoclassical economics, national culture, interest group pluralism, rational choice theory, and the like—the emphasis on a strong meritocratic state bureaucracy is well placed. There can be little serious question of the important roles played by national government bureaucracies and individual officials in the economic development of Northeast Asia; state bureaucrats there have frequently been in the economic driver's seat.[23]

All the same, developmental state theorists too often treat the national bureaucracy as totally depoliticized, socially disembodied, and in rational pursuit of a self-evident national interest—in short, the embodiment of Weber's "idealized" bureaucracy.[24] A close reading of Weber makes it clear that "the rules" by which bureaucrats operate are generated outside the bureaucracy itself. However, neither Weber nor the developmental statists offer many clues as to the dynamic between such an external source of rules and the functioning of the economic bureaucracy. Developmental statists most often imply that top bureaucrats either generate their own agenda or operate in pursuit of self-evident and unproblematic national goals. Surely, few contend that bureaucrats take their orders from political officials (elected or otherwise). In Johnson's phrase, politicians merely reign, whereas the bureaucrats actually rule. But if not from the politicians, from whom do bureaucrats get their sense of direction? Or even if bureaucrats do make their own rules, with whose interests in mind are these rules developed and enforced?

The idea of the developmental state is presumed to be "plan rational." Left unaddressed is the question, rational *in whose interests*? The implied

22. Yun-Han Chu, "State Structure and Economic Adjustment in the East Asian Newly Industrializing Countries," *International Organization* 43, no. 4 (Autumn 1989): 658.

23. For my thinking on this problem, see among others, T. J. Pempel, *Policy and Politics in Japan: Creative Conservatism* (Philadelphia: Temple University Press, 1982), esp. chap. 2, and *The Japanese Civil Service and Economic Development: Catalysts of Development*, edited with Hyung-Ki Kim, Michio Muramatsu, and Kozo Yamamura (Oxford: Oxford University Press, 1994).

24. See H. H. Gerth and C. Wright Mills, eds., *From Max Weber: Essays in Sociology* (New York: Oxford University Press, 1958), chap. 8, pp. 196–244.

answer, of course, is "the national interest" or some depoliticized variation such as macroeconomic improvements, gross national product (GNP) growth, more technologically sophisticated plants, increased exports, improved living standards, and so forth. Such indicators are by no means irrelevant. But just as there are many versions of capitalism, so are there many versions of "economic development." Different capitalisms force one to confront the question, Capitalism in the interests of which specific socioeconomic sectors? Which sectors benefit most, and which are most noticeably disadvantaged by the specific economic strategies pursued by the bureaucrats of the developmental state? What are the socioeconomic underpinnings of the developmental state?

On this matter, developmental state theory is largely silent.[25] In its focus on international catch-up, the model of the developmental state downplays intranational political and economic conflict. Hence, in domestic terms, the model remains largely apolitical and socially disembodied. Domestic "politics" is examined principally in terms of intraelite relationships among bureaucrats, generals, politicians, business leaders, and the like. Largely absent are such broad social sectors as landowners, farmers, consumers, workers, small shopkeepers. Relatively unexamined are the relative resources and power bases of such diverse groups in different countries; the ways in which these relative power capabilities interact; the politics of socioeconomic coalition formation; how such politics enhance or retard the capacity of state bureaucrats to act autonomously; and the particular character of the economic transformations that emerge as a consequence.

One major result of such a depoliticized view is that the developmental state, as Bruce Cumings has suggested in this volume, too easily emerges as a "web without a spider." And it is precisely such an image that undergirds the conclusions of Karel van Wolferen about Japan as a "truncated pyramid" or Kent Calder's treatment of Japan as a "reactive state."[26]

A second serious flaw flows from the first, namely, the implication that for a nation-state anxious to emulate the East Asian successes, the lessons

25. An important exception is Frederic C. Deyo, *Beneath the Miracle: Labor Subordination in the New Asian Industrialism* (Berkeley: University of California Press, 1989). See also Chung-in Moon and Rashemi Prasad, "Beyond the Developmental State: Networks, Politics, and Institutions," *Governance* 7, no. 4 (October 1994): 367, where the authors state explicitly their recognition that "social actors in the developmental states are not pacified agents of the state. They also control resources of strategic value to others over which they are perpetually engaged in negotiations of reciprocal exchange." See also Cheng-tian Kuo, *Global Competitiveness and Industrial Growth in Taiwan and the Philippines* (Pittsburgh: University of Pittsburgh Press, 1994), chap. 1.

26. Karel van Wolferen, *The Enigma of Japanese Power* (New York: Vintage, 1990); Kent E. Calder, "Japanese Foreign Economic Policy Formation: Explaining the Reactive State," *World Politics* 40, no. 4 (July 1988): 517–41.

are rather self-evident: stronger states and more industrial policy.[27] Obviously, no articulator of the developmental state with whom I am familiar puts the point quite so simplistically. Yet, the underlying message of the developmental state is not radically at odds with even this bold formulation.[28] For all developmental statists, a key to economic development is the insulation of state bureaucrats.

Clearly, the developmental state is not the fragmented apparatus advocated by the Federalist planners for the United States. Nor is it the representational state sensitive to pressures from public opinion, elections, interest groups, social pluralism, protest movements, or regional diversity. Rather, it is the state poised for steamroller action. Yet bureaucratic autonomy and mandarinate competence in the absence of numerous other conditions are thin reeds on which to rest a strategy of economic development. Its apolitical undergirdings make the developmental state a concept easily mobilized in the service of bureaucratic authoritarianism and antirepresentational politics, with few guarantees of positive economic consequences.

Finally, there is the question of the international political environment within which the developmental state thrives. By and large, despite an agenda that concentrates on international catch-up, the developmental state is assessed largely in terms of its domestic context. When developmental statists examine the hurdles that state bureaucrats must clear in carrying out their particular agendas, they mainly focus on domestic problems such as business organization; allocation of scarce capital, energy resources, and technology; infrastructure development; tax credits; budgetary incentives; mass education; labor regulations; foreign direct investment; and the like. Far less attention is given to the strategic goals of competing powers and superpowers; regional power balances; cross-na-

27. I take this to be at least the implicit suggestion of Robert H. Bates, who finds most African governments both highly fragmented and unstable and hence driven to spend in ways designed to maintain them in power with the result that they are incapable of longer-term planning. Moreover, they extract at such rapid rates as to reduce private investment incentives. What is politically rational becomes economically irrational. See his *Markets and States in Tropical Africa: The Political Basis of Agricultural Policies* (Berkeley: University of California Press, 1981); *Essays on the Political Economy of Rural Africa* (Cambridge: Cambridge University Press, 1983); and "Governments and Agricultural Markets in Africa," in Bates, ed., *Toward a Political Economy of Development* (Berkeley: University of California Press, 1988), pp. 331–58. Among the more persuasive items on the desirability of industrial policy for the United States, see, for example, John Zysman and Laura Tyson, eds., *American Industry in International Competition: Government Policies and Corporate Strategies* (Ithaca: Cornell University Press, 1983), and Stephen Cohen and John Zysman, *Manufacturing Matters: The Myth of a Post-Industrial Economy* (New York: Basic, 1987).

28. Wade, *Governing the Market*, is more sensitive to the problem of the political, class, and socioeconomic underpinnings of bureaucratic actions. See especially chapter 8. Yet Wade also eschews an explicit embrace of the terminological "developmental state."

tional rules and relations governing trade, investment, energy, and environmental pollution; the actions of multinational corporations and transnational nongovernmental organizations; foreign aid; and so forth.

Yet the modern state, like the mythological Janus, has two faces. One looks inward toward domestic society; the other turns outward toward the international arena. Both faces are part of the same head, yet students of the state too often become so entranced by one half of this visage that the other is ignored, leaving one side alone to represent the totality of "the state."

Because a fundamental goal of the developmental state is the improvement of its economic conditions *relative to other states,* any country aspiring to development must choose its strategy within the broader context of regional and international power balances. Such conditions are constantly in flux, at certain times offering far greater opportunities for marginal or industrializing countries than at others. Economic options will be highly contingent on the broader external arena within which any industrializing nation's leaders must operate.

Limits exist to what any concept can sensibly incorporate, and the contributions made by the developmental state are many. But, ultimately, low sensitivity to international factors works against the broader applicability of the notion of the developmental state, primarily by assuming that nation-states interested in development all start from more or less comparable international positions and are equally advantaged or disadvantaged. What counts, it is assumed, is getting their domestic act together, after which moving forward is the easy task. This has hardly been the case in the real world.

Certainly a fundamental question that must be confronted is whether the "developmental state" is a semipermanent option available to countries regardless of international conditions or whether the most successful embodiments of the "developmental state" have been historical anomalies unlikely to be imitated in the future.

The Developmental State and Four East Asian Puzzles

The various macroeconomic statistics on Japan, Taiwan, and Korea have become boringly familiar even to those who are not specialists on the region. Japan's gross national product grew at an average of about 11 percent per year from 1952 until 1973 while its share of world trade quadrupled from about 2 percent to about 8 percent. Even more impressive was its performance over the next decade and a half, until the bursting of the bubble in 1990. While Japan's absolute rate of growth had slowed in the 1970s and 1980s, it still exceeded that for most other industrialized countries. Moreover, Japan's trade balance became increasingly positive; its currency essentially tripled in international purchasing power; domestic inflation remained low; gross investment soared; manufacturing productivity improved rapidly; and overseas investment expanded at a rate unmatched by any other industrialized country. By most comparative indices, Japan's was the industrialized world's most successful economy during the decade of the 1980s.[29]

In 1950, South Korea had a per capita income of $146, roughly in the ballpark with Kenya ($129) and Nigeria ($150) and just slightly behind Egypt ($203). Taiwan ranked somewhat ahead of these countries with $224, but behind Brazil ($373), about one-half the level of Mexico ($562), and only about 25 percent of Argentina ($907).[30] For the next four decades Taiwan's GNP grew at an average of 8.7 percent per year; exports expanded at 20 percent per year; and the industrial share of production increased from 25 percent to 45 percent.[31] Korea's growth was slower to start, but from 1961 to 1991 it rose by 8.4 percent per year. Both countries roared past others that were once their economic peers. Despite some slowing in the 1990s, both countries were enjoying growth rates of over 6 percent in 1997. Indeed, South Korea had become sufficiently strong to acquire membership in the Organization for Economic Cooperation and Development (OECD). While Korean and Taiwanese lifestyles remained less luxurious than those in most southern European countries, they were superior to those in most of the non-oil-producing countries in Africa, Asia, and Latin America and closing fast on many of the less rich European countries.

For their growth and economic transformation, all three countries have relied heavily on the export of manufactured goods. Indeed, export-oriented development has become so linked in the public mind with the hypergrowth of Japan, Korea, and Taiwan that it has become "a new development orthodoxy."[32] In the early 1990s, for example, U.N. trade system data shows that Japan accounted for 14 percent of the world's manufactured exports, and Taiwan and Korea accounted for another 8 percent; Mexico, by way of contrast, accounted for only 0.4 percent. From another perspective, Taiwan, Korea, and Hong Kong together ac-

29. Lucy Gorham, *No Longer Leading—a Scorecard on U.S. Economic Performance and the Role of the Public Sector Compared with Japan, West Germany, and Sweden* (Washington, D.C.: Economic Policy Institute, 1988), pp. 1–44.

30. These figures and this formulation are based on Chalmers Johnson, "Political Institutions and Economic Performance: The Government-Business Relationship in Japan, South Korea, and Taiwan," in Frederic C. Deyo, ed., *The Political Economy of the New Asian Industrialism* (Ithaca: Cornell University Press, 1987), p. 136.

31. Tun-jen Cheng, "Democratizing the Quasi-Leninist Regime in Taiwan," *World Politics* 41, no. 4 (July 1989): 481.

32. Haggard, "The Newly Industrializing Countries in the International System," p. 344.

count for more manufactured exports than do all Latin American countries combined.

Even though Japan, South Korea, and Taiwan have shared high growth and won the label of "developmental states," the three countries differ significantly from one another in both the *structures* and the *strategies* of their respective states, with little commonality in their institutional and structural properties. Moreover, the tools of statecraft utilized by the three have been rather different, as have state-societal interactions. And with the exception of a common devotion to export-led growth, the three have followed rather different economic strategies. This poses the first East Asian puzzle: despite sharing the common label of "developmental state," the three states differ substantially from one another.

Japan is a constitutional democracy, deeply embedded in Japanese society, providing the standard guarantees of individual and civil liberties found in North American and Western European democracies.[33] As such this places important constraints on the autonomy of the Japanese state. In contrast, the Taiwanese state was imposed on a society in which it had no previous power base.[34] Moreover, until the very late 1980s, Taiwan had an extremely powerful president with a wide range of emergency powers.[35] He was supported in his authoritarian rule by what Tun-jen Cheng correctly identifies as a "quasi-Leninist" party, the Knomintang (KMT).[36] Korea, in turn, has experienced a succession of regimes, several straightforward military dictatorships interspersed with others such as the Park regime that were closer to autocratic one-person rule. The military has been highly interventionist in Korea, highly dependent on the KMT in Taiwan, and virtually impotent in Japan. Thus, if all three countries might generically be said to have had "strong states," the specific structural underpinnings of that strength have been quite disparate.

All three have also been highly creative in the generation and channeling of capital. Yet, capital mobilization had different institutional roots and forms. In Japan, most banks are private and often linked to industrial groups, but the keystone of the system, the Bank of Japan, is controlled by the government's Ministry of Finance, while the public postal savings sys-

---

33. See the essays in Takashi Ishida and Ellis Krauss, eds., *Democracy in Japan* (Pittsburgh: University of Pittsburgh Press, 1990), for a generally positive assessment of Japanese democracy, whereas a contrasting, largely class-based view is presented in Gavan McCormack and Yoshio Sugimoto, eds., *Democracy in Contemporary Japan* (Armonk, N.Y.: M. E. Sharpe, 1986). I make my own views quite explicit in "Japanese Democracy: A Comparative Perspective," in Craig Garby and Mary Brown Bullock, eds., *Japan—a New Kind of Superpower?* (Baltimore: Johns Hopkins University Press, 1994).

34. Thomas Gold, *State and Society in the Taiwan Miracle* (Armonk, N.Y.: M. E. Sharpe, 1986), pp. 19–20.

35. Ibid., p. 60.

36. Tun-jen Cheng, "Democratizing the Quasi-Leninist Regime in Taiwan," pp. 471–499.

tem is a key component of the entire system; foreign capital inflows have been limited. In South Korea, considerable capital has been raised abroad and almost all banking was privatized, yet government oversight has been critical in directing capital to desired sectors.[37] In Taiwan, the KMT is in charge; capital control by local Taiwanese bankers was minimized in favor of mainlander control, and finance and industry were kept as separate spheres.[38] Clearly, financial structures are quite different in all three countries.

If the core institutional structures of these states have been different, so were *state strategies.* In Taiwan since the 1950s, the government has pursued a policy of letting interest rates rise to quite high market levels; in Japan and Korea the government long sought to keep interest rates below international rates, if not negative in real terms. Taiwan's companies have been small and equity-based (although several of the largest have been KMT-owned), whereas Korea's, after the 1960s, became quite large and debt-laden.

Japan's corporate groups (*keiretsu*) served in many ways as the model for Korea's *chaebol,* but the huge Japanese groups all revolve around a central banking organization as the prime lender for group members; in Korea no such banks form a comparable financial core.[39] Furthermore, Japanese companies were debt driven in the 1960s and 1970s, making them highly vulnerable to manipulation by the state through capital availability and domestically controlled interest rates. By the 1980s, however, these companies were relying more heavily on retained earnings and equity financing, which gave them far more autonomy from state capital controls.

The export-orientation critical to all three economies is centralized in Korea, decentralized in Taiwan, and oligopolistic and highly competitive in Japan. When the 1973 oil crisis struck all three, state responses could not have been more different: Korea expanded and inflated, while Tai-

---

37. Byung-Sun Choi, "Financial Policy and Big Business in Korea: The Perils of Financial Regulation," in Stephan Haggard, Chung H. Lee, and Sylvia Maxfield, eds., *The Politics of Finance in Developing Countries* (Ithaca: Cornell University Press, 1993), pp. 23–54.

38. Tun-jen Cheng, "Guarding the Commanding Heights: The State as Banker in Taiwan," in Haggard, Lee, and Maxfield, eds., *The Politics of Finance in Developing Countries,* pp. 55–92.

39. It could be argued, however, that the key to both Japanese and Korean industrial groups is the trading company, a trait common to both.

40. Heng-seng Cheng, "Alternative Balance of Payments Adjustment Experience: Korea and Taiwan, 1973–1977," *Economic Review,* Federal Reserve Bank of San Francisco (Summer 1978): 57–62, as quoted in Tun-jen Cheng, "Political Regimes and Development Strategies: Korea and Taiwan," in Gary Gereffi and Donald Wyman, eds., *Manufacturing Miracles: Paths of Industrialization in Latin America and East Asia* (Princeton: Princeton University Press, 1990), p. 163.

wan contracted and stabilized;[40] Japan confronted massive inflation but began extensive deficit financing to cover the social costs of inflation control.

Japan eschewed foreign investment and foreign borrowing with consistency from the turn of the century until the 1980s and has hardly had the welcome mat out even since then;[41] instead, the country borrowed technology without the encumbering adjuncts of capital and managerial control.[42] In contrast, Taiwan was an early advocate of the export-free zone, setting up the first such zone in East Asia at Kaohsiung in 1965 and welcoming foreign firms and foreign direct investment ever since. Although more skeptical of foreign firms, Korea has relied extensively on foreign borrowing for long-term investment, borrowing its way out of balance-of-payments crises, particularly during the 1980s.[43]

Finally, the economies of the three differ vastly in size. In 1995, Japan had an economy of some $4.7 trillion, about seventeen times as large as Taiwan's and ten times as large as Korea's. As a member of various international economic policymaking bodies, most particularly the G-5 and G-7, the Japanese state is organizationally positioned to play an important role in the making of internationally influential economic policies on matters of trade, exchange rates, and the like; Taiwan and South Korea are not.

Clearly, Japan is one of the world's most powerful capitalist democracies; Korea and Taiwan still lack such economic muscle. While many South Korean companies are quite large by so-called Third World standards, only eleven are listed among the Fortune 500's largest companies; Taiwan lists four. In contrast, there are over 150 Japanese companies on the list. Finally, economic size is relevant in terms of domestic markets, which have played very different roles in the overall successes of the three

41. See, for example, T. C. Smith, *Political Change and Industrial Development in Japan: Government Enterprise, 1868–1880* (Stanford: Stanford University Press, 1955); Mark Mason, *United States Direct Investment in Japan* (Cambridge: Harvard University Press, 1992); and Dennis J. Encarnation and Mark Mason, "Neither MITI nor America: The Political Economy of Capital Liberalization in Japan," *International Organization* 44, no. 1 (Winter 1990): 25–54.

42. Richard J. Samuels, *"Rich Nation, Strong Army": National Security and the Technological Transformation of Japan* (Ithaca: Cornell University Press, 1994), esp. chaps. 8, 9.

43. Amsden, *Asia's Next Giant*, p. 94. Herman M. Schwartz, *In the Dominions of Debt: Historical Perspectives on Dependent Development* (Ithaca: Cornell University Press, 1989), chap. 7. Haggard and Cheng sum up the Korean policy as follows: "a consistent effort to invite foreign investment into targeted sectors while steadily tightening the criteria governing their operation, protecting domestic producers from competition in the home market, and forcing local equity participation." Stephan Haggard and Tun-jen Cheng, "State and Foreign Capital in the East Asian NICs," in Deyo, ed., *Political Economy of the New Asian Industrialism*, p. 113.

states. Development of products first for the domestic market and only then for the world was characteristic of Japanese policies; such a reliance on domestic market predominance was less easy for either Taiwanese or Korean companies.

Such data point to the problem of categorization: to what extent are these three states similar or different? Economic catch-up and state intervention suggest similarity. But numerous specific features of their political and economic structures underscore important differences. Compared with most other countries, the three share important similarities in history, geography, culture, and economic success. But their differences in state structure and state strategy make any links between East Asian economic success and some single type of "state" at best problematic. Unraveling this puzzle is important not simply for understanding the three countries themselves but more significantly for resolving several of the ambiguities identified in the concept of the developmental state.

A second and related puzzle concerns changes over time. The widespread images of "Japan, Inc." and "Korea, Inc." convey an aura of unchanging permanence that obscures the tremendous changes that took place in state structures and strategies in all three countries between the 1950s and the 1990s. A few highlights are relevant. From the 1950s until the 1970s in Japan macroeconomic policy relied on, among other things, a fixed and artificially depressed exchange rate, tight governmental control over the credit and monetary supply, high levels of protection for both agriculture and industry, severe restrictions on capital movements into and out of the country, low government expenditures, minimal public debt, and overbalanced budgets. By the mid-1990s, these had given way to a floating and ever more highly valued yen sustained by periodic Bank of Japan intervention; an expansion of borrowing opportunities for industries at home and abroad; lower tariffs and fewer quotas on manufactured imports than in almost any other industrialized country; liberalization of the capital, bond, and securities markets; the widespread expansion of Japanese investment and manufacturing operations throughout the world; extensive strategic alliances with non-Japanese companies; as well as a substantial increase in government spending as a proportion of GNP, in public debt, and in deficit financing.[11] In the years

44. T. J. Pempel, "Japan's Creative Conservatism: Continuity under Challenge," in Francis G. Castles, ed., *The Comparative History of Public Policy* (Oxford: Polity Press, 1989), pp. 153, 168–79. See also Hugh Patrick and Henry Rosovsky, eds., *Asia's New Giant* (Washington, D.C.: Brookings Institution, 1976), esp. chap. 1; Yamamura and Yasuba, eds., *The Political Economy of Japan*, vol. 1, *The Domestic Transformation*; Shinkawa Muneyuki, *Zaisei Hattan to Zeisei Kaikaku* (The collapse of public finance and the reform of the tax system) (Tokyo: Iwanami Shoten, 1989); and Nihon Keizai Shimbunsha, ed., *Shinnihon Keizai* (The restructuring of Japan's economy) (Tokyo: Nihonkeizai Shimbunsha, 1988).

following the bursting of the economic bubble, policy variously centered on keeping the stock market afloat; on fiscal tightness and tax hikes followed by economic stimulation through tax cuts and public works; on cutting sector-by-sector trade deals with the United States; and on bailing out the decimated financial system.

Politically, during the 1980s Japan saw a relative diminution of bureaucratic power and a corresponding rise in the power of the ruling Liberal Democratic Party (LDP).[45] Then, following the fragmentation of the LDP, the bureaucracy appeared to have regained substantial policy autonomy, only to be resubjected to a barrage of political attacks in the late 1990s. There has been a major overhaul in the organization of the nation's labor movement. The political system has withstood the rise and demise of a massive movement against the Japan Security Treaty, at least two major student movements, and an antipollution movement. There was also a brief flirtation with and a subsequent rollback in an expanded system of pensions and health care that, had it been left intact, could well have put Japan on the path to becoming a "superwelfare state."[46] In addition, Japan has been subjected to and has responded to strong pressures from the United States to restrict "voluntarily" many of its exports and more recently to expand its domestic spending.[47] Japan in the late 1990s is quite different from Japan in the 1950s, 1960s, or 1970s.

Changes in Taiwan and Korea have been drastic as well. U.S. foreign aid was a key ingredient in strengthening both state bureaucrats and the national economies of both countries into the 1960s. Aid to Taiwan over the period 1950–64 was $1.5 billion, or about ten dollars for every person on the island.[48] In addition, over $2.5 billion in military equipment was provided, vastly relieving the Taiwanese government of using scarce domestic capital to procure such equipment on the open market at higher prices.

In the case of Korea, from 1953 to 1958 the average annual inflow of aid from the United States represented $270 million, or roughly twelve

45. Sato and Matsuzaki, *Jiminto Seiken.*

46. Compare the popular government notion that Japan should become a "welfare society" (that is, not a welfare state). Japan Ministry of Economic Planning Agency, *New Economic and Social Seven-Year Plan* (Tokyo: Economic Planning Agency, 1979); Nakagawa Yatsuhiro "Japan, the Welfare Super-Power," *Journal of Japanese Studies* 5, no. 1 (1979): 5–51.

47. One is hard pressed to refrain from suggesting that U.S. demands that Japan increase its public spending for various internal improvements such as bridges, schools, highways, and apartment complexes must surely have come as a result of the success of Washington's Japan lobby. Surely, the Liberal Democratic Party must have felt like Brer Rabbit crying, "Please don't throw me in the briar patch." LDP power long rested on precisely such pork barrel projects.

48. Neil H. Jacoby, *U.S. Aid to Taiwan* (New York: Praeger, 1966), p. 38.

dollars per capita, nearly 15 percent of the average annual GNP and over 80 percent of foreign exchange.[49] The civilian component of this important source of revenue ended in the mid-1960s, eliminating a key ingredient of domestic and foreign economic policies.[50]

Both the Taiwanese and Korean governments pursued import substitution policies from the end of World War II into the early 1960s (1964 for South Korea; 1960 for Taiwan). But import substitution gave way to export-led growth policies in the 1970s. For Korea, much like Japan, a devalued currency and severe barriers against the import of foreign consumer and manufactured goods were critical components of policy. When South Korea shifted to export-led growth, the state channeled investment funds to specific firms in targeted industries using a vast array of export and investment subsidies.[51] In addition, Korea followed a policy of national champions with the adoption of its new policy under the Heavy and Chemical Industry Plan of 1973.

Finally, Korea and Taiwan both shifted away from authoritarian structures to increased political competition in the late 1980s and early 1990s, with the transition to democracy and free elections coming in South Korea in 1987 and in Taiwan in 1996.

Such shifts in political structure and economic policy are themselves a puzzle: why the shifts, and what did they mean? In particular, why the openings and increased flexibilities, when presumably the states in all three countries should have been in positions of heightened strength and greater ability to harden their shells? But combined with the first puzzle, these shifts create a broader question: With all these differences and changes over time, should one consider the three countries as still constituting the separate category implied by the label "developmental state"? Or do they represent three somewhat idiosyncratic versions of more classic categories such as capitalism, developing economies, authoritarianism (either of the "soft" or "hard" versions), parliamentary democracy, or the like?

Still a third puzzle arises in conjunction with the interactions between each of the three Northeast Asian states and the United States and secon-

49. Amsden, *Asia's Next Giant*, p. 39. Bruce Cumings notes the scale of this aid: the Republic of Korea (ROK) plus Taiwan received a total of nearly $20 billion in civilian and military aid. The ROK's total of nearly $6 billion in economic grants and aid from 1946 to 1978 compares with a total for all Africa of $6.89 billion and for all Latin America of $14.8 billion. Military deliveries to the two countries were three times greater than those for all Africa and Latin America combined. Cumings, "The Origins and Development of the Northeast Asian Political Economy: Industrial Sectors, Product Cycles, and Political Consequences," in Deyo, ed., *Beneath the Miracle*, p. 67.

50. It is important to note that in the case of Korea, however, normalization of relations with Japan in 1965 led to massive infusions of Japanese aid and investment, much of it replacing that from the United States. In addition, a $4 billion military aid arrangement with Japan in 1983 also provided a major boost to the Korean budget.

51. Schwartz, *In the Dominions of Debt*, p. 246.

darily between South Korea and Taiwan, on the one hand, and the United States and Japan, on the other. During the mid-1940s all three states were economically prostrate. Theories of domestic politics alone would have predicted the virtual impossibility of emerging from this condition. Far more plausible would have been predictions of the long-term success of the Philippines, with its Americanist culture and political structures and a GNP per capita vastly ahead of Japan, South Korea, and Taiwan.

Yet the three countries advanced well beyond any probable projections based on their relative world strength in the 1950s. Most important, all three did more than simply advance their own economic well-being in the face of the structural impediments of the international system; they were voluntarily helped in their efforts by the system's hegemon. It is hard to imagine the economic successes of these three had the United States not been so anxious to assist their economic enrichment. Moreover, the generosity shown at the height of the cold war had given way to self-interested protectionism and overt attacks by the United States on many of the key economic strategies of all three states from the late 1970s into the 1990s. Alterations in international political conditions were vital to the changing fortunes of the three countries.

Finally, these three Asian success stories present a fourth puzzle. Their macroeconomic growth is impressive and has been subjected to extensive analysis. Far more paradoxical is the fact that such growth was accompanied by relatively high levels of social equality, despite the fact that on almost any ideological scale all three countries would be ranked from highly conservative to overtly authoritarian. The left has been politically weak in all three, and none has anything resembling a "welfare state." Yet, Japan has social equality levels as measured by the Gini index comparable with these of Sweden or Norway, rather than the more conservative countries such as Canada, the United Kingdom, the United States, or West Germany.[52] And in contrast to Latin American countries such as Brazil and Argentina with Gini index figures around .60, Taiwan's has been low and has fallen to just below .30, whereas South Korea's has been in the range of .33–.35 since the mid-1960s.[53]

---

52. This point is explored at length in Pempel, "Japan's Creative Conservatism," pp. 149–91. See also Malcolm Sawyer, *Income Distribution in the OECD Countries* (Paris: OECD, 1976), and Sidney Verba et al., *Elites and the Idea of Equality* (Cambridge: Harvard University Press, 1987).

53. A useful comparative table summarizing findings on Gini indexes for several major newly industrializing countries is presented in Stephan Haggard, *Pathways from the Periphery: The Politics of Growth in the Newly Industrializing Countries* (Ithaca: Cornell University Press, 1990), p. 226. See also Hagen Koo, "The Political Economy of Income Distribution in South Korea: The Impact of the State's Industrialization Policies," *World Development* 12 (1984): 1029–37; Peter Evans, "Class, State, and Dependence in Asia: Lessons for Latin

Relatively egalitarian income structures are paralleled by widespread improvements in human well-being. Thus, a Japanese child born in the early 1990s had an expected lifespan of nearly 80 years, the highest in the world; a Taiwanese child could expect to live 74 years, only a year less than an American or a German and 15 years longer than a Taiwanese born in 1952; South Koreans could anticipate 70 years on earth, up from 58 in 1965.[54] In all three countries, unemployment is typically between 1 and 4 percent, consumer goods are widespread, crime rates are low, and education is pervasive and relatively egalitarian. While Japan, South Korea, and Taiwan have hardly eradicated class differences, gaps in the living conditions of rich and poor are far less extreme than in many other parts of the world, including within many of the OECD democracies.

This, then, is the final paradox of East Asian development: high growth with high levels of social equality and social well-being despite the absence of a powerful Left or an institutionalized welfare state. Why such equality despite the absence of political conditions traditionally presumed to be equality's preconditions? In more practical terms, absent constraints from democratic institutions or the political Left, why didn't the ruling elites of these three countries simply take the money and run?[55]

Unraveling these puzzles requires more than simply an examination of the three countries themselves. It rests on a deeper appreciation of the dual nature of the state, in both its domestic and its international roles. What one face of the state does is quite frequently in response to what its other face has seen.[56] The unraveling also requires that one look beyond the state as a reified concept separate from society. As I will argue in the next section, while state institutions have clearly played a vital role in the economic successes of all three countries in East Asia, that success springs not simply from the *states* but also from the more complex *regimes* of which the state is but a part. In this sense it requires a sensitivity to the interactions between "state" and "society," as well as a sensitivity to domestic and international conditions. It is in this context that the notion of regime seems most helpful.

Americanists," in Deyo, ed., *Political Economy of the New Asian Industrialism*, pp. 217–20; and Schwartz, *In the Dominions of Debt*, p. 266.

54. Information on Taiwan and South Korea from the *Economist*, July 14, 1990, p. 19.

55. This is not to dismiss the realities of political corruption in all three countries: none are ruled by saints; bribes and consequent scandals are not unheard of; and very few of their politically powerful are poor. But none of these countries has witnessed the systematic looting of the national treasury that has been so endemic to many other countries.

56. This point is nicely developed in game theoretic terms by Robert D. Putnam, "Diplomacy and Domestic Politics: The Logic of Two-Level Games," *International Organization* 42, no. 4 (Autumn 1988). See also Peter B. Evans, Harold K. Jacobson, and Robert D. Putnam, eds., *Double-Edged Diplomacy: International Bargaining and Domestic Politics* (Berkeley: University of California Press, 1993).

THE CHARACTER OF THE EAST ASIAN REGIMES

Understanding the contemporary economic successes of Japan, Taiwan, and South Korea requires one to drop the artificial dichotomies between "state" and "society" and between "domestic" and "international." In fact, the relative strengths of "state" and "society" as well as of "domestic" and "international" influences are not constants but variables that can be mapped along a continuum. As Peter Evans has shown with regard to state-society relations, most countries identified as having "developmental states" have states and societies that are mutually "embedded."[57] And George Tsebelis has noted that politicians are invariably involved in "nested games" such that domestic and international political "games" are considered simultaneously, with the conflicts and payoffs from one influencing considerations in the other.[58] Understanding this complex interplay requires a focus not simply on "the state" but also on the state as situated internationally and as embedded in domestic society for each of the three regimes. Key to this mixture is the concept of "regime."

A regime functions above the day-to-day hubbub of microlevel politics. In this sense, it is more than the government of the day. But it is also far less, in substance or in longevity, than a complete constitutional order or a political community. "Regime" involves a sustained fusion among the institutions of the state, particular segments of the socioeconomic order, and a particular bias in public policy orientation. Together, this mixture provides a pattern of elements so unified as a whole that its properties cannot be fully appreciated by a simple summation of its parts. "Regime" in this sense equates with such terms as "gestalt," "system," or "weltanschauung" and results in what E. E. Schattschneider would call a prevailing "mobilization of bias."[59] Metaphorically speaking, a constitutional order changes when the entire character of the game changes; governments change whenever the players in the game change. In between these two levels are regimes, which change when the nature of the rules of the game change.

57. Peter Evans, *Embedded Autonomy: States and Industrial Transformation* (Princeton: Princeton University Press, 1995).

58. George Tsebelis, *Nested Games: Rational Choice in Comparative Politics* (Berkeley: University of California Press, 1990).

59. Compare David Easton, *A Systems Analysis of Political Life* (New York: John Wiley, 1965), pp. 190–211. In an early treatment of the notion of regime, John G. Ruggie gave the following definition: regimes were "sets of mutual expectations, generally agreed-to rules, regulations and plans, in accordance with which organizational energies and financial commitments are allocated." "International Responses to Technology: Concepts and Trends," *International Organization* 29 (Summer 1975): 569, as cited by Robert Keohane and Joseph Nye, *Power and Interdependence: World Politics in Transition* (Boston: Little, Brown, 1977), p. 20. E. E. Schattschneider, *The Semi-Sovereign People* (New York: Holt, Rinehart and Winston, 1960), p. 71.

Regimes are based on the interactions of specific social sectors and key state institutions. They rest on the mutual penetration of specific sectors of state and society particularly around commonly accepted principles for organizing the nation's political economy and its public policy profile. These fusions of state and society are reflected in specific public policy profiles akin to what Antonio Gramsci called "hegemonic projects,"—that is, broad and coherent thrusts or biases in the behavior of nation-states. Implicit in this notion of regime is the expectation that specific components of state and societal power will be mutually reinforcing (though not necessarily without challenge) and that public actions will reflect this interaction. In short, the character of a regime is determined by the societal coalitional base on which a state rests, the power of that state (both domestically and internationally), and the institutionalization and bias of the public policies that result.

For any government to endure and function effectively it must establish, maintain, and reward a particular socioeconomic support base. That base may be broad or narrow; it may rest on any combination of pillars, from voting strength to worker support to police power to the confidence of capital. In any capitalist economy, the latter is critical. Moreover, support from other sectors such as agriculture, labor, the military, middle-class professionals, and the like can be essential to a regime's longevity even if the contributions of such groups do not rest simply on the votes of their members. In this sense a regime involves the creation of a particular social and normative order. A regime thus persists over time periods that correspond to long-standing historical arrangements such as prevailed under the Red-Green coalition in Scandinavia, the New Deal coalition in the United States, the lib-lab coalition in turn-of-the-century England, or the business-agricultural coalitions that have prevailed in much of twentieth-century Australia and New Zealand.

For a regime to gain the kind of stability that allows it to transcend mundane daily politics and become more than a government of the day, it must do several things. First, it must forge a socioeconomic support coalition that commands more in the way of politically relevant resources than the coalition(s) supporting its opponents. Second, a regime must be able to define the central issues in politics, that is, set the content of the nation's political agenda, defining and pressing its own issues at the expense of its opponents. Third, a regime must be able to put forward a legitimating ideology that plausibly presents the interests of its supporters as general or common interests.[60] Finally, a regime must be able to deliver

60. In this sense, there is a similarity to the term "regime" as used in international politics, that is, "regimes are social institutions . . . which are recognized patterns of behavior or practice around which expectations converge." Oran R. Young, "Regime Dynamics: The

benefits to its supporters that reward them for their support. A regime is sustained to the extent that these supporters are given long-term benefits, not simply short-term profits. And these payoffs must come in ways that do not engender sufficient hostility by the regime's opponents that they revolt or exit.

The exchange relationship between incumbents and supporters is the essence of state action. Incumbents require political supporters to survive, and the supporters, in turn, must be provided with incentives sufficient to prevent their shifting support to other potential officeholders.[61]

Furthermore, if a regime is to develop what I have elsewhere called a "virtuous cycle" of support—use of governmental machinery to reward supporters, and the generation of further support—its policies should be in the long-term benefit of the national economy. Hence, for a regime to gain long-term predominance and equilibrium, it must be continually about the business of reinforcing itself.[62]

Japan, South Korea, and Taiwan share several essential regime traits. Common to all three are certain historical and ideological features quite different from the industrializing efforts of industrialized democracies in Europe and North America and of countries in much of the rest of the world. Just as the European nation-states were historically and internationally conditioned by their mixture of common and unique experiences, so were those of Japan, Korea, and Taiwan. But the forces acting on these latter three were significantly different from those affecting regimes formed earlier and in a different sociohistorical milieu. As a consequence, all three countries are different in several fundamental ways from their counterparts elsewhere.

Eight features are both common to the three countries and sufficiently different from the experiences of other industrialized and industrializing countries to warrant particular attention. These are idealized summations of what are highly variable conditions. As such, the mixture within each

---

Rise and Fall of International Regimes," *International Organization* 36, no. 2 (Spring 1982): 277. It is somewhat close also to Steven D. Krasner's definition: "principles, norms, rules, and decision-making procedures around which actor expectations converge in a given issue-area." See Krasner, "Structural Causes and Regime Consequences: Regimes as Intervening Variables," *International Organization* 36, no. 2 (Spring 1982): 185. Krasner, however, stresses beliefs and expectations, whereas Young focuses on social institutions; my usage, while not ignoring expectations, is also institutional in character.

61. Peter Evans, "The State as Problem and Solution: Predation, Embedded Autonomy, and Structural Change," in Stephan Haggard and Robert R. Kaufman, eds., *The Politics of Economic Adjustment* (Princeton: Princeton University Press, 1992), p. 146.

62. T. J. Pempel, "Introduction: Uncommon Democracies: The One-Party Dominant Regimes," in Pempel, ed., *Uncommon Democracies: The One-Party Dominant Regimes* (Ithaca: Cornell University Press, 1990), p. 16.

of the three regimes is somewhat particular, and each regime is distinct from the other two. At the same time, all three cluster at the end points of all these variables, in a combination that makes them unique as a group from most other regimes.

1. All three have "strong states"—that is, states in which technocrats and bureaucrats enjoy disproportionately high levels of power and wield a variety of tools to enforce their will. State actors are also relatively free from major populist pressures, most especially from organized labor and organized peasants.
2. There is no sharp dichotomy between state and society. The presence of semipermanent socioeconomic coalitions closely linked to state institutions makes such a reified bifurcation meaningless.
3. All three underwent land reforms that virtually eliminated large landholders as major elements in the sociopolitical landscape. Moreover, with limited natural resources and small land areas, none of the three is a major exporter of agricultural products or natural resources.
4. All have domestic power structures that, for males at least, are open to entry largely (though by no means exclusively) on the basis of individual merit rather than ascriptive traits such as social class.
5. The regimes in all three have taken on what Bob Jessop might call "hegemonic projects" that entail two essential elements: first, the enhancement of their national economic competitiveness through the development of internationally marketable goods, and second, an ideologically and economically rooted opposition to communism, socialism, and big states.[63]
6. In conjunction with the project of improved economic competitiveness, all three reject the deified Western concept of "the market," opting instead for active market manipulation, but in ways that are market enhancing rather than market rejecting.
7. To the extent that they have been successful in advancing their overall production, national income per capita, and shares of world trade, all three have also done so relatively free from the compromising effects of international capital penetration. In particular, the three regimes have retained highly effective filters over foreign direct investment and foreign capital flows.
8. All three are exceptionally closely linked both in economic and security policies with the United States. Moreover, Taiwan and South Korea are similarly linked to Japan.

63. Bob Jessop, "Accumulation Strategies, State Forms, and Hegemonic Projects," *Kapitalistate* 10/11 (1983): 89–101.

Naturally, there is more to the story of these three countries than is implied in the above summary; similarly, interrelationships among all eight traits make the isolation of any one of them meaningless for anything but analytic purposes. Collectively, however, they constitute core traits that make the three regimes rather similar to one another and quite distinct from most other nation-states.[64] They also form the heart of a political explanation for economic success of all three.

In his classic study, Alexander Gerschenkron suggested, among other things, that late industrializers would feel strong economic pressures toward the centralization of the institutions of both capital and administration.[65] Certainly the strong state apparatuses and strong centralized banking systems of Japan, South Korea, and Taiwan are congruent with such a prediction. But timing alone explains tendencies at best, as can be seen from the fact that Nigeria, Egypt, and Mexico also began their industrialization efforts historically "late" but look nothing like the three Asian success stories.

Japan was by far the earliest of the three to begin industrialization, and it did so in a manner that explicitly positioned it between the laissez-faire capitalist mode of England and the dirigiste mode of the Soviet Union. The Meiji state in the late nineteenth century was given extensive formal powers and with time and practice added additional informal powers to its repertoire. But as Bert Rockman has colorfully observed, "state strength" in itself may be meaningless without an economic base: "the hangman's noose may be the major production function of a state with few other goods to produce. . . . But that is entirely sufficient to make for a powerful state."[66] The nineteenth-century Japanese state pursued rapid, national, and defensive industrialization in large measure to avoid the colonization that was besetting its neighbor China, along with Africa, Southeast Asia, and much of the rest of the world. The Meiji state set up model factories, encouraged cartelization, created a strong central bank, and sought to provide coherent "top-down" direction to the nation's economy.

In doing so, it also abjured most state ownership, selling off its model factories at bargain prices to privately owned industrial cartels (*zaibatsu*).

64. I do not wish to enter into the debate about whether Singapore, Malaysia, Thailand, Indonesia, and perhaps North Korea and China also share these traits and should be included in the collection of "developmental regimes." In general I can accept the notion that many of these have certain regime traits in common with Japan, South Korea, and Taiwan. At the same time, I believe that certain conditions affecting most of these other regimes make them sufficiently different to require separate treatment.

65. Alexander Gerschenkron, *Economic Backwardness in Historical Perspective* (Cambridge: Harvard University Press, 1962).

66. Bert A. Rockman, "Minding the State—or a State of Mind?" *Comparative Political Studies* 23, no. 1 (April 1990): 31.

This, along with subsequent close collaboration between big business and the state, forged the ties of "reciprocal consent" that, although often challenged and frequently readjusted, have never since been broken.[67] Large landowners and the military establishment formed the additional key elements in the prewar Japanese regime that eventually led the country into authoritarianism and aggression.

Although landlord class was eliminated by an extensive land reform in 1947 and the military was removed from formal power by the U.S. Occupation and the new constitution, the basic alliance between strong state institutions and large, oligopolistic industrial groups was reaffirmed following World War II. The government resumed its economic orchestration in an effort to overcome the war damage and once again to propel Japan to "catch up" with the West. An electoral coalition heavily dependent on small-scale farmers, plus small and medium-size businesses dependent on protectionism, state subsidy, and conservative cultural values, as well as a mutually dependent relationship with heavy industry and finance capital, forged a virtually unshakable system of single-party dominance that prevailed from 1955 to 1993.[68] Thus, while Japanese state/governmental institutions have been critical to national success, state officials would have been far less influential were it not for the interactive network linking them to key segments of society through a powerful political party.

Colonialism provided the central mechanism whereby the Japanese model was first influential over both Korea and Taiwan.[69] As Atul Kohli explains in Chapter 4 of this volume, Japan's colonial bureaucrats brought with them industry, commerce, transportation, and communications and created strong, well-educated, local bureaucracies in their two colonies. Under Japanese occupation, the Korean state was expanded in size, became highly centralized, and reached down to every village in the form of a police force and an agricultural extension service.[70] Similarly in Taiwan, the reach of the state was long and pervasive: cadastral surveys, railroads, ports, schools, and scientific agricultural improvements were a positive face of the strong state, paralleled by the often less welcome police, tax collectors, and military. In addition, Japan emphasized industrial development under strong colonial state auspices, particularly in the 1930s.[71] Moreover, unlike its European colonialist counterparts, Japan in

---

67. Richard J. Samuels, *The Business of the Japanese State: Energy Markets in Comparative and Historical Perspective* (Ithaca: Cornell University Press, 1987), chap. 1.

68. This theme is explored in the Japanese case and in the broader comparative context of Sweden, Israel, and Italy in Pempel, ed., *Uncommon Democracies*.

69. Cumings, "Northeast Asian Political Economy."

70. Amsden, *Asia's Next Giant*, p. 34.

71. It is useful in this regard to note that in Korea and Taiwan during this period, the colonial state did indeed stand rather apart from Korean and Taiwanese societies.

both of its colonies developed complex financial systems, as well as heavy industry, including steel, chemicals, hydroelectric facilities, metallurgy, and transportation.[72]

Growing in part out of this legacy, both South Korea and Taiwan emerged in the postwar periods with "strong states" that had highly trained technocrats in well-institutionalized government offices as well as the makings of a sophisticated industrial infrastructure. Government bureaucrats in both countries were drawn from a highly educated technocratic elite, and the civil services in both were suffused with extensive military influence, in personnel and as the model for emulation. The result was what Hagen Koo called the "hyper-militarization" of both countries' bureaucracies and their controls over society.[73]

In Taiwan, the colonial Japanese bureaucracy was supplemented by that of the Leninist-based Kuomintang run by the Chinese mainlanders who arrived in the late 1940s. As Cumings has noted in Taiwan, the KMT "had finally found a part of China where its bureaucracy was not hamstrung by provincial warlords and landlords."[74] (In addition, Japanese bureaucrats remained in Taiwan well into 1946 to train Taiwanese replacements, while native bureaucrats continued in office.) The KMT penetrated in every corner of Taiwanese society through youth corps, farmers groups, and party-controlled workers groups. Most of the industrial enterprises inherited from Japanese colonial rule remained state owned and state run. The KMT itself acquired about a dozen important enterprises and thus was able to sustain an economic base relatively independent of private capital.[75]

In South Korea the process was a bit slower, but after the war with North Korea, few doubted the strength of the South Korean state during its initial efforts at import substitution, then a deepening of industrialization, and then, finally, export-led growth. As Amsden has noted: "Korea is evidence for the proposition that if and when late industrialization arrives, the driving force behind it is a strong interventionist state. The need to intervene is greater than in the past because the curses of backwardness are greater."[76] In Korea, the grip of the state over the economy and business was tight, direct, and heavy. Meanwhile, in Taiwan, "the state

72. Cumings, "Northeast Asian Political Economy," pp. 55–56; Samuel P. S. Ho, *The Economic Development of Taiwan, 1860–1970* (New Haven: Yale University Press, 1978), pp. 70–90.

73. Hagen Koo, "The Interplay of State, Social Class, and World System in East Asian Development: The Cases of South Korea and Taiwan," in Deyo, ed., *Political Economy of the New Asian Industrialism*, p. 172.

74. Cumings, "Northeast Asian Political Economy," p. 65.

75. Cheng, "Political Regimes and Development Strategies," pp. 17–18.

76. Amsden, *Asia's Next Giant*, p. 55.

dominated the heights of the economy and accounted for a sizable and crucial portion of industrial production."[77]

The highly concentrated Korean chaebol, such as Samsung, Hyundai and Daewoo, and large-scale Taiwanese enterprises, such as Tatung, have been close collaborators with the two states. Both are patterned on the prewar Japanese zaibatsu or the contemporary Japanese keiretsu. Cartelization and oligopoly mark the business sectors in both countries, though far more in South Korea than in Taiwan.[78] But as Meredith Woo-Cumings has shown for Korea, by the early 1960s, both business cartels and the state economic bodies were equally committed to high growth, realizing that they would have to sink or swim together.[79]

Important to the subsequent socioeconomic base of all three regimes was the fact that landlords were largely eliminated as a powerful political force in the period following World War II. As noted above, the Americans carried out such reforms in Japan (although Japanese officials had initiated the process prior to defeat). In Taiwan, the mainlanders left their landlord supporters behind on the mainland where they underwent "reform" by the Communists. And on Taiwan itself, the KMT had no political reason to ally with domestic landlords. It was far easier to carry out a reform that transferred land and power to KMT hands. In South Korea as well, an extensive land reform was carried out following the war.

Land reform, combined with the fact that none of the three countries had a strong natural resource base, eased the politics of industrialization. Pro-industry policies could go forward without running headlong into powerful domestic opposition anxious to protect plantation or tenant agriculture at the expense of manufacturing and industrial development. In these respects, all three regimes were created under socioeconomic conditions quite different from those that have prevailed in much of Latin America, the Philippines, South Asia, or Africa.

In large part because of their cohesive socioeconomic coalitions, all three governments were well equipped with a variety of tools to shape their national economies in cohesion with the private sector. All three regimes embraced state planning and intervention, rejecting the notion of a "free world market" in goods. (Their concentration on differentiate

77. Gold, *State and Society in the Taiwan Miracle*, p. 75.

78. Amsden notes, for example, that in Taiwan virtually every major export has been cartelized at one time or another: "textiles, canned mushrooms and asparagus, rubber, steel, paper products and cement." Alice H. Amsden, "The State and Taiwan's Economic Development," in Peter B. Evans, Dietrich Rueschemeyer and Theda Skocpol, eds., *Bringing the State Back In* (Cambridge: Cambridge University Press, 1985), p. 90.

79. Woo, *Race to the Swift*, p. 149.

manufactured goods makes this vastly more plausible than would a regime based on the export of more generic agricultural or mining goods.) State bureaucracies developed a host of enhancements for exports.[80]

Andrew Shonfeld, John Kenneth Galbraith, and James O'Connor are among those who have shown the extensive level of planning in all capitalist states, even those most religiously genuflecting before the idol of "free markets."[81] For the most part, however, such planning is by the private, highly concentrated sectors of industry and banking. These sectors are by no means opposed to planning; for all of them, planning and prediction are essential to stable and regularized growth and profits. What they most frequently oppose is any government or public sector planning that constricts their opportunities for profit. Yet such worries emerge largely because public sector planning in most capitalist democracies runs the risk of being subject to the whimsicality of electorally sensitive politicians tempted to offer short-term payoffs to voters by extracting resources from or exerting increased policy controls over precisely those private sector companies which are themselves most dependent on planning. In short, big business and finance most fear not planning per se but public sector planning, with its vulnerability to electoral swings or political caprice and its potentially antibusiness bias.

The dominant regimes in Japan, Korea, and Taiwan, however, have been heavily insulated from collective action by popular sectors, which in turn has severely mitigated such business sector fears. Moreover, government planning has almost always taken a "pro-business" direction. This is not to ignore the important role played by state discipline of private firms. Indeed, the willingness of the state in all three regimes to punish recalcitrant firms—often only as examples—has been vital to the overall acceptance and success of macrolevel, state-led incentives. But none of the three governments has been systematically hostile to the broad interests of big capital and big finance.

The insulation of state planners and big business leaders from effective popular protests has been particularly vital in this orientation, which stands in sharp contrast to the situation in most of the industrialized

80. Robert Wade, "Dirigisme Taiwan-Style," *IDS Bulletin* 15, no. 2 (1984): 66. Chalmers Johnson, "Political Institutions and Economic Performance: The Government-Business Relationship in Japan, South Korea, and Taiwan," in Deyo, ed., *Political Economy of the New Asian Industrialism*, p. 147; Hyug Baeg Im, "The Rise of Bureaucratic Authoritarianism in South Korea," *World Politics* 39, no. 2 (January 1987): 244.

81. Andrew Shonfeld, *Modern Capitalism* (Oxford, Oxford University Press, 1969); Galbraith, *The New Industrial State;* James O'Connor, *The Fiscal Crisis of the State* (New York: St. Martin's, 1973).

democracies.[82] In Northeast Asia, unlike in Europe or even Latin America, organized labor has traditionally been extremely weak. Popular class or mass organizations find it difficult to gain institutional expression. Taiwan, South Korea, and Japan have long resisted organized union or other mass actions. Again in this regard, the three countries stand quite apart from the Euro-American experience, as well as the situation in Latin America.

In South Korea, for example, President Rhee was able to push through a series of constitutional amendments that weakened the legislature and strengthened the executive. He and subsequent executives were also able to draw on the strong police, army, and civilian bureaucracy (and later the Korean Central Intelligence Agency) to minimize the political viability of popular institutions. This pattern lasted with only minor fluctuations until the 1987 presidential election. For most of its postwar history, Korea has been either a military-dominated or an executive-led, single-party regime. Taiwan is only beginning to show vague hints of political democratization following decades of overt authoritarianism. Neither government is institutionally structured for sensitivity to mass influence, and neither has been seriously threatened to date by the possibility of popular control over the directions given to government-led economic transformation. Japan, arguably as formally representative and free a political democracy as any in the industrialized world, nonetheless forged a tight conservative coalition that for most of the postwar period was also invulnerable to most mass politics. For all three regimes, therefore, big capital's fear of public sector planning was mitigated by the knowledge that government planning would rarely be used against business and for labor or other popular or "antibusiness" sectors.

Organized labor was slow to develop in Japan. Strong state repression combined with entrepreneurial paternalism through the prewar period.[83] As a result, only about 7 percent of the workforce was unionized in the 1930s. During the early U.S. Occupation, union membership leaped to over 50 percent, but then, first the U.S. Occupation and later the Japanese government during the late 1950s and early 1960s broke the most radical of the country's unions. Within Japan's larger firms, labor did become paternally integrated through enterprise unions, but this plant-level bargaining power rarely translated into serious political influence at

82. An important treatment of the ways in which regimes were shaped by such popular sectors and efforts to deal with them in the advanced industrials is Gregory M. Luebbert, *Liberalism, Fascism, or Social Democracy: Social Classes and the Political Origins of Regimes in Interwar Europe* (New York: Oxford University Press, 1991).

83. See, for example, Sheldon Garon, *The State and Labor in Modern Japan* (Princeton: Princeton University Press, 1987), and Andrew Gordon, *The Evolution of Labor Relations in Japan: Heavy Industry, 1853–1955* (Cambridge: Harvard University Press, 1985).

the level of national policymaking. As of the late 1990s, fewer than 26 percent of the workforce was unionized, and more important for political and economic planning purposes, until 1993 (with the exception of a six-month interregnum in 1947–48, when all government policies were subject to veto by the American Occupation) Japan never had a labor-backed government. In the 1990s, labor's advocates pointed with optimism to the unification of much of Japan's labor movement into a single national federation, Rengo, as a sign of possible influence for the labor movement. But the government's administrative reform program during the early 1980s eviscerated the most militant public sector unions, leaving Rengo as a potentially influential, but hardly antiregime, force. Whatever influence Rengo has exerted has been within the broadly accepted parameters of the dominant conservative regime. Certainly the experience of the nominally socialist-led, three-party coalition under Prime Minister Murayama Tomiichi did nothing to carry out European-style, pro-labor and antibusiness policies. Quite the contrary, Murayama virtually renounced all the principles on which the original Japan Socialist Party had initially been formed.

If labor was politically weak in Japan, it was far weaker in South Korea and Taiwan. Virtually none of the limited benefits enjoyed by Japanese labor were available to its counterparts in the early 1990s. Union membership stood at approximately 10 percent of the workforce in South Korea; there were no minimum-wage standards, and strikes and closed shops had long been outlawed. "The labor movement had always been subject to various state controls, through limits on organization and strike activity, through informal penetration, and through government participation in the settlement of disputes; under the new government [of Chun in 1980], the system of industrial relations became even more repressive."[84] Even the liberalization following 1987 subsequently gave way to massive police interventions to break up serious strikes in the 1990s and to antilabor laws in 1996. Only with the election of Kim Dae-Jung in 1997 did Korean labor seem to have an official governmental ally.

In Taiwan, the incoming Chinese nationalist government brought with it most of the repressive labor legislation enacted on the mainland during the protracted civil war.[85] As in Korea until 1987, strikes and collective bargaining were illegal, and unions remained under strong Kuomintang controls, including party control over leadership selection and all union activities.[86] Like Japan, oppressive political conditions were mitigated by

84. Stephan Haggard and Chung-in Moon, "Institutions and Economic Policy: Theory and a Korean Case Study," *World Politics* 42, no. 2 (January 1990): 220.

85. Frederic C. Deyo, "State and Labor: Modes of Political Exclusion in East Asian Development," in Deyo, ed., *The Political Economy of the New Asian Industrialism*, p. 184.

86. Johnson, "Political Institutions and Economic Performance," p. 150.

elements of firm-level paternalism, but this was a long way from collective political influence.

The close cooperation among the state and big business, small farmers, and shopkeepers in all three countries, combined with the systematic exclusion of other popular sectors, especially organized labor, should not disguise the subtle fact that all three regimes remain rather open to *individual* penetration and to *sectoral absorption*. In both ways these regimes demonstrated a certain openness and flexibility that make them hard to disengage from.

Even more fundamental, the low levels of ethnic, religious, linguistic, racial, and other noneconomic divergences in Japan, South Korea, and Taiwan contrast starkly with conditions facing other developing countries, where such differences have often superseded any sense of overriding common nationhood that is the precursor to political and economic legitimacy. Instead, there is a lack of the psychological and emotional integration that Benedict Anderson sees as critical to the creation of the "imagined community" which is the precondition for the modern nation-state.[87] In Japan, Korea, and Taiwan, however, little question exists about the bonds of nationhood, making it much easier for governments and individual businesses to adopt principles of individual, meritocratic mobility.[88]

This is not to accept at face value the prevailing ideologies in Japan, South Korea, and Taiwan stressing family-like unity among all segments of society, such as the "New Life Movement" in Taiwan or the "New Spirit Movement" in South Korea during the 1970s. In all three countries, a seductiveness exists to the overriding sense of nationalism and unity that such slogans seek to convey. That state and society are one, that "all of us" are "in the same boat," and that "we share the same goals" are difficult ideas to dispel in such culturally homogeneous countries.[89] Yet there has been a systematic reduction in rigid class divisions within all three countries, which have manifested comparatively high levels of economic egalitarianism. The pockets of rural power and inequality present in many other late industrializers were forcefully reduced, and high growth has

87. Benedict Anderson, *Imagined Communities* (London: Verso, 1983).

88. This is in dramatic contrast to, for example, Sri Lanka, which after independence from Britain attempted to follow such principles of individual mobility only to find that minority Tamils were "overly" represented in government offices. The result was a series of policies designed to set special advantages for the Buddhist majority, which eventually led to the Tamil effort at cessation and to the long-running civil war. In the Taiwanese case, there was a long-standing effort by former mainlanders to keep local Taiwanese from positions of power, but with the presidency of Lee Tung-hue there has been much more integration.

89. This is clearly much less true for the case of Taiwan, where there is still strong cleavage between the former mainlanders and the indigenous population. At the same time, individual mobility and greed are pervasively seductive among both groups.

been conducive to a sense of regular and steady improvements in personal lifestyles. The result has been the broadscale internalization of official pronouncements that all citizens are in the same boat. Such relative harmonization between state and society, Daniel I. Okimoto has argued, creates a "societal state."[90] Because that societal state is open to individual penetration without the dangers of a politicizing ethnic or linguistic confrontation, societal improvement can be seen as and can actually be relatively generic in quality. In contrast, economic failure is largely accepted as the consequence of personal failures or misfortune, not systematic unfairness in the system as a whole.

Further enhancing egalitarianism and individual mobility in these countries has been the educational system. Mass education was a key component of Japan's nineteenth-century industrialization; by the turn of the century virtually all Japanese children between the ages of six and thirteen were in school, and the level of literacy was at least as high as in most Western countries. Formal educational credentials became a broadly accepted channel for individual mobility into government and the larger business firms.

Japanese colonialism carried this pattern to Taiwan and Korea, and it is a tradition that has been built on indigenously ever since. And as Cumings has noted, the formal school system is bolstered by mass conscription into the military, which provides general education, disciplined training, and national indoctrination to a mass of young people, while rearing officers and managers who later populate state bureaucracies and big corporations.[91]

Education in all three countries has been heavily geared toward the production of technicians, engineers, and businesspeople, which in turn has also been conducive to economic growth based on manufacturing prowess. Education can be a vexing problem for many countries, as can be seen in India, where middle-class aspirations have replicated the British colonial heritage: go to university and become a lawyer, accountant, or civil servant. Indian education (like Britain's) has put far less emphasis on becoming an engineer, a technician, or an entrepreneur. Any such orientations in Taiwan were overcome by the government policy to expand vocational training on a massive scale and to restrict the number of universities.[92] None of the three regimes in question is staggering under the burden of a well-educated but unemployable and economically

90. Daniel I. Okimoto, "Political Inclusivity: The Domestic Structure of Trade," in Takashi Inoguchi and Daniel I. Okimoto, eds., *The Political Economy of Japan*, vol. 2, *The Changing International Context* (Stanford: Stanford University Press, 1988).

91. Cumings, "Northeast Asian Political Economy," p. 69.

92. Jennie Hay Woo, "Education and Economic Growth in Taiwan—a Case of Successful Planning," *World Development* 19, no. 8 (August 1991): 1029–44.

unproductive professional class that has proven so detrimental to industrial transformation and manufacturing vitality in much of South Asia, Latin America, North Africa, and the Middle East.

An important component of education is East Asia has been the relatively egalitarian inclusion of females. (Though none of the three is a model of gender equality, they are far more equal in their treatment of females than most African, Latin American, South Asian, or Middle Eastern countries.) Thus, as Gustav Papanek notes, in most of East Asia from 55 to 63 percent of girls were in primary school in the 1950s, even outside Japan, whereas in India it was 14 percent, and in Pakistan, only 6 percent. By the 1970s, all children in Taiwan and South Korea (as well as the rest of East Asia) were in primary schools, and a third or more were in secondary schools. In contrast, India had only 50 percent of girls in primary schools, while in Bangladesh it was 34 percent and Pakistan 22 percent, with even wider gaps at the level of secondary education.[93] Furthermore, in East Asia the widespread educational system contributes to mass socialization into the prevailing values of the predominant regime, unifying society and providing a girder of underlying societal support. In all three countries as a result, education has served as an important conduit for individual mobility and as a strong underpinning for both industrial development and regime continuity.

Educational channels for individual mobility are complemented by a fine-tuned capacity for sectoral absorption. Over time, all three regimes have shown themselves highly adept at co-opting former political opponents. As most opposition leaders are frozen out of state office, potential opposition groups find it extremely difficult over time to challenge the regime from the outside. Eventually, it becomes highly seductive to enter into various pacts, alliances, and other collaborative arrangements, thus sweeping former opponents into an acceptance of much of the regime's agenda.[94]

Japan's conservative coalition was perhaps the most adept of the three in this regard. The experience of organized labor has been cited above. In addition, one can note the experience of citizens movements formed around environmental issues and around numerous interest groups that once took positions hostile to the regime and a decade or two later were regularly dealing with it on its own terms.[95] One can also point to the

93. Gustav Papanek, "The New Asian Capitalism: An Economic Portrait," in Peter Berger and Hsin-Huang Michael Hsiao, eds., *In Search of an East Asian Development Model* (New Brunswick, N.J.: Transaction, 1988), p. 67.

94. This point is developed extensively for Japan in T. J. Pempel, "The Dilemma of Parliamentary Opposition," *Polity* 8 (Fall 1985): 63–79. It also forms an important part of my concluding essay on one-party dominant regimes in *Uncommon Democracies*.

95. Muramatsu Michio, Itō Mitsutoshi, and Tsujinaka Yutaka, *Sengo Nihon no Atsuryoku Dantai* (Postwar Japanese pressure groups) (Tokyo: Toyo Keizai Shimposha, 1986).

seeming facility with which a fragmented LDP was able in 1993–94 to forge a coalition with its long-standing ideological nemesis, the Democratic Socialist Party of Japan, and reemerge as the key power in government.

The recent experiences of Korea and Taiwan suggest a certain effort to replicate some of the political structures which have so insulated Japan's politics from popular forces and which have been so absorptive of opponents. The KMT has always served as a sponge for upwardly mobile and ambitious individuals in Taiwan. With political liberalization in 1983, Taiwan revised its electoral laws to create a single-vote, multimember district system similar to that which so effectively aided conservative political dominance in Japan.[96] The system provides low entry barriers to new parties, strong rewards to very large parties, and severely penalizes medium-size parties such as the Democratic Progressive Party.[97] Thus far, the electoral system in Taiwan has had an effect similar to Japan's, namely buffering government from the potential power of elections and opposition parties.

Similarly, in South Korea former President Roh Tae Woo managed a merger of three parties into the Democratic Liberal Party, thereby consolidating a support base analogous to that of Japan, while simultaneously isolating the remaining opposition parties. Two of the absorbed opposition parties had shortly before been vowing unalterable opposition to the regime. Suddenly, they were part of it. Before the presidential election of Kim Dae-jung, the party appeared likely to replicate the long dominance of Japan's LDP.

Conducive to the broad sense of national integration and the delegitimation of potential opposition has been what could be called a "hegemonic project," a set of broadscale goals to which important segments of the regime are singularly dedicated and which provides a goal around which to mobilize collective national energy. Although by no means absolute and unrelated to other nationally articulated goals, rapid economic development based on export-led growth has been a key ingredient in the hegemonic project of all three regimes. In Japan, the acceptance of such an economic agenda was virtually unadulterated by other goals during the 1950s and 1960s. It was most vividly articulated in Prime Minister Ikeda's goal of "doubling the national income in ten years" (1960–70). High growth was so widely accepted and pursued that the clichés of "Japan, Inc." and "economic animal" became pervasive epithets worldwide. Subsequent efforts to modulate the singular focus on

96. Arendt Lijphart et al., "The Limited Vote and the Single Nontransferable Vote: Lessons from the Japanese and Spanish Examples," in Bernard Grofman and Arendt Lijphart, eds., *Electoral Laws and Their Political Consequences* (New York: Agathon Press, 1986), pp. 154–69.

97. Tun-jen Cheng, "Democratizing the Quasi-Leninist Regime in Taiwan," p. 495.

high growth came with the environmental movement of the early 1970s, the greater concern with effective use of leisure time in the early 1980s, and the ambulatory search for a new international role for Japan during the late 1980s and early 1990s. Yet the leitmotiv of economic growth has run consistently through all these other orientations. Until the economic bubble burst in 1990 (and for many people long after), it was widely accepted among Japanese that theirs was the world's most dynamic and creative economy and that any future role for the country would have to be predicated on that economic dynamism.[98]

National cohesion around the project of economic growth was helped by the pervasive anticommunism of all three regimes, particularly before the fall of the Berlin Wall in 1989. In Japan, overt anticommunism was widely manifested during the height of the cold war and during the period of bipolar confrontation between Japanese conservatives and the organized political Left into the mid-1960s. This bipolarity was modulated somewhat with time, but the underlying logic continued into the 1980s sweeping along with it virtually all elements of socialism or social democracy. Most indicative of its power were widespread political and business protestations against the coming of the so-called British disease—high social spending, severe labor-management confrontations, and a sapping of economic vitality. The pervasive acceptance of a philosophy of economic growth over economic redistribution could be seen in the relative ease with which the government carried out its programs of administrative reform, sharp budget cuts, and a rollback of the nation's embryonic welfare programs.[99]

Anticommunism was an even more defining property of the regimes in Taiwan and South Korea. Both were founded at the height of East-West tensions, and each faced a tangible enemy in charge of a part of its claimed national territory against which its domestic anticommunism could be readily directed. Spurred in part by U.S. government AID (Agency for International Development) missions, as well as by those of the World Bank, both countries adopted this strategy with vigor. As Woo-Cumings noted for South Korea, economic growth was transformed into a symbol able to mobilize the public: "That symbol in Korea was a number: a talismanic double-digit GNP growth figure that was the Korean score in the race to catch up with Japan and also to surpass the DPRK's [North Korea's] economic performance."[100]

98. This obviously oversimplifies a great deal of Japanese thinking. But it is also relevant that current debates over Japan's new international role hinge most centrally on how it can fruitfully use its economic wealth—in foreign aid, in solving the Latin American debt crisis, in keeping the U.S. domestic debt funded, in defusing North Korean nuclear potential, and so forth.

99. On these economic measures see Shindo Muneyuki, *Zaisei Hattan to Zeisei Kaikaku* (Tokyo: Iwanami Shoten, 1989).

100. Woo, *Race to the Swift*, p. 98.

From the 1960s onward, economic success served as the self-justification for broad, antileftist policies. Cumings notes that in Korea, "the state's relative autonomy from particularistic economic interests, combined with the exclusion of workers and farmers, gives it the capacity to look after the whole in the interest of, but not necessarily at the behest of, certain of the parts."[101] Woo-Cumings has called the result "a social constituency for the state."[102]

The collective mobilization for economic advancement, however, has not been of the laissez-faire variety given such ideological stature in the United States or the United Kingdom. Instead, as I noted in my treatment of the developmental state, the economic policies of all three countries, despite their specific differences, has been "market sustaining" or "market conforming." Each regime has operated with an eye toward world markets, especially in manufacturing and particularly as regards quality and price, and has sought to develop product competitiveness on those bases.

As Johnson has noted, none of these three sees any incompatibility between state control and market competitiveness: "One of the things a state committed to development must do is develop a market system, and it does this to the extent that its policies reduce the uncertainties or risks faced by entrepreneurs, generate and disseminate information about investment and sales opportunities, and instill an expansionist psychology in the people. Once a market system has begun to function, the state must then be prepared to be surprised by the opportunities that open up to it, ones that it never imagined but that entrepreneurs have discovered."[103] An important component of this market compatibility has been the willingness of state officials to exercise discipline not only over labor but over business as well. Government programs were often generous to favored industrial sectors, but international competitiveness was expected in return. Poor performers were penalized; good performers were rewarded. In this way, state authority reinforced market principles, but principles of an international, rather than a domestic, marketplace.

As each of the three states has served as disciplinarian over domestic industries, so too they have functioned as gatekeepers between domestic society and the external world of states and markets. This has by no means been a Sisyphean task. All three have been greatly helped in their external activities by the United States.

External aid, especially from the United States, was critical to the economic success of the three countries. That aid initially came in the form

101. Cumings, "Northeast Asian Political Economy," p. 73.
102. Woo (Woo-Cumings), *Race to the Swift.*
103. Johnson, "Political Institutions and Economic Performance," p. 141.

of military and financial assistance immediately after World War II. And virtually all such aid was filtered through government offices, thereby reinforcing state powers at an important early stage in the regimes' histories. As noted above, since 1945, South Korea has received some $13 billion in American assistance; Taiwan has received about $5.6 billion ($600 per capita in the ROK, $425 per capita in Taiwan).[104] More than two-thirds of Japan's imports in 1947 were covered by U.S. aid; subsequently, Japan benefited tremendously from military procurements during the Korean and Vietnam Wars, and indeed those clearly were two undeniable catalysts to Japan's subsequent and uninterrupted growth.[105] Even more important, over the bulk of the postwar period, American assistance involved opening its own domestic markets to the products of all three on terms that were exceedingly generous and by no means based on reciprocity.

As has been frequently pointed out, such aid resulted from U.S. concerns with world security and strategic alliances. American policies were predicated on the conviction that economic growth by its strategic allies would defuse the potential appeal of anticapitalist ideologies and political parties and contribute mightily to the development of markets for U.S. goods and to overall U.S. economic strength.[106] The long-term strategic and economic hegemony of the United States was congruent with a certain component of short-term generosity.

An important element of this generosity involved a U.S. willingness to allow the governments of Japan, South Korea, and Taiwan not only to fashion export policies that took advantage of the relatively open U.S. and world markets but also to exercise selective protection over their own domestic economies from unwanted foreign investment. In much of Europe and Latin America, U.S. multinationals had been heavy investors in key sectors from at least the early years after World War II; moreover, capital markets there were substantially internationalized. In striking contrast, within Japan, Korea, and Taiwan the governments were able to exercise far greater control over investment capital.

In the Japanese case, this control took several forms. The yen was intimately linked to the dollar at an undervalued and export-enhancing rate of ¥360. The Foreign Exchange and Control Law of 1949 provided a

104. Cumings, "Northeast Asian Political Economy," p. 67.

105. Yutaka Kosai and Yoshitaro Ogino, *The Contemporary Japanese Economy* (Armonk, N.Y.: M. E. Sharpe, 1984); Takafusa Nakamura, *The Postwar Japanese Economy* (Tokyo: University of Tokyo Press, 1981).

106. Philip Armstrong, Andrew Glyn, and John Harrison, *Capitalism since World War II*; Robert Gilpin, *Political Economy of International Relations* (Princeton: Princeton University Press, 1987) chaps. 4, 5; Robert O. Keohane, "Hegemonic Leadership and U.S. Foreign Economic Policy in the 'Long Decade,'" in William P. Avery and David P. Rapkin, eds., *America in a Changing World Economy* (New York: Longman, 1982), chap. 3.

basis for keeping out foreign companies wishing to repatriate profits in dollars (which meant virtually all companies), as well as a means for the Japanese government to reward or punish exporting companies. When liberalization became inevitable in the mid-1960s, Japanese companies were allowed, by ignoring antimonopoly regulations, to engage in extensive cross-holding of one another's stocks, principally to prevent hostile foreign buyouts of Japanese companies. This policy required close coordination among government agencies and with the industrial groups.[107] Meanwhile, insulation of Japan's capital markets kept interest rates low for savers and underwrote exceptionally low rates of interest to favored users of capital. Within this context, the Bank of Japan followed a systematic policy of overloans and "window guidance," designed systematically to encourage industrial expansion and exports.[108]

In South Korea, the government relied heavily on foreign loan capital. The country's security dependence on both the United States and Japan gave Korea access to loan capital in both countries on favorable terms.[109] But most critical to the development of the state was the fact that the government, especially the Economic Planning Board (EPB), controlled the access to and usage of these foreign funds. The EPB also had to approve all proposals for foreign direct investment and technology transfer agreements. The Korean state initially used its powers over these areas to protect infant industries and to keep the Korean populace insulated from foreign consumer goods, and later to move capital into heavy and chemical industries.

In Taiwan the state initially owned many important firms, but large-scale divestment took place in the 1950s, in part owing to new U.S. aid packages. Always more liberal than South Korea toward foreign investment, with numerous export-processing zones (EPs), Taiwan still followed policies that were far from laissez-faire. In both Korea and Taiwan, foreign investors in the export-processing zones were required to export all their output, and both governments made similarly successful demands for investments outside the zones. Taiwan has had local-content

107. Encarnation and Mason point out, however, that when foreign technologies were desired by Japan's "local oligopolists," these latter became important manipulative intermediaries between foreign multinationals and the Japanese government. See "Neither MITI nor America."

108. This summary is based in part on Pempel, "Japanese Foreign Economic Policy"; John Zysman, *Governments, Markets, and Growth: Financial Systems and the Politics of Industrial Change* (Ithaca: Cornell University Press, 1983); and Peter Drucker, "Financial Systems: Europe, America, Japan," in Ezra Vogel, ed., *Modern Japanese Organization and Decision-Making* (Berkeley: University of California Press, 1975).

109. This was especially true after the normalization of relations between Japan and Korea in 1965. The settlement resulted in a highly conflictual contest domestically, however. Haggard, *Pathways from the Periphery*, pp. 197–98.

requirements for a limited range of goods and has made successful demands for local sourcing.[110] Incentives for foreign investors were under government control through the Statute for the Encouragement of Investment. Targeted sectors were all but guaranteed entry; others had to make a special case. The Investment Commission controlled joint ventures and, as did MITI for Japanese industry during much of the 1950s and 1960s, often played a role in negotiating terms more favorable than would be dictated by the simple bargaining power of the two contracting firms.[111] In addition, the state monopolized the banking sector through its ownership of banks moved from the mainland and through majority shares confiscated from Japanese partners in private local banks. Taiwanese bankers were thus state employees keeping finance highly amenable to state policies.[112]

State control over foreign direct investment by South Korea and Taiwan has also been a complement to diplomacy. For Taiwan in particular, the threat of international isolation as a result of most Western states' recognition of the People's Republic of China (PRC) was acute. But by selectively opening up various investment opportunities to the multinationals of major North American and European countries, "economic hostages" were created to ensure a measure of political influence not otherwise possible. South Korea followed much the same strategy after President Carter raised the specter of withdrawing U.S. troops from the peninsula.[113]

The ability to export goods to the United States and the other advanced industrialized countries, combined with the capacity to maintain protected manufacturing and capital markets at home, was vital to the economic success of Japan, South Korea, and Taiwan. Doing so allowed all three to take advantage of relatively open markets worldwide as a means by which to advance their own domestic transformations. In addition, the strategic sustenance given to the three regimes by the U.S. military was of great importance. Military objectives ensured that America would be the external patron for regime success in Northeast Asia; America's strategic policies opened up space for these three countries to pursue their own economic policies. Japan's overall international muscle allowed it some measure of independence from the

110. Ibid., p. 199.

111. Haggard and Cheng, "State and Foreign Capital in the East Asian NICs," pp. 115–16.

112. Gold, *State and Society in the Taiwan Miracle*, p. 108.

113. In this context it is also important at least to note that Japan has begun to fill some of the power vacuum left by a withdrawing United States. This has been true of its expanding foreign aid to both countries, the expansion of its defense perimeter, and especially by its granting in 1983 to South Korea the sum of $4 billion in "aid," a package that was clearly tied to the military barrier provided by Korea for Japan.

United States from early on, but as late as the early 1980s, South Korea and Taiwan could probably not have remained in existence without the international support provided by both the markets and the military of the United States.

Yet a particular economic dependence on the United States remained for Japan as well. The extent of this dependence can be appreciated by a simple question: which country is Japan's number two export market? Virtually every follower of contemporary economic events knows that the United States is Japan's largest export market; generally, the United States took 30–35 percent of Japan's exports for most of the postwar period. In contrast, Japan's number two market, most often South Korea but sometimes (West) Germany, rarely took more than 5 percent of Japan's total exports. In short, the U.S. market was consistently five and a half to six times larger than Japan's number two outlet. In addition, Japan was vitally dependent on U.S. suppliers of food and oil. Thus Japan achieved the status of "world economic superstar" mostly in terms of its GNP, capital holdings, and per capita income; it was far less a world economic power in terms of diversified market sales.

The United States was also the largest market by far for Korea and Taiwan, taking an even larger 38–45 percent of both countries' exports. The second largest partner for each was typically Japan, which absorbed 12–20 percent of their exports. Although such figures do not show quite as large a margin as between Japan's number one and number two markets, an even greater gap exists for South Korea and Taiwan between their number two and number three export markets.[114] Thus, the economic prowess of both these countries is similarly constrained by their one-way trade links to the United States, although these are complemented by links to Japan.[115]

Canada and Mexico are the only other countries more singularly dependent on the U.S. market. No other Western European, African, Australasian, or Middle Eastern countries bear any comparable levels of single-market dependence for their exports. The closest parallel to Japan's singular dependence on the United States in the late 1980s was Bulgaria, which in 1987 sent 52 percent of its goods to the USSR and 5 percent to

114. Data based on Yano Tsuneta Kinenkai, ed., *Nihon Kokusei Zue, 1993* (Tokyo: Kokuseisha, 1993), p. 404, and Keizai Koho Center, *Japan, 1994* (Tokyo: KKC, 1994), pp. 38–39. When I first did this comparison using 1988 data, Hong Kong was the third largest market for Korea and Taiwan behind the United States and Japan. In 1994, Hong Kong was ahead of Japan as an export market for Taiwan, but it remained South Korea's third largest market.

115. This point is different from, but coherent with, that of Walter Hatch and Kozo Yamamura, *Asia in Japan's Embrace* (Cambridge: Cambridge University Press, 1997). They are concerned with showing the ways in which growth throughout Asia, especially in Southeast Asia, is linked to production networks of Japanese-owned firms.

East Germany. And, indeed, it is the former Eastern European bloc that most resembles the trade patterns of South Korea and Taiwan.[116]

When one adds in the security dependence of all three regimes on the United States, as well as foreign direct investments and other capital linkages, it is clear that though their respective states may demonstrate a great deal of control and independence vis-à-vis many segments of domestic society, these are hardly states with the level of autonomy idealized in most literature on international state theory. These regimes are highly dependent on the United States, with Korea and Taiwan secondarily dependent on Japan.[117]

Such dependence helps to explain the shifts in U.S. policy toward all three and the subsequent diffusion of their economic activities during the 1990s. When security concerns were predominant in U.S. foreign policy, the economic growth of Northeast Asia was taken as an inevitable desideratum by U.S. policymakers, even if that growth came at the expense of certain U.S. manufacturers or industries. This orientation began to change with the recognition of the PRC, the loss of the war in Vietnam, the articulation of the Nixon Doctrine and finally the Clintonesque embrace of the amuletic slogan, "It's the economy, stupid." America's changed perspectives eventually crystallized into a drumbeat of pressure on all three countries to open specific segments of their domestic markets to American products and investments, while restricting the quantities of certain exports to the U.S. market. (Japan went on to follow the U.S. lead, negotiating voluntary export agreements with South Korea on textiles in the late 1980s.) It played out subsequently in U.S., G-7, and International Monetary Fund pressures on Japan and South Korea for comprehensive overhauls of their entire financial structures and their policies concerning foreign direct investment in the 1997–98 period.

Overall, therefore, the picture of the regimes that emerges in these three countries is one quite different from the regimes in Europe or most of the so-called Third World. Certainly Japan, the closest approximation of the other advanced industrialized states, has never gone through the stage of being a "social welfare state,"[118] nor has it had the experience of having to accommodate organized labor in one or another form of state-

116. The closest is Austria, with 35 percent going to West Germany and 10 percent to Italy. *Nihon Kokusei Zue*, 1989, pp. 399–400.

117. T. J. Pempel, "Trans-Pacific Torii: Japan and the Emerging Asian Regionalism," in Peter J. Katzenstein and Takashi Shiraishi, eds., *Network Power: Japan in Asia* (Ithaca: Cornell University Press, 1997), pp. 47–82.

118. See, however, the rather stateless argument of Nakagawa that Japan is a "super welfare state," which rests on arguments about private spending for health, education, and the like. Nakagawa, "Japan, the Welfare Super Power," pp. 5–51.

directed neo-or liberal corporatism.[119] It certainly has shown only limited inclinations towards socioeconomic pluralism.

While South Korea and Taiwan unquestionably show similarities to the bureaucratic-authoritarian states of Latin America, they are quite different in having pursued strategies of export-led growth and in having exerted far greater state control over their capital markets and over foreign direct investment. As Evans notes, the transnational corporation came to Korea and Taiwan only in the mid-1960s, by which time "worldwide norms governing relations between Third World states and the transnationals were quite different" from what they had been when U.S. firms entered Latin America.[120] As a result many of the baneful effects attributed to transnational corporations were less severe during the rapid growth periods of South Korea and Taiwan.

The experiences of Japan, South Korea, and Taiwan suggest the absence of generalizable patterns of development that blend them conveniently into typologies based on the Western European or Latin American experiences. Rather, the numerous comparabilities in the regimes in the three countries suggest that they do form the core of a specific type of regime, but these similarities go well beyond those articulated as part of "the developmental state."

One of the main conclusions that emerges from the above analysis is that Japan, South Korea, and Taiwan have pursued a particular approach to capitalism, one in which the government is not driven by presumptions about the desirability of competition as a device to improve choice and lower prices for domestic consumers. Instead, the three Asian countries have created a capitalism with few national political guarantees for organized labor, little impetus toward the social welfare state, high degrees of mercantilism, limited penetration by foreign investment, and few of the problems associated with neocorporatist European planning or extensive public entitlements. They have also generated capitalisms that has been exceptionally dependent on access to the U.S. market (and for Korea and Taiwan, on the Japanese market as well).

They also differ in the international arena. Although the situation changed somewhat in the 1990s, for most of the postwar period all three countries had state bureaucracies that buffered their domestic economies from international financial and capital markets, while domestic industri-

---

119. T. J. Pempel and Keiichi Tsunekawa, "Corporatism without Labor? The Japanese Anomaly," in Philippe Schmitter and Gerhard Lehmbruch, eds., *Trends toward Corporatist Intermediation* (Beverley Hills: Sage, 1979), pp. 231–70.

120. Evans, "Class, State, and Dependence," 206–7.

alists and financiers collaborated in the pursuit of national economic independence. As a result, all three countries reached the 1990s relatively free of the threat of leveraged buyouts, hostile takeovers, and the loss of national control over key industrial sectors. Only with the sweeping Asian financial crisis later in that decade did these principles become subject to major external pressures, particularly in South Korea and Japan.

Furthermore, in comparison with many countries anxious to transform themselves economically, all three underwent successful agrarian reform thus eliminating one of the most powerful impediments to economic growth based on rapid industrialization. Successful export drives, instead of import substitution, in turn expanded the size of their domestic economic pies, substantially reducing some of the worst pressures over issues of distribution and redistribution. Meanwhile, the relative openness of elite positions and the political capacity to absorb potential challengers to regime hegemony mitigated the extremes of domestic political tensions.

How these dynamics will play out in the future is, of course, unclear. What is evident is that both the international economic conditions and the domestic political economies of Japan, Taiwan, and South Korea had changed appreciably by the late 1990s. Whether the tremendous economic successes of the three can continue at their torrid, earlier pace has become highly questionable: the so-called Asian meltdown of 1997–98 makes this particularly clear. At the same time, these states have also reached substantially higher levels of GNP, substantially more sophisticated economies, and far deeper levels of political coherence and stability than virtually anyone would have predicted for them as recently as the 1960s. Firms in all three countries have increased their overseas investment and entered into a host of important cross-national alliances. Hence, despite any future problems the economies of these three countries may confront, all will be facing them from substantially more advantageous positions than they had two or three decades earlier. In this sense, their "developmental regimes" have achieved their most important raisons d'être.

Yet the "developmental regime" may be quite bound by time and geography. It is highly unlikely that potential emulators of the Northeast Asian political economies will enjoy anything like the same favorable international conditions as did Japan, Korea, and Taiwan. When paired with their own deep social divisions, the new international conditions make it this particularly difficult to imagine.

Nor is it likely that the developmental regimes themselves will remain unaltered. Japan, mainly, but the other two to a lesser degree, has begun restructuring its regimes and policies. Liberalization in trade, finance, and investment criteria has advanced in Japan, Korea, and Taiwan. Moreover, all three have witnessed the rise of middle classes no longer fully content with the blind acceptance of the *hegemonic project* of growth for its own sake. Newly created and newly empowered groups have been pressing for changes in state structures and regime policies. In particular, such groups have been poised to challenge the "soft authoritarianism" on which the three regimes initially rested. As Inge once suggested, "A man may build himself a throne of bayonets, but he cannot sit on it." Fundamental changes in the underlying characteristics of these three regimes seem inevitable and under way.

CHAPTER SIX

The Economic Theory of the Developmental State

Ha-Joon Chang

The idea that the state should play a leading role in economic development was central to early development economics.[1] The "Big Push" theory of industrialization put forward by Paul Rosenstein-Rodan and Tibor Scitovsky accorded a crucial role to the state in the developmental process as the coordinator of complementary investment decisions.[2] Alexander Gerschenkron constructed his theory of late development around the increasing need for state involvement in industrial financing that arises from the continuous increase in the minimum efficient scale of production owing to the nature of modern technical progress.[3] Paul Baran identified the absence of such a nationalistic developmental state as found in early capitalist Europe or Meiji Japan as the major cause for the underdevelopment of many poor countries.[4] Gunnar Myrdal argued

1. Of course, the idea was not invented by early development economics of the 1950s and the 1960s. A similar view on the role of the state had been proposed by the German historical school, represented by Friedrich List, who in turn was influenced by the American economists of the eighteenth century such as Alexander Hamilton. See Chalmers Johnson, *MITI and the Japanese Miracle: The Growth of Industrial Policy, 1925–1975* (Stanford: Stanford University Press, 1982), p. 18, and Christopher Freeman, "New Technology and Catching-Up," *European Journal of Development Research* 1, no. 1 (1989). Some trace these ideas back even further, to sixteenth-century Europe—especially England and Venice. See Erik Reinert, "Catching-Up from Way Behind: A Third World Perspective on First World History," in Jan Fargerberg, Bart Verspagen, and Nick von Tunzelmann, eds., *The Dynamics of Technology, Trade, and Growth* (Aldershot: Edward Elgar, 1994).

2. Paul Rosenstein-Rodan, "Problems of Industrialisation of Eastern and South-Eastern Europe," *Economic Journal* 53 (June–September 1943); Tibor Scitovsky, "Two Concepts of External Economies," *Journal of Political Economy* 62, no. 2 (1954).

3. Alexander Gerschenkron, *Economic Backwardness in Historical Perspective* (1962; Cambridge: Harvard University Press, Belknap Press, 1966).

4. Paul Baran, *The Political Economy of Growth* (New York: Monthly Review Press, 1957).

that a major reason for the economic stagnation of many developing countries was the absence of a "hard" state that can override conservative interests in favor of social reform and economic transformation.[5] Simon Kuznets, someone who is not usually associated with the idea of the developmental state, also emphasized the role of the state as the mediator of political conflicts between the "winners" and the "losers" in the process of growth and structural change.[6] Common to all these was the notion that economic development requires a state which can create and regulate the economic and political relationships that can support sustained industrialization—or, in short, a developmental state.

In the late 1970s, however, the tide started turning against the developmental state. Between the late 1970s and the early 1990s, across all social sciences but particularly in economics, there has been a spectacular upsurge of so-called neoliberal ideas, advocating individualism, market liberalization, and contraction of the state.[7] As a result of its rather "unorthodox" nature up to this period, development economics was exposed to a particularly savage attack by the neoliberal "counterrevolutionaries."[8] The main target of this attack was the developmental state, which, as we said earlier, was at the core of many early development theories. The neoliberals not only argued against particular interventionist policies such as import substitution industrialization and financial "repression," but by questioning the fundamentals of political economy behind the traditional notion of the developmental state, they also tried to undermine the very notion that the state could play any positive role (except in the areas of law and order and possibly of physical infrastructure).

Politically, the neoliberal attack centered on the notion of the state as a guardian of public interest, however we define the public interest. Its contention was that the universally valid assumption of self-seeking motives by individuals should also be applied to politics as well as to economics and that it is therefore wrong to believe that the objective of the state, which is ultimately determined by certain individuals, will be commensurate with what is good for society. On this premise, various models of

5. Gunnar Myrdal, *Asian Drama: An Inquiry into the Poverty of Nations* (New York: Twentieth Century Fund, 1968).

6. Simon Kuznets, "Innovations and Adjustment in Economic Growth," in *Population, Capital, and Growth* (London: Heinemann, 1973).

7. For some critical assessments of these ideas, see Ha-Joon Chang, "Explaining 'Flexible Rigidities' in East Asia," in Tony Killick, ed., *The Flexible Economy* (London: Routledge, 1995), and Ha-Joon Chang and Bob Rowthorn, introduction to *Role of the State in Economic Change*, ed. Chang and Rowthorn (Oxford: Oxford University Press, 1995).

8. For surveys, see Albert Hirschman, "The Rise and Decline of Development Economics," in *Essays in Trespassing* (Cambridge: Cambridge University Press, 1981); John Toye, *Dilemmas of Development* (Oxford: Blackwell, 1987); and Tony Killick, *A Reaction Too Far* (London: Overseas Development Institute, 1991).

neo-liberal political economy characterized the state as an organization controlled by interest groups, politicians, or bureaucrats who utilize it for their own self interests, producing socially undesirable outcomes.[9] The possibility that at least some states may be run and influenced by groups whose objectives are not mere self-enrichment or personal aggrandizement but less personal things such as welfare statism or economic modernization was not even seriously contemplated on the ground of the alleged self-seeking motives behind all human actions.

Economically, the neoliberals made the very notion of *developmental* goals redundant by according theoretical primacy to "static" efficiency over "dynamic" efficiency. In the neoliberal models inhabited by agents with perfect foresight, every short-run move is made after taking all its future consequences into account, and therefore the distinction between the short term and the long term is ultimately meaningless.[10] The neoliberals therefore regard the price mechanism as capable of achieving not only optimal short-term allocative efficiency (by not admitting market failures of any significant scale) but also optimal long-run dynamic efficiency. The upshot is that no need exists to discuss "developmental goals" as a separate notion and that letting the price mechanism reign is the best developmental policy. Consequently, the notion of the developmental state became at best redundant and at worst misleading, and the only viable and desirable path to development lay in following the "invisible hand" of market forces, which could not be controlled by the state.

In terms of policy proposal, the neoliberal argument had two closely interrelated components—one more "economic" and the other more "political." The more economic component was the recommendation for a wholesale *liberalization*—often summarized in the phrase, "getting the prices right."[11] "Right prices," to the neoliberals, are the prices that will

9. For a critical review, see Ha-Joon Chang, *The Political Economy of Industrial Policy* (London: Macmillan, 1994), chap. 1.

10. Those neoliberals who are influenced by the Austrian school (for example, Friedrich Hayek, Ludwig Mises, Israel Kirzner) will not agree with this "perfect foresight" assumption. At the same time, they would not accept that there can be any "goal" (short-term or long-term, developmental or not) that can be pursued in a meaningful way by the state at the systemic level. This is because they believe that the "spontaneous order" that emerges out of a *complex* system like the modern industrial economy is beyond all human comprehension and hence cannot be "rationally" constructed. For a classic summary of this view, see Friedrich Hayek, *The Fatal Conceit* (London: Routledge, 1988). Although, in my opinion, the Austrian variety of neoliberalism is much more profound than the neoclassical version in many ways, it remains a minority opinion. Therefore I will not discuss it in any detail. For a critique of the Austrian notion of development, see Ha-Joon Chang, "State, Institutions, and Structural Change," *Structural Change and Economic Dynamics* 5, no. 2 (1994).

11. For a critique, see Alice H. Amsden, *Asia's Next Giant: South Korea and Late Industrialization* (New York: Oxford University Press, 1989). Privatization is another, perhaps politically more prominent, plank in the neoliberal policy recommendation, but it is less central to the issue of the developmental state. The early mainstream position that unequivocally

prevail in totally unregulated (domestic and international) markets. Domestically, "getting the prices right" means deregulation of various product and factor markets. On the international front, this means the opening up of trade and following the comparative advantage dictated by the country's resource endowments (technology is not an issue, as it is assumed to be accessible to everyone on equal terms). In practice, the upshot is that, given their abundant labor, the developing countries are recommended to specialize in labor-intensive products and wind down those capital-intensive industries "wrongly" promoted by past policies.

The more political component of the neoliberal recommendation was *depoliticization* of the economic policymaking and implementation process. The neoliberals see any political determination of economic outcome as essentially leading either to social waste (for example, the rent-seeking theory) or to the dominance of minority interest over the majority interest (for example, the regulatory capture theory, the predatory state theory, the self-seeking bureaucrats theory). They argue, therefore, that any pursuit of self-interests that is not disciplined by market forces (politics being the most dominant form of such pursuit) will lead to socially harmful results, making it necessary to depoliticize the economy. In their view depoliticization is to be achieved through the contraction of the state (through deregulation and opening up) as well as through the destruction (or at the least restrictions) of interest groups.

A CRITIQUE OF THE NEOLIBERAL PROPOSAL

The Limits to Liberalization

The neoliberals recommend a wholesale market liberalization, which, they argue, will allow countries to reduce "wastes" in their economic systems, making them use resources in the most efficient way. To many people in the developing countries, such a proposal has a strong appeal, in view of the apparently enormous "wastes" that have been created by previous interventionist policies in many of these countries—excess ca-

---

supports privatization in developing countries is best set out in World Bank, *World Development Report, 1983* (New York: Oxford University Press, 1983). Critics of this position can be found in Paul Cook and Colin Kirkpatrick, eds., *Privatization in Less Developed Countries* (New York: Harvester Wheatsheaf, 1988), and Ha-Joon Chang and Ajit Singh, "Public Enterprises in Developing Countries and Economic Efficiency: A Critical Examination of Analytical, Empirical, and Policy Issues," *UNCTAD Review* 4 (1993). More recently, the World Bank produced a new report espousing a less extreme position, *Bureaucrats in Business* (New York: Oxford University Press, 1995). However, this report still does not fully address the earlier criticisms. See Ha-Joon Chang and Ajit Singh, "Can the Large Firms Be Run without Being Bureaucratic?" *Journal of International Development* 9, no. 6 (1997).

pacity, protection of high-cost producers, resources spent in seeking protection and privilege (the so-called rent-seeking costs), and so on. On a closer look, however, this view reveals some fundamental problems.

The first problem with the neoliberal argument for liberalization is that of "market failures," in the sense that individually rational decisions made in a decentralized manner in response to price signals can lead to collectively inefficient outcomes.[12] In other words, there are many good reasons for a state to intervene that even the neoliberals cannot reject.[13] Of course, most neoliberals brush aside the importance of market failures on the ground that they are few and far between in real life, or assert that the alternative (namely, state intervention of some sort) is even worse, because it will result in what they call "government failure."[14] Whichever way they try to evade this problem, the fact remains that areas exist in which the market mechanism simply does not work. In the absence of concrete empirical evidence, the neoliberal argument that market failures are either insignificant or the lesser of the two evils remains a pure assertion.

More important, the neoliberals put emphasis on the attainment of static allocative efficiency at the cost of dynamic efficiency (which is closely related to developmental goals). They usually do not differentiate between these notions of efficiency, sometimes misleading one to believe that achieving static allocative efficiency will automatically lead to dynamic efficiency.[15] However, there is neither a coherent theoretical case nor robust empirical evidence for this to be the case.[16] Even if it was true that a more deregulated economy will lead to higher allocative efficiency (this is not necessarily the case, as I argue in note 13), there is no theory that tells us that it will lead to higher dynamic efficiency. For example, as Joseph Schumpeter and his followers have argued, innovation often requires

12. For a good summary, see Andrew Schotter, *Free Market Economics: A Critical Appraisal* (New York: St. Martin's Press, 1985).

13. What is known among the economists as the Second Best Theorem informs us that liberalizing more (but not all) markets does not necessarily guarantee higher allocative efficiency. In other words, as far as a total liberalization is not possible, there is no *guarantee* that a (partial) liberalization will bring about an improvement, even in terms of static allocative efficiency. On this point, see Ha-Joon Chang, "The Political Economy of Industrial Policy in Korea," *Cambridge Journal of Economics* 16, no. 2 (1993): 133.

14. Anne O. Krueger, "Government Failures in Development," *Journal of Economic Perspectives* 4, 3 (1990). For criticisms, see Helen Shapiro and Lance Taylor, "The State and Industrial Strategy," *World Development* 18, no. 6 (1990), and Ha-Joon Chang, *The Political Economy of Industrial Policy*, chaps. 1–2.

15. World Bank, *World Development Report* (New York: Oxford University Press, 1983), and ibid., 1991.

16. Lance Taylor, "Review of *World Development Report,* 1991 by the World Bank," *Economic Development and Cultural Change* 41, no. 2 (1993).

complex institutional arrangements that cannot be provided by arm's-length market relationships and maximum price competition, which the neoliberals aim to attain through liberalization.[17] This means that there may be certain trade-offs between static and dynamic efficiencies.[18]

Even if "freeing the market" were the best path to economic development, there is still the problem of defining what constitutes a "free market,"[19] because it is impossible to determine how "free" a particular market is without making moral judgments regarding the legitimacy of the system of rights underlying that market. For example, is a (hypothetical) labor market that is subject to laws banning child labor (and no other regulation) a "free" labor market? Most people living in twentieth-century OECD (Organization for Economic Cooperation and Development) economies would regard it as a "free" market, whereas the nineteenth-century English capitalists (or indeed many twentieth-century Third World capitalists) would regard it as a "regulated" market. This shows that what a society regards as the *legitimate* system of rights differs across time and place and that a "free" market cannot be defined without reference to the system of rights regarded as legitimate by the society in question. As there are always disputes and struggles going on about defining the legitimate system of rights, defining how "free" a market is may not be as obvious as the neoliberals think.

Moreover, the neoliberal recommendation for liberalization lacks any institutional specifications for the "free economy." From their recommendation it is not clear what kind of markets are necessary, who should be allowed to participate in which markets, what rights and duties each should have, and who is going to regulate these relationships and how. When it comes to practical policy suggestions, their recommendation amounts to the proposition that developing countries should copy the Anglo-Saxon economic institutions characterized by arm's-length relationships between contracting partners (and very highly stylized versions of them at that).[20] However, as demonstrated by recent theoretical developments in

17. Joseph Schumpeter, *Capitalism, Socialism, and Democracy* (New York: Harper and Brothers, 1942). More recent works in this vein can be found in Bengt-Åke Lundvall, ed., *National Systems of Innovation* (London: Pinter, 1992), and Richard Nelson, ed., *National Innovation Systems* (Oxford: Oxford University Press, 1993). This is not to argue that more oligopolistic market structures or more "relational" contracting arrangements will *necessarily* lead to a higher rate of innovation.

18. For more details, see Ha-Joon Chang, "Political Economy of Industrial Policy in Korea," pp. 133–34.

19. For a more detailed discussion, see Ha-Joon Chang, "The Economics and Politics of Regulation," *Cambridge Journal of Economics* 21, no. 6 (1997).

20. It is understandable, given their political biases, that the neoliberal economists do not recognize the positive role of strong centralized unions (as in Scandinavia), but it is cu-

institutional economics, many economic problems require institutional solutions that go beyond arm's-length contracts—relational contracting, networks, and hierarchies.[21] Also, many more recent studies have shown that a considerable degree of diversity exists in institutional configuration, even among the "market" economies.[22] The neoliberal belief that there is only one "correct" theory which prescribes one "correct" institutional configuration applicable to any country is unwarranted.[23] Their assertion that this configuration is exemplified by the Anglo-Saxon economies is especially inappropriate, when many Anglo-Saxon people themselves have been questioning whether "other" (say, the German or the Japanese) ways of organizing the capitalist economy may be superior to their way.

Thus, the neoliberal recommendation for market liberalization has some critical limitations. In addition to the rather well known problem that it underestimates the extent of market failures, it does not ade-

---

rious that they also ignore the positive role of industry associations or centralized employers associations (as in many Continental European and East Asian economies), even if this is presumably a very "pro-business" thing. It is also worth noting that the neoliberal recommendation for financial liberalization is based on the model of the Anglo-Saxon financial system with an arm's-length relationship between the firms and the banks, not the bank-dominated German one or the state-dominated French or Japanese one. There is, of course, no mention of the possibility that the other systems may be superior to the Anglo-Saxon system in many ways. On the diversity of financial institutions across capitalist economies, see John Zysman, *Governments, Markets, and Growth: Financial Systems and the Politics of Industrial Change* (Oxford: Martin Robertson, 1983).

21. For example, see Richard Langlois, ed., *Economics as a Process* (Cambridge: Cambridge University Press, 1986).

22. Zysman, *Governments, Markets, and Growth;* Peter Katzenstein, *Small States in World Markets* (Ithaca: Cornell University Press, 1985); and Jukka Pekkarinen, Matti Pohjola, and Bob Rowthorn, eds., *Social Corporatism* (Oxford: Oxford University Press, 1992), are early examples. More recent examples include Suzanne Berger and Ronald Dore, eds., *Global Capitalism and National Diversity* (Cambridge: MIT Press, 1996); Ha-Joon Chang, "Markets, Madness, and Many Middle Ways: Some Reflections on the Institutional Diversity of Capitalism," in Philip Arestis, Gabriel Palma, and Malcolm Sawyer, eds., *Essays in Honour of Geoff Harcourt,* vol. 2, *Markets, Unemployment, and Economic Policy* (London: Routledge, 1997); and Colin Crouch and Wolfgang Streeck, eds., *Political Economy of Modern Capitalism* (London: Sage, 1997).

23. Ha-Joon Chang and Richard Kozul-Wright, "Organising Development: Comparing the National Systems of Entrepreneurship in Sweden and South Korea," *Journal of Development Studies* 30, no. 4 (1994). One obvious reason for this diversity is that conditions facing different countries, on the one hand, and the "raw material" from which these institutions are to be built (for example, political culture, social norms), on the other hand, are different across countries, which means that different countries require different institutional configurations to deal with their problems. This is widely acknowledged—even by some neoliberals. Unfortunately this acknowledgment is made in a way that is highly biased toward the Anglo-Saxon model. For example, people who recommend that less developed countries (LDCs) institute an Anglo-Saxon type of stock market would wince at the suggestion that they may be advised to institute, say, Japanese lifetime employment schemes.

quately address the question of dynamic efficiency, it does not tell us what exactly is a free market (in terms of the rights-duties system underlying it), and it does not tell us what it means to "liberalize" in institutional terms other than trying to replicate some highly idealized version of Anglo-Saxon economic institutions.

The Limits to Depoliticization

The neoliberal attack was, more than anything else, a "political economy" attack. The neoliberals argued that the apparent policy "errors" in many less developed countries (LDCs) had deeper causes than the technical incompetence of their bureaucracies or the "irrational" goals imposed by the political rulers, namely, the nature of interest groups and the nature of the state.[24] This was something of a fresh look, at the subject, which had been slowly taken over by technocratic approaches during the 1960s and the 1970s (recall the developments of mathematical programming, social cost-benefit analysis, and computable general equilibrium models in this period), reducing the problem of development to that of accounting and balancing.[25]

Another claim of the neoliberal political economy was that it was "populist" in advocating the interests of the "silent majority," namely, the rural poor and unskilled urban workers. Adherents argued that in most developing countries the urban interest groups—protected oligopolies and the labor aristocracy in the "modern" sector—have disproportionate access to the government decision-making machine. Hence governments in developing countries adopt policies that support uncompetitive industries employing overpaid skilled workers, imposing the costs on powerless rural populations and unskilled workers in the forms of high manufacturing prices and high unemployment.[26] By adding a dose of populism to their conservatism, the neoliberals could boast of their "political correct-

24. This is reminiscent of the Dependency Theory, which regarded "irrational" policies as the outcome of the manipulation of the state apparatus by the "comprador" ruling elite. On this point, see John Toye, "Is There a New Political Economy of Development?" in Christopher Colclough and John James Manor, eds., *States or Markets? Neo-liberalism and the Development of Policy Debate* (Oxford: Clarendon Press, 1991).

25. It was probably for the same reason that the Dependency Theory, which also was a political economy critique of early development economics, was popular during the early days of neoliberal counterrevolution.

26. This is the so-called urban bias argument. See Michael Lipton, *Why Poor People Stay Poor: A Study of Urban Bias in World Development* (London: Temple Smith, 1977); Robert Bates, *Markets and States in Tropical Africa* (Berkeley: University of California Press, 1981); and World Bank, *World Development Report* (New York: Oxford University Press, 1990). For a critique, see Terry Byres, "Of Neo-populist Pipe-Dreams: Daedalus in the Third World and the Myth of Urban Bias," *Journal of Peasant Studies* 2 (1979).

ness" and chastise advocates of "structuralist" policies as defenders of the "conservative interests" of big government, big business, and big labor.[27]

Having launched a "political" economy attack, however, the neoliberal political economists wanted to get rid of politics altogether by depoliticizing the economy, for they regarded politics as an "irrational" corrupting force that prevents a rational management of the economy. The neoliberals hold that the conflicting desires of different individuals and groups can be best reconciled by the "invisible hand" of the competitive market and that "political" resolutions of these differences will subject the process to abuses by those with privileged access to political power. On this view, a competitive market populated by "insignificant" agents provides an "objective" solution that cannot be politically manipulated, whereas state intervention opens the door for sectional interests to assert themselves through their influences on the state decisions regarding the distribution of resources.

Thus, the argument goes, if the pursuit of self-interests by individuals leads to socially beneficial outcomes in the market and socially harmful results in politics (by "corrupting" economic policies of the government), would it not be better to depoliticize the economy by emasculating those who can exercise political influence on government economic policies (namely, politicians, bureaucrats, and interest groups)? This is a powerful argument. In my opinion, this recommendation, rather than its proposal for market liberalization, will remain the most long-lasting legacy of the neoliberal counterrevolution. The recommendation is not without serious problems, however.

First, the fundamental assumption behind the neoliberal political economy is that self-interest prevails in the polity in the same manner as in the economy. But the validity of the self-interest assumption is problematic even in the realm of "pure" economics (if such a thing exists).[28] When it comes to politics, it becomes even more so. Rightly or wrongly, politicians and bureaucrats regard themselves as guardians of public interests, while many interest groups would also regard at least part of their activities as serving some "public" purpose. This is partly because the process of "political" (as opposed to "economic") socialization inculcates less self-oriented views into people but also because there are more institutional constraints on self-seeking in politics than in the marketplace.

Second, it is not clear whether a thorough depoliticization is a politi-

27. Ha-Joon Chang, "Review of *New Directions in Development Economics*, edited by A. K. Dutt and K. Jameson," *International Review of Applied Economics* 7, no. 2 (1993).

28. Michael McPherson, "Limits of Self-Seeking: The Role of Morality in Economic Life," in David Colander, ed., *Neoclassical Political Economy* (Cambridge: Ballinger Publishing, 1984).

cally feasible option. For good or bad reasons, all countries have accumulated politically organized groups and have developed ways to modify certain market outcomes "politically". Some of these could be easily eliminated, whereas others may be so entrenched that they can be eliminated only at very high political and economic costs: hence the apparent paradox that radical economic liberalization frequently requires harsh authoritarian politics, as well as a high degree of depoliticization.[29] The liberalization attempts by the Pinochet regime in Chile is a classic example. But in the end, depoliticization can never be complete in practice, and at best it amounts to destroying certain interest groups (say, labor unions) while allowing others to exercise their powers even more (say, capitalist groupings).

Third, it is not clear whether depoliticization is an "economically" attractive option (see "Conflict Management," below, for a more systematic argument). In a world full of assets with limited mobility (highly task-specific equipment, very firm-specific or industry-specific skills), those who own such assets will have a large incentive to resist the economic changes that will threaten their positions. This will not be a problem, of course, *if* the complete depoliticization envisaged by the neoliberals can be achieved, as then the only alternative for the losers is to accept the market outcome (whatever they may want). However, if such a high degree of depoliticization is not obtainable, the losers can at least obstruct the necessary changes, if not completely thwart them. In such a case, a more overtly political management of the developmental process may be better, if it is done *in a forward-looking manner*. Empirical studies show that in some of the more successful economies (the East Asian countries and the Scandinavian countries), structural changes have been managed in a highly politicized way, especially in times of economic crisis that call for large-scale and rapid change.[30]

To summarize, given that the degree of depoliticization envisaged in the blueprint for the neoliberal "brave new world" is not practicable, politicizing certain "economic" decisions may not only be inevitable but also desirable, because the world is full of assets with limited mobility and owners who are (naturally) determined to prevent changes that threaten their current positions. Of course, politicization of economic policymaking and implementation processes can lead to the abuse of state power by certain powerful groups, as the neoliberals fear. Indeed, there may be a case for a certain degree of depoliticization under certain cir-

---

29. See also Andrew Gamble, *The Free Economy and the Strong State: The Politics of Thatcherism* (London: Macmillan, 1988).

30. For a summary of the literature, see Chang, "State, Institutions, and Structural Change."

cumstances.[31] The appropriate way to deal with the danger of overpoliti-cization is to reform the state so that it can become better at "politically" managing the economy without too much costs.

RECONSTRUCTING THE DEVELOPMENTAL STATE

In the previous section I argued that the neoliberal critique of the developmental state is based on shaky grounds. Despite the pretense that long-run developmental goals can be achieved simply by attaining maximum allocative efficiency in the short run, such goals cannot be met simply by "getting the prices right." Neoliberals insist that an activist state will inevitably lead to the "corruption" of economic policymaking (which is true to an extent under certain conditions), but an explicitly "political" management of the economy may be better in a world full of assets with limited mobility, as far as this is done with an eye to long-term "developmental" goals.

The above points to one direction: namely, the need for the reconstruction of the developmental state. This state takes the goals of long-term growth and structural change seriously, "politically" manages the economy to ease the conflicts inevitable during the process of such change (but with a firm eye on the long-term goals), and engages in institutional adaptation and innovation to achieve those goals. In the following I outline what I think are the necessary functions that such a state must perform.

Coordination for Change

The most important insight from early development economics was that systemic changes need coordination. For example, the basic insight behind the Big Push theories was that people in developing countries do not invest in new industries because they do not know whether other, complementary investments will come along; therefore there needs to be a centralized coordination of investment plans. This insight has been more or less forgotten in the neoliberal upsurge. The neoliberal belief, in contrast, is that once people are allowed to pursue their interests to the maximum extent, all possible improvements can and will be achieved through totally decentralized, voluntary private contracting.

As recent developments in the literature on technical change have informed us, however, the existence of a better alternative does not neces-

31. For example, this especially applied to the communist economies before their recent collapse.

sarily mean the advent of a change, and a centralized coordination may be needed for that alternative to be realized.[32] When interdependence prevails between economic agents, changes would not automatically be made without the (explicit and implicit) guarantee of complementing changes. As Moses Abramovitz argues, if "the capital stock of a country consists of an intricate web of interlocking elements," then "it is difficult to replace one part of the complex with more modern and efficient elements *without a costly rebuilding of other components.* . . . "[T]his may be handled efficiently if all the costs and benefits are internal to a firm," but when the capital stock is *"interdependent in use but divided in ownership"* and thus the accompanying costs and benefits of change are divided among different firms and industries, "the adaptation of old capital structures to new technologies may be a difficult and halting process."[33]

Although it is possible that the potential investors in complementary projects devise a contract between themselves, such a contract may be costly to draw up and monitor, especially when it involves a large number of agents. State intervention in this case may cut the transaction costs involved in such contracts sharply. Such intervention need not involve financial resources like subsidies. Governmental announcement, as in the French and East Asian "indicative planning" exercises, may suffice, if it can provide "focal points" for coordination between complementary investments.[34] Of course, financial incentives provided by the state—say, for cooperative research in new industries—may make the state's commitment to its announcement more credible by serving as a "signaling" device. Thus, industrial policy that coordinates complementary investment decisions may be essential for, rather than an obstacle to, economic change in a world of interdependence.

Provision of Vision

The developmental process requires more than what I have just described—namely, coordinating a simultaneous move from a low-equilib-

32. For a more detailed discussion, see Chang, The *Political Economy of Industrial Policy*, pp. 74–76. As the famous story of the QWERTY keyboard tells us, people do not invest in a superior technology in the face of what economists call "network externalities," because a unilateral change may penalize them. See Paul David, "Clio and the Economics of QWERTY," *American Economic Review* 75, no. 2 (1985).

33. Moses Abramovitz, "Catching Up, Forging Ahead, and Falling Behind," *Journal of Economic History* 46, no. 2 (1986): 401–2; italics mine.

34. Chang, *The Political Economy of Industrial Policy*, p. 53. On the practice of indicative planning in France, see Stephen Cohen, *Modern Capitalist Planning: The French Model*, 2d ed. (Berkeley: University of California Press, 1977), and Peter Hall, *Governing the Economy* (Cambridge: Polity Press, 1987). On Japan, see Johnson, *MITI and the Japanese Miracle*. On Korea, see Chang, "The Political Economy of Industrial Policy in Korea."

rium to a high-equilibrium state.[35] This is because economic development, as Albert Hirschman said a long time ago in his critique of Big Push models, "depends not so much on finding optimal combinations for given resources and factors of production as on calling forth and enlisting for development purposes resources and abilities that are hidden, scattered, or badly utilised."[36] If we agree with this view of development, the problem facing a state promoting development is not only that of identifying and moving to an optimal state in a given "choice set" but also that of formulating the "choice set" itself.

As there are certain decisions that can be made sensibly only at the national level, the state, as the sole agent that has the potential (if not the actuality) of representing the national interest, has to formulate the choice sets required for those decisions by providing a "vision" for the future of the economy.[37] This vision has to be such that it should be able to address the issues of long-term development, which, as I argued earlier, cannot be dealt with adequately by blindly following current price signals. This means that there is an important "entrepreneurial" dimension in the role of the developmental state.

Seeing the state as an entrepreneurial agent which provides vision means that, unlike in the early Big Push theory, what the state should do to promote development becomes much less obvious; therefore there is a danger of its "entrepreneurial vision" proving wrong later. This does not mean, however, that the state should not perform such function, because *any* entrepreneurial vision, be it private or public, runs the danger of proving wrong.[38] In fact, in a world where there is no such danger, entrepreneurship would have been redundant in the first place, for if there is perfect foresight, no one can introduce an element of "surprise" into the world, which is the essence of entrepreneurship. Thus, what is necessary is not to dismiss state entrepreneurship as risky but to build a mechanism that will enable the state to put together and compare different visions

35. As interpreted by Joseph Stiglitz, "Alternative Tactics and Strategies in Economic Development," in A. K. Dutt and K. Jameson, eds., *New Directions in Development Economics* (Aldershot: Edward Elgar, 1992).

36. Albert Hirschman, *The Strategy of Economic Development* (New Haven: Yale University Press, 1958), p. 5.

37. Chang, "State, Institutions, and Structural Change"; Ha-Joon Chang and Bob Rowthorn, "Role of the State in Economic Change: Entrepreneurship and Conflict Management," in Chang and Rowthorn, eds., *Role of the State in Economic Change*.

38. Nevertheless, such a problem is significantly abated under the condition of late development, when the late developer can watch the leaders and learn from their experiences. On this point, see R. Dore, *Flexible Rigidities: Industrial Policy and Structural Adjustment in the Japanese Economy, 1970–80* (London: Athlone Press, 1986), p. 135, and Chang, *The Political Economy of Industrial Policy*, p. 81.

that exist in the society and to create a consensus out of them. Japan provides useful lessons of how to do this.[39]

Institution Building

If the "entrepreneurial vision" held by the state is to be realized, the state, as the ultimate guarantor of property (and other) rights, has to provide necessary institutions to make it a reality. In fact, the success of private entrepreneurship itself also critically depends on the construction of new institutional vehicles for the realization of its vision. This is another important function of the developmental state.

It is well known that many developmental states, from nineteenth-century Germany to present-day Korea, have played a crucial role in institution building. They adapted institutions from advanced countries (for example, "model factories" in Prussia or Meiji Japan, Korea learning the art of industrial policy from Japan) and invented new institutions (for instance, codetermination in Germany, lifetime employment in Japan, export-monitoring system in Korea), which proved critical for their development. In addition, now increasingly more people point out that even the apparently "nondevelopmental states" of the United Kingdom and the United States engaged in extensive institution-building, at least in the initial stages of their development.[40]

Institution building is by no means easy and cannot result in "optimal" outcomes. The process of institutional adaptation and innovation is an uncertain process, and it is by no means clear that what the state thinks are "good" institutions will in fact be good for the society.[11] Nevertheless, this does not mean that such an attempt at institution building should be abandoned, for such problems are common to all cases of adaptation and

39. See Johnson, *MITI and the Japanese Miracle*; Dore, *Flexible Rigidities*; Geoffrey Renshaw, *Adjustment and Economic Performance in Industrialised Countries* (Geneva: International Labour Office, 1986); and Daniel Okimoto, *Between MITI and the Market: Japanese Industrial Policy for High Technology* (Stanford: Stanford University Press, 1989). "Consensus" should not be interpreted as an outcome of a harmonious decision-making process involving all relevant agents. In the real world, consensus typically emerges out of a conflict-ridden process that often excludes many potentially relevant agents from the decision-making process. Indeed, a large part of politics is about deciding who is going to be included in or excluded from the decision-making process.

40. On the United Kingdom, see Karl Polanyi, *The Great Transformation* (Boston: Beacon Press, 1957), and R. Coase, *The Firm, the Market, and the Law* (Chicago: University of Chicago Press, 1988); on the United States, see R. Kozul-Wright, "The Myth of Anglo-Saxon Capitalism: Reconstructing the History of the American State," in Chang and Rowthorn, eds., *Role of the State in Economic Change*.

41. The Austrian school was extremely skeptical of attempts at state-led institution building, or what they call "rational constructivism."

innovation, whether they be technological or organizational or performed by business enterprises or by the state.[42] Another difficulty in the process of institution building is the possibility of many conflicts, partly owing disagreements over the acceptable distribution of property (and other) rights that will result from the new institutions and partly owing to the fact that different institutional structures have assorted implications for various objectives (growth, equity, efficiency), which groups value differently.[43] Such conflicts can easily thwart institutional changes that bring about improvements. To summarize, the uncertainty and the conflicts inherent in the process of institution building mean that, although necessary, institution building by the state (or for that matter by anyone) cannot be expected to produce "optimal" outcomes.

Conflict Management

Economic development involves shifting resources from such low-productivity activities as agriculture into high-productivity activities like manufacturing. With perfectly mobile factors of production, this shift should not cause a problem, as owners of those productive assets needing alternative employment will easily be able to switch to the next best option, whose return will be only "marginally" lower (in a perfectly competitive economy). But when the mobility of certain physical and human assets is limited, their owners will face the prospect of "obsolescence, unemployment and income differentials," *if* they accept the market outcome.[44] For this reason, those who have invested in particular physical capital, skills, contractual relationships, and even political patronage are likely to resist changes, thereby often provoking counteractions from other groups. This makes the developmental process potentially very conflictual. Dealing with the conflicts that arise out of such resistance and the counteractions to them is another important function of the developmental state.

The question is not whether the state should be involved in such conflicts, because, as the ultimate guarantor of property and other rights in the society, it is bound to be. The real question is how the state can man-

42. Essays in Eric Hobsbawm and Terence Ranger, eds., *The Invention of Tradition* (Cambridge: Cambridge University Press, 1983), show how even many cultural "traditions" have been "invented" through conscious effort.

43. For example, take the case of monopolies. If "allocative efficiency" is the ideal, one should destroy all monopolies. If faster technical progress is the objective, one may want to be more permissive to monopolies. Alternatively, one may want to restrict monopolies for the sake of equity. Now, different groups will value these objectives (allocative efficiency, technical progress, and equity) variously, but there is no theory that tells us how much weight each of them should have. Thus there is no "scientific" solution to this conflict.

44. Kuznets, "Innovations and Adjustment," p. 204.

age such conflict in a forward-looking manner or, more concrete, help different groups in the society to come to an (explicit or implicit) agreement by which the losers would accept the need for adjustment and the gainers would compensate them for the burdens of such adjustment.[45]

As the neoliberals will be only too eager to point out, state management of conflict will involve some degree of "politicization" of economic policymaking, and I agree that excessive politicization may be undesirable in many respects.[46] But the boundary between the economic and the political is not something "naturally" given but something that can vary across time and place.[47] In the end, all prices are *potentially* political, and there is no "scientific" rule that will tell us which prices should be "political" and which should not be. In all capitalist economies, the two critical prices that affect almost every sector—namely, wages (especially when considering immigration control and labor standards) and interest rates—are politically determined to a very large degree. When we add to them those numerous regulations in the product markets regarding safety, pollution, import contents, and so on, there is virtually no price that is free from politics.[48] If this is the case, little reason exists to assume any inherent supremacy of the "market solution" over a more politicized management of the economy, as the neoliberals would have one believe.

Conflict management should not be seen as simply the "social" or "human" dimension of an essentially economic adjustment—as implied by discussion of a safety net in Eastern European reform or "adjustment with human face" in International Monetary Fund stabilization programs in LDCs. The state in its role as the conflict manager can be seen as providing "insurance" to the members of the society by providing them a governance structure that will guarantee some "fair" level of income to all under even the most adverse circumstances. This insurance function of the state is related to, but by no means the same as, the notion that the welfare state improves allocative efficiency through the pooling of risk. For one thing, a state that pools risk through the welfare state is dealing

45. On different methods of conflict management, see Chang, "State, Institutions, and Structural Change."

46. For example, in the former Communist countries, excessive politicization created numerous problems, such as the "waste" of time and resources in bargaining, the difficulty of setting "objective" performance standards, the difficulty of containing certain redistributive demands, and so on.

47. In many developing countries, strikes are banned, and therefore striking, an activity that is regarded as "economic" in most OECD economies, becomes a "political" act.

48. A vivid example of this is the political row surrounding coal mine closures in Britain in 1992. During the process of the debate, it slowly emerged that the allegedly "objective" world market prices of coal, which the "politically" protected British miners were told to accept, are in fact determined by the "political" decisions of the German government to subsidize its coal, of the French government to subsidize its export of nuclear electricity, and of the Colombian government to allow child labor in its coal mines.

with calculable risks, whereas a state that provides governance through conflict management is dealing with uncertain contingencies, which do not permit probabilistic calculation. Moreover, such an insurance function can improve the productivity of the economy in the medium to long run by encouraging risk taking in general (the good, old "socialization of risk" for investment activities) and investments in assets with limited mobility (a point that has rarely been discussed before)—although it can harm the economy when it creates too much room for "moral hazard." In societies in which the state fails to manage conflict in an appropriate way, people will be reluctant to take risks or commit their resources in specific investments, thus the dynamism of the economy may suffer.[49]

CONCLUSION

In this chapter I have questioned the validity of the neoliberal policy proposal on the grounds that the degree of market liberalization and depoliticization envisaged in the neoliberal scheme is neither feasible nor desirable. I have tried to show the continuing need for a developmental state, something that has been disparaged and made redundant by the neoliberals. What I suggested as the central functions of the developmental state go far beyond correcting for market failures in the conventional sense. They include coordination for large-scale changes, provision of "entrepreneurial" vision, institution building, and conflict management, which, with the possible exception of the first function, cannot be easily accommodated within the narrow confines of mainstream economics. I contend that an approach richer in institutional texture and more sophisticated in its understanding of politics is called for.

Making a case for the developmental state does not necessarily mean ignoring the costs associated with active interventionist policies. Such costs are real and can be important in certain cases, although they are not usually as high as the neoliberals make them out to be. Various costs associated with informational problems in relation to policy design and implementation and with rent seeking need to be considered. The danger of the expropriation of the state apparatus by various individuals and groups (including the political rulers and the bureaucrats) for their "sectional" interests has to be taken seriously as well.

The appropriate response to the above-mentioned problems of state intervention should be the reform of the state in order that it can prop-

49. For example, in some developing countries the lack of a reliable mechanism for conflict resolution discourages industrial investments and encourages the holding of such liquid assets as gold, foreign currency, and, if the government is expected to last for at least the foreseeable future, money.

erly deal with such dangers, rather than a wholesale "rolling back" of the state. As I have discussed in my previous work, there are many relatively simple institutional changes that can reduce various costs associated with state intervention.[50] Examples of successful state reform that produced effective developmental states, as seen in nineteenth-century Prussia, Meiji Japan, postwar France, post-1949 Taiwan, or post-1961 Korea, may be relatively rare, but they are still numerous enough to give us some hope that such reform is indeed feasible and can lead to remarkable outcomes.

50. Chang, *The Political Economy of Industrial Policy*, pp. 33–44 and 79–89.

CHAPTER SEVEN

The Economics of Successful State Intervention in Industrial Transformation

Juhana Vartiainen

Whether economic growth and successful structural change can be explained by skillful state policies or private transactions coordinated by a decentralized and parametric price system is a classic controversy within economics and political science. Economists and social scientists tend to read the empirical literature on growth and development according to this normative question, and academic discussions on this issue often result in generalized verdicts on the merits of "interventionism" versus "liberalism." Although sometimes hidden and sometimes more explicit, there is nevertheless a strong, normative endeavor in much of economics and political science. In the case of development economics, this programmatic struggle is reinforced by the connection between dominant economic doctrines and the policies of international development agencies such as the International Monetary Fund (IMF) and the World Bank.[1] Accordingly, skirmishes about academic respectability have direct repercussions on political strategies.

Furthermore, the controversy is laden with an aspect of competition between academic disciplines and their paradigmatic modes of discourse. Economists and political scientists writing about the proper way of examining economic development often plead implicitly for the general applicability of the approaches typical of their disciplines. Although both

1. See Thomas J. Biersteker, "Reducing the Role of the State in the Economy: A Conceptual Exploration of IMF and World Bank Prescriptions," *International Studies Quarterly* 34 (1990): 477–92; Thomas J. Biersteker, "The 'Triumph' of Neoclassical Economics in the Developing World: Policy Convergence and Bases of Governance in the International Economic Order," in J. A. Rosenau and E. O. Czempiel, eds., *Governance without Government* (Cambridge: Cambridge University Press, 1992).

sides nurture their minorities, this state of affairs tends to place most economists in the liberal-neoclassical camp, whereas political and social scientists are more prone to stress the importance of political and social institutions as substantive causal factors and of historical-institutional and comparative analyses as indispensable methodological tools. A browse through the development literature shows, for example, that many of the political scientists' best contributions are hardly touched on the economic literature, while much of good development economics is unknown to political scientists.

To readers familiar with the historical analyses of such writers as Max Weber, Karl Polanyi, and Alexander Gerschenkron, it is striking how little attention the neoclassical-neoutilitarian approach pays to the importance of social and political institutions and cultural norms in fostering economic development and sustaining exchange transactions. It is hard not to feel a bit outraged by the cheerful dismissal within the neoutilitarian credo of the entire pedigree of historical sociology and political philosophy that has illuminated the *complementary* natures and roles of the marketplace, on the one hand, and the rational and rule-bound state bureaucracy, on the other. To Weber, the two were the twin, necessary components and complementary preconditions of modern capitalism. Weber's analysis concerns first and foremost the mature European countries, but the same insights are applicable to newly industrialized and developing countries. In a more recent contribution, Peter Evans argues convincingly that the problems of African predatory states should be seen as examples of too little, not too much, bureaucracy in the Weberian sense.[2] To sustain the norms that are conducive to a well-functioning market economy and to encourage the buildup of new industries, there should be a competent state bureaucracy, the modus operandi of which should *not* follow the logic of individual utility maximization. Evans nicely makes the point that it is precisely a pattern of individual optimization that permeates the administration of those weak African states which may be justly characterized as predatory.

On the political philosophy circuit, there is the respectable tradition of corporatist theorizing, starting perhaps with Hegel, that emphasizes the dangers of alienation and the deracination of people in societies organized around market exchange.[3] Moreover, this tradition stresses the importance of popular movements, corporatist organizations, and other social organizations and networks in *sustaining* the workings of modern

---

2. Peter Evans, *Embedded Autonomy: States and Industrial Transformation* (Princeton: Princeton University Press, 1995).

3. See Shlomo Avineri, *Hegel's Theory of the Modern State* (London: Cambridge University Press, 1972), esp. chaps. 2 and 7–9.

capitalism.[1] Thus, sociologists and economic historians have always questioned even the politically dominant view that the industrialization of early developers was an essentially market-driven and "spontaneous" process.[5] These arguments are no less pertinent for the study of the experiences of late industrializers, the main objects of interest in this essay.

On the other hand, the critique against the neoclassical approach seems to dismiss much of good economics altogether. An institutionally oriented economist (as am I) need not buy the entire political Weltanschauung of neoclassical economics and neoutilitarian politics to appreciate the strength of some new economic ideas for development issues.

Hence, much unused but fertile territory exists between the extreme positions. I shall try to show in this essay that many more recent and even less recent developments *within economics* provide credibility to the interventionist-political perspective on economic development. Without abandoning the idea that agents behave more or less rationally, there is a lot to be said, from the point of view of economics, for the proposition that strongly interventionist strategies for economic development can be successful and that not all the observed successes are purely idiosyncratic and contingent occurrences. Modern economics is indeed far more interesting than the straw man criticized by many political scientists. In the following section I offer a biased (without apology) survey of some of these economic ideas and discussions, then consolidating these arguments with the help of two rather verbal economic "models." I thus demonstrate that the concept of increasing returns to scale from some technological externality can provide a positive explanation for the occurrence of etatist intervention and corporatist concertation as well as a normative argument for the possibilities of interventionist policies.

4. For the modern economic view of corporatism, see Jukka Pekkarinen, Matti Pohjola, and Bob Rowthorn, *Social Corporatism: A Superior Economic System?* WIDER Studies in Development Economics (Oxford: Clarendon Press, 1992).

5. Barry Supple surveys the attitudes of economic historians whose theoretical positions have been influenced by classical authors such as Alexander Gerschenkron and Friedrich List. Supple emphasizes that the role of the state in industrialization has not been limited to the provision of a basic legal framework, public order, and external security. The state has actively encouraged public services and other institutions favorable to industrialization and has even undertaken direct organizational activities in production. The Hungarian historians Iván Berend and György Ránki arrive at essentially similar conclusions in their study of several peripheral European economies. Nobel laureate Douglass North also emphasizes the importance of institutional frameworks. See Barry Supple, "The State and the Industrial Revolution, 1700–1914," in Carlo M. Cipolla, ed., *The Fontana Economic History of Europe*, vol. 3, *The Industrial Revolution* (London: Collins/Fontana, 1980); Iván T. Berend and György Ránki, *The European Periphery and Industrialization, 1780–1914* (Cambridge: Cambridge University Press, 1982); and Douglass C. North, *Institutions, Institutional Change, and Economic Performance* (Cambridge: Cambridge University Press, 1990). See also Linda Weiss and John M. Hobson, *States and Economic Development: A Comparative Historical Analysis* (Cambridge: Polity Press, 1995), for a more recent contribution of similar tenor.

The following two sections are thus concerned with the potential role of the state in enhancing economic development, as seen in light of some more recent economic ideas. I then move away from this normative discussion toward more positive and empirical questions, first enumerating a set of stylized facts about successful cases of state-sponsored industrialization. I use these facts to show how the policies and political contradictions predicted by theory turn up in economic policy experiences and also, to answer the question, What factors are conducive to success in policy intervention? I then present a tentative list of "preconditions" for success, arguing that, provided these conditions are met, there is a lot of freedom in the choice of specific policy packages.

I concentrate on the experiences of four countries in particular: Taiwan, Korea, Finland, and Austria. While the growth performances of the first two countries have been proclaimed as among the very best, Finland and Austria also boast performances above the average for industrial countries. Yet what the four countries have in common is that they underwent clear and rapid structural changes and late industrialization from the 1950s through the 1970s. In all of them, the state played a very active role in this transformation. The choice of Taiwan and Korea as objects for study is, of course, not very original. But I hope to shed some new light even on these two cases and, at the same time, make the perhaps more original point that similar elements of successful developmental etatism can be seen in the two European cases. In all four cases, we see a strong and bureaucratic state planning the economy in cooperation with a corporatist network while never questioning, however, a basic commitment to respect the private property rights of capitalism. Furthermore, the four countries have found themselves in a challenging position within international geopolitics. I provide a detailed description of the experiences of these individual countries.

The focal point of the stories and theoretical models in this essay is the theme of capital accumulation. In a nutshell, I suggest a rudimentary "economic theory" of capital accumulation in a successful developmental state. My method consists of some modeling plus straightforward qualitative observation, comparative description, and interpretation of observations according to models and economic ideas. Thus, there is no pretension to generality in the sense adopted by modern universalist economics or statistical analysis. Indeed, such theories as the ones presented here are by necessity more particular and casuistic than the grand achievements of general equilibrium theory.

Yet I believe we can learn a great deal even from such unsystematic theorizing in conjunction with comparative-institutional observation.[6] In this

6. The methodological prejudices of neoclassical economics are illustrated by the status accorded to different, purely mathematical models. When I presented the ideas in this essay

I deviate from the expanding industry of recent econometric growth studies. Comparisons of long-run growth rates in different countries, now based on the new, large Penn World Table data set, are very interesting but fragile, as Ross Levine and David Renelt have shown.[7] As Jon Elster argues, entire societies are so complex that overall explanations of their performances are necessarily problematic.[8] The commonplace statistical methodology employed in economics implicitly assumes that "countries" are appropriate units of analysis, which seems to presuppose that they are, in fact, generated by a common mechanism and sampled from a superpopulation of "potential" countries. Whereas firms and households and even industries can perhaps be assumed to behave in ways that are so universal that similar economic models apply to all, this assumption is much more dubious for such incredibly complex entities as countries and societies. The alternative, also advocated by Elster, is to look at *mechanisms*, particular and partial causal relationships that may be corroborated by all kinds of arguments, ranging from social theory and statistical inference to common sense and historical description.

---

to an audience of economists in a more formal way, one of my commentators pointed out that the model amounted merely to a kind of "internal consistency check" of interventionist-corporatist theories. While there may be some truth to this criticism, one wonders whether the same characterization would be applied to, for example, Debreu's *Theory of Value*. The latter, of course, is a "consistency check" as well, albeit an intellectually impressive one. At least in the economic literature, it seems that authors who explore noncompetitive models always have to provide an empirical legitimation for their endeavors, whereas competitive models are used without apology to infer even empirical conclusions and policy prescriptions. It is rarely asked whether the validity of the competitive assumptions has been checked empirically. It is also noteworthy how fast the assumptions of increasing returns and growth externalities (see the next section) have become generally fashionable in academic economics after they were more thoroughly analyzed by skillful neoclassical *theoreticians* such as Robert Lucas and Paul Romer. Nicholas Kaldor had already sketched the implications of similar assumptions in the 1950s, but his ideas remained part of the post-Keynesian dissidence. See Kaldor, *Further Essays in Economic Theory* (Duckworth, 1978).

7. Levine and Renelt examine the robustness of the results generated by the new empirical growth literature. Their method is to use E. E. Leamer's extreme bound analysis to assess whether reported statistical regularities between growth rates and various explanatory variables are robust. Supposing one wants to examine the robustness of one particular explanatory variable, Leamer's method consists of varying a set of other explanatory variables and establishing lower and upper bounds for the coefficient of the variable of interest. The correlation between the variable and the regression is said to be robust if the coefficient remains significant (and of the same sign) at the extreme bounds. Levine and Renelt find that there is generally no strong relationship between the policy indicators and growth. See Ross Levine and David Renelt, "A Sensitivity Analysis of Cross-Country Growth Regressions," *American Economic Review* 82, no. 4 (September 1992): 942–64. For a critique of empirical growth studies, see also Gregory Mankiw, "The Growth of Nations," *Brookings Papers on Economic Activity* 1 (1995): 275–326.

8. Jon Elster, *Political Psychology* (Cambridge: Cambridge University Press, 1993).

ECONOMIC ARGUMENTS

While a deeper understanding of incentive mechanisms and information economics has discredited the feasibility of comprehensive central planning and public ownership as viable economic strategies, the emphasis of the most interesting modern economics has also shifted in a way that makes the interventionist case more appealing than it used to be.[9] In this section, I will survey a number of economic arguments and theories that emphasize the role of the state in economic development, both in the *normative* sense that states may improve economic performance and in the *positive* sense that social scientists should not be surprised that structural economic transformations are often associated with interventionist economic policies.

To economists, this section may appear loose and speculative. However, I aim to present a kind of exploration or brainstorming session to underline the fact that much in modern economics lends credibility to a more "political" view of the economy (and of economic development in particular) than what is implied by the neoclassical-Walrasian model. The neoclassical-Walrasian view basically considers state intervention as a "distortion," whereas the Weltanschauung I want to bring forward unavoidably allows the state to occupy a prominent role at the center of the stage.

Exploiting Economic Externalities

New theories of *endogenous growth* have pointed out the potentially great significance of various externalities related to the accumulation of human capital and the level of technical knowledge. These aspects of economic development are now taken seriously in growth theory.[10] While no single and unifying theory of endogenous growth yet exists, it is already possible to learn from this literature. Many of the models share such assumptions as increasing returns to scale associated with levels of various capital stocks, be they tangible or intangible. Models of endoge-

9. Joseph Stiglitz, *Whither Socialism?* (Cambridge: MIT Press, 1994).
10. The classic papers of new growth theory are Paul Romer, "Increasing Returns and Long-Run Growth," *Journal of Political Economy* 94, no. 5 (1986): 1002–37; Paul Romer, "Endogenous Technological Change," *Journal of Political Economy* 98, no. 5 (1990): 71–102; and Robert Lucas, "On the Mechanics of Economic Development," *Journal of Monetary Economics* 22 (1988): 3–42. It is fair to say, however, that these basic ideas were already present in Nicholas Kaldor's writings (see esp. chapters 1, 2, and 7 in Kaldor, *Economic Theory*). Technical progress that is embodied in equipment investment and the importance of increasing returns to scale for endogenous growth play an important part in Kaldor's analysis: "Once, however, we allow for increasing returns, the forces making for continuous changes are endogenous—they are engendered from within the economic system" (p. 186).

nous growth can often have multiple equilibria and can generate both the possibility of discrete jumps between stationary states or accumulation regimes as well as "thresholds" in economic growth. Their assumptions contradict the usual neoclassical assumptions.

Furthermore, in general these models lead to the conclusion that an economy's growth performance can be enhanced by various interventions, such as subsidies to investment in sectors with high potential for spillovers or subsidies to education or research. In the presence of externalities, firms cannot fully internalize the effects of their investment on the economy-wide stock of technical expertise; similarly, individuals cannot fully internalize the effect of their increased human capital on the economy-wide stock of skills.

Of course, no proof exists that this new "view" of the economy is more correct than the Solow model generated by traditional neoclassical assumptions. To some authors, the new view makes better sense of the different countries' growth performances than does the neoclassical growth model. The empirical evidence is not unequivocal, however, and I shall not survey the literature here.[11]

The new views also strike a chord with many classical empirically and institutionally oriented studies of economic transformations and phases of economic growth. As early as 1960, W. W. Rostow presented his theory of the stages of economic growth by which each "stage" of growth was characterized by various self-enforcing mechanisms.[12] Other, similar accounts of growth and development include Erik Dahmén's idea of a "developmental bloc" and the notion of "linkages" suggests by Albert Hirschman.[13] Similarly, Michael Porter outlines the idea of industrial "clusters" that generate an environment and a system of linkages favorable for industrial growth.[14] These empirically inspired notions of blocs,

11. Among those studies that support the "new" views is that of Costas Azariadis and Alan Drazen, who discuss the strong contribution of educational expenditures for economic growth and the existence of growth "thresholds." J. B. de Long and Lawrence Summers argue that machinery investment in particular has a strong effect on growth. A contrasting view arguing that the various countries' growth performances nevertheless fit into the neoclassical Solow model is presented by Nicholas Crafts. Gregory Mankiw articulates a kind of compromise position according to which the neoclassical scheme as such is adequate if one adopts a very broad view of the economy's capital stock. See Costas Azariadis and A. Drazen, "Threshold Externalities in Economic Development," *Quarterly Journal of Economics* 105 (1990): 501–26; J. B. de Long and Lawrence Summers, "Equipment Investment and Economic Growth," *Quarterly Journal of Economics* 106 (CVI) (May 1991): 445–503; Nicholas Crafts, "Productivity Growth Reconsidered," *Economic Policy* 15 (October 1992); and Mankiw, "Growth of Nations," 275–326.

12. W. W. Rostow, *The Stages of Economic Growth* (Cambridge: Cambridge University Press, 1960).

13. Erik Dahmén, *Entrepreneurial Activity and the Development of Swedish Industry, 1919–1939* (Stockholm: Industriens utredningsinstitut, 1951).

14. Michael Porter, *The Competitive Advantage of Nations* (London: Macmillan, 1990).

clusters, and linkages are obvious empirical candidates for counterparts to the theoretical notion of externality.

One important implication of these theories is they do not assume that a decentralized price mechanism will select an outcome from a set of dynamically efficient growth paths. It may be possible to believe the economists' standard Walrasian auctioneer story in the case of static markets, but it is much less plausible that decentralized markets will always coordinate the investment decisions of an economy such that a path will be selected on the frontiers of a dynamic production possibilities schedule. The functioning of markets in a static setting requires arbitrage and a matching of the supply and demand decisions of a large number of agents. Investment activities, by contrast, are often unique in character and take time. Furthermore, the profitability of an investment project may depend on the successful completion of another. At time zero, however, neither of the two may seem profitable on their own. The notion of a production possibility frontier is elusive in the sense that it depends on the flexibility of social arrangements and on the costs and means of transmitting information about production possibilities. Public policy may be needed to map out an economy's productive potential.

This input-output way of thinking about a national economy ill fits the dominant neoclassical economic theory. Yet, mapping an economy's resources and growth potentials in various industries has often been essential for successful industrial takeoffs. In the Nordic countries, for example, an extremely important aspect of economic development has been the creation of an institutional research structure to support the development of natural resources. In Finland, the management of the nation's most important resource endowment, the forests, was at an early stage organized on a half-public–half-corporatist basis.[15] We can interpret this as the mapping out of the production possibility frontier by public agents.

In a more recent contribution, Dani Rodrik interprets the Korean and Taiwanese performances as successful solutions to coordination problems. According to Rodrik, these countries had, by the 1950s, reached a stage at which high human capital and an equal distribution of income made it potentially profitable to increase the output of intermediate goods for manufacturing. Rodrik argues that many of these production processes were interdependent in such a way that the machinery and

---

15. In Sweden, the state was very active in developing similar institutions for other areas of productive potentials as early as between 1870 and 1914. State-sponsored organizations were created to map the country's mineral resources by using geologic surveys and similar bodies for research in hydrography and water technology. See Bo Södersten, "One Hundred Years of Swedish Economic Development," in Magnus Blomström and Patricio Meller, eds., *Diverging Paths: Comparing a Century of Scandinavian and Latin American Economic Development* (Washington, D.C.: Inter-American Development Bank, 1991).

human capital investments of individual firms and workers could appear profitable only if complementary investments were undertaken by other firms. Thus, the state played an extremely useful role in coordinating the economy's investment on a new, higher level.[16]

New ideas of growth generate powerful normative and political implications. If the related assumptions are true, one cannot presume that the market can generate a dynamically efficient outcome. The state has the potential for enhancing economic growth and development.

Mediation of Distributive Conflicts

One may also speculate about *positive* predictions of political and economic structures in small countries. This observation provides the bridge to the second family of economic theories, those related to *strategic distributional conflicts*.

The assumptions of increasing returns typically lead to outcomes that contradict assumptions of perfect competition. If, for example, industrial technology exhibits increasing returns to scale, a few large firms may dominate the economy. This is indeed the case in many small economies. As shown in the various essays of Jukka Pekkarinen, Matti Pohjola, and Bob Rowthorn and the related literature on corporatism, corporatist structures are typical for small economies.[17] One plausible explanation discussed in the literature hinges on economies of scale. If technologies imply increasing returns to scale along some intervals of the capital stock axis, some industry sizes are more advantageous than are others. Moreover, there may be a minimum size for manufacturing sectors below which they cannot operate profitably in the international market.[18] If this is the case, the structure of small economies will differ from that of large economies: small economies will be dominated by a few industries and will not be simply a mirror image of larger economies.

By the same token, if technological externalities exist such that industry-wide returns on research and development or equipment investments are larger than their private costs, then it may also be the case that successful economies will exhibit corporatist characteristics. Big oligopolistic

16. Dani Rodrik, "Getting Interventions Right: How South Korea and Taiwan Grew Rich," *Economic Policy* 20 (April 1995).

17. Pekkarinen, Pohjola, and Rowthorn, eds., *Social Corporatism*. See also discussions by Peter Katzenstein in *Corporatism and Change: Austria, Switzerland, and the Politics of Industry* (Ithaca: Cornell University Press, 1984), and *Small States in World Markets* (Ithaca: Cornell University Press, 1985).

18. See Michael Landesmann and Juhana Vartiainen, "Social Corporatism and Long-Term Economic Performance," in Pekkarinen, Pohjola, and Rowthorn, eds., *Social Corporatism*.

or monopolistic firms will do better than small firms, and industrial associations that coordinate members' research activities will have a raison d'être. Industries will try to organize research activities on a collective basis, obtain state support for the buildup of infrastructure, seek the help of state diplomacy in their exploration of export markets, and will depend by and large on state authorities in myriad ways.

Such observations make sense of economic history. State-sponsored infrastructure and research activity, all-encompassing export organizations, big mercantile companies, and political management of economic change have always been an integral part of economic development. This observation is particularly lucid in successful examples of late industrialization. In the Asian success stories, the large but diversified business groups, with close ties to political decision-making bodies, have been the most important engines of economic growth.

To take this speculative exploration further, such an economic structure may have far-reaching implications for the *political systems* of small economies. In small countries such as the Nordic ones, successful firms and industries are important and "big" actors in the political and economic arenas.[19] Big actors such as export industries in small economies act *strategically* vis-à-vis other groups. This influences the behavior of *other* societal agents. For example, labor, farmers, or banks may be better off organizing themselves. Indeed, in Finland and other Nordic countries, an all-encompassing corporatist mobilization of the major agents of the economy was undertaken from the turn of the century onward.[20] Thus, we can expect that such economic structures lead to *corporatist* politics with *strategic* distributional conflicts.

Economic game theories have cast light on problems of distribution and strategic action in corporatist economies with organized agents.[21] Typical corporatist actors are big firms, labor unions, and their federations and industrial and employer organizations.

To continue this speculative reasoning one more step, consider the implications of these arguments for the role of the state. First, the problem with a corporatist economy is that it may be generically inefficient in generating economic change. This assertion may sound loose, but it follows directly from the theoretical characterization of the corporatist economy

19. For more empirical arguments on the politics of corporatism, see Katzenstein, *Small States in World Markets.*

20. For Finland, see Jukka Pekkarinen and Juhana Vartiainen, *Suomen talouspolitiikan pitkä linja* (The long line of Finnish economic policy) (Helsinki: WSOY, 1992), and Jan Otto Andersson, Pekka Kosonen, and Juhana Vartiainen, "The Finnish Model of Economic and Social Policy: From Emulation to Crash," Research Report A:401 (Department of Economics, Åbo Akademi University, 1993). For Sweden, for example, see H. de Geer, *The Rise and Fall of the Swedish Model* (Stockholm: Carden Publications and the FA Institute, 1992).

21. See Pekkarinen, Pohjola, and Rowthorn, *Social Corporatism.*

as a game with a moderate number of players. It is well known that there is no general theorem or outcome in game theory that would show equilibrium outcomes to be generally efficient. On the contrary, the few general results of game theory suggest that equilibrium outcomes are often, *not* efficient overall. While this is often true of Nash equilibria in one-shot games, it may also be true for repeated games and truly dynamic games.

How can we concretize this to understand the problem of capital accumulation? Basically, inefficiency results from the dependency of future returns on today's investments on the strategic reactions of other agents. In other words, when Walrasian assumptions are not met, the social returns and costs of investments do not correspond with the private returns and costs as perceived by the players. Nash equilibria in dynamic games typically result in investments and other sacrifices for the future remaining too low because the agents in question cannot be assured that they will enjoy returns that correspond with the costs of optimal investments.[22] A paradigmatic example is the game between a trade union and a firm or an industry. The entrepreneurs do not want to invest as much as society's welfare would warrant because they anticipate that organized labor will ex post expropriate the quasi rent associated with the new machines.[23] Hence, there is regular role for the state to step into as the mediator and use policy instruments to generate dynamically efficient economic outcomes.

The foregoing is, again, essentially a normative argument. Yet, there is room for a positive prediction as well. Even in a liberal political culture, in which officials may have been reluctant to operate an active interventionist policy, the state can in a corporatist society easily become a forum or a playing field for strategic distributional conflicts. In the economic and political arenas, corporatist agents assume political importance. The state becomes a component of the corporate agenda. The managers of strategically important industries and the leaders of powerful trade unions know that the state authorities cannot dismiss their demands and will try to influence policymaking. Conflicts between opposing interest groups will then easily assume a political character. The ideal role of the state is to act as mediator or as partner in social partnership that should lead to acceptable bargains in income distribution.

22. For a thorough analysis of capital accumulation problems in economies with organized labor and capital, see Juhana Vartiainen, "Capital Accumulation in a Corporatist Economy," *Lecture Notes in Economics and Mathematical Systems* 383 (Heidelberg: Springer-Verlag, 1992).

23. See Frederick van der Ploeg, "Trade Unions, Investment, and Employment," *European Economic Review* 31 (1987).

Why the State? Incompleteness of Contracts and Uncertainty

What would make the state a potentially useful player in a game between such organized agents as export firms, farmers, workers, and banks? Again, one can appeal to some ideas in economics, namely, those related to *incompleteness of contracts* and *uncertainty*. Suppose that the agents in an economy want to embark on an ambitious program of industrialization and economic restructuring. Such a program may unambiguously increase the expected aggregate income of the economy. But this in itself does not ensure that all parties want to cooperate. First, not everybody gains; some individuals may find their professions obsolete, and some industries may disappear. Second, nobody can predict the final outcome with certainty. There is uncertainty as to how much each party will benefit.

If this setup is seen as a game between rational agents who can communicate with one another, what prevents the agents from reaching an efficient agreement? The point is that efficiency may require that the parties can contract on an extremely wide set of variables. As new industries emerge and old ones disappear, it should be possible to compensate the losers. The structure of transactions and property rights may, however, rule out such bargains. The state should therefore be seen as a *general coordinator* which has the largest potential set of instruments for creating acceptable outcomes and which can undertake at least some action in all kinds of originally unforeseeable contingencies.

The state is empowered with a usefully *wide* mandate to promote efficiency and resist socially harmful, unilateral collective action. There is no axiom that the state always will and always is able to carry out that task. Nevertheless, of all social institutions, the state is the only one with the institutional and jurisdictional form to permit such an interpretation. From the point of view of its "principal," the citizen, the state in a modern society seems to be the only institution against which everybody has a claim.[24]

These rather general speculations may be relevant for understanding the processes of growth and capital accumulation. To get industrialization under way, the state must mobilize and organize the economy, act to build a coherent corporatist structure with which it can work, and design growth-promoting policies. This means that it must also be able to deal

24. From the point of view of game theory, the state can be identified with the "grand coalition." In this sense, a functioning state is a precondition for efficiency. If, for some reason, the grand coalition is unable to "meet" and ensure that all participants improve on a prospective distribution through joint collective action, there is no guarantee that the economic outcome is collectively rational.

with the inevitable distributional conflicts. The state must cope with the inherent paradox that rapid structural change requires extensive social organization and political coordination of resources, which at the same time may aggravate problems of inefficient corporatism and unilateral interest group action aimed at redistributive rent seeking.

To sum up, this "increasing returns-corporatism-interventionist" synthesis suggests that the political economy of small corporatist economies is organized around two themes: the exploitation of economies of scale and the management of strategic conflict between organized interest groups. Both these themes point to an extended role for the state. If the firms themselves do not exploit the economies of scale—via, for instance, coordinated investment policies, joint research, or mergers—it is rational for the state to operate an active industrial policy. If the economies of scale indeed lead to an oligopolistic economic structure and a corporatist political structure, the state cannot easily avoid the role of arbiter and manager of inevitable strategic conflicts.

TWO ECONOMIC EXAMPLES

The foregoing arguments may seem extremely loose and abstract. To make them more definite and precise, I present two economic examples, both of which illustrate the relevance of the above arguments for problems of capital accumulation.

Example 1: The Economic Logic of Income Policies and Credit Rationing

To concretize the reasoning on the incompleteness of contracts, consider the following economic model, explored more thoroughly in my work elsewhere:[25] Imagine an economy with the "Nordic" characteristic of workers organized in a powerful trade union federation and able to determine their wages. The economy consists of many neoclassical firms, each identified with a stock of machines, K (capital). The firms use a homogeneous labor force that sells an undifferentiated labor service. The firms take the wage as given and increase their labor to the point where labor's marginal product is equal to the wage costs. The workers of each firm are organized in a trade union, and the workers' unions are in turn organized within a centralized peak federation. Capital and financial

25. Juhana Vartiainen, "Can Nordic Social Corporatism Survive? Challenges to the Labor Market" (1996), in David F. Good and Randall W. Kindley, eds., *The Challenge of Globalization and Institution Building. Lessons from Small European States* (Boulder, Colo.: Westview Press, 1997).

markets are not integrated with the rest of the world, and the interest rate can be determined by national monetary policy.

As I explained above, such a corporatist economy generically suffers from underinvestment, because the determination of income distribution is a process separate from that of investment and capital accumulation. In my model of centralized corporatism, I assume that the wage is set by the trade union at the central level. The firms take as given the wages set by the union, working out their optimal investment plans to maximize their profits. Suppose that increasing the capital stock imposes an adjustment cost on the firm. Standard dynamic programming techniques can be used to show for each long-run wage level, w, there is an optimal long-run stock of capital, K, which maximizes the profits of the shareholders.[26] Figure 1 presents the situation of this corporatist economy in a graphical form. The horizontal axis measures the capital stock of the economy, and the vertical axis measures the wage. The decreasing curve, $ST(K)$, depicts those combinations of steady state (long-run equilibrium) wage and capital that are compatible with the firms' optimal investment plans.

The problem is that the points on this curve are, in general, inefficient steady states.[27] Both parties would be better off if the workers moderated their wage demands and the firm invested more than what is implied by dynamic optimization. One can show that there is a locus of combinations of steady state wages and capital stocks that correspond with the dynamically efficient steady states.[28] This is depicted as $EFF(K)$ in Figure 1. The economy may end up at a point such as (K^*, w^*) on this curve.

26. Suppose that the firm earns profits (P) net of investment costs, $P(K, w)$, where K is the stock of capital and w is the wage. In addition, the firm must pay the investment bill, $C(I)$, where I is the increase in the capital stock and C is a convex cost function. The capital stock obeys the transition equation $K_{t+1} = K_t(1 - \delta) + I_t$, where t is time and δ is the rate of depreciation. If the wage is w^* and the firm discounts the future with a factor β, the firm's investment program should maximize $\Sigma_t [P(K_t, w^*_t) - C(I_t)]\beta^t$ subject to the transition equation. Standard dynamic programming techniques show that the firm's optimal investment leads to a steady state level of capital that depends negatively on the wage level. By manipulating the first-order conditions generated by the Bellman equation, one can derive the condition $P_K = BC'(\delta K)$, where $B = [1 - \beta(1 - \delta)]/\beta$ is a term that depends on the discount factor (that is, the interest rate) and P_K is the marginal revenue product of capital, which depends on the wage.

27. This argument is a version of Ian MacDonald and Robert Solow's model with "capital" in place of "employment." See Ian MacDonald and Robert Solow, "Wage Bargaining and Employment," *American Economic Review* 31 (1981).

28. This is derived by solving the problem of a Pareto dictator who chooses sequences of w and I to maximize a weighted sum of both parties' utilities: max $\rho \Sigma_t [P(K_t, W_t) - C(I_t)]\beta^t + (1 - \rho) \Sigma_t R(K_t, w_t)\beta^t$, where ρ and $1 - \rho$ are the welfare weights of the two parties. The manipulation of the related Bellman equation generates a relationship between wage and capital stock at the steady state; however, now wage and capital stock are increasing functions of each other.

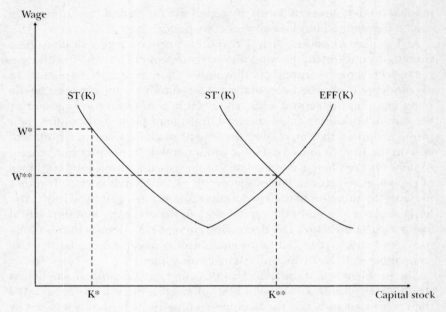

Credit rationing and wage moderation as a class compromise

An *efficient* program that generates a point on the curve *EFF(K)* would require that *wages and investment be bargained simultaneously.*[29] Yet such an agreement is difficult to implement within the institutions of capitalism, because the investment decisions of the firms must in the last instance be accepted by the shareholders of each firm. A central trade union federation cannot make a contract with *every* firm. One obvious way out is to reach for a *political* solution mediated by the state. For example, the state can use credit rationing and selective regulation of the credit market to lower the effective interest rate costs incurred by the firms. At the same time, it can agree with the workers' trade union federation on wage moderation, either directly or by using its tax instruments. Decreasing the interest rate moves the curve *ST(K)* outward.[30] By rationing interest rates downward, the state can move the curve to the position *ST(K)*. This is the investment part of the class compromise. If the political system and the

29. This is shown, for example, in my earlier work, but it is generally not surprising that efficient arrangements can be reached if all parties can contract on all variables. See Vartiainen, "Capital Accumulation in a Corporatist Economy."

30. When the firm is risk neutral, the discount factor β is equal to $1/(1-r)$, where r is the interest rate. When this holds, the owner of the firm is able to break even if he or she borrows to buy the firm at the start of the period and uses the profit stream to meet interest payments on the loan.

corporatist network work rationally, the economy is able to attain a point such as *(K**, w**)* on the efficient curve. Which specific point is attained and what the implied profits and wage rates are depend on the political strengths of the parties.

I see this as a reasonable interpretation of the Finnish (or Nordic) class compromise. As explained below, economy-wide wage settlements, selective credit rationing, and allocation of credit to manufacturing industries were a staple part of Finnish economic policy after World War II. A similar logic can be seen in the Korean and Taiwanese cases, although they employed much more authoritarian measures to contain workers' aspirations. What we see is essentially a political bargain whereby the state uses instruments that would otherwise never be part of a private contract.

Example 2: The Economic Logic of Corporatism and Price Rationing

I will now outline another model of a small economy that captures some of the economic characteristics I have described above. This model has been more fully exposed in another essay.[31] Consider a small and oligopolistic economy that consists of a moderate number of productive sectors. Each sector produces a good by using such resources as labor and capital. The technology of each sector exhibits increasing returns to scale. For example, one may assume that there are spillovers owing to the fact that when engineers are trained to operate a machine in one firm, they may exchange their ideas with their colleagues in other firms and can thereby improve the use of similar or almost similar machines in other firms.

The goods produced in the various sectors are traded in a commodities market that equilibrates supply and demand. The owners of the firms in each sector are confronted with the question of how much they should invest at the cost of foregone consumption. With increasing returns to scale, the individual investment decisions are in general not socially optimal. Investment is generally too low and the economy has the potential to grow faster with subsidization. There are certainly many ways for the state to improve this situation. It may, for example, levy a lump sum tax and then subsidize investment in each sector. This requires knowledge of the technology of each sector and capacity to operate a selective industrial policy. These informational assumptions are severe.

A scenario that is at least as likely is one in which firms in each sector get together and exploit their economies of scale. If the shareholder-en-

31. Juhana Vartiainen, "Understanding State-Led Late Industrialization" (1996), in Villy Bergström, ed., *Government and Growth*, FIEF Studies in Labor Markets and Economic Policy (Oxford: Clarendon Press, 1997).

trepreneurs understand the technology and the scope for increasing returns, it is better for them to socialize their investment decisions in order
to realize the growth potential of the economy. This may mean that they
organize themselves into corporations that coordinate their investment
and research policies. It might also mean that over the course of time the
industry would become a monopoly.

If the number of sectors in the economy is not too large, however, the
industries can gain strategic importance. Accordingly, in the planning of
their investment decisions, they will also take into account the relationship between their supply of goods and the price they can command.
Thus, even if they can exploit the scale factor of their technology, they
may be inclined to cut down output in order to exploit the consumers
and the owners of the other sectors. Although strategic organization may
help in exploiting economies of scale, it may create new problems of
strategic conflicts. Now, in such a simple model an easy way for the state
to improve the economy's performance is to *ration* the prices of the goods
produced by these industries; by so doing, the scope for strategic action
for the monopolistic industry is limited, yet the incentives for exploiting
the economies of scale are not diminished. Thus, the state may have to
become active simply to contain the strategic conflicts that arise from a
corporatist structure. Again, such an economic outcome is not feasible
without a state that has the mandate and the prerogative to ration the
prices of goods. The corporations must not be able to manipulate the
state.

This example may be a bit abstract, but I think it captures many of the
East Asian characteristics. While state authorities have consistently encouraged the exploitation of economies of scale, they have also tried with
mixed success to safeguard their ability to discipline big corporations—
the *chaebol* and the *zaibatsu* in the Asian cases—and prevent them from
using their strategic muscle to seek rents at the expense of others.

In the Scandinavian countries, the goals of industrial policy have also
been defined in terms of productive efficiency and economies of scale
rather than in terms of competition, allocative efficiency, and antitrust
objectives. Scandinavian industrial policy has "concentrated on structural
efficiency of various industries and on policy measures that should be
taken to promote more rational industrial structures."[32] This strategy relies heavily on the assumption that there are important economies of
scale in many production sectors.[33] For example, the Swedish government has concentrated its activities on influencing the speed of structural
rationalization and investment in new plants. A variety of subsidies and

32. Lennart Hjalmarsson, "The Scandinavian Model of Industrial Policy," in Blomström
and Meller, eds., *Diverging Paths*, p. 245.
33. See ibid., p. 246, for references.

other selective measures have been used to enhance productivity. The growth of firm size has been encouraged. A competitive environment as an objective per se has not been altogether neglected but, rather, taken for granted by a small open economy. The same can be said of Finland, where industrial policy has not until recently been very concerned with the creation of competitive conditions.

The real world, of course, has far more variables than this example. Yet, it is easy enough to imagine empirical counterparts to the mechanisms analyzed in the context of this model. In sum, the model suggests that:

- the state may attempt to operate a selective industrial policy (compare subsidies with investment in the model) if it perceives positive technological externalities;
- the state may operate a policy of low interest rates to affect investment;
- it may be advantageous for the state to encourage the buildup of corporatist structures (if the state authorities understand that their knowledge of the technology is less perfect than that of the industrialists themselves); however,
- the corporatist structure may lead to strategic conflicts that the state may have to mitigate either through selective industrial policies or administrative rationing of those prices that are seen as the strategic variables; therefore,
- the state must be strong enough to impose its own policies and commit to them.

STYLIZED FACTS OF SUCCESS CASES

I have argued that normatively the state has the economic potential for improving economic performance and positively one may predict that the state becomes enmeshed with strategic conflicts of distribution. I have also presented economic examples that illustrate these general arguments. Consideration now turns to the experiences of the four success cases in light of the theoretical discussion. After laying down a list of stylized facts, I offer a tentative "theory" of why the state in these countries was able to implement a successful developmental strategy, also suggesting that the conditions predicted by the theories presented above have indeed been at the center stage in these countries.

To introduce the arguments, consider first some stylized facts. The experiences of the four case countries exhibit at least the following common characteristics that may have been associated with "mechanisms" of success in state-led industrialization:

In the left margin, handwritten: *These points are the exact opposite of what a neo-liberalist would prescribe.*

1. The state has been so powerful and interventionist that the practical organization of new investment has at times resembled that of planned economies.
2. The four countries have extremely organized, corporatist economies in which strategic decisions of economic and industrial policy have been taken in concertation with the state and organized interest groups of business and labor.
3. Political and collective decisions have regulated both the channeling of surplus from savings to the needs of capital accumulation and the distributional conflict around the functional distribution of income.
4. Despite extensive etatist planning, the state and the political establishment have ultimately been committed to the liberal market order and have respected private property as a principal solution.
5. For various historical reasons, the state has been strong politically and endowed with a large and competent bureaucracy.
6. In international politics, all four countries were situated in a contested border zone between the two ideological blocks of capitalism and communism and were confronted with the threat of loss of sovereignty.

DETERMINANTS OF SUCCESS

The above observations lend support to a rudimentary theory of the "successful developmental state." This theory predicts that state intervention and even planning can be very successful if long-run incentives for private entrepreneurship are not weakened; a competent and meritocratic bureaucracy sets state policy independent of organized interest groups and does not aim at maximizing the revenues of its individual members; the state can manage a coherent and balanced corporatist network of organized interests; the state and its various corporatist partners are endowed with tools for allocating finance and regulating the functional distribution of income; and the nation is confronted with a fragile position in international politics such that the consequences of economic failure are fatal. An emerging literature within political science seeks to clarify the role of the state in economic development and reinterpret the clumsy conceptual apparatus related to the question of whether the state is "strong" or "weak." Even at the risk of entering an industry with decreasing returns, let me generalize from these points and suggest factors that I see as essential for successful state intervention in economic development:

1. There is a state that is "strong" in the sense that its internal modus operandi is insulated from both the market and the logic of individual utility maximization. In other words, the state apparatus must be *bureaucratic and meritocratic* enough to impose its collective objectives onto its individual civil servants.

2. The state should be endowed with *thick external ties to the economy's organized agents* such as corporations, industrialists associations, and trade unions. This perhaps requires a certain degree of initial economic maturity and corporatist organization of the economy. This notion corresponds with what Peter Evans calls "embeddedness."[34]

3. There is a relationship of *mutual dependence* or *mutual balance* between the state and the rest of the economy. The state bureaucrats must be able to "discipline" economic actors such as firms and trade unions, while appreciating that their privileged positions ultimately depend on the success of the economy. Such a balance may reflect an underlying political commitment to honor private property rights in the long run, but it might also be strengthened by an *external challenge* to the nation.

The Bureaucratic Tradition and a Contact Network

As emphasized in the Weberian tradition, rational management of the economy requires a meritocratic bureaucracy that is sufficiently competent and autonomous to obey its own logic, which is necessarily not one of individual utility maximization. The Weberian professional bureaucracy consists of career civil servants who are committed to their tasks and prestigious enough not to be easily corrupted by outside interests. Such a meritocratic civil service is also able to reproduce itself, for its prestige makes it possible to recruit from the nation's most talented.

Thus the quality of state institutions genuinely depends on history and traditions. In a political culture where public service is held in high esteem, it is easier to recruit from among the best minds, which has already been pointed out by Chalmers Johnson in his classic study of the Japanese MITI and is similarly emphasized by Robert Wade's study of Taiwan and Alice Amsden's study of Korea.[35] In Japan, Korea, and Taiwan, the indus-

---

34. Peter Evans, *Embedded Autonomy: States and Industrial Transformation* (Princeton: Princeton University Press, 1995).

35. Chalmers Johnson, *MITI and the Japanese Miracle: The Growth of Industrial Policy, 1925–1975* (Stanford: Stanford University Press, 1982); Robert Wade, *Governing the Market: Economic Theory and the Role of Government in East Asian Industrialization* (Princeton: Princeton University Press, 1990); Alice H. Amsden, *Asia's Next Giant: South Korea and Late Industrialization* (New York: Oxford University Press, 1989).

trial pilot agencies were continuously able to retain their prestige and recruit able personnel. Corruption and mediocrity are self-enforcing phenomena as well: mediocre administrations can, at best, attract mediocre people, and corrupt regimes attract corrupt people and encourage the corruption even of those who originally tried to enforce the common interests.

Neoclassical policy prescriptions might accentuate a degeneration of state institution. The distrust of any mode of social conduct that is not conditioned by individual market incentives is perhaps revealing of a hidden political agenda. Indeed, neoclassical economists need not look very far to find a cornerstone of the capitalist economy that is not full of privately maximizing individuals: the private firm. The private firm is a prime example of an *organization* in which individual agents must obey the demands of collective corporate interests.

Our success cases have all "enjoyed" the services of a competent and prestigious administrative bureaucracy able to design and carry out successful industrial policies. A successful state must be able to formulate credible and consistent policies that do not change overnight. This is precisely what bold and insensitive bureaucracies are good at.

Weak states tend to have bureaucracies that behave according to the economic logic of individual maximization. Their most extreme forms are seen in the militarily strong but otherwise weak African states, where even administrative behavior is aimed at individual revenue maximization. Evans describes at length the Zairian state, where "everything is for sale" and "personalism and plundering at the top destroys any possibility of rule governed behavior in the lower levels of the bureaucracy, giving individual maximization free rein underneath."[36] As Evans points out, it is not bureaucracy but its absence that makes the state rapacious.

Another less extreme case in point is related to the "industrial organization of corruption" as analyzed by Andrei Shleifer and Robert Vishny.[37] The economy may tolerate a reasonable amount of corruption as long as it is organized by a "monopoly" such that an entrepreneur need not bribe a thousand officials to get a project completed. This is one more argument for a strong, centralized bureaucracy. A strong bureaucracy may harass the prospective entrepreneur with red tape, but if the individual bureaucrats are well monitored within the system, the economic costs of corruption will remain moderate. The monopolistic bureaucrat of the strong state may expropriate a part of the economic surplus related to an investment project, but if the project is economically sound, it will be car-

36. Evans, *Embedded Autonomy*, p. 46.
37. Andrei Shleifer and Robert Vishny, "Corruption," *Quarterly Journal of Economics* 109 (1993): 599–617.

ried out anyway. With the uncontrolled bureaucracy of a weak state, however, the entrepreneur must bribe every official that can block the investment. Accordingly, these competing bureaucrats together impose a much higher economic cost.[38]

The second factor, embeddedness, is one that repeatedly comes consistently forward in the empirically and historically oriented studies of successful state intervention, which is not surprising in light of my discussion of economic externalities. If the state is to coordinate investment and map out the economy's productive potential, it must be able to gather a large amount of information. In this way, the state bureaucracy can at least sketch a potential input-output table for the economy. This factor has been emphasized by many political scientists, perhaps most consistently by Evans in his conception of "embeddedness." If the state wants to have a say in the running of the economy, it has to talk to somebody.

In our country cases, the state has thus been involved in economic planning of some sort in cooperation with the economy's private actors. Often, this planning has taken place within informal networks where industrialists, civil servants, bankers, and policymakers have coordinated their decisions.

Mutual Balance and Incentives

Most important, there must be an appropriate balance of forces between the state apparatus and private economic actors. Both must feel that their own success depends on the fortunes of the other partner. The state bureaucracy should be able to discipline private economic actors but should *not* be able to afford an economic failure. A political coalition that defeats the business community is not useful for accumulating productive capital. On the other hand, if the business side of the partnership feels that it can hijack and manipulate the state, it will not shape its investment policies in a way that contributes to national industrialization. Thus, instead of talking about the "weakness" and "strength" of states, we need to analyze the equilibrium of forces between the state and the economy's organized agents. While this notion is still tentative and I have no systematic theory or body of evidence to support it, I would like to draw attention to two factors that have been of importance in creating the right balance of forces and, consequently, the right environment for economic intervention.

38. For Korea, see Amsden, *Asia's Next Giant*, and Jung-en Woo, *Race to the Swift : State and Finance in Korean Industrialization* (New York: Columbia University Press, 1991). For Taiwan, see Wade, *Governing the Market*. For Austria, see Katzenstein, *Corporatism and Change* and *Small States in World Markets*.

First, although all our success cases operated policies that amounted to far-reaching planning, none of them questioned the commitment to private property rights as a long-run solution. There was no master plan to build socialism, although the management of the economy at times was not very different from that of a planned economy. This is an issue that the economic discussion on planning versus markets has failed to appreciate fully. The question of whether "planning can work" may depend on whether it is attempted as a temporary way of organizing a transition to a modern market economy or as a fundamental "system" solution. In the former case, which applies to all our case countries, the prospective entrepreneur can count on the system's commitment to keep the incentives of private entrepreneurship alive. In such a situation even extensive and direct administrative interference may be tolerable. In the latter case, the prospect of ever being able to recover the returns of today's investments is poor, and the environment for entrepreneurship is wrought with much more uncertainty.

Therefore, basic political commitments may be as important as specific policies. Paradoxically, a regime that is fundamentally committed to respect private property and the private ownership of productive assets may successfully use wide-ranging planning and other radical methods of political intervention. These are accepted by capitalists as temporary measures. A left-wing regime, on the other hand, ardent in its antimarket rhetoric, loses the confidence of domestic investors even if the practical policy package is not very radical and comprehensive. Thus, "right-wing" interventionism may have a built-in advantage over its "left-wing" counterpart. Peter Katzenstein's work shows that there has at times been more planning in the Austrian economy than in some of its nominally socialist neighbors.[39] Similarly, the accounts by Wade and Amsden show that Taiwan and Korea were not much behind the German Democratic Republic in overall dirigisme.[40] Yet, Austria, Taiwan, and Korea were also committed to and successful in becoming capitalist economies. Another example is that of Peru during the years of President Alan Garcia (1985–88). Garcia's aim was to mobilize domestic investors in a national program of industrial restructuring. Although his policies would probably not have been more interventionist than those of Taiwan and Korea, Garcia's basic political orientation and anti-IMF rhetoric aroused the suspicions of the national elites, and his economic policy resulted in failure.[11]

39. Katzenstein, *Corporatism and Change*.
40. Wade, *Governing the Market*; Amsden, *Asia's Next Giant*.
41. Of course, Garcia's explicit political project of reneging foreign debt was a clear break from the market-oriented rules of the game. Although stopping the interest payments on foreign debt increased the scope for short-term industrial policy, a rational domestic investor in Peru must have pondered whether a regime not committed to the fundamental property rights of capitalism would, in the future, guarantee a fair return on his own investment.

The experience of Austria is also instructive in this respect. In that country, a very extensive program of nationalization was undertaken at the end of World War II and again in 1955, when the Soviet army withdrew from Austria and many enterprises that had been in its zone of occupation fell into Austrian hands. However, this was not seen as primarily an ideological decision, and it did not seem to hamper the willingness of entrepreneurs to cooperate with the state within the corporatist power structure.

Second, the role of an external political challenge has been prominent in all four success cases. The four countries have been situated within a contested border zone of the world's two ideological blocs and have been challenged by far more powerful countries. The very existence of South Korea has been dependent on the constellations of international politics and on the willingness of the United States to maintain its military presence in the area. A similar story might apply to Taiwan, the existence of which has been continuously put into question. Taiwanese rulers have been faced with the challenges of Mainland China and an outright economic failure could become the very end of the Taiwanese state. In addition, the Taiwanese political elite represent an immigrant minority on the island, thus they cannot be sure of their support even at home.

Finland and Austria have also shared a precarious international position. After World War II, both countries found themselves in the border zone of two political power blocs, and both have had a history of bitter internal conflicts and civil war. For Finland, successful industrialization and integration of economic system with Western European economies were powerful political objectives as well as economic motivations. The buildup of state-led corporatist structures from the 1960s onward was a conscious political mobilization project encouraged by the state as well as by many employers.[12] The encompassing nature of Austrian corporatism probably also owes something to a political project of national integration and mobilization (see below).

Thus, these countries could ill afford an economic failure. This factor is also perfectly understandable in light of modern economics and rational-choice theory, provided one is willing to buy the framework of a small economy with an organized, corporatist structure.[13] Whatever incentive there may otherwise be for the individual bureaucrat to take advantage of his or her position or for the large firm to take advantage of its market power, such free riding is not rational if it is generally understood that overall economic failure results in national catastrophe. Hence, an external threat to the nation-state may change the payoffs to the agents in a

42. Max Jakobson, *Vallanvaihto* (Helsinki: Otava, 1992).
43. See Vartiainen, "Understanding State-Led Late Industrialization," for a formal analysis.

fortuitous way. Formally, this can be illustrated by a kind of prisoners' dilemma. Suppose that there are two industrial sectors in the economy, each with two options: either "Invest a Lot" or "Seek Rents" (the latter alternative may entail low investment but high pricing, for example). Typically, one might expect that the table of payoffs in such a game might look like the following:

Table 1.

Industry 1	Industry 2	
	Seek rents	Invest a lot
Seek rents	Poor, poor	Excellent, miserable
Invest a lot	Miserable, excellent	Good, good

In this table, the first entry in each cell is the payoff of Industry 1 and the second is that of Industry 2. The entries are meant to convey preference ordering according to which "excellent" is best for both parties and "miserable" is worst, with "good" in between. It is well known that the Nash equilibrium and dominated equilibrium of such a game is "Seek Rents, Seek Rents," which does not yield a Pareto optimal outcome. If it is clear to all participants that the very existence of the nation is threatened unless everybody invests a lot, the table might read instead:

Table 2.

Industry 1	Industry 2	
	Seek rents	Invest a lot
Seek rents	Miserable, miserable	Miserable, miserable
Invest a lot	Miserable, miserable	Good, good

In this game, the strategy pair "Invest a Lot, Invest a Lot" is a form of equilibrium.[11] Note that this second table describes an economy with altogether less favorable economic opportunities. However, the crucial point is that failure has become more expensive. In political terms, this means that the political authorities have an easy job in persuading the industrialists to undertake large investment programs at the expense of short-term profitability. Thus, external threats can improve the state's bargaining position vis-à-vis the economy's organized agents.

Again, we can use the analogy of a private firm. Neoclassical economics and neoliberal-neoutilitarian policymakers are generally unconcerned with the eventual internal bureaucracies of private firms because there is

44. As is, of course, every other cell as well.

supposedly an extremely severe external constraint—market competition—that eliminates inefficient "corporate bureaucracies."

Economic analyses are oriented toward evaluating the specific policies that have been implemented in different countries. The study of different country cases, however, suggests that much freedom is most likely involved in choosing the specific policy packages meant to enhance development. Provided that specific conditions—such as the three discussed earlier in this section—are met to a reasonable degree, it is perhaps not decisive whether investment in new industries is boosted by direct economic planning, subsidies to research and development, selective credit rationing, or direct state ownership.

AN OVERVIEW OF COUNTRY EXPERIENCES

In this section I describe the individual experiences of each country case in light of the foregoing discussion. I pay relatively more attention to Finland and Austria because many excellent analyses have already been devoted to the two Asian miracles.[15]

Korea

The case of Korea illustrates most of the elements outlined above. The Korean state has been very strong not only toward labor but also toward business. While it has offered large rewards for successful entrepreneurs, the Korean state has also had the ability to discipline business: "Where Korea differs from most other late industrializing countries is in the discipline its state exercises over private firms."[46]

Alice Amsden and Meredith Woo-Cumings (Jung-en Woo) have traced the historical roots of the Korean state's strength in their separate discussions of Korea's industrialization. Japanese colonization of Korea left a vacuum of power after World War II, and the state was able to establish its power in the 1960s because of the weakness of Korea's social classes. The landlord aristocracy had been dispersed by land reform, the working class was too small and too weak to pose a serious challenge, and capitalists had become dependent on government subsidies. The military government nationalized the banks in 1961, which gave the state the power to determine the allocation and timing of industrial investment.

Thus, the strength of the Korean state has never been questioned in the postwar period. At the same time, the state has been subject to checks and

---

45. See Woo, *Race to the Swift*; Amsden, *Asia's Next Giant*; and Wade, *Governing the Market*.
46. Amsden, *Asia's Next Giant*, p. 14.

balances that have prevented it from degenerating into pervasive corruption. Amsde emphasizes the role of the student movement as well as that of external poressures and the U.S. administration. The students' movement was important because it presented the state with the constant threat of rebellion, which in turn "disciplined" the government against the worst excesses of power. Because the Korean strategy of industrialization relied on the rapid education of a class of salaried engineers and other white-collar workers, the students found themselves in a pivotal position.

The external challenge factor has also been critical.[17] The challenge posed by the North Korean regime may have compelled South Korean leaders to pay more attention to overall performance and efficiency than they would have otherwise. South Korea has not been a real democracy until recently, and it is instructive to consider what may have prevented economic degeneration in the hands of an authoritarian state apparatus. The student movement may have played a role in controlling the actions of the state, but the external challenge of North Korea and dependency on the U.S. military commitment were probably more important factors.

Taiwan

Robert Wade and Alice Amsden have both analyzed the state-led industralization phase in Taiwan.[18] In the late 1940s, agriculture was still by far the most important sector in Taiwan, accounting for 90 percent of its exports. Several multiyear Economic Plans between 1953 and 1968 brought about remarkably rapid industrialization. In accordance with the "Scandinavian-Asian" model of industrial policy outlined above, Taiwanese industrial policies have emphasized the sectoral promotion of productivity at the expense of domestic competition.

Taiwan shares the legacy of Japanese colonialism with Korea. The strength of the Taiwanese state derives from the "invasion" of the island by the two million military and civilian Nationalist mainlanders in 1949 after the defeat of the Nationalist army. The islanders had no army or powerful political structure to challenge the position of the Nationalist forces, and the Nationalist-mainlander government was granted unusually wide latitude for maneuver.[19] The monopolies originally owned by the Japanese colonialists were passed to the incoming government, which then established multiyear development plans. Although they were not very detailed, these government initiatives laid the foundation for several

---

47. See in particular the account by Woo, *Race to the Swift*, who eloquently describes the strategic aspects of Korean policymaking in the cold war international environment.

48. Wade, *Governing the Market*; Amsden, *Asia's Next Giant*.

49. Wade, *Governing the Market*, p. 75.

branches of production (that is, plastics, fibers, cement, and textiles). In the 1960s and 1970s, new export sectors such as steel, automobiles, and shipbuilding were boosted, motivated partly by the idea of import substitution. Throughout this period, the government intervened heavily in favor of export industries. An impressive economic bureaucracy was set up to manage the governing of the economy.

In Taiwan's case, too, the Nationalist rulers were faced with a severe external challenge. As the claimants of legal rule in mainland China, they could ill afford a failure in economic management. A challenge, external to the Nationalist Party but internal to Taiwanese society, was constituted by the native Taiwanese islanders, whom the Nationalists excluded from power positions.[50]

Finland

Finland provides an example of state-led corporatist industrialization in which all the elements analyzed in this essay have been present. Although its severe crisis in the early 1990s has blurred the picture, Finland's economic performance during the postwar period has unquestionably been very successful. The breakthrough of industrialization in Finland took place later than in the other Nordic countries. In the 1930s, the economy was predominantly agrarian, and as late as 1950, more than half the population and 40 percent of output were still in the primary sector. Per capita gross domestic product was only half that of Sweden.[51] By the late 1970s, however, Finland had become a mature industrial economy.

Finland came out of World War II in a very vulnerable position between the power blocs of international politics. The victorious Soviet Union did not invade the country, but throughout the next forty years, Finland was within the sphere of influence in Soviet foreign policy. Immediately after the war, the Soviet Union imposed a heavy war indemnity that required an extremely rapid buildup of industrial production. The way in which this challenge was tackled alludes to the particular organization of economic management that was to prevail for the entire period of state-led industrialization. The organization of industrial production was thrust to a joint committee of civil servants, private industrialists, and bankers.

This starting point led to a conscious program of state-sponsored industrialization and the construction of a corporatist structure that was actively encouraged by the state. In the early 1950s, a strategic decision was made not to decrease taxes to prewar levels but to use the surplus created

50. Ibid., p. 237.
51. See Andersson, Kosonen, and Vartiainen, "The Finnish Model of Economic and Social Policy."

by the subtraction of war expenditures from the budget to increase investment by state-owned and private companies.[52] This decision, combined with a tradition of fiscal orthodoxy, led to continuous structural budget surpluses. Thus, the Finnish state became an important generation of net savings for the economy. The structural budget surplus did not vanish until the 1980s, and public savings accounted for as much as 30 percent of aggregate savings during the 1950s and 1960s.[53] President Urho Kekkonen also thought that the trade unions would moderate their wage claims if a larger share of savings and investment was undertaken by the state.

The first phase of industrialization in the 1950s and early 1960s was characterized by active and direct state participation in the diversification of the economy.[54] Several new state-owned companies were established, and old ones were developed.[55] The 1950s in particular were a period in which wages as well as prices were regulated according to a political bargain made by political parties as well as corporatist bodies (compare the corporatist solution with price rationing in the model). Typically, the state would encourage long-term wage contracts with low-wage increases and would then also regulate the prices of basic agricultural products such as milk. At the same time, it invested heavily in state-owned companies as monetary authorities channeled cheap finance to manufacturing investments.

Concerning decision-making institutions, one finds both an efficient bureaucratic tradition and a powerful corporatist network at work. The prestige and strength of the civil service have been emphasized repeatedly by Finnish historians. This tradition dates back to the Autonomy Period from 1809 to 1917, when Finland was under Russia's rule. Throughout this period, the civil service was in Finnish hands, and its legalistic tradition provided a protective shield against the imperialistic aspirations of Russian politics. This is one important factor that explains the relatively powerful and respected position of the Finnish civil service vis-à-vis government and parliamentary institutions. The civil service has played an important role in economic policy throughout the postwar years. In comparison with East Asian countries, one may say that the Finnish state, if understood as the political power of a parliamentarian government, has

52. A classical reference on this issue is *Onko maallamme malttia vaurastua* (Has our country the patience to prosper) (Helsinki: Otava, 1952), written by Urho Kekkonen (who was later to become president), which endorses a state-led investment strategy.

53. See Katri Kosonen, "Savings and Economic Growth from a Nordic Perspective," in Pekkarinen, Pohjola, and Rowthorn, eds., *Social Corporatism*.

54. See Andersson, Kosonen, and Vartiainen, "The Finnish Model of Economic and Social Policy," p. 13.

55. The most important examples include Neste, which established a monopoly on oil refining and then continued into different lines of petrochemicals and plastics.

been relatively weak, whereas business corporations and a relatively autonomous bureaucracy have been very strong.

Corporatist structures had already been erected during the interwar years and were actively continued in the 1950s and the 1960s. Similarly to Austria, key economic decisions have been made within an informal network encompassing leaders of powerful business corporations, monetary authorities at the central bank, and top civil servants as well as government officials.

These patterns are characteristic of corporatist concertation in which the state is but one actor among many. But there is no doubt about the essential mechanisms: Finnish industrialization was "managed" by a handful of corporatist leaders, top civil servants, bankers, central bankers, and government officials. This half-official–half-corporatist decision-making structure dates back to the very birth of the independent state. The victorious White (bourgeois) side of the civil war of 1918 was an improvised organization of the military, bankers, industrialists, and right-wing politicians. Generally distrustful of republican democracy, this organization established a constitution that set clear checks and balances for proper political intervention in the economy. The rights to private property in particular have enjoyed strict constitutional protection. This can be seen as an important ingredient in the "basic commitment" discussed above that has probably been especially crucial for a country situated within a contested zone between the world's ideological blocs.

Banks have been an important headquarters for economic management. The credit markets were rationed until the 1980s, and as in Taiwan and Korea, credit was allocated to productive manufacturing investment, while the households' demands for credit exceeded supply. From the 1930s onward, the central bank became an authoritative agent of economic policy, well endowed with ties to the business community. The central bank also directly financed a number of selected economic activities. As in Korea, Finnish business was highly leveraged and, then in line with monetary policy.

From the aftermath of the civil war of 1918, Finnish corporatism had acquired a pro-business character. However, when the Finnish Left and the trade union movement strengthened after World War II, they became gradually immersed into the established decision-making institutions. The state did not resist the buildup of a coherent corporatist structure on the "labor" side (that is, the comprehensive unionization of Finnish workers). On the contrary, authorities actively encouraged the buildup during the 1960s, when the unionization rate increased from under 40 percent to almost 80 percent.[56] This had an economic and a political logic, both fitting well into the stylized story of managed industrialization of a small

56. See Pekkarinen and Vartiainen, *Suomen talouspolitiikan pitkä linja.*

and vulnerable economy. From the point of view of state authorities and the employers, the inclusion of workers in a corporatist structure provided protection against communist influences and a measure to contain potentially dangerous political pressures. In economic terms, it was seen as a means of controlling wage inflation and distributive shares and limiting industrial conflicts. The official acceptance of trade union organization found its concrete expression in the introduction in 1967 of the tax deduction on trade union membership fees.

Finally, we see at work the phenomenon of old power networks being dissolved by the outcome of the war. Finland's defeat in the war against the Soviet Union discredited the bourgeois parties, and from then on, the business community felt much more insecure and in need of political support. This facilitated the practical management of the economy. In fact, much in the Finnish experience rings a bell for scholars of the Korean experience. Both countries were confronted with a difficult international situation, but both turned it to their advantage. As Woo-Cumings describes at length, Korea's precarious position also made it possible for the Korean leadership to exploit the country's strategic significance and squeeze out subsidy money from the U.S. administration.[57] In a similar way, Finland was to become a kind of "showpiece" for Soviet postwar diplomacy. Trade with the Soviet Union greatly enhanced the etatist aspects of Finnish economic management. This trade was organized politically, and close ties with the political elites became a source of lucrative business contracts as well.

Austria

The Austrian economy also underwent a process of late industrialization after World War II. In contrast to Czechoslovakia, Austria had never been part of the industrialized core area of Central Europe, and the outcome of the war left Austria with an economy that still relied to a great extent on agricultural output and primary production. Furthermore, the Potsdam Agreement of 1945 gave the Soviets the right to seize German assets in their occupation zone. As a result, many Austrian factories were effectively dismantled, and machinery parts were sent to the Soviet Union.[58] The period from the late 1940s to the 1970s, however, became one of heavy expansion for manufacturing industries. Iron and steel production, as well as the manufacturing of aluminum products, expanded particularly rapidly.

57. Woo, *Race to the Swift*.
58. Lars Mjöset, "The Irish Economy in Comparative Institutional Perspective," *National Economic and Social Council* 93 (1992): 164.

Most of the mechanisms discussed earlier can be seen at work in Austria. The legal and formal institutions that have carried out political intervention in the economy have been more similar to those of Finland than to those of the East Asian cases. The Austrian state has been relatively weak in comparison with various semiofficial corporations. Nevertheless, the Austrian state and civil society corporations have merged with each other in a remarkable way. In broad terms, the Austrian and the Finnish cases are reminiscent of each other.

Austria, too, had to struggle for survival from 1945 to 1952. After liberation from Nazi rule, the economy was in chaos, and the country did not enjoy full sovereignty. The Allied (including Soviet) forces occupied Austria until 1955. As in the other cases treated in this section, it is fair to say that an economic failure could have led to further losses of sovereignty.

This critical starting point led to a remarkable mobilization of the nation's resources and the adoption of an industrialization strategy that depended on state action and corporatist concertation. This was as much a response to external challenges as it was a reflection of the country's history. There had been a tragic civil war in 1934 when the Social Democrats, having been subjected to increasing provocation by the Nazis, took to arms. The victory of the conservative forces led to an authoritarian government, and the Austrian state's half-hearted attempt to counter Nazi-German infiltration was unsuccessful. Germany annexed the country in 1938. Therefore, there were ample lessons of the dangers of internal strife and external threats. With reference to the discussion earlier in this section, one can say that the outcome of the war produced a situation in which established internal power blocs were disrupted. "Denazification" laws passed in 1946 and 1947 formally eliminated Nazi influence from the public life of Austria, and the labor movement had to reconstruct itself after years of repression.

The management of the Austrian economy has typically taken place within an informal border zone of public decision making and private decision making. Yet, there has been a strong centralization of power in economic policymaking, which, as far as the practical results are concerned, has been equivalent to a strong state. Whether all these decisions have been made within the formal jurisdiction of state activities is then of secondary importance. As Katzenstein maintains, this concentration of power occurs in a political setting that does distinguish between public and private: "Lines of formal authority are typically blurred. As bodies of public law, some of Austria's major interest groups exercise, in addition to their normal, autonomous operations, administrative powers delegated by the state."[59] A typical institution in this respect is the Joint Com-

59. Katzenstein, *Corporatism and Change*, p. 66.

mission, which joins both state representatives and industrial organizations in deliberations on income and other economic policies.

The political management of the economy has included nationalization of a large part of the Austrian economy. At the end of World War II, the newly established Parliament decided to nationalize most of the assets seized by the Germans after the Anschluss of 1938. Similarly, when the Soviet Union withdrew its forces from Austria in 1955, many of the enterprises formerly in the Soviet zone of influence fell into the hands of Austrian state. This vast nationalization reinforces the argument that state-led economic management can be perfectly acceptable from the point of view of private capitalists as long as it is not motivated by a socialist ideology. It was clear in Austria that these nationalizations were not a reflection of ideological class struggle but expressions of the struggle for national independence.[60]

Austrian economic policy has exhibited important elements of planning and political intervention. There has been extensive regulation of prices and wages by political-corporatist bodies. The first wage/price agreements in 1947 were responses to the inflationary chaos of the immediate postwar period. This coordination was institutionalized in 1951. Remarkably, even the business community has by and large accepted the political-corporatist determination of prices. Finally, public ownership of a large part of the banking sector and the rationing of credit markets have "socialized" a number of investment decisions. This political determination of investment has introduced another instrument that has eased the finalization of corporatist agreements.

Many authors have emphasized the weakness of the Austrian state vis-à-vis civil society corporations. I have argued above that this weakness is somewhat illusory, because the state and corporations have merged with each other and power has been centralized. Furthermore, Austria has enjoyed a strong administrative tradition that dates back to the mercantilist unification of the most important German parts of the Habsburg Empire in the eighteenth century.[61] The Austrian civil service is well known for its great competence and is intimately involved in relations with business and trade unions. Measured by the number of officials per capita, Austria's welfare bureaucracy is larger than that of any other Western European country.[62] Hence, again we see a competent bureaucracy richly endowed with formal and informal ties with organized economic agents. The East Asian one-party state is substituted in Austria with a network of

60. In this respect, it is important to note that the nationalization laws were passed unanimously by the Austrian parliament. See ibid., p. 49.

61. Ibid., p. 63.

62. Ibid.

corporatist arrangements and a state influenced by two remarkably stable political parties.

I have tried to make sense of some successful developmental states with the help of economic theory. Although I have not considered the large body of data on failure cases, the three criteria or "mechanisms of success" I have discussed may be equally useful for telling a "failure story" according to the absence of one or more of these factors.

Can the success cases be generalized to produce "recipes" for success? It must be emphasized that the analyzes in this chapter relate to specific stages of economic development. Forces that generate long-run growth are distinct and still largely unknown. However, many theoretical and empirical arguments dress the importance of thresholds and qualitative leaps. The examination of particular phases of industrialization and structural change is therefore an extremely important task for development economics. Whether the state-led strategies analyzed in this essay can generate growth in the long run is an altogether different question. Studies by Katzenstein and many others have pointed out the weaknesses of state-led strategies in the long term. In the Austrian case, for example, Katzenstein argues that the economy's ability to produce innovations has not been very good.[63]

There are also a number of compositional fallacies involved in the idea that East Asian or Finnish experiences can be generalized. First, these countries took advantage of a particularly favorable phase in the world economy. Second, Taiwan and Korea have protected and subsidized their growing industries in many ways. If all developing countries attempted to run similarly aggressive industrial policies, the international market would become much more difficult to penetrate for anybody.

The idiosyncratic nature of some of the proposed "mechanisms of success" also renders the idea of replication meaningless. I have suggested that the external threats posed by international politics may have consolidated political institutions to produce positive results. Yet, one would not wish to live in a world so politically unstable that the threat of conflict and destruction would be a major motive for economic development. I also posited that former political upheavals might have produced situations in these countries in which economically enlightened state bureaucrats had ample room for maneuvering. By the same token, development policies cannot be built on exceptional upheavals.

Not all the suggested mechanisms are self-defeating, however. The experiences of the case countries suggest that a coherent and meritocratic bureaucracy dealing with a well-organized corporatist network can pro-

63. Ibid.

duce good results. Mainstream development policies advocated today by developed countries perhaps pay too much attention to the creation of free exchange at the expense of social and political institutions that create stability, order, and political acceptance of structural change.[64] The incredibly complex system of implicit and explicit contracts and moral rules of which a mature market economy consists contains a substantial hidden order that has developed, whether spontaneously or not, over decades and centuries. In countries where such a system is not yet in place, a one-sided emphasis on "freedom" of transactions may be ill placed. The predatory states of Africa offer ample evidence of individual optimization operating at all levels of state institutions. The economic costs of a competent bureaucracy, on the other hand, may be small when compared with the benefits it can bring about if it imposes a stable set of rules within which people can operate.

64. See Biersteker, "Reducing the Role of the State in the Economy" and "'Triumph' of Neoclassical Economics in the Developing World."

CHAPTER EIGHT

The French Developmental State as Myth and Moral Ambition

Michael Loriaux

There are striking resemblances between the political economies of Japan and France—similar elites, similar interventionist institutions, similar patterns of national preference. Does this mean that France is a developmental state? If so, we cannot treat the developmental state as simply an East Asian idiosyncrasy but must apprehend it as a more general category of political economy.

To determine if France is a developmental state, we need a definition. The term "developmental state" refers to a kind of capitalist political economy that is characterized by the preponderance of a certain kind of actor, which pursues a certain kind of ambition using a certain kind of power. The actor is the state bureaucracy. Moreover, it is a particular type of state bureaucracy, composed of the nation's best and brightest, as identified by their performance in the nation's elite universities, and co-opted into administrative careers that, as Ben Schneider shows in his study of Latin America, are not subject to the whims of political fortune. This state bureaucracy is activated by a certain kind of ambition. That ambition is not only one of economic growth but also one of protection and promotion of national interests, as perceived or determined by the administrative elite. The developmental state elite often directs its attention to perceived vulnerabilities, such as dependence on foreign suppliers of energy or the stuff of military power. As Meredith Woo-Cumings observes in the introduction, that ambition can assume revolutionary dimensions when the state bureaucracy seeks to address those vulnerabilities by promoting radical change in social structures and norms. Finally, to accomplish its ambitions, the state bureaucracy disposes of a certain kind of power. That power is, first, the power to intervene in economic life by regulating international transactions and domestic prices and, more typically, by controlling or guiding industrial investment. But no less important to the state elite is the power that comes from being "well-connected" to powerful actors in politics and business. Woo-Cumings describes the developmental state as a seamless web of political, bureaucratic, and money influences.

Is France, then, by this definition, a developmental state? In the first two parts of this chapter, I argue that France was, between 1945 and 1985, not only a developmental state but the very paradigm of the developmental state. Japan was a pale second. I develop this argument, first, by examining France's administrative elite and its interventionist powers in this period and, second, by looking at the particular kind of ambition it pursued.

In the third part of this chapter, however, I qualify this claim, as do many of the contributors to this volume, though they are generally sympathetic to the notion of the developmental state. In other chapters we learn that the developmental state arises in a certain kind of international context, presupposes a certain kind of discourse, and exhibits certain kinds of pathologies that threaten its existence. All these qualifications apply to the French case. The developmental state in France, as in T. J. Pempel's Japan, arose within the framework of a hegemonic international political economy that made possible the coexistence of developmental nationalism and growing openness in world trade. It also arose within a certain discursive context, which was characterized not only by the axiomatic acceptance of private property and the free market, as Bruce Cumings observes, but also by a nonideological pragmatism that could be achieved in Europe only after war had broken the deadlock between the ideologies of Left and Right. Finally, the developmental state exhibits pathologies, of which the three that have posed the greatest threat to its existence are authoritarianism, corruption, and the generation of rents. Not only are these pathologies present in the French case, particularly the last two, but they have also come to dominate political debate in France.

Armed with this understanding of the developmental state in France, I turn in the concluding part of this chapter to the main question of this volume: is the concept of the developmental state still relevant? Liberalization in the world economy and liberalism in the American academy have colluded to contest its relevance. Moreover, the need, felt by its advocates, to surround the concept with qualifying statements suggests that the developmental state's existence depends on conditions that may no longer obtain.

To my mind, the question of the developmental state's relevance has an important ontological dimension. If the developmental state is conceptualized as a "natural kind" of political society, the structure and logic of which are amenable to elucidation by behavioral science, then the concept is open to criticism. But I claim that the developmental state exists not as a "natural kind" of political society but as a "moral ambition," informed "mythological" conceptualization of how the world works and what can be achieved in it. The myth and moral ambition of the developmental state are kept alive by institutional routines, discursive habits, and supportive structural conditions in the international political economy. Only the latter, the external structural conditions, have become unfriendly to the developmental state in the last decade. The myth and moral ambition of the developmental state, however, endure within the protective environment of domestic institutional and discursive practices. Indeed, there is good reason to believe that they will prove resurgent as the structure of the international political economy itself undergoes change once again.

FRANCE AS THE PARADIGM OF THE DEVELOPMENTAL STATE

France, as stated above, is a paradigmatic case of the developmental state as characterized by the preponderance of a certain kind of actor, pursuing a certain kind of ambition, and employing a certain kind of power.

The State Bureaucracy in France

France's state bureaucracy is powerful and pervasive. It is more influential than its East Asian counterparts. The administrative elite is recruited from France's grandes écoles, which are specialized professional schools that function independently of the French university system.[1] University studies lead too often to occupational uncertainty. But the grandes écoles lead to a secure career path dotted with well-paid and prestigious positions in the civil service, politics, and business. Unlike the universities, to which the postsecondary school diploma—the baccalaureate—gives direct access, the grandes écoles require a highly selective entrance examination. Candidates typically prepare for that exam by taking two or three years of classes beyond the high school baccalaureate in an *école prépara-*

1. The locus classicus of work on the French civil service in English is Ezra Suleiman, *Politics, Power, and Bureaucracy in France: The Administrative Elite* (Princeton: Princeton University Press, 1974), and Suleiman, *Elites in French Society: The Politics of Survival* (Princeton: Princeton University Press, 1978); see also Pierre Birnbaum, *Les Sommets de l'État: Essai sur l'élite au pouvoir* (Paris: Seuil, 1977), and Pierre Rosanvallon, *L'État en France de 1789 à nos jours* (Paris: Seuil, 1992).

toire (preparatory school), adjoined to most of the more selective secondary schools, or *lycées*. Entry into a preparatory school itself requires a highly selective exam.

Not all grandes Écoles, however, feed the ranks of the administrative elite. The École Normale Supérieure supplies the universities with faculty, and the Hautes Études Commerciales prepares its students for business careers. The principal nurseries of France's civil servants are the École Polytechnique for the mathematically minded and the École Nationale d'Administration for the less technically inclined. The École Polytechnique (or "X," from the crossed cannons that form its emblem) was founded during the Napoleonic era to supply Napoleon's Grande Armée with engineers. The *polytechnicien* still receives primarily an engineering education, although economics has been added to the curriculum in recognition of the fact that many of its graduates go on to be something besides engineers. After *Polytechnique*, the graduate may continue in the military or buy back his or her contract and embark on a nonmilitary career. The most ambitious students, however, choose to take yet more exams in order to continue their education in a second grande école. The scientifically inclined polytechniciens will want to matriculate in one of the *écoles d'application*, such as the School of Mining, the School of Civil Engineering (*Ponts et Chausées*), the School of Armaments, or Telecommunications. All these schools lead to careers in the technical ministries. Other graduates of X, however, who like Valéry Giscard-d'Estaing are more attracted to affairs of state, will abandon the technical route and continue their instruction at the École Nationale d'Administration.

The école Nationale d'Administration (ENA) was founded after World War II to provide the nontechnical ministries with personnel who would approach their job in the same scientific spirit as the polytechniciens in the more technical ministries. The education provided at ENA focuses primarily on economics and "administrative science." The school has positioned itself as the principal supplier of nontechnical personnel to top administrative positions. The Institut d'Études Politiques, so well known to American exchange students, used to enjoy that position. Today, however, it acts chiefly as preparation for the entrance exam to ENA.

Upon graduation the top students of these two schools are co-opted by the Grands Corps of experts and civil servants that constitute the higher administration. The most important of these are the nontechnical corps: l'Inspection des Finances, the Corps Diplomatique, the Cours des Comptes, the Conseil d'État, and the Corps Préfectoral. Graduates of the *écoles d'application*, on the other hand, generally join the technical Grands Corps of the civil service: the *Corps des Mines*, which supplies staff to the Ministry of Industry; the Corps des Ponts et Chaussées, which serves the

Ministry of Public Works; and the Corps des Télécommunications, which monopolizes positions in the Ministry of Post and Telecommunications.

Co-optation into a Grands Corps brings a job with tenure. But members of the Grands Corps can take extended leave from their administrative appointment without giving up tenure. While on leave they are free to try their chances in business or politics or to take on other administrative assignments outside the particular function of the corps, notably in the cabinet of a government minister. To do so involves no professional risk, because administrators can reclaim their job in the *corps* if they should decide (say, after an unsuccessful election) to return. It was once common for the elite civil servant to take leave to accept a "retirement" position in a large firm. This practice is called *pantouflage* (from *pantoufles*, meaning "slippers"), and corresponds to the "golden parachute" of the Japanese. But the golden parachute of the French can be used again and again, a fact that has encouraged France's administrative elite to jump younger and more often. France has become a country that is governed by its youth. The director of the powerful public works firm, the Compagnie Générale des Eaux, is a thirty-eight-year-old graduate of X and ENA, *Inspecteur des Finances,* who first took leave from his administrative position to enter the cabinet of Finance minister Édouard Balladur at the age of twenty-eight. His career path is particularly brilliant, but not atypical. The Grands Corps confers on its youthful elite a striking degree of independence and an insufferable degree of self-confidence that can generate a sort of brash and bold experimentalism in public policy that looks very "un-European" and, one might say, somewhat East Asian.

Because the system of the Grands Corps confers a high degree of flexibility on the civil servant's career path, one finds the administrative elite not only in the upper reaches of the state but throughout the world of politics and business. This is particularly true of the most prestigious of the Grands Corps, the Inspection des Finances, members of which dominate ministerial cabinets and abound on the boards of large firms, both public and private, and in the inner circles of France's principal political parties. As of this writing, *enarques* (the somewhat satirical designation of ENA graduates) direct Renault; Peugeot; the petroleum firm Elf-Aquitaine; the two largest deposit banks, the Banque Nationale de Paris and the Société Générale; as well as one of France's principal insurance companies, the Union des Assurances de Paris. Peter Hall (citing Pierre Birnbaum) reports that 4 percent of the heads of private banks came from the civil service in 1954 but that 30 percent came from the civil service in 1974. In the mid-1970s, 43 percent of the heads of the hundred largest corporations in France had at one time been civil servants. In 1996, 43 percent of France's two hundred top chief executive officers come from the ranks of the higher civil service, up from 41 percent in 1985, despite the privatization of many of France's state-owned firms in the late 1980s and early 1990s.[2]

In government, the four most prestigious nontechnical corps supply approximately two-thirds of the personnel of ministerial cabinets. As for politics, France, in the words of one sociologist, is a "republic of valedictorians."[3] The three principal candidates in the 1995 presidential election were all énarques: Lionel Jospin, the candidate of the Socialist Party, and Jacques Chirac and Édouard Balladur, rival representatives of the Gaullist Rassemblement pour la République (RPR). Chirac began his political career in the cabinet of Prime Minister Georges Pompidou at the age of thirty. Gossip regarding future presidential elections focuses on Socialist énarques Laurent Fabius and Martine Aubry, Gaullist énarques Alain Juppé and Pierre Séguin, and Giscardian énarque François Léotard. Fabius was co-opted into the inner political circle of François Mitterrand in 1975, at the age of twenty-seven. As president, Mitterrand named three énarques from the same class of 1980 to important ministerial portfolios: Michel Sapin, Ségolene Royale, and Frédérique Bredin—none yet forty years old.

The énarques owe their power not only to their (somewhat overblown) reputation for brilliance but also to the fact that they are classmates of powerful people who, in turn, owe their power to the same fact. Sociologists Michel Bauer and Bénédicte Bertin-Mourot characterize France as a society of "castes." Power and privilege are distributed on the basis not of one's birth but of one's diploma. There is little or no mobility between educational castes. Within this caste system, the énarque is the Brahmin.

The pervasiveness and power of France's civil service elite create a political economy in which the boundary between public and private is extraordinarily porous. As Hall writes, "To a degree present in few other nations, the management of French industrial strategy became a cooperative endeavor between civil servants and industrialists."[4] Indeed,

2. Peter Hall, *Governing the Economy: The Politics of State Intervention in Britain and France* (New York: Oxford University Press, 1986), p. 168; Michel Bauer and Bénédicte Bertin-Mourot, *Radiographie des grands patrons français* (Paris: L'Harmattan, 1997). Twenty-six percent rose up in the firm's own ranks, and 31 percent were chosen from among the firm's principal owners.

3. Michel Bauer, interviewed in *Le Nouvel Observateur*, February 16–22, 1995. See François Bazin and Joseph Macé-Scaron, *Les Politocrates* (Paris: Seuil, 1994). Michel Bauer and Bénédicte Bertin-Mourot, *Les 200: Comment on devient un grand patron* (Paris: Seuil, 1987), and, by the same authors, *L'ENA: Est-elle une business school?* (Paris: Centre National de la Recherche Scientifique, 1993), and "*L'accès au sommet des grandes enterprises françaises, 1985–1994* (Paris: Centre National de la Recherche Scientifique, 1995).

4. Hall, *Governing the Economy*, p. 168.

the civil servants quite often are the industrialists. "The . . . interpenetration of administrative and industrial technocracies," notes one observer, "has no equivalent in the Western world, not even in Japan."[5]

The Interventionist Power of the French State: Planning and the Public Sector

The developmental state endows a more or less politically independent elite state bureaucracy with two kinds of power: good connections and interventionist tools. I touched on good connections in the preceding section. In this section and the next I turn to the state's interventionist tools, beginning with economic planning and the public industrial sector and concluding with a look at what was for several decades the state's most powerful tool: its capacity to influence investment through its control over credit allocation.

Chalmers Johnson characterizes the developmental state as "plan rational." France, unlike other states that have been characterized as developmental, has actually used formal economic planning since World War II.[6] But the French case suggests that we should employ the term "plan rationality" with care. It refers more to an ambition than to a result or a process.

Planning was inaugurated after World War II and remains in effect to this day. Planning in France has always been "indicative" rather than imperative and has never threatened the centrality of either the market or private capital in the French political economy. The first three plans of economic development sought to promote overall expansion of the economy by funneling investment to basic industries. Because this policy had the effect of increasing French demand for imported goods, it depended on the government's capacity to control transactions across its borders with quotas and tariffs. When trade liberalization stripped away France's capacity to exert such control, the French reformed the plan and used it to promote the competitiveness of selected French firms on internationalized markets. The plan fostered contractual agreements with French firms, according to which the state provided them with financial support to implement firm-specific strategies approved by the state. Such agreements produced a series of mergers in the 1960s and 1970s designed to develop "national champion" firms, as I discuss below.

---

5. Christian Stoffaës, "Industrial Policy in the High Technology Industries," in William J. Adams and Christian Stoffaës, eds., *French Industrial Policy* (Washington, D.C.: Brookings Institution, 1986), p. 43.

6. On Johnson, see the introduction to this volume by Meredith Woo-Cumings; Hall, *Governing the Economy*, chap. 6.

Businesspeople have never felt any real compunction to refer to the plan except as an expression of the medium-term intentions of the state with regard to public procurement and subsidies.[7] In the estimate of Pierre Rosanvallon, the "latent functions" of the plan—the promotion of alliances between industrial sectors and the state to reform industrial structures, a certain "apprenticeship" in social change—were more important than its putative role of economic coordination.[8] Planning, moreover, proved ineffectual with regard to achieving more abstract macroeconomic objectives, such as price stability, demand management, and employment, which were more sensitive to short-term pressures. Planning lost much of its attractiveness during the 1970s when France confronted problems that called for radical change in the thrust of fiscal and monetary policy. Industrial policy turned its back on the plan and focused on the more immediate problems of preserving employment and propping up firms threatened by bankruptcy.[9]

The Socialist electoral victory of 1981 resurrected planning. Priority programs (*programmes prioritaires d'exécution*) committed the state to fund projects on a multiyear basis to shelter them from the impact of external shocks. Planning contracts (*contrats de plan*), signed between the state and chosen industrial firms, provided financial support to firms to pursue certain state goals while leaving firm management largely autonomous in determining how those goals would be achieved. Though the government had nationalized the largest industrial firms, it made clear that it wanted to respect the individual firm's decision-making autonomy and confine the state to a role of sympathetic and supportive stockholder. But liberalization in the mid-1980s has again raised questions regarding the usefulness of the plan.

The state derived greater interventionist power from the fact that it owned a number of large industrial firms. France's large public sector was created in four waves. Subsidized services and defense industries were brought under state ownership in the 1930s,[10] when the French unified the national railway system under the aegis of the Société Nationale des Chemins de Fer (SNCF) and nationalized a number of aeronautical firms. The second wave occurred in the aftermath of World War II and was con-

---

7. See John H. McArthur and Bruce R. Scott, *Industrial Planning in France* (Boston: Division of Research, Graduate School of Business Administration, Harvard University, 1969). François Caron, *Histoire économique de la France, XIXe–XXe siècles* (Paris: Armand Colin, 1981), pp. 247–49.

8. Rosanvallon, *L'État en France*, pp. 247–48.

9. Suzanne Berger, "Lame Ducks and National Champions: Industrial Policy in the Fifth Republic," in Stanley Hoffmann and William Andrews, eds., *The Fifth Republic at Twenty* (Albany: State University of New York Press, 1981).

10. Caron, *Histoire économique*, pp. 225–27.

siderably more extensive. The state nationalized much of the energy sector, which it brought under the control of three large public firms: the Charbonnages de France (coal); Gaz de France (natural gas); and électricité de France. The state also nationalized a sizable fraction of the financial sector, including the central bank, the Banque de France, and the three main deposit banks, Crédit Lyonnais, Société Générale, and Banque de Paris et des Pays Bas. Through these nationalizations the state sought to bring supply-side factors—energy, capital, and transportation—under its direct control to hasten economic reconstruction and modernization. The automobile firm Renault was also nationalized at this time, but as punishment for the collaborationist politics of its owners rather than for economic reasons.

The third wave occurred during the presidency of Charles de Gaulle (1958–69), who, rather than nationalize existing industries, created a number of new public firms in high-tech sectors: Aérospatiale in the aerospace industry, *Cogéma* in nuclear materials, and CII in information processing. De Gaulle also created a number of government laboratories and research centers in applied sciences: the Commissariat à l'énergie Atomique (nuclear engineering and materials); the Centre National d'études Spatiales (space launchers and satellites); the Centre National d'études des Télécommunications; as well as national laboratories in oceanology, information processing, and the biological sciences.

The fourth and most extensive wave of nationalizations occurred in 1982 following the electoral victory of the Socialist leader, François Mitterrand. Mitterrand added twelve major industrial companies to the public sector. Among these were five major industrial conglomerates (Saint-Gobain-Pont-à-Mousson, Rhône-Poulenc, Péchiney-Ugine-Kuhlmann, Compagnie Générale d'Électricité, and Thomson); two steel companies (Usinor and Sacilor); two high-technology defense companies (Dassault and Matra); three subsidiaries or affiliates of foreign-based multinationals (Compagnie Générale de Constructions Téléphoniques, CII-Honeywell-Bull, and Roussel-Uclaf); thirty-six commercial banks; and two major investment banks (Suez and Paribas). The nationalizations reinforced the public sector's existing dominance in some areas—transportation, communications, energy, banking, and insurance—and made it newly ascendant in others—basic industries, high-technology industries, capital goods industries (mechanical equipment, and so forth), and the automobile industry. Following the nationalizations, public enterprises employed 750,000 people in France and another 250,000 abroad, produced 25 percent of domestic industrial output, and produced fifty percent of output in sectors in which there was considerable industrial concentration, such as where production was capital intensive, and in sectors in which investment in research and development was high, or in which the propensity to export was high.[11]

Throughout the post–World War II period, the French used their large public sector advantageously to manage the supply-side factors of industrial growth, as a tool of macroeconomic policy, and to restructure French industry to enhance its competitiveness on international markets. The French used the state's control over supply-side factors, such as energy and transportation, to promote economic development by keeping costs low. Between 1959 and 1974, the prices of goods and services produced by the state sector actually diminished by 20 percent relative to the prices of goods and services as a whole. Energy prices fell by 30 percent.[12] The state also used its control over supply-side factors to bolster anticyclical policy. As a rule, the investment effort of France's state-owned industries was greater—sometimes significantly greater—than that of private firms. The rate of investment of public firms (that is, the ratio of the firm's investment in fixed capital to its value added) fluctuated in the mid-40 percent range throughout the 1960s and 1970s, reaching a maximum of 54 percent in 1979–80 in reaction to the second oil shock. The rate of investment of private firms, in contrast, generally fluctuated between 15 and 20 percent. The state has sometimes made very sophisticated use of its public sector to support macroeconomic policy. In the mid-1970s, in the wake of the OPEC (Organization of Petroleum Exporting Countries) shock, the French adopted a policy of heavy borrowing on foreign capital markets, the purpose of which was twofold: to bring capital into the French economy at a time when the oil crisis was causing money to leave the country in large volumes, and to strengthen foreign demand for the floating franc by converting borrowed currencies into francs (and thus to prevent the franc from depreciating against the dollar, which was used to import oil). Because of the crisis, the demand for capital by private firms was weak. The state therefore encouraged and even directed state-owned firms to be the instrument of this policy.[13]

The Interventionist Power of the French State: Subsidies and Control over Credit Allocation

Although state ownership of industrial and financial firms provided the state with a more flexible and powerful interventionist tool than indica-

11. Christian Stoffaës, "Postscript," in Adams and Stoffaës, *French Industrial Policy*, pp. 201–2.

12. Michel Pébereau, *La politique économique de la France: Les instruments* (Paris: Armond Colin, 1985), pp. 17–24.

13. Michael Loriaux, *France after Hegemony: International Change and Financial Reform* (Ithaca: Cornell University Press, 1991), pp. 34–38.

tive planning, the principal instrument of industrial policy, in France as in other developmental states, has traditionally assumed the form of subsidy programs and credit controls. The Fund for Economic and Social Development (Fonds de Développement Économique et Social, or FDES) which appropriates money directly from the state budget, was the workhorse of industrial policy under the Fourth Republic (1945–58). Its importance declined under de Gaulle, who sought to balance the budget. But the oil and monetary crises of the mid-1970s and the subsequent need to reform finances and reorganize industry gave the fund new life. In 1974–75 alone, the fund funneled Fr 3 billion to the automobile industry and steel.

The fund also backed up a number of subsidy programs that were created in the wake of the oil crisis. The Interministerial Committee for Industrial Restructuring (CIRI) was created in 1974 to help small and medium-size firms, particularly when jobs were at risk. The Interministerial Orientation Committee for the Development of Strategic Industries (CODIS) subsidizes investment in innovative technologies. Like CIRI, it draws its funds primarily from the FDES, but concentrates its attention on large firms. The Interministerial Committee for the Development of Investment and Defense of Employment (CIDISE) supports investment in medium-size firms. The Special Fund for Industrial Adaptation (FSAI), created in 1978, was designed to promote investment in regions where unemployment was high. Most of its aid has gone to shipbuilding and the automobile industry. The Institute for Industrial Development (IDI) was created in the 1970s to perform the same mission as CIDISE, but in a reversal of roles it has focused to a large extent on declining industries. Finally, the National Agency for the Promotion of Research (ANVAR), whose role has grown considerably in recent years, directs its aid toward small and medium-size firms that invest in innovative products or techniques.

For the most part, these subsidy programs survived liberalization in the mid-1980s. Inversely, liberalization all but eliminated what had served as the chief tool of state intervention for almost three decades: the capacity to control the allocation of credit by banks and other financial institutions. France has a dozen or more public and parapublic financial institutions that are either state-owned or operate under a charter. They include the Caisse des Dépôts et Consignations (CDC), which acts as the "bank" for local administrations; the Crédit National, which specializes in industrial loans; and the Crédit Foncier, which specializes in home mortgages. Law requires that state and parastate financial institutions, including the post office (which, as in most European countries, manages checking accounts), deposit a part of their resources with the Treasury. The Treasury, in turn, keeps an account of its own with the post office to pay government fees and salaries and facilitate the collection of revenues. The banking system was partially integrated into this "Treasury circuit" in fulfillment of the requirement that banks retain a certain fraction of their reserves in Treasury bonds. This crisscrossing of liabilities between the Treasury, the post office, the banks, and the semipublic financial institutions allowed Treasury officials in the 1950s to draw on multiple accounts to finance public spending without issuing bonds or relying on inflationary financing and thus to transform short-term deposits into long-term loans and even subsidies. The Treasury used money deposited in post office accounts in much the same way that a bank uses its reserve assets to create more money—that is, by inscribing transfers onto the post office accounts of households (the salaries of civil servants, for example) and firms (subsidies and grants). But because the money borrowed by the Treasury from one of these institutions to pay off the state's creditors ultimately found its way back to the banks, the post office, or one of the financial institutions that composed the Treasury circuit, a fraction of the money that was created made its way ipso facto back to the Treasury. Thus the Treasury had the unusual capacity to feed its "reserves" with money of its own creation. In technical terms, the credit multiplier was, theoretically, nonexistent.[14] Properly handled, the Treasury circuit offered policymakers a tool that they could use to redistribute money while both avoiding the political liability of increasing state income through higher taxes and containing the dangers of inflationary financing.[15]

De Gaulle's fiscal conservatism made it impossible for the Treasury in the 1960s to continue to serve as the French economy's principal source of capital. But bank reforms in 1966–67 allowed the French to disengage the Treasury from industrial policy while keeping intact the interventionist logic of the Treasury circuit.[16] The reforms moved the main site of "transformation" of short-term capital into long-term loans to the banks. They encouraged the banks to extend medium-term loans to certain types of activity by extending the eligibility of such loans for rediscounting at the central bank. Simultaneously, the state discouraged the banks from making other types of loans by placing quantitative restrictions on the overall growth of credit. Those restrictions were referred to as encadrement du crédit. Encadrement du crédit supplied the state with a powerful financial tool of interventionism. In effect, the state merely had to exonerate a particular sector from encadrement to attract credit to it.

14. See Loriaux, *France after Hegemony*, pp. 65–72, 150–53.
15. See Edgar Faure, *Mémoires* (Paris: Plon, 1982), 1:457; Jean-Pierre Patat and Michel Lutfalla, *Histoire monétaire de la France au XXᵉ siècle* (Paris: Économica, 1986), pp. 140–41.
16. Patat and Lutfalla, *Histoire monétaire*, p. 163.

By declaring loans to that sector eligible for discount by the central bank, the state could make the attraction irresistible.

THE DEVELOPMENTAL STATE AND INDUSTRIALIZATION IN FRANCE

The frequent application of the concept of the developmental state to the newly industrialized countries of East Asia has caused it to become associated with the idea of late industrial development. That association has exposed the concept to criticism. One can establish a link between developmentalism and late and rapid industrialization only by advancing the counterfactual claim that "if the developmental state did not exist, late industrialization would not have occurred." That claim is difficult to prove.

The comparison with France lets one explore and clarify what claims can be made about the developmental state and its link to industrialization. What the French case shows is (a) that industrialization was well advanced in France before the developmental state was in place; (b) that the developmental state, once in place, probably did not accelerate French economic growth; and (c) that the state bureaucratic elite was motivated by ambitions that were more complex than simple economic or industrial development, aiming instead at promoting a *certain kind* of industrial development.

France as a "Late Industrializer"

In this section I deal with the first two claims (a and b), reserving the third (c) for the next section. To begin, it is necessary to clear up a common misconception. France is not, properly speaking, a "late industrializer." Industrialization in France was well under way by 1810.[17] France is occasionally mischaracterized as such in the political science literature, and the mischaracterization is sometimes used to lend credence to the idea that late industrialization breeds industrial policies that are funded by state-controlled bank credit. Alexander Gerschenkron is sometimes awarded paternity for this claim, but all that Gerschenkron says in his sparse references to the French experience is that investment banks helped France (and Germany) overcome England's short industrial head start. But even this observation squares imperfectly with the historical record. It is true that France experimented with long-and medium-term credit institutions backed by state charter and guarantees, particularly

17. See Albert Soboul, "La reprise économique et la stabilisation sociale, 1797–1815," in Fernand Braudel and Ernest Labrousse, *Histoire économique et sociale de la France* (Paris: Presses Universitaires de France, 1976), tome 3, vol. 1, pt. 1, bk. 1, chap. 2, pp. 105–12.

under the Second Republic (1851–71). Industrialization, however, owed much more to industrial self-financing than it did to bank financing. The chartered banks preferred to invest in railroads and public works rather than in industry.[18] Gerschenkron's paradigmatic investment bank, the Crédit Mobilier of the brothers Péreire, went belly up less than twenty years after its founding when the French government, fearing monetary instability more than some putative industrial late start, refused the bank permission to raise funds through bond issues.[19] Later in the century, institutional savings, though voluminous, generally ended up in government bonds—even foreign government (Russian)bonds—rather than in industrial investment.

It is true that industrialization in France was hampered by the lesser abundance of coal reserves, slow population growth, and the fact that France, by its climate and soil, had an authentic agricultural vocation, which was not the case for either England or Germany.[20] Thus people migrated less from the farm to the factory in nineteenth-century France than they did in England and Germany. Half of Britain's population was urban by the middle of the nineteenth century. France's population did not reach that benchmark until the interwar period. As for coal, the major deposits straddled the Belgian border. The veins were thin and difficult to exploit. The iron deposits of Lorraine were largely in German hands between 1871 and 1914, and technology was not able to rid the ore of impurities efficiently until late in the nineteenth century. For these reasons, French iron and steel manufacturing did not take off until the early twentieth century.[21]

Nevertheless, France did industrialize in the nineteenth and early twentieth centuries, and it did so with little intervention by the state. The textile industry mechanized in the early nineteenth century, producing the same spillover effects as in England, though on a smaller scale. The construction of the railroads in the mid–nineteenth century relayed textiles as the motor of industrialization.[22] The state intervened modestly, but importantly, to provide the economy with infrastructure. It built and owned

18. Caron, *Histoire économique*, pp. 8.6–89; André Broder, "Le commerce extérieur: L'Échec de la conquête d'une position internationale," in Braudel and Labrousse, *Histoire économique et sociale de la France*, tome 3, vol. 7, pt. 2, bk. 7, chap. 3, pp. 332–34; see especially ibid., chap. 4, 5, and 6, by Maurice Lévy-Leboyer. On state support for railway construction in the nineteenth century, see Pierre Léon, "La conquête de l'espace national," in ibid., chap. 1, pp. 260–62.

19. See Caron, *Histoire économique de la France*, pp. 53–55.

20. See André Armengaud, "Le rôle de la démographie," in Braudel and Labrousse, *Histoire économique et sociale de la France*, tome 3, vol. 1, pt. 1, bk. 2, chap. 2.

21. Maurice Niveau, *Histoire des faits économiques contemporains* (Paris: Presses Universitaires de France), p. 58.

22. Ibid., p. 62. Caron, *Histoire économique*, pp. 67–76.

the rails, the roads, and the canals but awarded their exploitation to private capital. Despite the state's modest role, polytechniciens and engineers of the Grands Corps figured prominently in French industrialization. They did so, however, as private entrepreneurs rather than as state officials, particularly in the latter half of the century. The French phenomenon of the polytechnicien rising rapidly in the managerial hierarchy of the industrial firm makes its first appearance at this time, particularly in the mechanical industries, steel, and chemicals.[23]

Industrialization accelerated in the decades preceding and following World War I. When the "second industrial revolution" commenced, spurred by the development of the chemical industries, electrification, and the internal combustion engine, France lagged behind no one.[24] The French introduced mining technology that was in advance of anything used in Great Britain or Germany. The postwar expropriation of Deutsche Bank holdings in the Turkish Petroleum Company, which had already begun to exploit fields in Iraq, gave France's petroleum industry a boost. France became Europe's leader in the automobile industry, second in the world only to the United States. Renault was Europe's main constructor of taxis and internal combustion engines for ships and airplanes as well as automobiles. André Citroën was the first European constructor to reorganize his automobile shop on the Fordist model and mass-produce cars. Electrification advanced rapidly, spurred in part by the electrification of the railroads. The increase in the demand for electricity was met by constructing hydroelectric facilities in the Alps and along the border of the Massif Central.

France's chemical industry, which had long been a tributary to German industry, experienced rapid growth after the war. Kuhlmann assumed a leadership position in the production of paints and chemical fertilizers, and Saint-Gobain branched out from its traditional base in glass and began to produce artificial textiles, assuming international dimensions. The Compagnie d'Alais, Froges, et Camargue—the future Péchiney—assumed a position of leadership in the production of aluminum. Aided by the construction of hydroelectric plants, France was second only to Germany in the production of aluminum, a great consumer of electrical power, during the interwar period. The dynamism of the French economy was apparent as well in steel, for which France was, in 1929, the second largest producer in Europe—behind Germany but tied with Great Britain. The Schneider empire, at the heart of which was Le Creusot, dominated the French steel industry. Schneider expanded his foreign holdings to include petroleum refineries in Hungary, aluminum plants in Rumania, and coal mines in Belgium, Luxembourg, and the Saar, as well as the Skoda firm in Czecho-

23. Caron, *Histoire économique*, pp. 77–78, 80–81.
24. Ibid., pp. 142–44. Claude Fohlen, *La France de l'entre-deux-guerres* (Paris: Castermann, 1966), pp. 67–89.

slovakia. The expansion of Schneider's empire was sufficient to compel the German steel magnate, Stinnes, to enter into cartel agreements with it.

Banks became more involved in industrial development after the war.[25] The French banking system was patterned after the English system, however, with its strict distinction between business banks and deposit banks and with the corresponding restrictions that were placed on deposit banks regarding long-term lending and industrial investment. The German universal bank was unknown in France. Nevertheless, France, like England and unlike Germany, was a financial powerhouse. France's financial power was uncontested on the Continent. France, the land of banks, was commonly contrasted with Germany, the land of factories. The principal business banks, the Banque de l'Union Parisienne, and the Banque de Paris et des Pays-Bas, were directly involved in the financing of new investment. The older, established banks, Crédit Lyonnais and Société Générale, created subsidiaries that specialized in the extension of medium-term credits to finance industrial investment.

The French economy grew at an annual rhythm of 4.6 percent between 1923 and 1929—twice as fast as before the war.[26] It was recognizably "modern" in its organization and in the goods it provided to the market. In 1931, 18 percent of industrial labor was employed by firms of five hundred workers or more, up from 10 percent in 1906. The very large firms, such as one might encounter in Germany or the United States, were still relatively rare—only thirty French firms employed more than five thousand workers—but movement toward financial concentration was rapid. The aluminum market was dominated by two firms; chemicals, by three; and electrical power, by two. Concentration was apparent even to the consumer who now ran errands in retail chains such as Monoprix and Prisunic.

France's industrial firms entered into transnational market agreements. France's steel industry had already organized before the war and again in 1919 to limit competition. In 1926, however, French steel producers joined their counterparts in Belgium, Luxembourg, Germany, and the Saar to create an international steel cartel: 43.1 percent of the market going to Germany, and 31.1 percent to France. During this same period, French industrial leaders, having already experimented with sectoral organization, came together across sectoral boundaries to create the Confédération Générale de la Production Française in 1919 and began to act as an interest group vis-à-vis the French government.

25. Jean Bouvier, "L'extension des réseaux de circulation de la monnaie et de l'épargne," in Braudel and Labrousse, *Histoire économique et sociale de la France*, tome 4, vol. 1, pt. 1, bk. 2, chap. 3, pp. 168–92; Pierre Léon, "Le moteur de l'industrialisation, L'entreprise industrielle," in ibid., tome 3, vol. 2, pt. 2, bk. 2, chap. 2, pp. 520–32.

26. See François Caron, "Dynamisme et freinage de la croissance industrielle," in ibid., tome 4, vol. 1, pt. 1, bk. 2, chap. 5.

Throughout this period, French industrial development proceeded with little direct state intervention. The state continued to assume an entrepreneurial role in the construction of infrastructure. It established semipublic energy firms, such as the Compagnie National du Rhône in 1921 and the Énergie Électrique de la Moyenne Dordogne in 1928 to facilitate the construction of hydroelectric projects that stretched the capacities of private capital. But, though the state's involvement in transportation and energy were vital, they were not unusual and not significantly less "liberal" than comparable undertakings by American federal and state governments. Economic thinking in governmental circles was primitive. Conservatives such as Raymond Poincaré and Pierre Laval concentrated their energies on building confidence in the currency and eliminating budget deficits. Such progressives as Léon Blum intervened by decree to increase wages and shorten working hours. But industrial policy was a concept that was almost entirely ignored.

It is only after Liberation that the developmental state made its appearance. The École Nationale d'Administration was created in 1945, planning was introduced in the same year, and by 1951 the civil service elite was piecing together the Treasury circuit. State policy after the war was highly interventionist. State interventionism accompanied thirty years of rapid economic growth and full employment. But did state interventionism cause that growth? French economic performance, when compared with that of European countries that adopted different approaches to policy, was not exceptional, as can be seen from Table 1, which presents a comparison of postwar economic growth rates in France and in other countries, and Table 2, which compares industrial labor productivity growth in France with that in other countries. Growth in the post–World War II era, moreover, had many causes, including rapid population growth, growth in the money supply, and the liberalization of world trade. We cannot attribute postwar economic growth unproblematically to the appearance of the developmental state in France.[27]

Table 1. Average annual rates, in percent, of growth in gross domestic product, 1949–1977

	1949–1959	1955–1968	1968–1973	1972–1977
France	4.5	5.7	6.0	3.2
Germany	7.4	5.1	5.1	2.2
United States	3.3	4.0	3.6	2.7
OECD		4.6	4.8	

Source: François Caron, *Histoire économique de la France, XIXᵉ–XXᵉ Siècles* (Paris: Armand Colin, 1981), p. 159.

27. See the analysis by Caron, *Histoire économique*, chap. 9 and pp. 185–88.

Table 2. Average annual rates, in percent, of labor productivity growth in industry, 1953–1973

Japan	France	Germany	Italy
8.9	5.4	5.0	5.0

Source: François Caron, *Histoire économique de la France, XIXᵉ–XXᵉ Siècles* (Paris: Armand Colin, 1981), p. 168.

The Moral Ambition of the Developmental State

The frequent association of the developmental state with rapid economic growth is both historically and theoretically contentious. But aggregate economic growth is not the only or even the primary ambition that animates the developmental state elite. Rather, the state elite is motivated by a particular kind of ambition: to provide the national community with a kind of moral good. It is in this regard that we can discern a close relationship between France, Japan, and the newly industrialized countries of Northeast Asia.

I use the term "moral good" loosely to designate a good whose pursuit cannot be justified purely in terms of economic theory. Such goods as "social stability," "social cohesion," and "self-sufficiency" are not valued solely or even primarily for the economic externalities they produce. Nor do such goods need to have any transcendental justification at all. They can be valued simply because they correspond to a customary good or social norm that has been constructed historically within a particular society. As Cumings observes, such goods can suppose a rather noncritical attitude toward axioms and assumptions that a geographical or ideological "outsider" may want to question. By characterizing such goods as "moral goods," I do not mean to discourage that interrogation. But our first task is to understand those "moral goods" as the actors themselves understand them, as well as to understand the actors' intentions. To do so we must set aside the categories and assumptions of textbook economics, and even the familiar tools of behavioral political science, to approach the phenomenon as, say, anthropologists, ever alert to the myths, rules, and norms that inform human action. Following Alasdair MacIntyre, we might define our task not as one of collecting data "in the hope of formulating causal generalizations" but as one of looking "at cases where a will to achieve the same end was realized with greater or lesser success in different cultural [or structural] contexts. . . . What we shall achieve if we study the projects springing from such intentions are two or more histories of these projects, and it is only after writing these histories that we shall be able to compare the different outcomes of the same intention."[28] Thus by collating the various national histories of the developmentalist ambition, we can determine if there is enough similarity in those intentions and in the conditions in which they have been successfully prosecuted to warrant the adoption of a category called the "developmental state."

According to this more historicist approach, the developmental state elite pursues moral goods whose definition is informed by a certain mythological construction of how the world works and what we can and should accomplish in it. I use the term "mythological" in two senses. First, I use it in the everyday sense to denote a conceptual construction of "the world" that may not be entirely accurate but that nevertheless has widespread appeal and influence. It might be thought of as a commonly accepted "misrepresentation." As a commonly accepted misrepresentation, the myth in social life nourishes routines and habits of thought and action, just as myths in religious life nourish rituals. Those routines can become so ingrained in social relations that people lose the urge or even the temptation to question the myths that legitimate and justify them. Therefore, when I claim that the French state elite pursues moral goods whose definition is informed by a certain mythology, I am claiming implicitly that the state elite's mythological construction of the world may not be accurate and should be challenged. But I would qualify this statement by pointing out, for reasons explained in the next two paragraphs, that we all labor under the spell of some mythological construction of the world. This applies to the developmental state's critics as well as to its apologists. It applies in particular to the developmental state's neoclassical and rational-choice critics, who, by my anthropological interpretation, are—like the rest of us—merely mythomaniacs of a particular kind.

The second sense, then, in which I use the term "myth" derives from recent developments in philosophy and social science. In the philosophy of science, the fortunes of philosophical realism have probably declined to the vanishing point. Realism as a philosophical project sought to prove that our knowledge of the world "refers" or "corresponds" more or less accurately to what "is really out there" and that we can determine how accurately our knowledge refers by subjecting it to scientific testing. The resurgence of skepticism in the last decades of the twentieth century, apparent particularly in the works of Thomas Kuhn and Paul Feyerabend, but not absent in those of Karl Popper and Imre Lakatos, has undermined realism's case and lent credence to the claim that knowledge

28. Alasdair MacIntyre, "Is a Science of Comparative Politics Possible?" in *Against the Self-Images of the Age: Essays on Ideology and Philosophy* (Notre Dame: University of Notre Dame Press, 1978), p. 272.

consists of a plurality of historically and culturally specific constructions of local worlds.[29] The ability of a knowledge claim to refer to the real world cannot, technically, be determined, and so we should treat the claim as a "practical" one rather than as an epistemological one. In other words, we should treat it as a claim whose value is most meaningfully assessed by simply applying it pragmatically—by "trying it out." The warrant for the knowledge claim is an instrumental one—it works or it fails to work.

In similar fashion, recent theorizing in social science maintains that the phenomena of the social world that we habitually treat as "external objects" (states, classes, markets) are also social constructs. They exist in the mind as "myths" that both explain the world to us and guide and constrain our action in it. As is all knowledge, such myths are historically constructed and meaningful only within a specific historical context. Within that context, they generate and justify routines (secular "rituals") that embed themselves in discursive habits and institutional procedures. Like the theoretical constructs of science, the discursive and institutional constructs of social life have only an "instrumental" or "pragmatic" warrant. They are "legitimated" if they "work." If they do not work, then they become subject to gradual change or are set aside consciously for purposes of more or less abrupt experimentation. By applying monetarist theory, for example, we can stop inflation. But monetarism's success in stopping inflation does not tell us that monetarism is "true." It merely tells us that monetarism is good at stopping inflation. Nevertheless, monetarism's success in stopping inflation lends authority and legitimacy to the myths that inform monetarist theory, such as the myth of the efficient market and the myth of the rationally expectant economic actor. If monetarism did not work, the myths that inform it would lose appeal and influence.[30]

Of course, there can be—and in modern times there generally is—sig-

29. See discussions in Ernan McMullin, ed., *Construction and Constraint: The Shaping of Scientific Rationality* (Notre Dame: University of Notre Dame Press, 1988), and Peter Galison and David J. Stump, eds., *The Disunity of Science: Boundaries, Contexts, and Power* (Stanford: Stanford University Press, 1996). On Popper, see discussion by Robert D'Amico, *Historicism and Knowledge* (New York: Routledge, 1989), chap. 1.

30. This approach has several sources; see esp. Anthony Giddens, *The Constitution of Society* (Berkeley: University of California Press, 1984). It has entered political science through international relations: see Friedrich Kratochwil, *Rules, Norms, and Decisions: On the Conditions of Practical and Legal Reasoning in International Relations and Domestic Affairs* (Cambridge: Cambridge University Press, 1989). On the threat of relativism in this perspective, see Richard Rorty, "Is Natural Science a Natural Kind?" in McMullin, ed., *Construction and Constraint*, and Charles Taylor, "Rationalism," in *Philosophy and the Human Sciences* (Cambridge: Cambridge University Press, 1985), chap. 4.

nificant disagreement about what it means for a mythologically informed social theory "to work." The pragmatic warrant generally produces convergence around the "best theory" in the natural sciences, because scientists tend to agree on the aims that they pursuing.[31] But it rarely produces convergence in the social sciences, because there is great disagreement regarding the ends that social theorizing is supposed to promote. Some people, for example, will maintain that a theory that stops inflation "works." Others, however, will contend that the theory that "works" will be the one that eliminates economic inequality, secures the economic self-sufficiency of the nation, or achieves some other good besides stable prices. Such people might well find monetarism inadequate, misleading, or even false (because, for example, the market tensions that feed inflation will "truly" disappear only in an egalitarian society). Given such disagreement regarding the good that social theorizing is supposed to achieve, the philosopher of science Mary Hesse argues that "the proposal of a social theory is more like the arguing of a political case than like a natural-science explanation."[32] The critical analysis of fact and value, in this view, are best pursued jointly and simultaneously. They are of necessity integrated into a broader political debate about how the world works and what we should do in it.[33]

Such observations as these affect how we conceptualize the task at hand. When we ask if the concept of the developmental state is still relevant, we mean to ask, in the most general terms, if it still has a (potentially) viable place in contemporary debate regarding the proper balance between the state and the market. That question can be broken down further. Do the myths that nourish the developmental state still have appeal and influence? Are the actions and theoretical visions that those myths, habits, and routines inform perceived "to work" according to some instrumental criterion? Is the moral good that the developmental state seeks to promote a compelling one?[34]

---

31. See Larry Laudan, *Science and Values: The Aims of Science and Their Role in Scientific Debate* (Berkeley: University of California Press, 1984).

32. Mary Hesse, "Theory and Value in the Social Sciences," in Christopher Hookway and Philip Pettit, *Action and Interpretation* (Cambridge, England: Cambridge University Press, 1978), p. 16.

33. Stephen Toulmin's analogy with legal debate is appropriate here. See Toulmin, *The Uses of Argument* (Cambridge: Cambridge University Press, 1958).

34. The question of the moral justification of developmentalism deserves much more attention than it receives in this chapter. But because the question of the developmental state is typically conceptualized as an empirical question, I fell compelled to remain generally loyal to accepted practice so as not to stray further from my assignment—which is simply to assess the appropriateness of the notion of the developmental state to the French case—than I already have.

The Origins of the Moral Ambition of French Developmentalism

Drawing on this conceptualization of out task, we must first try to discern the "myths" and "moral ambitions" that animate the French developmental state elite. Like anthropologists, we must draw on a wide range of field observations and distill from them some more or less succinct statement of what those myths and moral ambitions are. The documentary evidence contains no straightforward statement of the state elite's ambitions—there are no "ten commandments" of the developmental state. But as one becomes familiar with state elite thinking, one begins to perceive in outline four formative myths that emerge again and again in the literature: (1) the French state is creator and tutor of the nation; (2) the Grands Corps of the state are the repositories of a science of national development and flourishing; (3) economically, France shows a tendency toward stagnation, the result of its unwillingness to embrace innovative techniques and ideas; and (4) France's "stagnation" makes the French nation vulnerable to the "outside" world. These four myths inform the state's moral ambition, which is to use its science to preserve the "French nation" (itself a mythological construct) from the forces that threaten it. Note that the myth of France's "stagnation" goes directly counter to what I argued earlier in this chapter. The myths that inform elite thinking do not have to be "true." They have to "work" or risk being rejected, but they do not have to be true.

The first two myths hearken back to the revolution, which destroyed the institutional bases of the ancien régime and confronted the revolutionaries with the challenge of restoring political cohesion. Both the destructive and reconstructive aspects of nation building are exemplified by the abolition of the provinces, characterized by their idiosyncratic institutions, patois, and identities. Adrien-Cyprien Duquesnoy defended the creation of the new, more compact *départements* in these terms: "A new division of the territory should above all produce that inestimable advantage of melting the local and self-centered spirit into a public and national spirit, it should turn all the inhabitants of this commonwealth [cet empire] into Frenchmen; all those who, until today, were merely Provençaux, Normands, Parisians, or Lorrains."[35] The desire to turn "peasants into Frenchmen" conferred on the revolutionary state a tutelary mission.[36] "The specificity of the French state relative to the English or American state has its deepest origin in this fact. It lies not in some 'interventionist tradition' dating back to Colbert, but in its tutelary [*insti-*

35. Adrien-Cyprien Duquesnoy, quoted in Rosanvallon, *L'État en France*, p. 102; my translation.

36. See Eugen Joseph Weber, *Peasants into Frenchmen: The Modernization of Rural France, 1870–1914* (Stanford: Stanford University Press, 1976).

tutrice] dimensions which date back to the Revolution."[37] That tutelary mission first expressed itself in the 1794 goal of eradicating "the patois and generalizing the usage of the French language."[38] The eradication of regional patois consumed educational energies for the next century and a half, driving to extinction not only local peasant idioms but also literary languages endowed with a long and rich tradition, such as the *langue d'oc.* Under the Third Republic, the state pursued its tutelary ambition by using the school as the vehicle for promoting the civic virtues of nationalism and republicanism. Catholic resistance to republican schooling generated an authentic Kulturkampf that dominated political life during most of the Third Republic (1871–1940). The fossil remains of that struggle still resurface today.

The state's tutelary role encompassed more technical issues designed to promote the nation's material flourishing. The Grands Corps of state and army engineers, particularly the Corps des Mines, undertook to instruct French entrepreneurs in the use of the latest technological innovations.[39] Because the state had the power to award mining concessions, the Corps des Mines was given the responsibility to oversee mining operations. In that capacity, it oversaw mining safety, it instructed managers of metallurgical firms in innovative techniques, and it regulated prices and profits. "The figure of the military engineer was a kind of technical incarnation of the state."[40] The expectation that the state should exercise a tutelary role spread from schooling and mining and mechanical issues to other domains, such that it established a thick network of agricultural schools and laboratories. The discovery of the microbial nature of infectious disease gave rise to a number of projects to promote public health. For Rosanvallon, the hygienists of the late nineteenth century "prefigure the technocrats of the 1950s."[41]

The French developmental state is, in the simplest terms, the extension of the domain of competence of the Grands Corps from problems of engineering and issues of hygiene to questions of economic policy. That extension, however, did not occur until the mid–twentieth century. We do not find the global "economic engineering" in nineteenth-century France that we begin to see in Prussia and later in Germany. It is true that the industrial exploitation of the immense riches of the Ruhr, the dredging and canalization of the newly acquired Rhine, and the application of

37. Rosanvallon, *L'État en France*, p. 125.

38. Ibid., p. 103.

39. A particularly enlightening study of the historical "construction" of the technician's central and tutelary role in France can be found in Ken Alder, *Engineering the Revolution: Arms and Enlightenment in France, 1763–1815* (Princeton: Princeton University Press, 1997).

40. Rosanvallon, *L'État en France*, pp. 219–25; my translation.

41. Ibid., p. 132.

Germany's newfound industrial advantages to the perfecting of its military machine created an integrated engineering project that was impossible to ignore—a sort of military-industrial Suez Canal. France had no equivalent. It is no wonder, then, that the Japanese were more struck by the German than by French model.

But the sense of mission that manifests itself in the French technical corps in the nineteenth century did begin to spread to the administrative and financial Grands Corps after World War I. Experts denounced the disorganization and inefficiency of the state's efforts to finance and supply the war effort. Under the spell of Taylorism, critics called for the application of engineering science to problems of economic administration.[12] Disgruntled technocrats-without-a-mission coalesced in organizations such as "X-Crise" (Polytechnique-Crisis), and in journals such as the *Cahiers du Redressement Français* (Notebooks on French reinvigoration), they engaged in sympathetic debate regarding the virtues of economic planning, as advocated by the Belgian Socialist Henri de Man and applied experimentally in the Soviet Union. Prominent figures of the post–World War II order, Michel Debré, Alfred Sauvy, Robert Marjolin, and Pierre Mendès France, cut their mythological teeth in these circles.

The Climacteric of Developmentalism in France

France's humiliation in 1940 legitimated the technocratic myth of French stagnation. The Resistance called for a concerted effort to "modernize" France's political economy, society, and political institutions following the war. The term "modernization" took on the dimensions of a Wagnerian leitmotiv in post–World War II technocratic literature. It was the antidote to the mythological ailment that the technocrats called "Malthusianism," a symbolic term that referred not only to slow population growth but also to low labor productivity, outdated technology, overcautious economic management, plethoric distribution networks, excessive administrative costs, and overreliance on protectionism.

The Resistance's program was "revolutionary" to the extent that its prescription against Malthusianism was to "modernize" France's political economy, its social relations, and its values. It called for the nationalization of major mining and petroleum companies, insurance companies, and banks; the development of an economic plan; recognition of independent trade unions; creation of a general system of social security; and educational reforms to promote an elite of merit rather than one of class. France's first plan called for investments over a four-year period that amounted to 25 percent of the French gross domestic product, requiring

42. Ibid., pp. 232–34.

imports (primarily of capital goods) worth an estimated $11 billion over a three-year period.

The developmental state was born of the Resistance and nurtured by the Fourth Republic (1945–58).[43] It implemented the plan, nationalized key industrial sectors, created ENA, and began piecing together the institutions of France's elaborate system of credit control. The Fourth Republic also pursued a number of grandiose projects that prefigured the more visible accomplishments of the Fifth Republic, foremost among which was the creation of France's ambitious nuclear weapons program. The Fourth Republic extended the state's tutelary ambition to the world of business and launched a vast program of productivity missions, whose purpose was to expose French entrepreneurs to innovative practices being used abroad.

But it is under the Fifth Republic that the French developmental state achieved its full realization, burgeoning into what Pierre Birnbaum has called a "republic of civil servants."[44] The new constitution enhanced the power of the executive, the site of administrative and economic science, and diminished the power of the legislative assembly, the site of "party" politics and ideological squabbling. Ministry staffs bulged with Grands Corps technocrats. The line between the political and the administrative faded to the vanishing point.[45] The myth of the tutelary state tending to the vulnerable nation endured and informed the tasks that de Gaulle and the technocrats assigned themselves. The first task was to adapt France's "stagnating" economy to the Common Market and the more open world economy that was emerging from the Kennedy Round trade negotiations. French trade patterns were undergoing a significant reorientation. The share of French exports to members of the franc zone (colonies and former colonies) fell from 42 percent in 1952 to 10 percent in 1970. Inversely, the share of exports to the industrialized countries of the Common Market rose from 16 to 50 percent in the same period. The second task was to counter what de Gaulle perceived to be America's hegemonic influence over France's economic development, as exemplified by the surge of direct American investment in French industrial firms. In response, the developmental state promoted mergers among industrial firms, using subsidies and subsidized credits, to foster the development of well-capitalized, "national champion" firms that could withstand interna-

43. The technocrats also profited from a number of initiatives pursued by Vichy. Many regulations were retained, and the state consulted the corporatist bodies that Vichy had set up to deliberate policy.

44. See Birnbaum, *Les sommets de l'État*, chap. 4; my translation.

45. Rosanvallon, *L'État en France*, pp. 90–92. Large ministerial staffs begin to make their appearance in 1945. It is only in 1958, however, that the *cabinet ministériel* becomes a deliberate piece in the machinery of the developmental state.

tional competition and defend themselves against foreign takeovers. Between 1950 and 1958, an annual average of 32 industrial mergers occurred each year. That figure climbed to 74 during the period 1959–65 and to 136 during the period 1966–72.[46] The third task was to assure France's self-sufficiency and independence in security by developing high technology. The state addressed this challenge by inaugurating a number of *grands projets*, such as development of the Caravelle medium-distance air carrier, the Concorde, and the Airbus (with other European partners). The Plan Calcul was launched in the mid-1960s following the U.S. government's refusal to authorize the sale of a supercomputer to the French Commissariat à l'Énergie Atomique. France also spearheaded the development of the highly successful European space launcher, Ariane; assumed a leading position in the construction of high-speed railways; and modernized its once miserable telecommunications system so as to become highly competitive on the international telecommunications system market.

The state redefined its priority tasks in subsequent years, but the myths of the tutelary state and the vulnerable nation forever informed its deliberations. In the aftermath of the 1973 oil shock, the state shifted its support to exporting industries that could help France pay off the energy bill and to the development of nuclear power to lessen France's vulnerability to shocks in the supply of foreign oil. In the 1980s, in the wake of liberalization in international financial markets, state policy focused once again on promoting mergers that would produce better capitalized firms which were less vulnerable to market-leveraged foreign takeovers.

CONDITIONS AND PATHOLOGIES OF FRENCH DEVELOPMENTALISM

The contributors to this book have attached a number of qualifications to the concept of the developmental state. It is important to examine those qualifications because they affect our appreciation of the concept's usefulness. The French case is particularly relevant to three of these claims: that the developmental state was predicated on the existence of a particular kind of international order; that the developmental state presupposes a certain kind of political discourse; and that the developmental state exhibits certain types of pathologies that threaten its existence.

The French Developmental State and American Hegemony

The French developmental state could not have arisen in the absence of the Pax Americana. American hegemony made possible the pursuit of

46. Ibid., pp. 259–62.

nationalist economic goals using inflationary financing in the framework of a world economy that was becoming increasingly open to trade.

The French developmental state was not inflationary in theory, but it was inflationary in practice. The Resistance program planned to finance state interventionism with money levied through reparations. Compensation, however, assumed the form not of reparations but of Marshall aid, on the one hand, and French access to German coal and steel markets through the European Coal and Steel Community, on the other. When Marshall aid ceased, the state elite had to locate new sources of financing for its developmental projects. Because the political class was timid in levying taxes, the state elite pieced together the Treasury circuit.

The Treasury circuit was not inherently inflationary, but it did deprive French finances and currency of a sound foundation. State interventionism and inflation caused France's once flourishing market for stocks and bonds to wither into insignificance. Industries grew dependent on institutional lenders for outside funds. As lending institutions developed a stake in the firms to which they lent, they developed a solicitude toward them that the more anonymous market for stocks and bonds would not have shown. That solicitude was enhanced by the state's influence and control over the activity of the lending institutions, which had the effect of endowing every bankruptcy with political significance. Subsequently, there were not many bankruptcies. Firms became accustomed to overdraft financing through accounts that both bank officials and government ministries conspired to keep open. Elsewhere I describe the development of an "overdraft economy" in France, in which economic activity, rather than being regulated and directed by market forces, was driven by the growing dependence of industry on credit accounts managed by lending institutions under direct or indirect state control. The overdraft economy became a source of "soft constraints," as described by Janos Kornai in his study of the socialist regimes of Eastern Europe. In the terms of my analysis, the overdraft economy generated "moral hazard" in the French political economy.[47]

The French overdraft economy was predicated on the state's capacity to channel and control rapid monetary growth so that it did not express itself in the form of price inflation. But when the dikes gave way, the state found itself ill-tooled to force the overflow back into its channels. Industrial borrowers, under the influence of moral hazard, responded to rising prices by increasing their demand for borrowed funds. In the absence of any sizable market for financial assets, increased borrowing had no me-

47. Loriaux, *France after Hegemony*, pp. 90–95, 284–88. For discussion of Kornai, see Ellen Comisso, "State Structures, Political Processes, and Collective Choice in CMEA States," in Comisso and Laura D'Andrea Tyson, eds., *Power, Purpose, and Collective Choice: Economic Strategy in the Socialist States* (Ithaca: Cornell University Press, 1986).

chanical impact on the conditions at which credit was supplied. On the contrary, banks, ministries, and the central bank typically responded to industrial duress with more solicitude, supplying the credit firms demanded at a price they could afford.

Thus, to a considerable degree, state intervention in the economy responded to and depended on inflationary growth in the money supply. But inflationary growth in the money supply was tolerable only because the international monetary order made it possible for France to achieve adjustment, on those occasions when the mechanisms of the Treasury circuit were overwhelmed, with the help of (and at the expense of) the international community. American hegemony provided a supportive monetary environment for the French overdraft economy by providing a key currency that could be used in international transactions, thus relieving France of some of the pressures of assuring the creditworthiness of its currency; by providing a lender of last resort in the form of the International Monetary Fund (and frequently in the form of the U.S. Treasury); and by organizing international recognition and active support of devaluing currencies. When the French overdraft economy spun out of control, as it did in 1948, 1954, 1957, 1969, and 1975, the only viable adjustment tool that the French disposed of was an external one—devaluation of the franc (or, as in 1954, manipulation of trade restrictions in a way that mimicked the effect of a devaluation). When that environment changed in the aftermath of the currency crises of the early 1970s, the French developmental state entered a period of hardship.

Developmentalism and the Advent of a "Depoliticized," Keynesian Economic Discourse

As Cumings remarks in Chapter 3 the rise of the developmental state presupposed the existence of a certain kind of discursive environment. That environment determined the questions one could legitimately ask and the questions that were considered "beyond the pale." It endowed terms that one, from the perspective of U.S. liberalism, might consider technical, such as "public service" and "planning," with emotional connotations that either facilitated, skewed, or otherwise prejudiced discussion and debate.

Political discourse before World War II was inimical to the full flourishing of developmental thinking. Both the Right and the Left distrusted the state. The non-Communist Left was still very much influenced by a long anarchical tradition that hearkened back to Proud'hon and the early-nineteenth-century Utopians. The Right professed a "natural law" kind of conservatism that identified a variety of threats to the "natural" social order, which ran the gamut from scheming Jesuits to stateless Jews to insurrectional Bolsheviks. Within the Left, the rift between the Communists and the non-Communists and, within the Right, the rift between the clerical and the anticlerical Right were no less wide or deep than the principal fracture between Left and Right. During the depression of the 1930s, ideological tensions flared into a "cold" civil war that left the population deeply divided as France faced the threat of invasion by Nazi Germany. Within this context, the discussion of possible state-directed technocratic solutions to social and economic problems was inevitably prefaced by the question, Who gets the state?

World War II brought a sea change to political discourse in France. The Soviet Union and the Communist Party exited the war victorious and martyred. The traditional "natural law" Right was the victim of the allied victory, both because of associations with Vichy and, outside the collaborationist Right, because of associations with the divisive politics of the Third Republic, which were now openly implicated in France's defeat and collapse in 1940. Not only did the demise of the natural law Right legitimate the idea of state activism, it also legitimated the idea of social and economic experimentation and the focus on progress and growth—on "movement" rather than "order." Simultaneously, American influence and prestige exposed the French to another kind of political discourse, a sort of mythical hands-on, pragmatic activism that "ignored ideological debates" to concentrate on "technical," managerial solutions to "real" problems, as opposed to speculative solutions to problems identified solely by philosophical rumination. The New Deal technocrats, in whose company Jean Monnet, the artisan of the first Plan of Reconstruction, passed the war years, glowed in the aura of the new pragmatism.

Just as Taylorism was the vehicle of the "nonideological, pragmatic" approach to policy in the 1920s, Keynesianism assumed that role after the war. It recast the issue of social justice and political order as a problem of economic regulation. The tutelary state understood that language. Here was a problem that the state, directed by proper experts trained in the science of economics, was qualified to address. For Pierre Mendès France: "From this theoretical system flow a number of practical solutions. All the financial institutions, the budget, credit, the currency, and taxes, assume a new meaning and a new function."[48] Keynesian theory informed the development of statistical observatories within the state. Alfred Sauvy inaugurated the national Institute for Demographic Studies in 1945. The Services des Études Economiques et Financières was established in 1952. The French state's hegemonic position in the collection and analysis of

48. Pierre Mendès France, *La science économique et l'action*, in *Oeuvres complètes* (Paris: Gallimard, 1984), See Peter Hall, ed., *The Political Power of Economic Ideas: Keynesianism across Nations* (Princeton: Princeton University Press, 1989).

economic statistics continues to distinguish it from many Western industrialized democracies.

The Pathologies of the Developmental State

Among the pathologies of the developmental state, Woo-Cumings invites us to distinguish the "bad" from the "ugly." Since France is not a military dictatorship (the "ugly" in East Asia), I use the term "bad" to refer to the fact that some actors have better access than others to the state's favors, giving rise to complaints of injustice, arbitrariness, and inefficiency, reserving the term "ugly" to refer to the scandals of influence peddling and abuse of power that have gained notoriety since the mid-1980s.

Students of the French political economy have examined the "bad" in some detail. The "soft constraints" generated by the French overdraft economy, rather than enhance the interventionist power (conceived as both autonomy and capacity) of the state, facilitated the "capture" of ministries by industrial clienteles. Indeed, one of the advantages of the inflation-financed overdraft economy, from the perspective of the politician, was the ease with which one could avoid making hard choices.

Jack Hayward has examined French efforts to come to grips with the challenge of industrial retrenchment in the late 1970s and early 1980s. For Hayward, the French state was handicapped by the "enduringly fragmented nature of the very state machine that aspires to impart unity to a pluralistic whole." The state was fragmented into a number of area-specific policymaking subsystems, each characterized by distinctive political institutions, processes, interpersonal relationships, and shared expectations and beliefs, the existence and activity of which tended in time to become ends in themselves. Hayward borrows the term "expenditure community" to convey the way in which "the policy that emerges depends upon the interpersonal sense of community of those who share in making it."[49]

Policy toward the steel industry provides an illustration. The French steel industry enjoyed a special relationship with the state for security as well as economic reasons. It was allowed to become highly indebted and thus dependent on the state for financial support. One would look in vain, however, for signs of this dependency in policy toward the industry. The state never leveraged financial dependency into control over steel policy. On the contrary, the industry's influence over policy actually grew as its financial situation worsened. Although Jacques Ferry, chairman of

49. Jack Hayward, *The State and the Market Economy: Industrial Patriotism and Economic Interventionism in France* (Brighton, England: Wheatsheaf, 1986), pp. 13, 16, and 101.

the steel industry's peak organization, the *chambre syndicale*, belonged to the elite caste that acceded to positions of leadership in business from positions in the Grands Corps of the civil service, he used his state connections to promote the interests of his new colleagues rather than to provide the latter with lectures on raison d'état. The industry made frequent requests for government aid and supported those requests with well-articulated and ambitious investment plans. The state repeatedly acquiesced to the industry's every demand for continued financial support, despite growing concern in government over the threat of overproduction. When the industry was nationalized in 1982, there ensued no real change in the basic pattern of state-industry relations. Despite the formal transformation of the relationship between state and industry from one of collaboration to one of subordination, the state continued to concede, at colossal cost, most of the industry's demands. Socialist policy toward steel displayed "the same institutionalized, systematic, congenital optimism that the main problem is securing public funds for an ambitious investment programme, rather than in tackling the fundamental problems."[50]

Harvey Feigenbaum also questions the interventionist autonomy and power of the French state in his examination of a sector that, far from being on the verge of collapse, was wallowing in the windfall profits generated by the oil crisis of 1973–75. The oil industry in France is dominated by two state-owned companies, the Compagnie Française des Pétroles (CFP) and *Essences et Lubrifiants de France—Entreprise de Recherches et d'Activités Pétrolières* (Elf-ERAP). Not only are these two industries state-owned, but they have traditionally also been directed by elite civil servants drawn either from the technical Grands Corps or, in the case of Elf-ERAP, from the Inspection des Finances. Feigenbaum asks a deceptively simple question: did the state's control over these oil companies cause them to behave differently during the oil crisis than privately owned companies? He gives us a provocatively simple answer: no, it did not. The state-owned petroleum companies, under the direction of elite civil servants, might have been expected to develop a strategy in response to the crisis that would address broader questions of national interest, but they did not. They acted no differently from the large, private, "Anglo-Saxon" companies in taking advantage of the crisis to maximize company profits. Asked why state dominance over the industry did not produce a more nationalist or mercantilist response to the crisis, Feigenbaum replies: "Market forces fragment capitalist interests and become reflected in the state through a division of labor in the policy process. This fragmentation is reinforced by competition among elites whose corps have colonized differ-

50. Ibid.

ent sectors. The dominant ideology of 'efficiency-promoting' profit centers justifies independent firms and thus reinforces the fragmentation of the state. Thus, even when some sectors pass into public hands, the doctrines of profit maximization and managerial autonomy serve to keep the state from posing any real threat to the private sector as a whole."[51]

Financial liberalization in the 1980s, the factors of which I will examine in the next section, caused the "bad" to turn "ugly." Scandal has rocked French politics in the last decade. Much of that scandal has been pedestrian: party hacks financing campaigns through graft in public procurement. But other scandals have tarnished the myth of the state as tutor and guardian of the nation, producing a rift between elite and citizen that became a campaign issue in the 1995 presidential elections.

The "ugly" begins with the privatization of industries and banks in 1986 and 1993 under conservative governments. The Right was and is ideologically committed to liberalization. But the Right's leading representatives are civil servants who have been socialized into the myth of the guardian and tutelary state. The Right could not simply privatize state-owned industries by selling off equity on the stock market. It had to manage the sale of its stock in public firms with care, seeking to create "stable" or "hard-core" stockholders in the newly privatized firms to assure that they did not fall into the hands of foreign investors. Its point of reference was the German or Japanese model, according to which the principal stockholders in industry are German or Japanese banks and financial institutions. The government conceived the "hard core" as a small association of French financial institutions or industrial firms that could be expected not to sell their holdings in a newly privatized firm on the open market. To implement the plan, the directors of the firms to be privatized were replaced by people who were committed to the policy and who had the capacity to make it work. The overwhelming majority of these new directors were elite civil servants.

But the hard cores fizzled. Like Thomas Becket, who disappointed his king by taking his episcopal duties seriously, many of the technocrats whom the state parachuted into the chair of newly privatized firms turned into capitalists. They sold their holdings, in response not only to market opportunity but also to opportunities that would never have arisen in less state-centric economies in which insider trading is regulated and the ability of managers to deal in stock options closely scrutinized.[52] In France, insider trading is a novel concept that has only begun to inform new reg-

51. Harvey B. Feigenbaum, *The Politics of Public Enterprise: Oil and the French State* (Princeton: Princeton University Press, 1985), p. 173.

52. Airy Routier, "Le scandale des stock-options à la française," *Le Nouvel Observateur*, June 8–14, 1995. Laure Panerai, "Hauts salaires: Toujours plus!" *Le Nouvel Observateur*, June 22–28, 1995.

ulation. Given the incestuous relations among the elite, however, it is not certain that it can be regulated.

Perhaps the French public could have forgiven the elite its moment of weakness had it proven successful in achieving its goal of making French firms vibrant players in the new, more open global market. But many elites failed dismally and embarrassingly. Jean-Yves Haberer, énarque, inspecteur des finances, and former director of the Treasury, was placed at the head of France's largest deposit bank, the Crédit Lyonnais, by the Socialist government. Following liberalization, Haberer engaged in a kind of cowboy capitalism (which, symbolically, included the acquisition of Metro-Goldwyn-Mayer). Many of the bank's loans and investments failed during the post–Gulf War recession, generating losses totaling more than $4 billion by the end of 1993. The bank's losses were such that the state had to devise a bailout plan that requires more than $14 billion in public money. Haberer was relieved of his duties and replaced by Jean Peyrelevade, former director of the Banque Worms. Peyrelevade was the type of administrator that the crisis required. Under his direction, the Banque Worms lost only about $1 billion in real estate speculation.[53]

The banking crisis of the Crédit Lyonnais has been the most serious one confronted by the French in modern times. But it is not unrepresentative of what went on in the world of French banking in the 1980s. The Banque Nationale de Paris, Paribas, and the insurance company Groupe d'Assurances National, all nationalized, all directed by members of France's civil service elite, together suffered losses of more than $4 billion in bad loans and investments. Management errors among France's major state-owned insurance companies have produced losses of about $12 billion.[54]

THE VIABILITY OF THE FRENCH DEVELOPMENTAL STATE

All these qualifying observations force us to ask if the concept of the developmental state is meaningful. Globalization has weakened the developmental state's "particular kind of power," and the state elite's inability to deal with globalization in a disinterested and effective manner tarnished the developmental myth. Inversely, however, the particular kind of actor and the specific sort of ambition that characterize the developmental state endure.

53. *Le Nouvel Observateur*, February 9–15, 1995, and March 23–29, 1995.
54. Thierry Philippon and Claude Soula, "Le sinistre du GAN," *Le Nouvel Observateur*, February 15–21, 1996.

The Structural Origins of "Globalization" and French Liberalization

To understand the enduring hold of the developmental myth, we must begin by acquiring a firmer grasp of the forces that threaten it. This notion of "globalization" is itself a myth. It evokes the image of relentless, one-directional change. I argue elsewhere, however, that globalization is better seen as a symptom of change in the structure of the international political economy.[55] And a structure that changes once can change again.

According to this interpretation, the French developmental state lost much of its power to intervene in finance because of change in the hegemonic structure of the international political economy. In the mid-1970s, the United States renounced its commitment to and support of international exchange rate stability. Henceforth, exchange rates floated, and monetary transactions took place on a more open and volatile currency market. Currencies (or blocs of currencies) fluctuated on this market, and the power of monetary officials to intervene to control the fluctuations was significantly curtailed.

Floating rates gave rise to the threat of destabilizing spirals of inflation and currency depreciation, notably in the trade-dependent economies of Western Europe. Depreciation under floating rates, moreover, did not supply the monetary "fix" that internationally coordinated and controlled devaluation did under fixed rates. Currency depreciation (like devaluation) raised the price of imported goods. But if the demand for those goods was inelastic (as it was for oil), currency depreciation resulted in a vicious circle as depreciation and inflation fed off each other. Inversely, attacking inflation caused the currency to appreciate, decreasing or negating whatever commercial benefits might have been sought in the first place. Overshooting of equilibrium currency values by an inherently nervous currency market ruled out "finessing" this dilemma through "fine-tuning."

Floating rates forced the French to strengthen the franc or face the prospect of chronic depreciation and instability. But the overdraft economy made it difficult to strengthen the franc. Soft constraints jeopardized the capacity of monetary officials to regulate and control monetary growth in a sustained fashion. Officials skillfully exploited their power to disconnect domestic from international interest rates, and they also propped up the franc through controlled, public sector borrowing on international financial markets. But as they did so, they reinforced the structural weaknesses of France's credit-based economy by validating industry's dependence on institutionally supplied credit. The expansionist

55. Michael Loriaux, Meredith Woo-Cumings, Kent Calder, Sylvia Maxfield, and Sofía Pérez, *Capital Ungoverned: Liberalizing Finance in Interventionist States* (Ithaca: Cornell University Press, 1997).

policies of the Socialists in the early 1980s increased that dependence. Growth in credit allocation grew by 18.8 percent between June 1981 and June 1982. In an economy in which new credit accounted for about 80 percent of growth in the money supply, government generosity produced money supply growth of 12.3 percent over the same period.

It was apparent to the Right by the late 1970s and to the Socialists by the mid-1980s that defending a strong franc meant that France had to rid itself of its overdraft economy and the soft constraints generated by that economy. Reform began with deregulation of the financial system. Special credit programs were dismantled; well-endowed, sectionally specific financial institutions, such as the Crédit Agricole and the Caisse des Dépôts et Consignations, were despecialized; and encadrement du crédit was abolished. These reforms tightened market-generated financial constraints on industrial firms while making financial resources previously earmarked for special uses available to the whole economy. Other reforms encouraged the banks to consolidate their financial base and to regulate their lending activity by relying more heavily on their reserves rather than on central bank refinancing of privileged credits.

Since 1983, the French have not deviated from their commitment to a strong franc, despite a rate of unemployment that has surpassed 12 percent, two major crises of the European Monetary System, and fears of worldwide deflation. The results, however, have been astonishing. Inflation after 1985 fell below the European Community (EC) average, and after 1991, it even fell below that of Germany. The balance of payments, though it experienced deficits during the rapid growth years 1987–90, was in the black in 1985–86 and has remained in the black since 1992, despite devaluations of the pound, the lira, and the peseta. Foreign sales of industrial goods, a sector in which France has traditionally been vulnerable, were particularly strong. Exports of French automobiles and machine tools rose dramatically in the early 1990s.

The Enduring Attraction of the Myth and Moral Ambition of the Developmental State

Structural change in the international political economy has weakened the state elite's interventionist powers. Incompetence and graft have tarnished the prestige of the developmental state elite. The developmental state's caste system of economic management has come under fire as mergers and international agreements have brought French firms in close contact with foreign firms that operate according to radically different standards. François Mitterrand, sensing the growing rift between the elite and the people, self-consciously sought prime ministers, Edith Cresson and Pierre Bérégovoy, outside the ranks of the elite. In a move replete with symbolism, he expelled ENA from its aristocratic quarters in Paris's seventh arrondissement and transferred it to Strasbourg. Jacques Chirac, énarque, inspecteur des finances, won the presidency in 1995 by making the attack on the bureaucratic elite a central part of his campaign. His gaffe in appointing Alain Juppé prime minister—a caricature of the self-sufficient, know-it-all énarque—brought the Socialists back to power in the 1997 legislative elections.

But the state elite's loss of power and prestige does not necessarily translate into the demise of the developmental state in France. The developmental state, I have argued, has three components: actor, power, and ambition. The actor has lost power and prestige, but the moral ambition of the developmental state and the mythological construction of the "world and how it works" that informs that ambition continue to draw nourishment from institutional routine and discursive habit.

The myth and ambition of the tutelary state are still very much alive in the Grands Corps. Occasional threats to close ENA pose no threat to them. The Harvard- or Chicago-trained economist of the future who enters the Inspection des Finances will be socialized into the same mythological culture as effectively as was the énarque in the past. Nor has liberalization affected the state elite's conviction that it possesses the scientific expertise to help France overcome its mythological stagnation, which is still very much part of French political discourse. It is true that the currently popular rendering of the myth of France's "stagnation" stresses the evils of *trop d'état*, or "too much state." But that interpretation does not contest the competence of the Grands Corps technicians to design reforms that preserve the "French nation" from external threats by adapting the political economy to the global economy. Moreover, discourse in the political realm, which tends to be very critical of the "Anglo-Saxon" style of capitalism, lends legitimacy to the state elite's enduring sense of mission.

Evidence of the lasting influence of developmental state mythology surfaces in a 1992 report of the Planning Commissariat, in which independent experts examine the role of the state in a time of economic liberalization and European integration and propose measures to "improve the state's efficacity." The report indicates that since 1983, the state "has renounced most of the instruments with which it could directly control markets: price controls, encadrement du crédit, administratively determined interest rates, exchange controls, and strict licensing [of foreign transactions]." It approves the reforms: "financial deregulation . . . has given rise to dynamic and unified capital markets, and the displacement of an overdraft economy [*économie d'endettement*], in which the state . . . played a determining role in the orientation of financial resources, by an economy that is financed increasingly by markets." The report also observes that liberalization and European integration brought with them the necessity, "recognized by the state itself, to delegate to other public authorities some of its own missions of public service."[56]

But the report goes on to ask if responsibilities that had once been considered incumbent on the "nation" should be surrendered to institutions at either the European or the local level, leading toward a more federal structure of the nation and a more confederal structure of the European Union, or whether, on the contrary, those responsibilities should remain centralized at the level of the state. The report retains the second hypothesis. The state, it claims, has a role to play as "the guarantor of social and territorial solidarity." Liberalization and European unification have not invalidated that justification. Rather, this "fundamental mission has assumed particular importance in today's world, given the development of a market economy."[57]

The authors of the report concede that the old interventionist model, which "for a long time had great advantages," is not adapted to a global economy. But their solution is to design a "strategic state" which is in close contact with a multiplicity of "poles of competence"—managerial, administrative, scientific, social—and which can coordinate the actions of those poles of competence in a way that favors an effective solidaristic response to external challenges. The strategic state would be leaner and more decentralized than the interventionist state, but it would be one in which economic planning would retain considerable importance and in which the central administration would coordinate the activity of relevant agents in pursuit of specific goals. There is, of course, good reason to entertain skepticism regarding the proposal. It is important to observe, however, that the Planning Commission was able without too much difficulty to find thirty outside experts, whose livelihoods were not affected by the future of the Planning Commission itself, who were willing to argue that planning and state involvement in economic life remain relevant and important.[58]

The Validation of the Myth by Practice

The strength of a myth depends on its capacity to "work," to deliver the goods that it promises. If the myth of the developmental state retains its

56. Commissariat Général du Plan, *Pour un état stratège, garant de l'intérêt général*, report of the Commission "État, administration et sevices publics de l'an 2000," Christian Blanc, chairman, (Paris: La Documentation Française, 1993), p. 16.

57. Ibid., pp. 29, 31.

58. Among the forty-six members of the commission were Christian Blanc, general director of Air France, whose mission was to prepare the airline for privatization; Michel Crozier, Harvard sociologist and critic of France's bureaucracy; Michel-Édouard Leclerc, who challenged the French regulatory state and commercial norms by pioneering discount shopping; and Pierre Rosanvallon, economic historian.

authority, it is because the developmental state has "worked" well enough to lend the myth credibility even in these times of liberalization and globalization. The myth of liberalism and the free market, inversely, has not "worked" so well that it has effectively discredited and displaced the myth of the developmental state. In other words, the success of neoclassical thinking has not been so overwhelming, nor the failure of developmentalism so complete, that we should simply declare the debate closed.

The French developmental state, I observed earlier, set out (a) to adapt France's "stagnating" economy to the Common Market and the more open world economy, (b) to counter what it perceived to be America's hegemonic influence over France's economic development, and (c) to assure France's self-sufficiency and independence in security by developing high technology. The French developmental state has had considerable success in meeting those goals. In the aerospace industry, France is a leader in the design and manufacture of aircraft engines, space launchers and satellites, and civil and business aircraft, and it enjoys a strong position in the production of helicopters, aircraft parts and equipment, military aircraft, and missiles and rockets. *Ariane* can launch civilian satellites at one-third the marginal cost of the American space shuttle. In the energy sector, France is a leader in oil and gas exploration and production, especially in offshore technologies, transport, and refining. France enjoys leadership in the area of transportation, particularly in railroad technology and the development of very fast trains.

In electronics France has enjoyed success in telecommunications, particularly in electronic switching systems, and in the development of computer software, but it can legitimately claim a position of world leadership in military electronics, including radio communications, guidance systems, and avionics. In the 1970s, the Ministry of the Post Office and Telecommunications successfully modernized France's notoriously antiquated telephone system. The new system was a technological marvel and generated significant export profits for the ministry. In the mid-1980s, the government merged the postal ministry with the Ministry of Industry, making possible the use of those profits to finance further research and development in the electronics and aerospace industries.

The capacity of the French state to propose and implement a coherent strategy of industrial development is particularly apparent in the area of nuclear energy. France has had unparalleled success in the production of nuclear materials, the construction of nuclear boilers, and nuclear engineering. The French developed an interest in nuclear energy in the 1960s, primarily as a spin-off of their nuclear weapons program. That interest sharpened following the OPEC crisis of 1973, when France was looking for ways to reduce its dependence on imported oil. By 1989, nuclear energy accounted for about 75 percent of all electricity produced in

France. As a result, the price of electricity in France is among the lowest in Europe.

The French developmental state has not been as successful in sectors that depend less on public procurement.[59] Efforts to save steel and ship-building ended in collapse. France's machine-tool industry, despite public solicitude, has traditionally been second-rate, though it has recently shown signs of renewal. The state's twenty-year effort to make *Bull* an international player in the computer industry has not succeeded, despite its efforts to bolster the firm by pushing CGE-Thomson out of computers and requiring that it concentrate its activities in the very successful civil telecommunications sector. Inversely, CGE, having bought up ITT's European operations, now occupies the number two spot in the industry worldwide, behind ATT. It does so without Thomson, which was split off and made to specialize in military electronics. Thomson, having acquired some operations from General Electric and the British firm Thorn-Emi, has become a world leader in the sector. *Bull*, meanwhile, though it profited briefly from the favorable world economy of the late 1980s, has not succeeded in establishing itself as a major or even significant player in the computer industry.[60]

Inversely, the state has had palpable success in its efforts to restructure French industry, making it more competitive and more resistant to foreign takeover. The 1981 nationalization of Rhône-Poulenc (itself a product of state-mediated mergers in 1961, 1969, and 1975) and *Péchiney-Ugine-Kuhlmann* (PUK; also a product of state-promoted mergers in 1961, 1967, and 1971) facilitated a reorganization that was long overdue in a sector that had fallen prey to prolonged decline. The state took chemical activities away from PUK and distributed them among three other chemical firms. These other firms, moreover, were restructured in a way that allowed each to corner some part of the sector: Elf-Aquitaine for chlorine and its derivatives, CDF-Chimie for fertilizers and organic chemicals, and Rhône-Poulenc for pharmaceuticals. Péchiney was left free to concentrate its energies on the production of aluminum and other nonferrous metals. It trimmed down its operations in France and enlarged its operations in Canada and Australia, where the cost of electricity (particularly important in the refining of aluminum) is lower. The firm climbed out of deficit in 1984 and began expanding in 1988, building a new plant in Dunkerque (after having shut down most of its operations in France) and acquiring ownership of American National Can. The acquisition of American Can made Péchiney the number one producer of aluminum cans in the world.

59. Stoffaës, "Industrial Policy," pp. 45–48.
60. Abdelilah Hamdouch, *L'État d'influence: Nationalisations et privatisations en France* (Paris: Presses du Centre National de la Recherche Scientifique, 1989), chap. 6.

Rhône-Poulenc, meanwhile, under state tutelage, withdrew from fertilizers and concentrated its activities on pharmaceutical goods, textiles, and biotechnology. Like Péchiney, it climbed out of the red in 1984 and embarked on a policy of expansion that included the acquisition of the farm chemical division of Union Carbide and, in Europe, certain pharmaceutical divisions of Monsanto. Elf-Aquitaine, which was given control over the production in France of chlorine and its derivatives, became the French national champion in industrial chemicals, returning to profitability in 1987. Finally, CDF-Chimie created in 1967, embarked on an aggressive policy of rationalization, acquisitions, and alliances. Having experienced balanced accounts in only five years after its foundation, the firm was producing profits in 1987.

This litany of achievements should not hide France's problems. Observers lament the low profitability of French firms and the enduring fact that France's largest firms remain small in international comparison. But the power to identify problems and provide those problems with solutions is ineluctably informed by our mythological constructions of the world and by the moral ambitions that nest within those constructions. The question I want to ask, then, is this: will the myth of the developmental state continue to inform French efforts to address French problems? Part of the answer lies in the observations of the preceding paragraphs, which suggest that little has occurred to delegitimate or discredit that myth.

International Structural Change and the Future of the French Developmental State

Both the myth and the moral ambition of the developmental state in France have survived the onslaught of globalization and liberalization, in part because success in a number of ventures has sustained the authority and legitimacy of the myth and the ambition. Structural change has weakened the state's interventionist powers. But a structure that changes once can change again. And structural change that was once inimical to the developmental state can be succeeded by structural change that is supportive of the developmental state. The contours of such a change are discernable even now in the growing regionalization of the world economy.[61]

France, like other Western European countries, is about 30 percent trade dependent. It conducts the lion's share of its trade, however, with other European countries. The European Union (EU) as a whole is about 8 percent trade dependent. Not only is European trade largely self-

61. See Robert Gilpin, *The Political Economy of International Relations* (Princeton: Princeton University Press, 1987), chaps. 9 and 10. The alert reader will recognize structuralism as part—indeed a key part—of the mythological vision that nourishes developmentalist thinking.

contained, but at this writing, France and other countries of the European Union remain committed to the goal of endowing the EU with a common currency. Economic regionalization on this scale amounts to a structural change in the world economy. The change, as it occurs, will have real repercussions on the French developmental state's capacity to realize its ambitions.

First, monetary union will loosen the interest rate constraint on state policy. Currently, speculation shifts assets largely between three refuge currencies: the dollar, the mark, and the yen. When speculative funds enter the mark, they bid the mark up relative to other European currencies, and other European governments must raise interest rates above German rates to stabilize their currencies. The single currency will eliminate that particular constraint. Second, monetary union will enable France to conduct most of its foreign trade in its own "national" currency, thus loosening the payments constraint on state policy. France will be in the enviable position of the United States, which, because it can pay for its imports in dollars, does not have to keep a constant eye on currency markets as it conducts foreign trade. Third, monetary union will make the EU as a whole a "large country" in economic terms—that is, a country whose size, self-sufficiency, and relative independence from foreign markets make it a "price maker" rather than a "price taker." This quality will endow it with the capacity to reinstate Keynesian demand management without encountering the international constraints that have ruled such policy out in the past decade. Finally, the commercial demand for the new currency will better counterbalance the speculative demand. At present, 40 percent of all international transactions employ the dollar; 27 percent, the mark; and 9 percent, the yen. After monetary unification, about half of all transactions would employ the Euro. All these factors point to the restoration of external conditions that will make it possible for the developmental state to influence investment. What instruments the state would use is an open question, but it appears likely that it will have greater leeway to develop and use such tools. That power would, of course, be constrained by EU rules and institutions, but those rules and institutions are themselves subject to evolution.

In sum, the "certain kind of actor" that characterizes the developmental state endures and is still activated by the "certain kind of ambition" that characterizes developmentalism. Although structural change in the international political economy has robbed this actor of much of its "particular kind of power," the regionalization of the world economy may well restore some or much of that power. The French case suggests, therefore, that the concept of the developmental state remains relevant, and predictions regarding the future course of the international political economy should not ignore it.

CHAPTER NINE

The Desarrollista *State in Brazil and Mexico*

Ben Ross Schneider

> For the knowledge of historical phenomena in their concrete-
> ness, the most general laws, because they are the most devoid of
> content are also the least valuable. The more comprehensive the
> validity—or scope—of a term, the more it leads us away from the
> richness of reality since in order to include the common ele-
> ments of the largest possible number of phenomena, it must nec-
> essarily be as abstract as possible and hence devoid of content.
>
> —MAX WEBER

Over thirty years ago Juan Linz divided the world's political systems into
three categories: totalitarian, authoritarian, and democratic.[1] On the economic side, others have categorized economies by the extent of state intervention in production: command, developmental, and market economies.[2]

I am grateful to Forrest Colburn, Atul Kohli, Kathleen Thelen, Kurt Weyland, Meredith
Woo-Cumings, and the volume authors for helpful comments, and to the Kellogg Institute
at the University of Notre Dame and the Institute for Policy Research at Northwestern University for research support. Weber is cited in Rogers Brubaker, "Rethinking Classical Theory: The Sociological Vision of Pierre Bourdieu," *Theory and Society* 14, no. 6 (November
1985): 770.

1. Juan Linz, "An Authoritarian Regime: Spain," in Erik Allardt and Yrjo Littunen, eds.,
Cleavages, Ideologies, and Party Systems (Helsinki: Academic Bookstore, 1964).

2. Chalmers Johnson, *MITI and the Japanese Miracle: The Growth of Industrial Policy,
1925–1975* (Stanford: Stanford University Press, 1982). See Fred Block, "The Roles of the
State in the Economy," in Neil Smelser and Richard Swedberg, eds., *Handbook of Economic Sociology* (Princeton: Princeton University Press, 1994), for a fivefold distinction among types
of states, as well as a critique of the entire analysis of state "intervention." In addition to the
three types noted here, Block includes social rights and macroeconomic stabilization states,

These typologies run along dimensions of more or less central state control of the economy and the political system. As Chalmers Johnson and Linz argue, however, developmental states and authoritarian regimes are not mere midpoints on continuous scales but rather discrete and distinctive systems. Table 1 provides some prominent examples of the nine types of political economies generated by crossing these two typologies.

The three cells along the diagonal from the top left to the bottom right include most of the political economies of the twentieth century. These cells also contain the most stable and presumably compatible combinations of economic and political systems. The concrete examples of countries outside these types (save the authoritarian-market cases) are short lived and seem to have tendencies that push them toward this diagonal. Along the diagonal, we still know more about the corner boxes of totalitarian-command and democratic-market systems than we do about authoritarian-developmental states.

"Developmental" has been applied to states such as those in Japan, Korea, Taiwan, and fascist Italy, but this type of state took a particular form, what I call the *desarrollista* state, in Mexico, Brazil, and other countries of Latin America.[3] The terms "developmentalism" and "developmental state" are not new to the social science debate on Latin America. In Brazil the analysis of developmentalism or national developmentalism was intense in the 1960s.[4] The concept of the developmental state, as opposed to more generalized Weltanschauung of developmentalism, first appeared in the late 1960s and early 1970s. In the context of Latin America, to my knowledge, Fernando Henrique Cardoso and Enzo Faletto make the first reference to "developmentalist states."[5] The Spanish version of their book appeared in 1971, though drafts of it were circulating as early as 1967. Even more explicitly, Soares used *desenvolvimentista* to describe many postwar states in Latin America and to distinguish them ana-

---

both of which are less central to the analysis of development or state intervention in production.

3. On Japan, Taiwan, and Korea, see Johnson, *MITI and the Japanese Miracle*; Chalmers Johnson, "Political Institutions and Economic Performance," in Frederic C. Deyo, ed., *The Political Economy of the New Asian Industrialism* (Ithaca: Cornell University Press, 1987); and Peter Evans, *Embedded Autonomy: States and Industrial Transformation* (Princeton: Princeton University Press, 1995); on Italy, see A. James Gregor, *Italian Fascism and Developmental Dictatorship* (Princeton: Princeton University Press, 1979). Although cumbersome, the Spanish and Portuguese adjectives, *desarrollista* and *desenvolvimentista*, respectively, are useful for distinguishing Latin American variants from other cases.

4. See, for example, Luciano Martins, *Industralização, burgesia nacional e desenvolvimento* (Rio de Janeiro: Saga, 1968), and for a full history, Ricardo Bielschowsky, *Pensamento econômico brasileiro: O Ciclo ideológico do desenvolvimentismo* (Rio de Janeiro: IPEA, 1988).

5. Fernando H. Cardoso and Enzo Faletto, *Dependency and Development in Latin America* (Berkeley: University of California Press, 1979), pp. 143–48.

Table 1. Political and economic typologies

Economy	Political System		
	Totalitarian	Authoritarian	Democratic
Command	Soviet Union and other Communist systems	Poland? (1980s)	United States and Britain during World Wars I and II
Developmental	Fascist Italy Nazi Germany	Brazil Mexico Korea Japan (pre-1945)	France Japan (postwar)
Market	China? (1980s)	Chile (1973–89) Pre-1945 Latin America Spain (1935–75)	OECD countries

lytically from classic minimal and welfare states.[6] Developmentalism was less central to earlier debates in Mexico and began to appear more often in the mid-1970s.[7] Despite the long currency in Latin America of the terms "developmentalism" and "developmental state," analyses have tended to focus on either the intellectual history of theories supporting developmentalism or on the consequences of state promotion of industry. Largely neglected has been a full reconstruction of how developmental states evolved historically as well as a fuller appreciation of the interaction between economic intervention and political exclusion.

In this chapter I abstract out of a comparison of Brazil and Mexico from the 1930s to the 1980s four essential characteristics of the state and its relations with the economy and the polity: (1) political capitalism, where profits and investment depended on decisions made in the state; (2) a dominant developmental discourse on the necessity of industrialization and of state intervention to promote it; (3) political exclusion of the majority of the adult population; and (4) a fluid, weakly institutionalized bureaucracy in which appointments structured power and representation. These components of the model of the desarrollista state illuminate the motivation behind the actions of state elites (developmentalism); the structure of power within the state (the appointive bureaucracy); and the predominant forms of state interaction with the economy (political capitalism) and with political and civil society (political exclusion). A major goal of this chapter is to examine these four characteristics in general, including an assessment of measurable indicators or thresholds, and in

6. Glaúcio Ary Dillon Soares, "O Novo Estado na América Latina," *Estudos CEBRAP* 13 (julho–setembro 1975): 62.

7. For example, María Guadalupe Acevedo de Silva, "Crisis del desarrollismo y transformación del aparato estatal: México, 1970–1975," *Revista Mexicana de Ciencias Políticas y Sociales* 21, no. 82 (October–December 1975): 133.

Brazil and Mexico. In this usage, the desarrollista state is an intensive, middle-range conceptualization that features a combination of elements peculiar to these political economies, though these four characteristics are useful in broader comparisons.[8] In particular, my formulation of the desarrollista state distinguishes Latin American and East Asian versions in terms of career patterns in the executive bureaucracy.

Another premise of my characterization is that the developmental state must be defined solely by traits of the state and its relations to society. More specifically, the desarrollista state is characterized by an exclusionary relationship to the polity (or "political society," in Alfred Stepan's terms) and an interventionist strategy of promoting the economy.[9] Here I differ with Johnson's formulation, which adds on several nonstate features including labor relations (though these are, of course, ultimately enforced by the state) and the structure of the private sector (the prominence of *zaibatsu*-like groups and the relative absence of foreign capital).[10] Other nonstate factors such as geopolitics, culture, class relations, and the nature of private firms should not enter into definitions of different kinds of states, though they obviously affect their performance.

This chapter has several potential contributions to make to the broader literature on the developmental state. First, it offers a non-Asian perspective, which given the exceptional performance of the Asian developmental states makes them less relevant for the study of the majority of other "normal" developing countries. Second, in this chapter I attempt to specify empirical criteria for identifying features of the developmental state. Previous analyses often do not provide clear empirical referents for the defining features of a developmental state, as in Johnson's original formulation: one historical case is defined as a developmental state, yet, to the frustration of the comparativist, without using indicators that travel easily to other regions. Lastly, these four characteristics are useful in broader comparisons between East Asia and Latin America and among Latin American and developing countries generally, as I discuss further in the conclusion. The first task, though, is to analyze the four components in Brazil and Mexico, beginning with political capitalism.

8. The concept is middle range in the sense that it is an "intra-area comparison among relatively homogeneous contexts." See Giovanni Sartori, "Concept Misformation in Comparative Politics," *American Political Science Review* 64, no. 4 (December 1970): 1044. Each level on Sartori's ladder of abstraction—global, middle range, and low level—has advantages and limitations. Global theories explain a few things in many countries; middle-level, "intensive" concepts illuminate more outcomes in fewer countries.

9. These definitional distinctions draw on Stepan's three-way distinction among the state (permanent executive, legal, and coercive bureaucracy); political society (parties, electoral system, and legislature); and civil society (organized groups). See Alfred Stepan, *Rethinking Military Politics: Brazil and the Southern Cone* (Princeton: Princeton University Press, 1988), pp. 3–4.

10. Johnson, "Political Institutions and Economic Performance."

Political Capitalism

Pervasive, discretionary control by the state over resource allocation politicizes capitalism. In political capitalism, accumulation (public and private) depends more on politics than markets. "Political capitalism" is Weber's term for wartime or booty capitalism, but it can be broadened, without being stretched, to include normal peacetime conditions.[11] States worldwide set rules for capitalist economies; in political capitalism, officials make rulings. Policymakers in political capitalism have a great deal of discretion: they award individual contracts, make loans, grant specific tax exemptions, approve import licenses, negotiate with multinational corporations (MNCs), and permit price increases on individual items. Creative officials can extend their discretion over even nominal entitlement programs by reinterpreting the implementation or manipulating disbursements.

For Brazil and Mexico there is relative consensus that capitalism was quite politicized or state controlled from the 1940s (or much earlier) until the 1990s.[12] Raymond Vernon claimed that there were two distinctive features of the Mexican economy: "first, the relative pervasiveness and vigor of the governments' regulatory measures; second, the extraordinary degree of particularity and discrimination in the application of those regulatory powers." A decade later Susan Purcell concluded that Mexico had "a form of state capitalism." José Luis Fiori argues that the state in Brazil promoted "politicized accumulation": "politicized because it responds to the determinations of a state much more than to rules of the market." Michael Barzelay coined the term "politicized market economy" for his analysis of Brazil in the 1970s and 1980s. Despite the apparent consensus, few analyses provided criteria for distinguishing political from nonpolitical forms of capitalism.[13]

Assessing the degree of political capitalism requires a qualitative analysis of resource flows through the "narrows" of the economy. Investment credit and foreign exchange constitute crucial narrows in most developing

11. H. H. Gerth and C. Wright Mills, eds., *From Max Weber: Essays in Sociology* (New York: Oxford University Press, 1946), pp. 66–67.

12. Maddison et al. offer the best succinct comparison of development in Brazil and Mexico. See Angus Maddison et al., *Brazil and Mexico* (New York: Oxford University Press, 1992).

13. Raymond Vernon, *The Dilemma of Mexico's Development* (Cambridge: Harvard University Press, 1963), p. 25; Susan Kaufman Purcell, *The Mexican Profit-Sharing Decision: Politics in an Authoritarian Regime* (Berkeley: University of California Press, 1975), p. 29; José Luis Fiori, "Sobre a crise do Estado brasileiro," *Revista de Economia Política* 9, no. 3 (July–September 1989): 105; and Michael Barzelay, *The Politicized Market Economy: Alcohol in Brazil's Energy Strategy* (Berkeley: University of California Press, 1986).

economies.[14] Particular economies suffer as well from their own peculiar scarcities. For example, in Mexico and other arid regions, water flows, physically and economically, through a narrows. Where governments have discretion over the distribution of water, hydraulic politics are intense and presumably salient in private decisions on agricultural investment. Because the overall extent and mix of discretion over scarce resource flows varies from country to country, no simple threshold can be applied, and it is probably best to think of capitalism as more or less politicized.

States politicize capitalism through direct investment in infrastructure and in state enterprises that ultimately trickles into the private sector as contracts for goods and services. In Brazil and Mexico the state accounted directly for around 40 percent of total investment for much of the postwar period.[15] Many businesses depended on the political decisions of how to spend this money. In her introduction, Meredith Woo-Cumings highlights the pivotal role of credit allocation by developmental states. In the Brazilian and Mexican desarrollista states, through their development banks, controlled most long-term credit to industry. Until the mid-1960s public bank resources in Mexico were greater than those in the private sector. The national development bank in Mexico, Nafinsa, alone accounted for 20 percent of total financing and 30 percent of all finance to industry.[16] From 1940 to 1970 only 10 percent or less of credit from private commercial banks went for medium-and long-term financing.[17] Moreover, as private banks grew, they lent proportionately less to industry.[18] Further subsidy and regulation influenced the allocation of much of the remaining, nominally private resources. Until the 1980s, a list of the major forms of indirect state control in both countries included tariff and nontariff barriers to imports, tax incentives, controls on interest

14. Perkins offers a longer list of measures to gauge the "relative importance of market and bureaucratic influences on enterprise behavior" including (1) the protected share of domestic production; (2) the degree of deviation of domestic prices from international prices; (3) the degree of sectoral concentration; (4) whether interest rates deviate from market rates; and (5) the rates of input inventories to inventories of final products. See Dwight Perkins, "Economic Systems Reform in Developing Countries," in Perkins and Michael Roemer, eds., *Reforming Economic Systems in Developing Countries* (Cambridge: Harvard University Press, 1991), p. 19.

15. On Mexico, see Dale Story, *Industry, the State, and Public Policy in Mexico* (Austin: University of Texas Press, 1986), p. 68. On Brazil, see Henri Reichstul and Luciano Coutinho, "Investimento estatal, 1974–1980: Ciclo e crise," in Luiz Gonzaga Belluzo and Renata Coutinho, eds., *Desenvolvimento capitalista no Brasil* (São Paulo: Brasilense, 1983), p. 45.

16. Frank Brandenburg, *The Making of Modern Mexico* (Englewood Cliffs, N.J: Prentice-Hall, 1964), p. 229.

17. Sylvia Maxfield, *Governing Capital: International Finance and Mexican Politics* (Ithaca: Cornell University Press, 1990), p. 67.

18. See also Eliza Willis, "The State as Banker," Ph.D. diss., University of Texas at Austin, 1986, and Miguel D. Ramírez, *Development Banking in Mexico: The Case of the Nacional Financiera, S.A.* (New York: Praeger, 1986).

rates, export subsidies, agricultural price supports, restrictions on MNCs, and wage and price controls. In Mexico, "the public sector [was] in a position to make or break any private firm."[19]

The Mexican and Brazilian economies were nonetheless still capitalist. Property, wealth, and profit were mostly private, and therefore capitalism set the overall parameters for the state and its policymakers. While the state provided much of total investment, the private sector often reaped the harvest. For instance, rates of return on state investment were usually lower than on private investment, often because state enterprises charged private customers low prices.[20] States may account for a large proportion of total investment but not enough to sustain rapid growth alone, and they depend on private investment to keep growth at a politically acceptable rate. Political capitalism thus involves heavy reciprocal constraints. State elites have enormous discretion and power over particular firms, yet they are structurally constrained to pursue policies conducive to private profit generally in order to increase total investment, especially as capital became more mobile over the 1970s and 1980s.

Multinational corporations further constrain the state. Their accumulation strategies are global, and they may not therefore invest in the domestic economy despite generous subsidies. They are also more likely to move new investment elsewhere in response to perceived political uncertainty. In large protected economies such as those of Brazil and Mexico, however, multinational firms came to resemble domestic firms in that production was for the local market, managers were often nationals, and, especially, most investment came from local profits.[21] For example, over the decade of the 1970s, reinvested profits accounted for 65 percent of the recorded value of U.S. investment in Latin America.[22] The far greater presence of MNCs distinguishes Latin America from Northeast Asia. But MNCs do not change the essence of political capitalism, which was similar across the two regions, though they do appear to affect greatly the effectiveness of developmental states.[23]

19. Vernon, *Dilemma of Mexico's Development*, p. 26.

20. See Peter Evans, *Dependent Development: The Alliance of Multinational, State, and Local Capital in Brazil* (Princeton: Princeton University Press, 1979), pp. 222–28, and Thomas J. Trebat, "Public Enterprise in Brazil and Mexico," in Thomas C. Bruneau and Philippe Faucher, eds., *Authoritarian Capitalism* (Boulder, Colo.: Westview, 1981).

21. See Gary Gereffi and Peter B. Evans, "Transnational Corporations, Dependent Development, and State Policy in the Semiperiphery: A Comparison of Brazil and Mexico," *Latin American Research Review* 16, no. 3 (1981): 31–64.

22. Sergio Bitar, "Corporaciones transnacionales y las nuevas relaciones de América Latina con Estados Unidos," *Economía de América Latina* 11 (1984): 99–124, as cited in Eduardo White, "The Question of Foreign Investments and the Economic Crisis in Latin America," in Richard E. Feinberg and Ricardo Ffrench-Davis, eds., *Development and External Debt in Latin America* (Notre Dame: University of Notre Dame Press, 1988), p. 164.

23. See Peter Evans, "Class, State, and Dependence in East Asia: Lessons for Latin Americanists," in Deyo, ed., *Political Economy of the New Asian Industrialism.*

Political capitalism has a profound impact on the political strategies of economic and state elites. Economic elites depend heavily on the state and have good reasons to lobby officials and to do so individually rather than collectively.[24] Moreover, state intervention increases political uncertainty for investors at the same time it reduces market uncertainty. For state elites, political capitalism provides a powerful array of sticks and carrots to influence the political as well as the economic behavior of economic elites. Unfortunately, most studies of the developmental state focus on their economic consequences to the neglect of their usually lasting political legacies.

DEVELOPMENTAL DISCOURSE

Widespread state intervention in the economy politicized capitalism; the dominant developmental discourse gave that intervention direction and legitimacy. Developmentalism is an ideology or world view that accords industrialization a higher priority than other societal goals and gives the state the leading role in promoting it. The criterion for evaluating policy is effectiveness, not efficiency.[25] Policymakers rely on straightforward quantitative measures such as increases in output or exports to evaluate progress. In an exemplary display of developmentalism, officials in Korea, infused with the competitive spirit of the Olympic games in 1988, constructed an electronic scoreboard in a central subway station that listed the participating countries, their capitals, flags, and incomes per head. In contrast, officials in liberal, socialist, or corporatist states evaluate policy in terms of overarching ideologies for which political leaders are often willing to suffer losses in production or competitiveness.[26]

In Brazil and Mexico after the depression of the 1930s, the prevailing diagnosis of the barriers to industrialization argued that the domestic bourgeoisie was incapable of generating self-sustaining industrialization. The state should lead and the bourgeoisie follow. This diagnosis spilled over into political discourse and reduced the legitimacy of private sector demands and by extension active political participation by the bourgeoisie. For example, at his inaugural address in 1934, the new Mexican president, Lázaro Cárdenas, stated: "The state alone embodies the general interest, and for this reason only the state has a vision of the whole. The state must continually broaden, increase and deepen its interven-

24. See Ben Ross Schneider, "Organized Business Politics in Democratic Brazil," *Journal of Interamerican Studies and World Affairs* 39, no. 4 (Winter 1997–98): 95–127.

25. Johnson, *MITI and the Japanese Miracle*, pp. 19–26.

26. See Ralf Dahrendorf, "Market and Plan: Two Types of Rationality," in *Essays in the Theory of Society* (Stanford: Stanford University Press, 1968).

tion." Public defense of the state's guiding role was constant. Nearly 40 years later, Luis Echeverría stated that it was the state's responsibility "to set the direction and rhythm of development" and to participate directly both "in the production and distribution of income."[27] These arguments fit preexisting, quasi-Rousseauian discourses that accorded the state the role of seeing to the national interest while other societal actors pursued their particularistic interests. The dominant discourses in Latin America had generally accorded the state primacy over social and economic interests, though before 1930 liberalism mounted a strong campaign to dislodge this dominant discourse.[28] Moreover, the state had been active, especially in Brazil, in promoting growth.[29]

Post-1940 developmentalism meshed with some preexisting discourses and practices, but it arose in the specific crises in international trade during World Wars I and II and the Great Depression, gaining theoretic and programmatic body in the analyses of Raúl Prebisch and the United Nations Economic Commission for Latin America (ECLA).[30] The growing consensus among elites was that Latin America could no longer rely on industrial countries to provide manufactured goods, nor could Latin America ever catch up to the rich countries without industrializing.

The military in some countries added national security concerns, though these were not as strong and immediate as they were later in East Asia.[31] Meredith Woo-Cumings has argued that national security concerns decisively influenced the course of economic policy in postwar Korea, an

27. Lázaro Cárdenas, cited in Nora Hamilton, *The Limits of State Autonomy: Post-Revolutionary Mexico* (Princeton: Princeton University Press, 1982), p. 129; Luis Echeverría, cited in Carlos Arriola, "Los grupos empresariales frente al Estado (1973–1975)," *Foro Internacional* 16, no. 4 (April–June 1976): 452.

28. Claudio Veliz, *The Centralist Tradition of Latin America* (Princeton: Princeton University Press, 1980); Alfred Stepan, *The State and Society* (Princeton: Princeton University Press, 1978).

29. See Steven Topik, "The Economic Role of the State in Liberal Regimes: Brazil and Mexico Compared, 1888–1910," in Joseph L. Love and Nils Jacobsen, eds., *Guiding the Invisible Hand* (New York: Praeger, 1988).

30. ECLA, is also known by its Spanish acronym CEPAL. On the history of developmentalism and the general intellectual history of development economics in Latin America, see Albert O. Hirschman, "Ideologies of Economic Development in Latin America," in *A Bias for Hope* (New Haven: Yale University Press, 1971); Thomas E. Skidmore, *Politics in Brazil, 1930–1964* (New York: Oxford University Press, 1967), esp. pp. 41–48, 87–90; Kathryn Sikkink, *Ideas and Institutions: Developmentalism in Brazil and Argentina* (Ithaca: Cornell University Press, 1991), esp. pp. 127–70; Bielschowsky, *Pensamento econômico brasileiro;* Maria de Lourdes Manzini Covre, *A fala dos homens: Análise do pensamento tecnocrático, 1964–1981* (São Paulo: Brasilense, 1983); Brandenburg, *Making of Modern Mexico;* Joseph L. Love, "Raúl Prebisch and the Origins of the Doctrine of Unequal Exchange," in James Dietz and James H. Street, eds., *Latin America's Economic Development* (Boulder, Colo.: Lynne Rienner, 1987): 81–86; and Sanford A. Mosk, *Industrial Revolution in Mexico* (Berkeley: University of California Press, 1950).

31. See Evans, "Class, State, and Dependence."

argument she further elaborates in the introduction to this volume.[32] In Latin America, military and security worries were more likely to be secondary and complementary to developmentalism emanating from other parts of the state and the private sector. In Brazil, where the level of military influence in economic policy was among the greatest in the developmentalist countries of Latin America, officers participated in economic policy through two principal avenues. First, in the 1930s the military developed interest and expertise in weapons industries, and generals became powerful lobbyists for sectoral policies in steel, petroleum, and, later, computers and aircraft.[33] A more general interest in industrialization among officers emerged later as the cold war intensified. By the 1950s and 1960s, generals in many countries had adopted the view that development was one effective antidote to communism. These concerns were much weaker in Mexico than in Brazil, where after the 1930s the military was not influential in economic policy and where security threats, communist or otherwise, were less salient political issues.

Most studies of postwar industrialization in Mexico and Brazil highlight the dominance of developmentalism. In his study of economic policymaking in Brazil in the 1950s, Nathaniel Leff examines the "modernizing nationalist ideology," which favored heavy industry, import substitution, and accorded an "ample role to the public sector." This ideology cut short debate because its "economic views have been virtually uncontested . . . since at least the early 1950s" and because the "economic intelligentsia also presented no critique or alternative."[34] The turmoil and coup of the 1960s temporarily unraveled the consensus. Beginning in the late 1960s the military revived developmentalism and silenced counterdiscourses from the left.[35]

In Mexico after the depression and World War II *técnicos* (technically trained officials) in the economic bureaucracy became increasingly partial to industrialization, restrictions on trade and foreign capital, and active state intervention to overcome the deficiencies of Mexican markets and capitalists.[36] For técnicos, "the word dirigiste has none of the invidious connotations which it usually carries in the French tongue."[37] Frank

32. Jung-en Woo [Meredith Woo-Cumings], *Race to the Swift: State and Finance in Korean Industrialization* (New York: Columbia University Press, 1991).

33. See Ben Ross Schneider, *Politics within the State: Elite Bureaucrats and Industrial Policy in Authoritarian Brazil* (Pittsburgh: University of Pittsburgh Press, 1991), and Emanuel Adler, *The Power of Ideology: The Quest for Technological Autonomy in Argentina and Brazil* (Berkeley: University of California Press, 1987).

34. Nathaniel H. Leff, *Economic Policy-Making and Development in Brazil, 1947–1964* (New York: John Wiley and Sons, 1968), pp. 4, 139–43.

35. See Covre, *A fala dos homens.*

36. Vernon, *Dilemma of Mexico's Development*, pp. 141–49.

37. Ibid., p. 149.

Brandenburg claims that "it was not until the post World War II years that industry managed to acquire a preferential role in economic development."[38] The two governments after 1940 made industrialization the central policy objective.[39] In 1946 Miguel Alemán took industrialization on the campaign trail as one of his three slogans and the only one relating to economics.[40] In his review of the literature, Edward Williams concludes that "the ideology of industrialization . . . began to take root during the Cárdenas regime" and later "became full fledged revolutionary dogma with the accession to power of Miguel Alemán in 1946." Brandenburg also notes the "primacy of the state in economic life" but argues that this is a centuries-old tradition. The most comprehensive study of Mexican business concludes that "most leading entrepreneurs accept the fact that Mexico has a mixed economic system. . . . Even in the 1980s, most businessmen still favor a substantial government role."[41]

Another way to assess the dominance of developmentalism is from the perspective of the eclipse of competing discourses, especially orthodox economics and liberalism, which had ardent albeit isolated backers in both countries. In Brazil one of the strong but ultimately unsuccessful candidates for the presidential elections of 1945 campaigned against developmentalism and the desarrollista state Vargas had been constructing and in favor of relying primarily on export agriculture.[42] In Brazil Eugênio Gudin and Octávio Bulhões were the leading liberal economists. They were both ministers in postwar governments but could do little more than stall developmentalism and increasing state intervention.[43] In Mexico the cleavage between monetarists and structuralists dominated struggles over discourse and policy.[44] However, the ascendant monetarists in the period of stabilizing development, including Antonio Ortíz Mena, a major figure among monetarists and finance minister from 1958 to 1970, were still moderate developmentalists.[45]

38. Brandenburg, *Making of Modern Mexico*, p. 214.

39. Mosk, *Industrial Revolution in Mexico*, pp. 53, 60–62.

40. See also Vernon, *Dilemma of Mexico's Development*, p. 88.

41. Edward J. Williams, "Mutation in the Mexican Revolution," *SECOLAS Annals* (March 1976): 35; Brandenburg, *Making of Modern Mexico*, p. 211; Roderic Ai Camp, *Entrepreneurs and Politics in Twentieth-Century Mexico* (New York: Oxford University Press, 1989), p. 45.

42. See John French, *The Brazilian Workers' ABC: Class Conflict and Alliances in Modern São Paulo* (Chapel Hill: University of North Carolina Press, 1992), pp. 114–16.

43. See Bieloschowsky, *Pensamento econômico brasileiro*.

44. Maxfield, *Governing Capital*.

45. Victor Urquidi, interview by author, November 6, 1991. The selective endorsement of U.S. hegemony and the cold war also reflects the strength of developmentalism. Political and economic elites accepted the struggle against communism and often paid lip service to the accompanying tenet of promoting free enterprise, but at the same time they systematically expanded the economic role of the state. Mexican nationalism, directed primarily against the United States, impeded open endorsement of the cold war aims of the United

A survey of elite opinion in authoritarian Brazil (1972–73) revealed widespread support for economic over social or political development. In terms of long-term priorities all groups (save church leaders and leaders of the opposition party) favored economic development, including Arena politicians (46 percent, $N = 33$), labor leaders (49 percent, $N = 53$), top civil servants (60 percent, $N = 40$), business executives (66 percent, $N = 84$), and managers of public companies (80 percent, $N = 15$).[46] In a broader survey in the 1960s in twelve Latin American countries including Brazil and Mexico, most managers ($N = 324$) favored state intervention to provide infrastructure, technical assistance and research, credit, tariff protection, tax exemptions, and overall planning. They were more ambivalent about state enterprises and thought them appropriate only when they did not compete with private firms. They also criticized inefficiency and politics in government but generally opposed inept intervention rather than intervention per se.[47] As late as 1982, a survey after the decision by the Mexican government to nationalize private banks revealed widespread support for the decision among all social groups: 72 percent of all respondents favored the nationalization, as did nearly two-thirds of business leaders and industrialists.[48]

A quantitative indicator of the dominance of developmentalism and the sincerity of political leaders who endorse it is the division of government spending between economic promotion and other expenditures. When the economic budget exceeds the military, social, and administrative budgets (singly, not in total), it is one strong indicator that the state has a developmental orientation (see Table 2 below). In contrast, administrative and military expenses are greatest in the classic state, while the social budget is highest in the welfare state.[49] Consistently high economic spending, over time, and across various governments and regimes, is a good indicator of how enduring and widely shared developmentalism is.

Quantitative thresholds require qualitative confirmation because strong developmental motivations can underlie apparently noneconomic spend-

States. Northern business especially was receptive to the free enterprise message, but they were unable to project their views nationally as a counter-discourse. In Brazil, the Sorbonne faction within the officer corps went furthest in endorsing the full package of cold war ideology, but they were a minority, and even some of their prominent members such as Ernesto Geisel turned out to be statists in practice. See Alfred Stepan, *The Military in Politics: Changing Patterns in Brazil* (Princeton: Princeton University Press, 1971), pp. 237–50.

46. Peter McDonough, *Power and Ideology in Brazil* (Princeton: Princeton University Press, 1981), p. 141.

47. Albert Lauterbach, "Government and Development: Managerial Attitudes in Latin America" *Journal of Inter-American Studies* 7, no. 2 (April 1965): 212–20.

48. Miguel Basáñez and Roderic A. Camp, "La nacionalización de la banca y la opinión pública en México," *Foro Internacional* 98 (October–December 1984): 208.

49. Soares, "O Novo Estado na América Latina," p. 62.

ing on education (such as funding foreign graduate study in engineering) or military training and research and development in high technology that has commercial applications. In Brazil, for example, the military government created "social" programs such as unemployment insurance in the form of funds on which beneficiaries could draw. In practice, other government agencies used unclaimed, accumulated funds to finance development projects. Moreover, developmentalists may prefer to rely on indirect forms of intervention, such as trade protection or credit rationing, which do not show up as large items in the government budget.

In the twentieth century most states were expected to facilitate growth and improve social welfare. The developmental state is peculiar in that state and other elites expect economic policies to transform the economy from a less to a more industrialized stage and tolerate enormous state discretion over resource allocation. Regulatory states may promote industrialization as a by-product, but it is not the primary goal, nor is it legitimate for officials to use state intervention to achieve it. Welfare states may be quite interventionist in the distribution, rather than production, of gross domestic product (GDP), and much if not most of the GDP may pass through the government. Moreover, officials lack discretion and measure success with indicators of social welfare rather than GDP per capita.

POLITICAL EXCLUSION

Political exclusion (or limited pluralism) exists when the majority of adults are denied the right to free and meaningful choices in regular elections—meaningful in that opposition candidates have a chance of coming to power, free in the limited sense of absence of direct coercion. Neither of these conditions exists in authoritarian regimes, which in most cases hold no elections. When they do, as in Brazil under the military, the opposition still has no chance of winning. Political exclusion is not limited to authoritarian regimes, however; many democracies inhibit, formally or informally, the participation of the majority of adults.[50] Property,

50. Many formal democracies in Latin America fit Linz's definition of authoritarian regimes as "political systems with limited, not responsible, political pluralism; without elaborate and guiding ideology (but with distinctive mentalities); without intensive nor extensive political mobilization (except some points in their development); and in which a leader (or occasionally a small group) exercises power within formally ill-defined limits but actually quite predictable ones." See Linz, "An Authoritarian Regime," p. 297. Other authors who define political systems in Latin America as exclusive regardless of regime type include Therborn, who uses the term "exclusivist," Soares, and especially Remmer. See Goran Therborn, "The Travail of Latin American Democracy," *New Left Review* 113/114 (January–April 1979): 71–109; Soares, "O Novo Estado na América Latina," p. 71; and Karen L. Remmer,

literacy, gender, party, or registration requirements can deny the franchise to the majority. Like developmentalism in economic policy, exclusion orients and motivates political activity on the part of state and political elites. Political exclusion was often more a question of practice and usually contradicted lip service to democracy. The generals in Brazil, for example, always claimed that they were in power temporarily in order to prepare Brazil for democracy.[51] Political leaders, after first paying homage to classic democratic precepts, often went on to qualify the type of democracy appropriate for the times or the country. Echeverría, for example, claimed that politics could not be left "to the free play of forces."[52] Political exclusion in the desarrollista state was enduring. The majority of adults in both Brazil and Mexico had either no real choice or no vote until the end of the twentieth century. In Brazil, literacy requirements excluded a majority of adults during the democratic period 1945–64. The eligible electorate grew from 13 percent of the total (not just adult) population in 1945 to 19 percent in 1960, levels that were low compared with other Latin American countries at similar levels of development.[53] In Mexico, formal restrictions on voting were fewer, but political elites maintained exclusion by denying opposition candidates any real chance of victory. Such other countries as Chile and Argentina alternated between exclusive authoritarian regimes and inclusive democracies. However, exclusionary periods were presumed to be temporary and extraordinary.

Clase política is an apt term to describe the exclusive political elite in Mexico and Brazil. Politicians in Brazil referred to themselves as members of such a class with unique rights and privileges. The press helped construct this "class." For instance, the Mexican daily *La Jornada* devoted a multipage section titled "Clase Política" to political intrigue and elite

"Exclusionary Democracy," *Studies in Comparative International Development* 20, no. 4 (Winter 1985–86): 64–85. Therborn also considers many democracies in Latin America "exclusivist," singling out Brazil, Mexico, and Costa Rica as the only "constitutional exclusivist regimes" in 1978 (p. 95, Table 3). Remmer uses Dahl's distinction between contestation and participation in defining democracy to create a two-dimensional classification of regime type: authoritarian versus democratic, and inclusionary versus exclusionary. The key category for the present discussion is exclusionary democracy, which included Brazil (1945–64). For 1980 Remmer classifies Brazil and Mexico as exclusionary authoritarian and inclusionary authoritarian, respectively (p. 75).

51. For an in-depth analysis of the "technocratic thought" of the military regime, see Covre, *A fala dos homens* (on democracy, see esp. pp. 234–70).

52. Cited in Arriola, "Los grupos empresariales frente al Estado," p. 452.

53. Philippe C. Schmitter, *Interest Conflict and Political Change in Brazil* (Stanford: Stanford University Press, 1971), p. 381. See also Olavo Brasil de Lima Jr., "Electoral Participation in Brazil (1945–78): The Legislation, the Party Systems, and Electoral Turnouts," *Luso-Brazilian Review* 20, no. 1 (Summer 1983): 73.

machinations.[54] The clase política was successful in controlling its membership and blunting nonelite challenges. Beyond crude devices such as limiting the electorate in Brazil or electoral fraud in Mexico, politicians in both countries devised more sophisticated techniques of manipulating elections. Basing electoral competition on clientelism and patronage shores up elite positions, because it favors those with access to resources and denies voters accountability. Political leaders co-opted rather than represented.[55] In both Brazil and Mexico, election was usually by appointment, which allowed elites to screen entry into the clase política and to co-opt challengers. In Mexico nomination by the Institutionalized Revolutionary Party (PRI) guaranteed electoral victory. Elections in Brazil were more open, but the many politicians who launched their electoral careers from executive positions testify to the electoral value of appointment.[56] The ambitious were more likely to enter the appointive bureaucracy than try to build grassroots support for a program.

Civil society posed little threat to this political elite. Local associations such as squatter settlements, religious groups, professional organizations, and labor unions had little independent power. Depending on the administration in power, the political elite attempted to co-opt their leadership, manipulate their finances, or intimidate and repress both leaders and members.[57] In Brazil, government officials successfully manipulated corporatist financial controls and legal restrictions on labor unions.[58] In Mexico PRI control of the Confederación de Trabajadores de México (CTM) is less formal and legal but more effective.[59]

In sum, political competition in the developmental state was restricted to a small group. Of course, these polities were not hermetic and static; several defects kept them in constant agitation (if not evolution). These exclusive polities lacked solid legitimacy, institutional mechanisms for resolving interelite conflict, and assurance of the continued acquiescence

54. For González, Mexico's clase política evolved out of the Revolutionary Family, took patrimonialist control of the state, and by the 1980s included four major factions: military, party, bureaucratic, and technocratic. See Jaime González Graf, "La crisis de la clase política," *Nexos* 136 (April 1989): 34–35.

55. Fernando H. Cardoso, *O modelo político brasileiro* (São Paulo: Difusão Européia do Livro, 1979), p. 43, and Simon Schwartzman, *As bases do autoritarismo brasileiro* (Rio de Janeiro: Editora Campus, 1982).

56. See Schneider, *Politics within the State*, pp. 243–44.

57. See Susan Eckstein, *The Poverty of Revolution: The State and the Urban Poor in Mexico* (Princeton: Princeton University Press, 1988).

58. See Kenneth P. Erickson, *The Brazilian Corporative State and Working-Class Politics* (Berkeley: University of California Press, 1977), and Youssef Cohen, *The Manipulation of Consent: The State and Working-Class Consciousness in Brazil* (Pittsburgh: University of Pittsburgh Press, 1989).

59. See Ruth Berins Collier, *The Contradictory Alliance: State-Labor Relations and Regime Change in Mexico* (Berkeley: International and Area Studies, University of California, 1992).

of nonelites. The clase política usually managed to stop threatening opposition but spent enormous energies re-creating internal accommodation while constantly checking over its shoulder.

THE APPOINTIVE BUREAUCRACY

By the 1980s the Brazilian and Mexican bureaucracies comprised thousands of agencies and employed millions of people. In 1988 public employment in Mexico totaled 4.4 million (including 2.7 million in the central government, 600,000 in state and local government, and 1 million in public enterprises) and accounted for one-fifth of total employment.[60] In Brazil in 1973, 9 percent of the economically active population, or 3.4 million people, worked in the public sector, though two-thirds of them worked in state and local government (1.4 million worked in public firms and other autonomous agencies at all levels of government).[61] Municipal, state, and federal employment grew to 4.3 million by 1984, and the largest state enterprises employed over 1 million people in addition.[62]

In these mammoth bureaucracies, formal organizations are fluid and flexible, save for such well-known exceptions as the Banco de México and the Brazilian National Bank for Economic and Social Development (BNDES), which prove the rule. Moreover, these bureaucracies suffered from a debilitating range of conventional pathologies: overcentralization, fragmentation, low professional ethics, high turnover, corruption, low salaries, and poor training. It is hardly surprising that bureaucracy enjoyed so little public esteem in either country.

Appointments gave this unwieldy mass dynamism and structure. In the desarrollista state, positions of power in the bureaucracy were distributed by direct personal, political appointment. One thousand appointments to the top three to four levels of the bureaucratic hierarchy is a rough threshold to define an appointive bureaucracy. Brazil, Mexico, most of Latin America and other developing countries, the United States, and all communist systems thus have appointive bureaucracies. About 50,000 positions are filled by political appointment in Brazil and Mexico. The incoming Collor administration estimated the number of political, confi-

60. Nafinsa (Nacional Financera), *La economía mexicana en cifras* (Mexico City: Nafinsa, 1990), p. 634.

61. Fernando Rezende and Flávio P. Castelo Branco, "O emprego público como instrumento de política econômico," in Rezende et al., *Aspectos da participação do governo na economia* (Rio de Janeiro: IPEA, 1976), pp. 46–47.

62. Antoninho Marmo Trevisan, "Operação desmonte, carga tributária e as estatais," *Economia em Perspectiva* 50 (September 1988): 2–3.

dence positions at 65,000.[63] An estimate for Mexico from the 1960s, when the bureaucracy was smaller, put the number at 25,000 (including 8,000 in the PRI bureaucracy).[64] Later observers put the total closer to 50,000.[65] Thousands of these appointments may be pure patronage pay-offs with little impact on policy, but all positions with any real power are open to appointment and subject to immediate dismissal. Even the Banco de México which by tradition has a meritocratic, career bureaucracy, was legally unprotected from the appointive powers of the president.[66] The extremely high number of appointments distinguishes Brazil and Mexico from most developed and many developing countries.

Appointments structure power and incentives inside and outside the bureaucracy. Subordinates can rise only through appointment, which helps focus their attention on those above them. The power to appoint and dismiss reinforces the top-down flow of power and gives superiors far more potential control over subordinates than they would have in a bureaucracy where promotion depends on impersonal criteria.[67] Given the dominance of the bureaucracy in the polity, appointment then becomes the primary means for gaining representation. Factions in the political elite maneuver to get their representatives designated, while ambitious bureaucrats seek outside support. The process often takes on the aura of an electoral campaign: the candidates for various positions (or any position) seek visibility, make speeches, and give interviews. Newspapers and magazines endorse or reject candidates, propose names, and circulate resumes. When the president has selected his subordinates (and they in turn theirs) the basic lines of representation and access are set until the next ministerial shakeup or presidential succession. In a famous quote, the politician último de Carvalho distilled the essence of power in the Brazilian political system into four verbs: appoint, dismiss, imprison, and release.

The key variable in distinguishing among bureaucracies is tenure. Bureaucrats in appointive bureaucracies have no job security and are thus constantly looking toward their next jobs and their next boss. In contrast, a key element of what Peter Evans calls Weberian bureaucracy is precisely job security.[68] Meritocratic recruitment and promotion are possible in both Weberian and appointive bureaucracies, but depoliticized adminis-

63. *Jornal do Brasil*, March 4, 1990, p. 4.

64. Brandenburg, *Making of Modern Mexico*, p. 157.

65. Gabriel Zaid, interview by author, Mexico City, July 4, 1989.

66. Employee of the Banco de México, interview by author, November 14, 1994.

67. See Schneider, *Politics within the State*, chap. 4, and Merilee Serrill Grindle, *Bureaucrats, Politicians, and Peasants in Mexico: A Case Study in Public Policy* (Berkeley: University of California Press, 1977), for full discussions of appointment relations.

68. Evans, *Embedded Autonomy*.

tration is possible only in the former. The distinction between Weberian bureaucracies in Asia versus politicized, appointive bureaucracies in Latin America is the crucial factor that differentiates developmental from desarrollista states. I return to these and other comparisons after examining the consolidation of desarrollista states in Brazil and Mexico and assessing further the interaction and synergy among the four components.

CONSOLIDATION

Several contributors to this volume have noted that developmental states are historically bounded phenomenon. What indicators do we use to set beginning and ending bounds? Determining the beginning and end of a multicomponent conceptualization of a type of state is at best difficult, especially when some components elude precise quantitative measurement.[69] The political components predate the full developmental state by decades if not centuries. The economic elements are harder to date. At the turn of the century the Brazilian and Mexican governments intervened in their economies but generally limited intervention in accordance with the dominant economic liberalism. From 1895 to 1910 government revenues ranged from 6 to 12 percent of GDP in Brazil and from 5 to 8 percent in Mexico.[70] The mid-1930s however mark a turning point in the goals and methods of state intervention. On the one hand, liberals could no longer hold out hope that the old international trading system would soon return. On the other hand, presidents Getúlio Vargas and Lázaro Cárdenas were moving increasingly, sometimes admittedly only in response to short-term crises, toward more systematic state intervention. This was a period throughout the world of political and economic redefinition. What gradually emerged from it in Brazil and Mexico was a particular form of developmental state.

Cárdenas dramatically increased and redirected government spending (see Table 2). He nearly doubled the total budget and expanded the share dedicated to economic development from an average of 25 percent (1924–34) to 38 percent for his term.[71] After Cárdenas, neither economic nor total spending fell until the 1980s. The 1938 nationalization of oil in Mexico marks qualitatively and certainly symbolically, if not

69. The "carbon" dating of regimes of accumulation in regulation theory and social structures of accumulation is also very problematic. See David M. Kotz, "Long Waves and Social Structures of Accumulation: A Critique and Reinterpretation," *Review of Radical Political Economics* 19, no. 4 (Winter 1987): esp. 27–34.

70. Topik, "Economic Role of the State," pp. 39–41, 125.

71. James Wilkie, *The Mexico Revolution: Federal Expenditures and Social Change since 1910* (Berkeley: University of California Press, 1967), pp. 22, 32.

Table 2. Government spending in Mexico, 1930–1990

	Economic	Social	Administrative	Per capita spending (in 1960 pesos)
	(percentage of actual government budget)			
Calles (1925–1928)	25	10	65	189
1929–1934*	25	15	60	188
Cárdenas (1935–1940)	38	18	44	264
Ávila Camacho (1941–1946)	39	17	44	287
Alemán (1947–1952)	52	13	35	400
Ruiz Cortines (1953–1958)	53	14	33	452
López Mateos (1959–1964)	39	20	41	689
Díaz Ordaz (1965–1970)	41	21	38	1,128
Echeverría (1971–1976)	45	24	31	1,689
López Portillo (1977–1982)				2,331

*Averages for three short presidencies in this period.

Sources: 1925–58, averages for each administration from James Wilkie, The Mexico Revolution: Federal Expenditures and Social Change since 1910 (Berkeley: University of California Press, 1967), p. 32; 1959–76, from James Wilkie, La revolución mexicana (Mexico: Fondo de Cultura Económica, 1978), as cited in Samuel Schmidt, The Deterioration of the Mexican Presidency (Tucson: University of Arizona Press, 1991), p. 40. Per capita spending in 1960 pesos from Dale Story, Industry, the State, and Public Policy in Mexico (Austin: University of Texas Press, 1986), p. 42. His data are reported at five-year intervals. Listed here is the latest figure for each administration.

quantitatively, a watershed in state intervention.[72] It created a lasting association between nationalism and state intervention. Some protective tariffs and tax exemptions for industry predate Cárdenas, but the flurry of legislation creating state-led import-substituting industrialization (ISI) came mostly in the late 1930s and 1940s.[73]

In Brazil, president Getúlio Vargas promoted a qualitative shift in government spending and intervention, though a recognizable and deliberate developmental state emerged only during the Estado Novo (1937–45).[74] From 1930 to 1945 various Vargas governments with strong military encouragement steadily created new ministries (for example, the Ministry of Labor, Industry, and Commerce in 1930), departments, councils (such as the National Petroleum Council in 1938), and state enter-

72. See especially Hamilton, Limits of State Autonomy, pp. 216–70.

73. See Story, Industry, the State, and Public Policy, p. 38, for a chronology of major policies.

74. Skidmore argues that "Vargas used the occasion of the war effort to elaborate a policy of industrialization, a goal toward which he had been moving since 1937, although as late as 1940 he had still not committed himself unequivocally to systematic industrial development." See Skidmore, Politics in Brazil, p. 45. Suzigan claims that from 1930 state intervention became deliberate (consciente) and "truly statizing" during the Estado Novo. See Wilson Suzigan, "As empresas do governo e o papel do Estado na economia Brasileira," in Rezende et al., Aspectos da participação do governo na economia, p. 85.

prises.[75] In symbolic terms the creation of National Steel Company (CSN) in 1941 and the successful construction of the mammoth steel works epitomized the dawn of a new era of state-led industrialization.

The triumph of developmental discourse is difficult to date with precision. Some subcomponents such as the primacy of the state over individual interest had deep historical roots. Equating autonomous industrialization with national security and welfare, however, is a postwar phenomenon. Overall, the period between the eclipse of liberalism in the early 1930s and the emergence of a coherent developmentalism backed by both theoretical elaboration and by state and societal actors in the 1950s is best characterized as one of contending discourses. But, the core ideas that would later flourish in the 1950s mostly date back to the 1930s. Prebisch, the foremost Latin American theorist of developmentalism, was implementing policies in the 1930s for which he would develop theoretical justification only later, out of power, in the 1940s and 1950s.[76]

The beginnings of the desarrollista state are thus visible in the 1930s. As part of a fully functioning development model, the core years date roughly from 1950 to 1980. Economic and industrial growth were rapid in the 1940s, which was more the result of international factors (in that World War II forced ISI in Brazil and Mexico) than directed state intervention. Mexico's default in August 1982 was the death knell for the desarrollista state, but inertia carried it on for several more years. By 1985 political leaders in both Brazil and Mexico were embarking on policies to dismantle one or more components of their desarrollista states. In Mexico, the first changes came in state intervention and hence political capitalism. In Brazil, the transition to civilian rule in 1985 led quickly to full political inclusion. Largely unreformed appointive bureaucracies survived intact in both countries through the 1990s, but by then the other elements were either weakened or on their way out.

Both countries moved closer to an ideal typical desarrollista state from the 1940s through the 1970s and then retreated in the 1980s. Systematic state intervention in the economy began in the 1930s and 1940s. The state role increased in the 1950s and 1960s through extensive protection and other ISI policies, and governments in the 1970s in both countries vastly expanded the number and scope of state enterprise. On the political side, nonelite participation expanded through the 1940s in Mexico and the 1960s in Brazil but then contracted until the 1970s, especially in Brazil. In the 1980s both systems experienced expanding but still limited pluralism.

75. Edson de Oliveira Nunes, "Bureaucratic Insulation and Clientelism in Contemporary Brazil: Uneven State-Building and the Taming of Modernity," Ph.D. diss. Department of Political Science, University of California, Berkeley, 1984, pp. 73–84; Suzigan, "As empresas do governo," pp. 85–87.

76. Love, "Raúl Prebisch," pp. 81–86.

SYSTEMIC INTERACTION

Table 3 provides a summary of the developmental state in Mexico and Brazil. Political capitalism and developmentalism affect the economy, whereas political exclusion and appointments are more political. In terms of differentiating structures and goals, political capitalism and the appointment bureaucracies are the structures through which elites pursued development and limited pluralism. Exclusion and developmentalism shaped the preferences or "ambitions," to borrow Michael Loriaux's term, especially of state and political elites, whereas the appointive bureaucracy and political capitalism influenced the strategies economic and state elites adopted to further their preferences.

The four components of the desarrollista state affect and often reinforce one another; they are parts of a system. In the introduction to this volume, Woo-Cumings writes that the developmental state is a "shorthand for the seamless web of political, bureaucratic, and money influences." Less a seamless web than a dense set of interrelationships, my conception of the desarrollista state tries to break out the analytically discrete components better to understand their interaction. This kind of systemic analysis is largely absent from research on developmental states in Latin America, which tends to focus much more on the bases of support and patterns of intervention in the economy.

The interactions among the four components are complex and multiple. Suffice it here to offer some examples and note that not all the interactions are equally significant. For instance, the effect of appointments on political capitalism is less than vice versa. It is the executive's control over resources that moves politics into the bureaucracy, and the executive bureaucracy dominates both politics and economics. The various entities of this bureaucracy run state enterprises and banks, fix tariffs, subsidize credit, and otherwise budget and plan government intervention into the economy. The legislature and judiciary are marginal in economic policy, and this exclusion dilutes their political relevance. The political elite therefore flocks to the executive that then dominates politics and further marginalizes the other branches. Politics becomes an essential part of doing business. In her study of Mexican industrialists, Flavia Derossi concluded that "when success and failure depend on political action as much as on productivity, entrepreneurs will remain 'power-oriented' more than 'production-oriented.' "[77]

The causal relations also operate in the reverse direction, though less strongly. The stakes in political capitalism are very high, so capitalists and

---

77. Flavia Derossi, *The Mexican Entrepreneur* (Paris: Organization for Economic Cooperation and Development, 1971), p. 66; see also Lauterbach, "Government and Development," p. 202.

Table 3. The Desarrollista state

	Politics	Economics
Structures	Appointive bureaucracy	Political capitalism
Elite goals	Political exclusion	Developmentalism

state actors want direct influence in appointments and through them control over the distribution of state resources. Political capitalism therefore makes it harder to reform an appointive bureaucracy. An innocuous-seeming proposal to create a career civil service is in fact a radical reform to redistribute power.[78] These difficulties and contending pressures are important to bear in mind when analyzing possibilities for administrative reform. Most analyses of developmental states in Asia emphasize Weberian bureaucracy.[79] By extrapolation the recommendation for Latin America would be that interventionist states require reforms to make them more Weberian. Yet, once states intervene extensively in the economy, they make such administrative reforms more politically costly and less likely.

Given that the politicization of capitalism focuses political activity on the executive bureaucracy, it is then appointments that structure access and representation for societal groups attempting to defend their interests. Appointments also distribute power in this politicized bureaucracy and present power holders (the appointers) with a sometimes difficult dilemma: how to balance representation and central control. This control and effective bureaucratic performances are crucial to elites with developmental goals. And, it is through appointments that top developmentalists communicate incentives to subordinates to make decisions that effectively promote industry.[80] Lastly, to the extent that representation is possible only through appointment, the appointive bureaucracy impedes mass participation, because appointment politics are opaque and restricted to elites. In this sense the appointive bureaucracy acts to exclude

78. Arellano and Guerrero argue that the proposal of the Zedillo government for administrative reform is unlikely to be implemented because it would do away with the appointive bureaucracy and therefore the basis for organizing power in the government and the ruling PRI. Of course, politicians and capitalists often want to use state resources for different ends, so that if either group lost influence it might be enlisted in a reform movement to reduce appointments and depoliticize distribution. See David Arellano and Juan Pablo Guerrero, "Unequal Advances and Unclear Intentions: The Mexican State Reform and the Managerialist Strategy," paper presented at the conference Political Economy of Administrative Reform in Developing Countries, Northwestern University, May 1997.

79. Alice H. Amsden, *Asia's Next Giant: South Korea and Late Industrialization* (New York: Oxford University Press, 1989); Johnson, *MITI and the Japanese Miracle*; and especially Evans, *Embedded Autonomy.*

80. Schneider, *Politics within the State,* chap. 4.

nonelites politically and to inhibit in a simple logistic way the expansion of pluralism.

The association between authoritarianism and industrialization has a long, unresolved history in social science theory. As suggested in Table 1, the association between the developmental state and authoritarianism seems historically to be a stable, if not necessary, combination. Of course, economic performance clearly varies independently of the type of political regime.[81] Yet there are mutually reinforcing tendencies between developmentalism, as ambition not outcome, and political exclusion. Johnson thinks so when he characterizes democratic Japan as a soft authoritarian regime. The developmental state in Japan appears to work because the system is not fully democratic. The two seem more closely related and mutually supportive in discourse than they may be in practice. Developmentalists regularly bemoan the messiness and sluggishness of democracy. Apologists for dictatorships just as regularly justify authoritarian means to promote development. The reinforcing pressures also work in the opposite direction. Dictators increasingly lost the means to legitimate their rule as the democratizing twentieth century progressed and were naturally drawn to developmentalism.[82] Maria Covre conducted an extensive analysis of the discourse of the military rulers in Brazil.[83] They began their rule by saying they were there to restore democracy. After several years they could no longer claim to be restoring democracy, and their discourse clearly shifted to extol the virtues of development and the advantages of military rule to achieve it.

Political capitalism also contributes to, or is functional for, political exclusion. Political capitalism was in large part the result of the sedimentation of myriad short-term decisions designed to meet particular economic problems. The result, as politicians are quick to realize, is that the state ends up with discretionary control throughout the economy that can easily be manipulated to stem political challenges. For those outside the elite, political capitalism also gives state actors resources for strengthening exclusionary clientelism. These funds do not usually promote real distribution but go to local elites who can effectively silence nonelites in their areas.

Among business people or the bourgeoisie, political capitalism can also blunt democratic impulses. Economic elites realize that they probably should not create trouble for a government that is reviewing their appli-

81. Karen L. Remmer, "Democracy and Economic Crisis," *World Politics* 42, no. 3 (April 1990): 315–35; Stephan Haggard, *Pathways from the Periphery: The Politics of Growth in the Newly Industrializing Countries* (Ithaca: Cornell University Press, 1990); Adam Przeworski and Fernando Limongi, "Political Regimes and Economic Growth," *Journal of Economic Perspectives* 7, no. 3 (Summer 1993): 51–69.

82. Samuel P. Huntington, *The Third Wave: Democratization in the Late Twentieth Century* (Norman: University of Oklahoma Press, 1991).

83. Covre, *A fala dos homens*, esp. pp. 117–25.

cations for subsidies. Political capitalism disaggregates business elites and forces them to work through ad hoc "bureaucratic rings."[84] Economic elites are thus poorly equipped to mount a collective challenge to authoritarian rule. Moreover, political capitalism makes business especially worried about the possibility that democracy would allow antibusiness politicians to oversee vast and deeply interventionist controls over the private economy. Big business in Mexico quickly retreated from active opposition to the PRI when the left emerged as the leading alternative to the PRI in the late 1980s.[85] There are limits, though, to the extent political capitalism shores up exclusion. At the limit, if business feels excluded, then economic elites become a powerful force for democracy.[86]

These, then, are some illustrative interactions among the four components of the desarrollista state. The analysis so far has emphasized similarities between Brazil and Mexico. In the following section I consider some distinctions between the empirical evolutions of the political economies of Brazil and Mexico.

Variations on the Theme

Brazil and Mexico had desarrollista states for most of the postwar period, but they differed from each other and from other developmental states. The PRI sharply distinguishes Mexico from Brazil. As a mass electoral force, the PRI appears to challenge the ideas of political exclusion and representation through the bureaucracy. Moreover, by channeling some demands and representation, the PRI eased pressure on appointments and shielded appointees from popular pressure, enabling them to carry out unpopular programs, particularly anti-inflation policies.[87] Yet, the very success of the PRI from the 1940s to the 1980s tended to move Mexico closer to the ideal typical desarrollista state. The PRI's quest for complete electoral dominance (*el carro completo*) stripped elections of meaning and thereby reduced the utility of politicians to other elites. In

84. See Cardoso, *O modelo político brasileiro.*

85. See Heredia Blanca, "Mexican Business and the State: The Political Economy of a 'Muddled' Transition," in Ernest Bartell and Leigh Payne, eds., *Business and Democracy in Latin America* (Pittsburgh: University of Pittsburgh Press, 1995).

86. See Stephan Haggard and Robert Kaufman, *The Political Economy of Democratic Transitions* (Princeton: Princeton University Press, 1995); Karen Remmer, "Democratization in Latin America," in Robert Slater, Barry Schutz, and Steven Dorr, eds., *Global Transformation and the Third World* (Boulder, Colo.: Lynne Rienner, 1993); and Catherine M. Conaghan, *Restructuring Domination: Industrialists and the State in Ecuador* (Pittsburgh: University of Pittsburgh Press, 1988).

87. See Ruth Berins Collier, "Popular Sector Incorporation and Political Supremacy: Regime Evolution in Brazil and Mexico," in Sylvia Ann Hewlett and Richard S. Weinert, eds., *Brazil and Mexico* (Philadelphia: Institute for the Study of Human Issues, 1982).

eliminating elections as a source of uncertainty, politicians did not secure a commensurate reward for their efforts but committed political suicide. In this sense, PRI dominance shifted political attention away from elections to the bureaucracy. Moreover, in co-opting or capturing popular-sector organizations, the PRI preempted nonelite challenges and reinforced political exclusion. At the same time, PRI dominance tarnished the revolutionary legitimacy of the political elite and encouraged them to rely more on nationalism, clientelism, and developmentalism.

The revolutionary ideology would seem to give Mexican political leaders a solid alternative legitimacy normally lacking in the developmental state, but paradoxically, it may have driven them to embrace developmentalism. To the extent that political leaders could not claim that past policies had advanced the revolutionary promise of social justice, they found it expedient to embrace developmentalism. From another perspective the revolutionary ideology embodied in the 1917 constitution is effective precisely because it embodies all the major "isms" of that era and can now be invoked in the service of communal, patrimonialist, socialist, and liberal projects.[88] In any event, the revolutionary ideology (in all its forms) filled Mexican ideological space. It could and did accommodate developmentalism but never allowed it the dominance achieved in Brazil.

Mexico's porous two-thousand-mile border with the United States enhances the structural power of business and thereby circumscribes state intervention and makes Mexican capitalism less political. The border limits the potential for state control of the economy, especially of the exit option for mobile resources; reduces the range of effective intervention; and hence predisposes state elites to more market-oriented policies in some areas. For example, exchange controls are costly to enforce and high inflation is more disruptive because of easier currency convertibility.[89] Policymakers had an indication of the significance of the border from the very beginning of the desarrollista state. Between 1935 and 1939 capitalists exported close to a billion pesos, more than twice the total deposits in the banking system.[90] In the explanation of different re-

88. González Graf, "Las crisis de la clase política," p. 35.

89. Maxfield argues that "the threat of flight to the dollar is more acute in Mexico than in other developing countries thanks to the two thousand mile U.S.-Mexican border . . . [which] heightens the threat of capital flight in response to unfavored policies." See *Governing Capital*, p. 71. She also quotes Cárdenas lamenting that "exchange controls can only work in highly disciplined countries where customs rules are well organized and borders can be effectively watched; exchange control in Mexico would surely be undermined by the black market" (p. 72). In some instances, however, the response of state officials to difficulties of control has been more interventionist than in Brazil, as in the bank nationalization of 1982 and the earlier policy of Mexicanization of MNCs. See Gereffi and Evans, "Transnational Corporations."

90. Juan M. Martínez Nava, *Conflicto Estado-empresarios en los gobiernos de Cárdenas, López Mateos y Echeverría* (México: Nueva Imagen, 1984), p. 104.

lations between business and government after 1940 in Brazil and Mexico, this border looms large.[91]

The Brazilian military has been a more visible protagonist in the desarrollista state than has its counterpart in Mexico. Brazilian military officers have since the 1920s propagated developmentalism, restricted political participation even in civilian regimes, and sought and achieved representation through appointment.[92] Overall, the military helped make Brazilian developmentalism more potent than the Mexican version.

In the democratic period 1945–64 Brazil appears to deviate from a pure case. Developmentalism and state intervention gained ground, but not without interruption. In fact, from the viewpoint of 1965, the previous twenty years seemed to be a merry-go-round in economic policy from liberal to developmental, to populist, and back. Formal literacy requirements and informal electoral coercion limited participation but not contestation, and the political system and exclusion were unstable. Before 1964, one can imagine several plausible alternative scenarios for Brazil; had Quadros not resigned, had Goulart not polarized politics, had the military not intervened. Yet in the period from 1930 to 1990 as a whole, developmentalism and exclusion were dominant, though there were more detours, fluctuations, and instability than in Mexico.

In terms of the appointive bureaucracy, state elites in Mexico managed to insulate the bureaucracy more from outside pressures and to institute more meritocratic promotion criteria, though more by custom than law. Lateral entry into high levels of the economic bureaucracy became rare, and outside economic and political elites could not pressure to have one of their own appointed to a top bureaucratic position. Meritocratic advancement became the informal norm in public banking and finance.

Overall, Brazil had a fuller desarrollista state than did Mexico. Brazil lacked a strong party (which could deflect some political attention from the bureaucracy), had greater control over its borders, and could therefore manipulate markets more to developmental and political ends. The Brazilian military invested a lot in discourse and helped create a stronger strain of developmentalism. Lastly, the appointive bureaucracy in Brazil was more open to outside infiltration and pressure and more politicized.

91. See Ben Ross Schneider, "Big Business and the Politics of Economic Reform: Confidence and Concertation in Brazil and Mexico," in Sylvia Maxfield and Schneider, eds., *Business and the State in Developing Countries* (Ithaca: Cornell University Press, 1997).

92. See Stepan, *Military in Politics,* and Edmundo Campos Coelho, *Em busca de identidade: O Exército na sociedade brasileira* (Rio de Janeiro: Forense Universitária, 1976).

The Desarrollista State in Comparative Perspective

The desarrollista state is an "intense" concept, in Giovanni Sartori's terms, designed to generate "rich, differentiated theory" applicable to a small range of cases.[93] Excluding one of the four components of the desarrollista state would leave a concept broader in coverage but weaker in analytic leverage. For instance, dropping the element of political capitalism would allow the inclusion of predominantly market economies such as small or open economies that are constantly subject to international market pressures as in countries of Central America, the Caribbean, or the entrepôt economies of Asia. But the dominant discourse in these countries is unlikely to be developmental, and hence the whole economic side of the desarrollista state is left out, and the general literature on authoritarianism is adequate to the task of analyzing the many governments with appointive bureaucracies that limit pluralism.

Dropping the condition of political exclusion allows the extension of the concept to include countries with strong parties and organizations such as labor unions in a vibrant civil society. In Argentina and Chile before the military coups of the 1970s, appointment relations structured the bureaucracies, capitalism was largely political, and developmentalism enjoyed wide though not hegemonic support.[94] Strong parties and unions, however, made elections more important and gave nonelites greater power, in turn encouraging the bourgeoisie to organize politically.

In these instances, nonelite power, democracy, and the elements of the desarrollista state created a volatile mix. Political capitalism contributed to polarization because economic elites had more reason to fear a leftist (or Peronist) electoral victory in that they depended so heavily on the state. Political capitalism can also exacerbate polarization by politicizing the labor movement. Because the state is so heavily involved in the economy—which means it also controls such variables as wages and prices that most affect workers—workers have strong incentives to organize to pressure the state, rather than employers. Unions target the state, and strikes become political weapons. Once polarization has taken hold, developmentalism becomes increasingly difficult because one or another faction will oppose almost any industrial policy on the grounds that it favors the opposition. Polarization also tends to strip the appointment bureaucracy

93. Sartori, "Concept Misformation in Comparative Politics"; see also Alexander L. George, "Case Studies and Theory Development: The Method of Structured, Focused Comparison," in Paul Gordon Lauren, ed., *Diplomacy* (New York: Free Press, 1979), p. 59.

94. On Chile, see Barbara Stallings, *Class Conflict and Economic Development in Chile, 1958–1973* (Stanford: Stanford University Press, 1978). On Argentina, see Sikkink, *Ideas and Institutions.*

of the flexible advantages it has in less antagonistic environments. In other words, authoritarianism and the desarrollista state may have an elective affinity because democracy so upsets the interaction among the four components: democratic conflict makes developmentalism contentious, political capitalism exacerbates polarization in a democracy, and political competition cripples the appointive bureaucracy.

Developmental discourse orients the desarrollista state. Without it (but with the other three components) the state would be more parasitic and rent seeking and less constrained by capitalism. Such predatory, kleptocratic states have appeared with greater frequency in Central America, the Caribbean, and Africa than in the larger countries of Latin America.[95] Of course, the constant temptation for illicit gain exists for all officials with discretion over direct or indirect resource allocation, and some officials succumb. Officials in successful developmental states often have strong ethical, ideological (discourse), career, or legal grounds for resisting the temptation, yet even here corruption has been endemic if not debilitating. Without an alternative discourse, leaders have the limitation of pluralism and retention of power as their only goals, and in such agrarian societies as Zaire, Ghana, Haiti, Paraguay, or pre-Sandinista Nicaragua, they found political capitalism and bureaucratic appointments useful in these pursuits.

Although the developmentalist discourse is, on the face of it, one of the common features of developmental states in both Asia and Latin America, the nationalism underlying the discourse, as emphasized by Woo-Cumings in the introduction, differs. In Asia, nationalism appears to have both stronger and deeper roots as well as more urgent and immediate stimulation. That is, Asian societies, especially Korea and Japan, are far more homogeneous and have far longer histories as discrete cultural units than do any of the societies of Latin America. What constitutes the essence of the Mexican nation has been a contested debate for much of this century, largely because of the unequal status of indigenous and mestizo cultures. Brazil has no comparable indigenous groups but was, especially earlier in this century, a patchwork of immigrant communities, the African the largest among them. Primary loyalties in both countries, as in others in Latin America, have often not been to shared vision of the nation.

In terms of immediate stimulus, Japanese colonialism and the cold war have been far more dramatic influences in Asia than American imperialism and economic dependency in Latin America. True, the United States did take half of Mexico's territory in the nineteenth century and sent troops into Mexico during the Mexican revolution. Still, this is a far cry from nearly half a century of brutal Japanese colonial rule of Korea. Simi-

95. See Evans, *Embedded Autonomy.*

larly, the Cuban revolution sent adrenaline through the veins of cold warriors and developmentalists in Latin America, but neither the fear was as enduring nor the threat as close as it was in divided Korea and Taiwan/China. In sum, despite moments of intense nationalist mobilization in Mexico and Brazil—the nationalization of the oil industries in the 1930s and 1950s, respectively, is the best example—nationalism was never consensual enough among nonelite groups or urgent enough among elites to provide the same impetus to developmentalism.

Creating a Weberian bureaucracy and insulating officials from appointment politics can give greater impetus to developmentalism, as in the cases of Taiwan and Korea, which otherwise resemble much more the desarrollista states discussed here. The absence of extensive appointments in these bureaucracies helped create a professional, committed, and less overtly politicized cadre of developmentalist officials (who in addition are more attuned to market concerns because of the vulnerability of their economies to international markets). In his comparative study of Brazil, Korea, and India, Evans argued that the "embedded autonomy" of Korean officials accounts for the greater effectiveness of the Korean developmental state.[96] Officials are embedded when they have enduring ties to dense networks of industrialists; they have autonomy when they have Weberian careers within the bureaucracy. The appointive bureaucracy, in contrast, undermines bureaucratic autonomy and generates high levels of circulation, which preclude embeddedness. Officials in an appointive bureaucracy rarely have the time to develop the long-term relations of trust and reciprocity with business that characterize developmental states in Asia because officials move to another job in another area of the state or the private sector whenever ministers or presidents change.

My first goal in this essay was to understand fully a few causal relationships within a limited range of variation, rather than generate concepts with broad coverage but, as Weber warned, "devoid of content." Nonetheless, the model of the desarrollista state can be useful in approaching broader comparative analysis by generating hypotheses and identifying primary causal variables. The comparison of East Asia and Latin America has attracted much attention, and explanations for their differing economic performance range from international factors to authoritarianism and to culture.[97] Fred Block has concluded that "there is reason to believe that most states aspire to be developmental states; the real issue are differences in capacities and effectiveness in their policies."[98] My approach

---

96. Ibid.

97. See Gary Gereffi and Donald Wyman, eds., *Manufacturing Miracles: Paths of Industrialization in Latin America and East Asia* (Princeton: Princeton University Press, 1990).

98. Block, "Roles of the State in the Economy," p. 705.

highlights the role of the bureaucracy (and a fuller appreciation of the strength of developmentalism). Explanations for the failure of ISI in Argentina and Chile also include economic constraints, policy failures, and bureaucratic dysfunctions. Comparisons with the model of the desarrollista state would recommend closer analysis of the greater political uncertainties due to political inclusion and political polarization, which in turn resulted in part from conflicts over developmentalism and political capitalism.

CHAPTER TEN

Embedded Particularism: India's Failed Developmental State

Ronald J. Herring

DEVELOPMENTAL STATE THEORIZING: THE IMPORTANCE OF FAILURE

India must be the most dramatic case of a failed developmental state. The historical context, international position, and ideas of empowering the state for widely shared developmental aspirations are congruent with the East Asian model. The state itself has remarkable human capacity and a surfeit of world-class economists. And yet the result of state-led development—decades of what came to be called the "license-permit-quota *raj* [rule]"—has been ultimately rejected by domestic critics and voters, as well as international technical elites. A turn from state to market, most dramatic since 1991, implies repudiation of what was once called the "Nehruvian consensus" for something more like the "Washington consensus." The financial crisis of faster-growing Asian nations in 1997 may give some pause—residues of the regulatory state and insulation from volatile capital markets arguably spared India the type of dramatic collapse visited upon its neighbors—but the perception of failure has dominated India's historically recent sweeping shift to liberalization as an antidote to its developmental state.

Failure is always relative. India's developmental state failed by measure of its own grand aspirations and in comparative growth terms, but not by standards of historical stagnation under colonial rule or by standards of upholding a responsible and democratic state. Its prominence in ideological battles over economic interventionism derived in part from its ideolog-

This paper has benefited from discussions with or comments from Chandra Mohan, Aseema Sinha, Vanita Shastri, Peter Katzenstein, Richard Bensel, Kaushik Basu, Mary Katzenstein, Manoj Srivastava, Atul Kohli, and Pranab Bardhan.

ically strategic position in the cold war. India was the "world's largest democracy," the counterpoint to "totalitarian," "red" China. But it was simultaneously the great Western hope, largely failed, for its leaders persisted in baiting and opposing the United States in particular, tilting toward the Soviet Union in economic relations, military alliance, and development strategy.[1] Liberalization in India came as a softer echo of the restructuring and collapse of the Soviet system and has served the same ideological functions for proponents of unfettered market capitalism.

What makes developmental state theorizing of interest comparatively is the argument that states make a difference in long-term economic performance—that is, variation across nations is neither randomly distributed over time and space nor simply the outcome of differential endowments operating through markets. In this sense, work on the developmental state joins the great debate between mercantilism and laissez-faire or the current neoliberal consensus and its critics. Its value is to force analysis beyond the sterile debate of states versus markets to ask questions about the character of the state, its projects, and its embeddedness in society.

Despite ambiguity over the generality and causal claims of developmental-state theory,[2] as well as real-world variation in characteristics of developmental states, the concept is important theoretically. To be of interest to the historical debate on the wealth of nations, however, the argument must rest on at least two assumptions: that states know what to do and are capable of doing it. There is then a cognitive question and a capacity question.

On the cognitive level, honesty should compel agnosticism about the determinants of anomalous economic growth., The big question of the causes of cross-sectional and temporal variation has been around at least since Adam Smith; we still lack parsimonious validated theory.[3] For so

1. See Dennis Kux, *India and the United States: Estranged Democracies* (Washington, D.C.: National Defense University Press, 1993). George Rosen's *Western Economists in Eastern Societies* (Baltimore: Johns Hopkins University Press, 1985) demonstrates concretely the greater permeability of the Pakistani economic establishment to American ideas in contrast to India, where the relationship was never one of hegemony and often one of reactive rejection.

2. I will not summarize the literature for reasons of efficiency; see Woo-Cumings's introduction to this volume. She does not see the causal connection to economic growth to be as important as do I.

3. Mrinal Datta-Chaudhuri provides a succinct overview of why development theorists thought the state was necessary in poor countries, how states have varied significantly in their capacity to intervene effectively, and why the specifically *political* economy of growth needed to explain these outcomes remains elusive. See Mrinal Datta-Chaudhuri, "Market Failure and Government Failure," *Journal of Economic Perspectives* 4, no. 3 (Summer 1990), and Dieter Senghaas, *The European Experience: A Historical Critique of Development Theory* (Leamington Spa: Berg, 1985). An instructive example of the concrete case is the multiple, conflicting, and overdetermined theorizing concerning the slowing of growth in industrial production in India after 1965; see Ashutosh Varshney, "Political Economy of Slow Industrial Growth," *Economic and Political Weekly*, September 1, 1984.

overdetermined and historically contingent a phenomenon, this outcome is almost inevitable. Yet for the developmental-state argument to be
valid, we must assume that successful states chose better strategies among
the many contenders—which have proliferated and changed over time.
Once a state (thinks it) knows what to do, the capacity to do it becomes
critical. It should then be possible to identify blockages in states that attempt a developmental role and fail.

The above presupposes that states are very important in achieving comparatively rapid economic growth; they may not be. Lester Thurow has
popularized the position that the United States commanded so rich a per
capita natural-resource base (the original inhabitants having been subjected to ethnic cleansing and dispossession) that it would have taken remarkable state blundering to have prevented rapid economic growth. No
developmental state was necessary, nor could any but the most extreme
developmental bungling prevent growth.[4] The sad truth is that we do not
know the necessary and sufficient conditions for more rapid than average
accumulation. Reciprocally, when growth rates fall below average, there is
uncertainty as to cause, though the development enterprise compels con-
sultants, academics, and international agencies to take assertive stances on
causes. In India, as in much of the world, the neoliberal zeitgeist has
placed the blame squarely on failed developmental states: interventionists
whose failed interventions illustrate the superiority of noninterventionist,
market-based strategies. My strategy is to compare the Indian experience
to a stylized version of developmental-state theory to illuminate both.

Developmental States and Growth States

No matter how obvious and important the distinction between growth
and development, the two are continually conflated. Development is
about realizing potential, creating the good society, over which there
is political conflict; growth is about accumulation.[5] Not all rapid growth is

4. This view is considered narrowly, and partly upheld, in Gavin Wright, "The Origins of
American Industrial Success, 1879–1940," *American Economic Review* 80, no. 4 (1990).
Wright curiously neglects the "natural resource" base represented by agriculture, which
would be crucial to the anomalous resource-base argument. Likewise, one could point to
nations such as Italy which suggest that a developmental state may not be necessary for success. The extremes of failure where too little state capacity clearly hinders growth are
discussed in Peter Evans, *Embedded Autonomy: States and Industrial Transformation* (Princeton:
Princeton University Press, 1995).

5. Gustavo Esteva observes, "Development, which had suffered the most dramatic and
grotesque metamorphosis of its history in Truman's hands, was impoverished even more in
the hands of its first promoters, who reduced it to *economic growth*." See Esteva's chapter in
Wolfgang Sachs, ed., *The Development Dictionary: A Guide to Knowledge as Power* (London: Zed,
1992), p. 12.

developmental—the analogy to cancer cells or endocrine malfunction is commonly made.

Conflations usually have causes. It is demonstrably true that global real-politik privileges accumulation, which dwarfs in importance any internally generated, normatively constituted notion of societal potential to be developed. States that dominate economies which are expanding wealth do better in the global hierarchy than states worrying about immunization of babies or clean drinking water in villages. No one much cares about what Henry Kissinger tellingly called "basket cases," those objects of "triage" in Garrett Hardin's "lifeboat ethics." The operating rules of the International Monetary Fund (IMF) had to be amended in 1979 precisely because the assumption of a universal agreement on maximizing Gross National Product (GNP) as the sole measure of "development" conflicted with at least the stated objective functions of many nations. "Adjustment with a human face" became the formulation of the liberalizing regime in India headed by Narasimha Rao in 1991. The reality is often adjustment for growth first, human face with what is left over, but the political reality is that states vary in how single-mindedly they pursue growth over other developmental projects.

Normatively and ideologically, for much of the former colonial world, the distinction between development and growth has been fundamental. Developmental states were ideologically legitimated by a distinction between themselves and the "night watchman" state that allows the evils of capitalism to accumulate with GNP, or the aggressive colonial state that altered society to enhance pernicious processes of accumulation. The peripheral developmental state was more likely to legitimate itself and perhaps to view its success in terms of broader economic desiderata: eradication of poverty and social indignities, balanced regional growth to bring up backward areas, and protection of traditional crafts and proto-industries on grounds of cultural identity and social justice. The notion of what a state should do was often forged in the dialectic of opposition to the colonial state. It was in mobilization of support to throw off a decidedly antidevelopmental colonial state that some of the core contradictions in India's developmental state emerged: a state committed to planning, yet too democratic, soft, and embedded to govern the market; a state too estranged from the business of the market and the least powerful economic actors to rely on sources of legitimation other than those of economic populism. The turn to liberalization should not be read, then, as an embrace of market society but as an admission that the alternative, in its specific national incarnation, was not working.

HOW BADLY HAS INDIA DONE?

In contrast to the very shaky foundations of sociopolitical analysis, assessments of economic performance should land us on firmer ground. Yet the project presupposes that we have a good way of measuring economic success. What if interventionist states have artificially lower growth rates as conventionally measured, because much economic activity is driven underground?[6] Perhaps the real economy has not done as badly as has the measured economy, in part because the state's reach so exceeded its grasp. But leaving aside the unmeasurable underground economy, the famous "Hindu rate of growth" (coined by the late Raj Krishna) of 3.5 percent per annum from 1950 to 1980 compares to a "Third World" growth rate of 4.9 percent per annum over the same period; the world economy was growing at 4.1 percent per annum.[7] India's figures in per capita terms look somewhat weaker comparatively because population growth has been relatively high.

Is the "Hindu rate of growth" too low? The Federal Reserve Bank of the United States begins putting on the brakes when growth rates approach 3.5 percent, fearing inflation and tight labor markets. What is too low a growth rate in India is too high in Washington. Where India's performance looks sluggish is *in comparison to developmental states* such as South Korea, which started developmentalism after the Second World War at India's income level and within decades attained incomes more than ten times India's level.[8]

Virtually all varieties of development theory emphasize a structural transformation in favor of industry. India's industrial growth rate from 1950 to 1975 was a robust 7 percent. Concern that the license-permit-quota raj was stifling growth focused on the drop in the rate of growth in industry after 1965—to 3.5 percent in the 1965–80 period. Yet this slug-

---

6. The "black economy" is very large in India; some popular estimates have put its size at half that of the visible, counted economy. If this were to be anywhere near true, estimates of performance over time would have to be radically altered in the direction of more favorable growth performance. Kamal Kabra, *The Black Economy in India* (Delhi: Chanakya Publications, 1982), in one of the early attempts to investigate the black economy systematically, concludes that the license-permit-quota raj was not responsible for the growth of the black economy. I find this argument unpersuasive, but the issue is unsettled.

7. It is reasonable to think of 1980 as the beginning of the rethinking of the Nehruvian developmental raj, as Indira Gandhi returned to power in Delhi and began making comparative reflections on growth—specifically with regard to South Korea—and entertained ideas of liberalization. Comparative growth data from World Bank's *World Development Report* (annual); Dalip S. Swamy, *The Political Economy of Industrialization* (New Delhi: Sage, 1994), chap. 1; Vanita Shastri, "The Political Economy of Policy Formation in India: The Case of Industrial Policy," draft of Ph.D. diss., Cornell University, defended September 21, 1994, p. 18 and passim.

8. For example, see Datta-Chaudhuri, "Market Failure and Government Failure."

gish performance, for which India became stereotyped, increased in the 1980s to 7.9 percent per annum. The period of significant liberalization since 1991 has deviated from the Hindu rate of growth; the growth path trend may be closer to 4–6 percent per annum, but there are serious questions of sustainability—and of causes, once favorable monsoons and other factors are figured in.[9]

Thus a very rough periodization indicates that India did reasonably well in terms of growth until the mid-1960s, during a period when the world economy was anomalously robust, then experienced a decline after 1965, especially in industrial growth, followed by a boom in the 1980s. The boom lead to unsustainable fiscal deficits, external debt, and a balance of payments crunch in 1991—the proximate causes of significant liberalization, after which the growth rate seems to have moved to a higher trend rate.

Because conventional wisdom among economists bemoans India's growth performance, it is useful to provide some perspective. Unlike the boom-and-bust states of Latin America, India was conservative in international financial behavior before the 1980s. The 1980s look very much like Reaganomics in the United States: rapid expansion built on unsustainable expansion of debt, both internal and external: a Keynesian boom. The result in India, unlike in the United States (which mints its own foreign exchange reserves), was a genuine financial crisis in the international sector. When the state was fiscally conservative, growth rates were fairly low, but the economic crises of more aggressive states were absent; when the state became more profligate, growth rates increased, but so too did symptoms of crisis. The crisis of faster-growing Asian states beginning in July 1997 illustrates the reality of Indian state managers' fear of dependence on volatile international capital flows.

Marxian and classical emphases on the size and mode of deployment of the economic surplus should then not be lost in the rush to credit or blame states for everything.[10] When the savings rate in India went up in the 1980s, so did the growth rate. The inward flow of investment following liberalization likewise made more capital available for growth. This suggests that the regulatory pathologies of statecraft may not be the whole story; forces emphasized in classical growth theory seem independently important: high rates of savings leading to high rates of growth.

Historical perspective of longer reach is also informative. India exited colonial rule with more than the usual obstacles: truly staggering rural

9. Prabat Patnaik and C. P. Chandrasekhar, "Indian Economy under 'Structural Adjustment,'" *Economic and Political Weekly*, November 25, 1995, pp. 3001–13.

10. See Paul Baran, *The Political Economy of Growth* (New York: Monthly Review Press, 1957).

poverty; low and unstable agricultural yields; dismemberment, which severed production and trade links and caused massive refugee flows when East and West Pakistan were hived off by Britain; and an economy that has often been described as a "gamble on the monsoons."[11] The dissolution of colonial rule—by a policy of "divide and quit"—left India with a difficult geopolitical position in the region and eventually in the global cold war. Confrontation with Pakistan was a consequence of partition; costly wars with Pakistan, armed by the United States, and unproductive military spending damaged development.

India's independent state had to build much from scratch. The state itself had to be built over a continental patchwork of colonial administrative divisions and "princely states" retained as feudal museums by the British for the convenience of "indirect rule." Empire also meant that Indian capital had decidedly superior exit options compared with business elites in East Asia. The empire spread Indian capital around the world, most visibly politically in Africa, where working in the English language and under English rules was no hindrance. Colonial education prepared businesspeople to work in England and the United States as well as the empire. The loss of capital was probably small, the loss of entrepreneurship very large. And no matter how badly the "Hindu rate of growth" fared in contemporaneous comparison, in longitudinal comparative terms it far outstripped the colonial rate of growth, which was very close to zero.

India's growth performance is also confused by an aggregation problem. No one ever says that "Europe did well from 1945 to 1990" but rather disaggregates experiences of Portugal, Sweden, Bulgaria, and France. Most Indian states are larger than most of these nations. Stagnation in Bihar is aggregated with vigorous growth in the Punjab or Maharashtra, yet all were subjected to similar policy from Delhi. That it is difficult to form and operate a continental-sized state and economy without imperial power is now becoming obvious to Europeans; the homogeneity of smaller countries in Asia was not in the cards after the colonial dissolution of the subcontinental piece of empire. Delhi looks out over a Europe and forged a state to deal with that reality; political management of the economy inevitably incurs a pluralism penalty.

India's developmental state thus faced extraordinary hurdles in comparative terms. State building is expensive; public resources have opportunity costs. Failure is then in part relative to difficulty of task and of aspiration. That growth could have been higher seems plausible, but not so

---

11. See Gunnar Myrdal, *Asian Drama: An Inquiry into the Poverty of Nations* (New York: Random House, 1968), vol. 1.

certain as liberal economists seem to think. More important than growth rates, which for all the reasons above remain elusive as explananda, is what the state did with its developmental aspirations.

CONCEPTUALIZING THE INDIAN STATE

Social scientists characterize large, complex entities—for example, "the state"—with summary designations that fit in two-by-two tables. Though this activity should make political scientists nervous, its popularity is just recompense for letting sociologists "bring the state back in." The state in India has been characterized in different ways, each telling us something of its multiple manifestations. Except as noted, these visions are not creatures of a unified analysis, but rather distinct strands in thinking about the state.

1) The "soft state" of Gunnar Myrdal's "Asian Drama" (1968). In the soft-state formulation, state capacity to act against powerful or even not-so-powerful interests in society is compromised across a range of issues. The Indian state is one that could not, for example, enforce prohibitions against "untouchability," collect overdues on state-supplied credit, or prevent the cutting of reserve forests or toxic desecration of the sacred Ganges River. Capacity is reduced by multiple interpenetrations of state and society; following Polanyi, I think of the state as *embedded* in society,[12] with variable degrees of autonomy (or "softness," reflexively) depending on issue area. Embeddedness varies with distance from the center until the "state" finally dissolves into the tissue of society at the local level. Softness, or incapacity, is not entirely due to embeddedness (or permeability or penetration), however, as there are identifiable bureaucratic pathologies: rigidity from routinization, hierarchical norms that induce conservatism and risk avoidance, extreme arrogance, and propensity for corruption.[13]

12. The use of "embedded" is not meant to be trendy but derives from Karl Polanyi's notion of allocative institutions being embedded in society before their extraction in the making of market society, after which a certain amount of reembedding of the market takes place as society "protects itself" from the disintegrating effects of market society. See Karl Polanyi, *The Great Transformation* (New York: Farrar and Rhinehart, 1944). India's administrative system as an "embedded bureaucracy" with regard to rural policy is developed in Ronald J. Herring, "Embedded Production Relations and the Rationality of Tenant Quiescence in Tenure Reform," *Journal of Peasant Studies* 8, no. 2 (January 1981), and Ronald J. Herring, *Land to the Tiller: The Political Economy of Agrarian Reform in South Asia* (New Haven: Yale University Press, 1983), chaps. 2, 3.

13. Herring, *Land to the Tiller*, chap. 2.

2) The pluralist class state. Overlapping with the soft-state perspective, pluralist accounts stress shifting power positions for various sectors of civil society depending on issue area. In Pranab Bardhan's version of Indian pluralism, a clear distinction is made between those groups with access to the state (the propertied elite and professional groups) and those without (the vast majority of the population).[14] Policy is the vector sum of bargaining among the three proprietary classes—owners of industry and agriculture and the professional elite—which exist in "uneasy alliance," united mostly by common interests in preserving privilege. Rent seeking is endemic, though on a larger scale than the literature typically stresses.[15]

3) The overextended state. The state is not so much co-opted, or penetrated, by interests in society as beleaguered by impossible tasks with which it cannot cope given its resources. Diversion of official energies into tasks which encounter the least resistance and match the exchange capabilities of officers with means of securing compliance are more common than policy achievement. Unity of the state dissolves as bureaucrats act rationally trying to make the best of situations in which they command inadequate resources and face unrealistic demands. The beleaguered state is the institutional embodiment of the accumulation of efforts to penetrate society too far, along too many dimensions, whether for legitimation or predation. Political parties are involved in the process for the patronage resources (nodes of discretionary authority) provided for their own projects (winning and retaining power).

In each of these formulations, dimensionality is crucial, yielding the obvious compromise: the "weak-strong state" of Lloyd and Susanne Rudolph.[16] The same state that cannot enforce minimum-wage or child-labor laws has proved capable of crushing a railway workers' strike, jailing the opposition, and defeating its neighbor in war. The state shows a different face to different sectors of society on different issues, much as severity of punishment for crime in the United States varies with the race and class of the criminal. The same Indian state, which could not uncover culprits in military procurement corruption at the highest levels, regularly managed to apprehend and murder agrarian radicals (shot "in en-

14. Pranab Bardhan, *The Political Economy of Development in India* (Oxford: Blackwell, 1984).

15. For an excellent summary and alternative treatments of the state in India, see Jayati Ghosh, "State Intervention in the Macroeconomy," in Prabhat Patnaik, ed., *Macroeconomics* (Delhi: Delhi University Press, 1995); for influential early treatment, see Anne O. Krueger, "The Political Economy of the Rent-Seeking Society," *American Economic Review* 64, 3 no. 1 (1974), and "Government Failures in Development," *Journal of Economic Perspectives* 4, no. 3 (Summer 1990).

16. Lloyd Rudolph and Susanne H. Rudolph, *In Pursuit of Laksmi: The Political Economy of the Indian State* (Chicago: University of Chicago Press, 1987).

counter with police"). State hardness and softness vary with branches of the state itself and with the sectors of society engaged. Lacking good measures of hardness and softness, the analysis often proceeds with some imprecision and opportunism.

4) The "imprisoned"—or structurally trapped—state. The number of people below a grotesque official poverty line in India is in the vicinity of 400 million. Growth and accumulation become imperatives not only because of the perceived political threats assumed to accompany destitution but also because the state itself is constrained in its own objectives by aggregate poverty. Its bureaucrats cannot be adequately compensated (relative to private sector salaries) or assured basic amenities (relative to expectations). The state legitimates its activities as necessary to alleviate destitution and backwardness, is unable to do so, and in the process becomes the captive of structural power in the economy: the first constraint is not to antagonize capital. Charles Lindblom analyzed this structural trap in an essay titled "The Market as Prison."[17]

5) The "iron-frame" state. In this perspective, the bureaucracy runs the country. Continuing the colonial legacy, the bureaucracy arrogates to itself the privilege of deciding how to rule; its autonomy began as extraordinary. In the frame's view, politicians "play to the gallery" and are incompetent, ignorant, and corrupt, thus their products are taken with a grain of salt by bureaucratic rulers. Populists come and go, but officialdom believes that it provides the continuity that *is* stateness. Yet the bureaucracy is clearly embedded in society and has felt (increasingly) for several decades the pressure of "political meddling": transfers of officers who offend local politicians or powerful segments of local society. No bureaucrat I know in India would disagree with the statement that the state is becoming less autonomous in this sense.

6) The contested federal state. Delhi's reach is sharply limited by dynamics in the States, where political forces are more populist and the local state is more permeated by groups with power. Comparatively few interest groups attain true national influence, whereas local politics caters to a mind-boggling array of organized interest and ephemeral "demand" groups. Announced policy change at the Centre may therefore translate

17. Poverty estimates in India—as elsewhere—are notoriously unreliable and politically sensitive. On the conceptual and technical problems, see Martin Ravallion, *Poverty Comparisons* (Chur, Switzerland: Harwood Academic Publishers, 1994). For a controversial comprehensive treatment of trends in India, see the World Bank, *India: Achievements and Challenges in Reducing Poverty* (Washington, D.C., 1997). Charles Lindblom, *Journal of Politics* 44, no. 2 (May 1982): 324–36.

into little in the periphery. Delhi has for decades been reluctant to come down too hard on State governments because of the fragile hold of regimes at the Centre and the propensity for desertion of politicians with secure local power bases. Thus there is no coherent state but a multiplicity of actors claiming state authority in a contested federalism.

There is some truth in all these perspectives on the Indian state; the difficulty in providing a summary categorization that permits comparison across states should give caution to generic state theorizing. Nevertheless, in explaining failures in growth, features of state structure highlighted by these perspectives are useful. Moreover, consistently lacking from dominant characterizations of the Indian literature is the "strong state" presumed to be crucial for successful developmental statism. More important that static categories is the process by which the state becomes differentially embedded in society and reconstituted by shifting political formations; contingency and process replace essential characteristics as explanation.

Developing the "License-Permit-Quota Raj": Logics of State Intervention

There are two logics of state interventionist developmentalism: one a rationalist planning mode, and the other a defensive reaction mode. Intervention in the defensive reaction mode follows Polanyi's historical observation that "market and regulation grew up together." In Polanyi's vision, societal vulnerability drives intervention to "reembed" markets in society. It is clear that a political economy of extensive intervention may be built on precisely this base, through the politics of protection from market dynamics and responses to "market failure."[18]

A positive state repertory of intervention, as opposed to Polanyi's defensive-reaction state, seemed historically appropriate to Indian elites. The attraction of the developmentalist argument for intervention—including central planning—seemed clear in the formative period of mobilization for independence. The success of the Soviet Union at a time when the capitalist world was sunk in depression, combined with the dominant theoretical literature, suggested that planning was the way to catch up.[19] The Keynesian revolution in theory and policy in the 1930s

18. Ronald J. Herring, "Explaining Sri Lanka's Exceptionalism: Popular Responses to Welfarism and the 'Open Economy,' " in John Walton and David Seddon, eds., *Free Markets and Food Riots: The Politics of Global Adjustment* (Oxford: Blackwell, 1994).

19. Polanyi, *Great Transformation*. On the evolution of congressional thinking about development, see Jawaharlal Nehru, *The Discovery of India* (New York: John Day, 1946); Daniel Thorner, *The Shaping of Modern India* (New Delhi: Allied Publishers, 1980; Francine Frankel,

further legitimated the notion of state responsibility for aggregate economic outcomes at the normative level, even in capitalist society, and bolstered the belief in the efficaciousness of the tools of the modern state.

Colonialism added two important elements to validate economic interventionism: a pervasive and strong state, and the legacy of cultural denigration and powerlessness—the acute awareness of national vulnerability in a hierarchical world system. Moreover, opposition to colonial rule had symbolically, politically, and economically centered the concept of *swadeshi* ("self-reliance"). It was understood that economic dependence on England was a linchpin of subordination. The cultural residue of international economic subordination has been so strong that the Congress finance minister of the liberalizing regime after 1991, Manmohan Singh, periodically derided in public speeches fears of economic openness as "the East-India-Company mentality" in his defenses of liberalization.[20]

Because the Congress Party led the struggle for independence, Congress economic philosophy was certain to drive India's development strategy. Economic philosophy was deeply split but consistent in several themes that placed development above growth. The Karachi platform of 1931 was clearly socialist: "land to the tiller and power to the people"; in the 1930s the socialist wing of the movement gained enormously. Despite their sometimes bitter disputes, both the Gandhi and Nehru wings of the party were convinced that at a normative level "profit" was wrong as first principle; both visions were more communitarian than individualist, despite deep differences on political economy.[21] The notion of what a developed society should be resonated with the otherwise conflicting main strands of political opposition to colonial rule: Gandhian "traditionalism" and Nehruvian socialism, both hostile to profit, both wary of the international system as a benign place for the poor and weak.

A National Planning Commission preceded independence; the Industrial Policy Resolution of 1948 called for a planning commission to be chaired by the prime minister. The Planning Commission of the independent state had been established by 1950, but under serious political opposition from the antisocialist section of the National Congress. Among the most important purposes of planning and extensive intervention were the goals of self-reliance, fairness, rooting out exploitation, balanced development across regions and sectors, and elimination of the worst forms of indignity and poverty. In a typical statement of its vision of

India's Political Economy, 1947–77: The Gradual Revolution (Princeton: Princeton University Press, 1978), chap. 3; and Myrdal, *Asian Drama.*

20. Ronald J. Herring, "Stealing Congress Thunder: The Rise to Power of a Communist Movement in South India," in Peter Merkl and Kay Lawson, eds., *When Parties Fail* (Princeton: Princeton University Press, 1988).

21. Frankel, *India's Political Economy*, p. 109.

postcolonial India, the All-India Congress Committee (AICC) stated in 1947: "Our aim should be to evolve a political system which will combine efficiency of administration with individual liberty and an economic structure which will yield maximum production without the concentration of private monopolies and the concentration of wealth and which will create the proper balance between urban and rural economies. Such a social structure can provide an alternative to the acquisitive economy of private capitalism and regimentation of a totalitarian state."[22]

Whether or not the state so conceived was at one with "socialist objectives,"[23] there is no question that policy was not single-mindedly accumulationist. Much of the effort was tragically ineffective (Sen), as resources were co-opted by local elites or simply wasted. Redistributive strategies that proved crucial in the East Asian cases were defeated by the federal structure of power or co-opted by gentry. Unlike East Asian states, India's "soft state" was not able to impose land reforms on recalcitrant State governments.[24] Nor despite its particular failings as a liberal democracy did the Indian state have the luxury of restricted franchise and authoritarian tools available to most of the current nations of the Organization for Economic Cooperation and Development (OECD) at comparable stages of development. Nation building and state building proceeded together in compressed time and with constitutionally limited powers.

Self-reliance was a crucial desideratum and in practice implied a closed economy. In contrast to Latin American states, India was notoriously tough on transnational corporations, leading to low rates of foreign direct investment, almost infinitesimally small until 1980. The strategy was import substitution. The virtually closed economy was legitimated not only by developmental logic but was as well a residue of state practice from the colonial period, especially the administrative dirigiste apparatus created during World War II. With low internal rates of savings, the relative absence of external investment was almost certain to depress growth rates in most models, whether Marxist or classical.[25] Likewise, the government's commitment to self-reliance resulted in very conservative international borrowing behavior until the 1980s, further restricting capital's cir-

22. From AICC, *Resolutions on Economic Policy and Programme, 1924–1954*, cited in Frankel, *India's Political Economy*, p. 18.

23. Swamy (*The Political Economy of Industrialization*, p. 16) argues that the Mahalanobis strategy *with land reforms* would not have failed so seriously. Datta-Chaudhuri ("Market Failure and Government Failure," p. 31) notes the "irony" of free-market dynamics in rural areas, where 80 percent of the population lived, in a "socialist" society in which socialism was reserved for the industrial sector. On the ambiguity of the commitment to land reform at the Centre, see Herring, *Land to the Tiller*, chap. 5, and, more generally, Frankel, *India's Political Economy*, chap. 4.

24. Herring, *Land to the Tiller*, chaps. 3, 5.

25. This argument obviously ignores the very early dependency arguments, most clearly associated with Andre Gunder Frank, that saw foreign investment as depressing growth.

cuit. Protection allowed infant industries the luxury of never growing up and soaked consumers with monopolistic high prices for inferior products.

Export pessimism dominated development planning in India, resonating with the theories and experiences of Latin America as filtered through Economic Commission for Latin America (ECLA), Prebisch et al. This outcome on the periphery is not surprising for the historical period. The greater puzzle may be why East Asian nations were less pessimistic; certainly similar signals of peripheral inferiority were received. The impossibility of autarky must be a conditioning factor; India was, in a sense, cursed for being a continental nation-in-making. The potential was simply so vast that it seemed possible to bypass external trade; self-reliance was thinkable in India, not in Japan or Korea.

Though self-portraits of regimes are inevitably self-serving, India's comparatively strenuous efforts in pursuit of both self-reliance and equity must have had costs. State energies have opportunity costs, as do state personnel and limited investment funds. That these efforts bore little fruit is a well-known but complicated story. What is usually characterized as a monolithic commitment to statist intervention obscures the historically actual lack of unity and will within an increasingly unstable political formation. Even in the heyday of Congress Party hegemony, Nehru's vision was contradicted by the powerful faction associated with Sardar Patel and then with the Swatantra (Freedom) Party, and later by Kamraj and regional bosses in the States.[26] There were always dissonant chords that undermined the purposive commitment to state control of economic growth that characterized the East Asian nations.

When Nehru died in 1964, these contradictions again asserted themselves; Congress electoral success declined, first in the States in 1967 and finally at the Centre. As modest growth failed to deliver on the noble promises of founders, much of the "developmental" activity of the state became politically necessary public consumption—in effect a political consequence of the failure of the growth state. Prospects for growth dimmed as populism consumed resources earmarked for investment.[27]

The closed and statist economic system was only in part an unfolding of the visions of Nehru and Mahalanobis. The politics of Polanyi's "defensive reactions" worked in a system in which economic policy was highly politicized—politicized in large measure because of the persistent ideological practice of the Congress political elite, which located historic failure in the central authority of colonial rulers and just as squarely located economic salvation in the political center of independent India. Over

26. Frankel, *India's Political Economy*, pp. 201–45.
27. Bardhan, *Political Economy of Development in India*.

time, the "license-permit-quota raj" graduated from an ideological caricature of conservative domestic capital to reality.

In the public sector, for example, state-owned enterprises (SOEs) were planned to control the commanding heights of the economy and to provide entrepreneurial energy where the private sector would or could not. Capital objected to the reservation of the core sector of the economy as state terrain but lacked the political power to reverse it. As the public sector evolved, however, it became as much hospital as commanding height, accumulating "sick" and failing enterprises (a process often called "lemon socialism"), *not* in Chalmers Johnson's "plan-rational" mode but as employer of last resort. It was hard for a firm of any importance to fail. Takeovers of "sick units" accounted for almost one-third of the financial losses of central public sector enterprises by 1991.[28] It was impossible to let capital fail; on closer inspection, India's "socialism" was a welfarist capitalism, for both workers and capitalists, though with sharply class-differentiated consequences. The Darwinian weeding of losers was truncated from the top.

Part of the argument for state-induced stagnation is that as SOEs increased their share of total investment and corporate assets (reaching a highpoint of about one-third), their operation constituted a special drain on economic surplus and the efficiency of its deployment; both Paul Baran and his bourgeois antagonists agreed that the result would be lower growth rates. In his enthusiasm for liberalization, Prime Minister Rajiv Gandhi figured that the public sector, including oil, brought a rate of return between 2 and 2.5 percent on invested capital, and without oil, a loss of 1 to 1.5 percent.[29]

Opportunity costs of public sector investments became more expensive as democracy spread down the social hierarchy and constituent States became more active developmental agents; patronage became a pervasive dynamic. However much the iron-frame state might be insulated from society, the SOEs clearly were not insulated, nor with the soft-budget constraint did the enterprises have much motivation to pursue either cost or allocative efficiency. As SOEs multiplied in the States, these dynamics were magnified.

Public investment thus encountered obstacles to efficiency: agents faced multiple principals with conflicting objectives. Domestic private investment was subject to extensive steering, monitoring, and regulation. The system was mind-numbingly complex. Before the advent of "broad banding," a separate license was required for altering a firm's product mix, even within licensed capacity. Administrative limits on investment, as

28. Shastri, "Political Economy of Policy Formation in India," p. 90.
29. Ibid., p. 170.

well as the firm-size level at which clearance had to be obtained, differentiated between "backward and nonbackward areas." In 1980, 87 districts were identified as "no-industry districts." Businesses willing to set up industry in those districts were given preferences in obtaining infrastructural development and licenses in addition to a relaxed limit on size of firm.[30]

Diversion from the path of single-willed growth commitment from the state almost certainly had consequences, difficult though these are to parse from overdetermined development patterns. First, the normatively appealing notion that affirmative action for depressed areas might mitigate historic disadvantages and reduce pockets of poverty must certainly have some growth consequences: all resources have opportunity costs. Second, regional-allocative and similar incentives deflect investment logic from that of the market to that of the administrative apparatus, as filtered through political processes. Third, nodes of discretionary authority created thereby breed corruption, or at a minimum invite political allocation.

Slowing of industrial growth in the mid-1960s could not be attributed, except ideologically, entirely to controls.[31] Certain crucial arenas of public investment declined; there were also two terrible droughts in the mid-1960s, which economic structure magnified into constraints on industrial growth. Foreign aid declined significantly in part because of two wars, themselves consumptive of resources. Whatever the real causes of the slowdown, Vanita Shastri has argued that the decline of industrial growth rates after 1995 facilitated stronger controls, not liberalization.[32] The full-blown license raj was then in part the consequence of the dialectics of politics and markets, not simply the plan-rational beginning point. The very embeddedness of the planning state in messy democratic politics—with regional pluralism and a contested federalism—renders a judgment on the merits of the planning model itself empirically problematic. What is of more importance is the operation of the regulatory regime in practice as an instance of embedded particularism.

EMBEDDED PARTICULARISM

In a speech on January 28, 1995, Congress finance minister Manmohan Singh said in explaining the risks and benefits of liberalization, "We should be careful not to replace an inefficient public sector by a regime

30. Ibid., p. 325.
31. For a review of the positions, see Varshney, "Political Economy of Slow Industrial Growth."
32. Shastri, "Political Economy of Policy Formation in India."

of crony capitalism."[33] What prompted this public expression of concern is presumably Singh's exquisite ethnographic sensibility of the way Indian state-society relations work in the field of economics; there was a real danger of the ancien régime spoiling the liberalization project on which so much was staked.

"Embedded particularism" implies persistence of state-society relations inimical to application of universalistic rules across cases—the effective homogenization of the subject and the case. India's state in the sense of bureaucracy was not set up for particularism but does suffer structurally from vertical and horizontal incoherence, much introduced by constitutional federalism, much by inadequate self-awareness in an extraordinarily complex organism operating over a continental political economy. These characteristics invite particularism.

The bureaucracy per se at independence certainly approached Ben Ross Schneider's "polar" case of bureaucratic autonomy on the "insulated, statist path."[34] Officials of the central administrative services have shared elite social origins and elite educational experiences. Recruited through highly competitive and meritocratic, though "generalist," exams, they circulated widely across agencies and could expect superior performance at each level to result in promotions until retirement from the civil service. By Schneider's criteria, the bureaucracy—and certainly the Indian Administrative Service—should be classified as corporate and autonomous. The iron frame was free from the appointive partisan instability of the civil service common in the Americas historically, increasing the potential autonomy of the state.

Corporate autonomy of the central bureaucracy in specifically economic affairs was reinforced by the very early emergence of a planning commission, chaired by the prime minister, with extraordinary powers. Nevertheless, India's constitution matters. Over time, autonomy and corporate cohesion were undermined by the federal structure of governance and the emergence of ever more bureaucracies at the State and local level. To take but one example, agriculture is designated a principal responsibility of the States (Article 246). Thus the property structure of the most important sector in terms of employment and low productivity was outside the scope of Delhi's effective control. The linkage and spread effects of planning are limited by structural disarticulation of the state. Even economic and social planning are on the "Concurrent" list, shared between States and Delhi. The powers reserved to the Union government alone touch only a fraction of the issues relevant to economic development.

33. Speech reported in *Business Standard* (New Delhi), February 6, 1995.
34. Ben Ross Schneider, "The Career Connection: A Comparative Analysis of Bureaucratic Preferences and Insulation," *Comparative Politics* 25, no. 3 (April 1993): 332.

Structurally, vertical and horizontal incoherence are built into the system through federalism, size, and scope: size because of the continental nation that the bureaucracy tries to rule; scope because of the extraordinary range and complexity of mandates in the Indian constitution and Five-Year Plans. The arrogance and distance of the iron frame produced popular political protest—inevitably so in a vigorous democracy—resulting in popular institutions demanding a share of control, embedding the bureaucracy more in society over time.[35]

A fragmented state produces one set of complications for developmental pacts that are common in East Asia; fragmented labor and capital exacerbate the problem. If the developmental state is to act in the interests of capital as a whole, there must be someone with whom to bargain and an agent to enforce bargains. Class formation among capitalists was hindered for various reasons. At the center, the bureaucracy was autonomous of capital as a class (though decidedly permeable to individual capitalists). This autonomy was reinforced by the disunity of capital, which grew in part from different strategies of how to cope with a state overtly hostile to private enterprise and yet staffed by individuals not at all hostile to individual capitalists or their fortunes and a hegemonic political party, the Congress, that needed their contributions to maintain an increasingly tenuous hold on hegemony. Fragmentation of Indian capital began with the continental scope of the political economy and the family/community-based development of business houses; it was reinforced by the zero-sum game of courting particular favors from the regulatory bureaucracy, a dynamic inherent in the license raj.

Emergence of class cohesion among capitalists was also hindered by divergent tactical vision among the major players in response to perceived state hostility and control. The groups formed around the family business empires of the Tatas and the Birlases took different stances, based on different visions of how to get along with the new state. The Tatas initiated the Forum for Free Enterprise (the "Bombay group"), which eventually formed the nucleus of the oppositional political party Swatantra to contest the premises of socialist development.[36] The Birlas backed the accommodationist policies of the rival national business organization (Federation of Indian Chambers of Commerce and Industry, or, FICCI). The

35. Again the Gandhian legacy, with a time delay, proved an important legitimation for bringing government closer to the grass roots. *Panchayati raj* institutions (elected local councils at various levels) have been uneven in development but have now virtually everywhere become a check on centralized district administration. For their developmental role in one state, see Ronald J. Herring and Rex M. Edwards, "Guaranteeing Employment to the Rural Poor: Social Functions and Class Interests in the Employment Guarantee Scheme in Western India," *World Development* 11, no. 7 (1983).

36. Howard L. Erdman, *The Swatantra Party and Indian Conservatism* (London: Cambridge University Press, 1967).

accommodationist strategy for capital was to work the system as individuals, not taking the rhetoric from Delhi too seriously; working the system entailed cultivating contacts in high places, maintaining "industrial embassies" in Delhi, and finding means of establishing exchange relations with individuals in the state.[37] The frequent movement of officials across departments contributed not only to absence of identification with the success of any particular agency or function but also to susceptibility to particularistic connections with private capital.

Embeddedness thus has to be disaggregated: the relations of the state-qua-officialdom to the capitalist class were not supportive, as the developmentalist-state literature suggests they must be. Bureaucrats looked down on capitalists—a view legitimated by both wings of the independence movement and culturally sanctioned as well. As an elite corps of self-confident generalists, however, the bureaucracy had no expertise to substitute for capitalists and little understanding of the enterprises (qua enterprises) they regulated. Yet individual capitalists were very much welcome on a selective basis; all the ties that make up particularism came into play: family connections, native place, school ties, marriage alliances, side-payments, and the like. Embeddedness thus worked against the sort of capital-state relationship that empowers the state to act against some in the interests of all. *Particularistic* embeddedness created in practice a porous state; regulations deterred some, delayed everyone, but in the final analysis only intermittently approached stated goals.

Liberalization

India's regulatory regime has long been the object of severe criticism in international development circles. Presumably the holders of state power within India had an interest in making the system work better: le-

---

37. On Swatantra, see ibid. Stanley Kochanek's classic work *Business and Politics in India* (Berkeley: University of California Press, 1974), p. 232 and passim, demonstrates that business as a class has not had collective influence but rather has sought and attained influence on individual matters of specific concern. Thus the "industrial embassies" have been more particularistic than class-solidaristic, more solicitous and accommodationist than confrontational. See also Shastri, "Political Economy of Policy Formation in India," pp. 285–87. The Confederation of Indian Industries (CII) may be changing that traditional pattern. The CII is more "modern" and internationalist than is traditional business; in Delhi its members are called the "tie-wallas" (because they wear suits) as opposed to the *dhoti-wallas* who wear traditional wraps. Shastri argues that the sort of business-state relation conducive to growth in the development state literature is emerging with the increasing prominence of the CII. My work on the role of CII in the Montreal Protocol supports this view; see Ronald J. Herring, "Market-Structuring Regulation and the Ozone Regime: Politics of the Montreal Protocol," in Mohammed H. I. Dore and Timothy D. Mount, eds., *Global Environmental Economics* (Oxford: Blackwell, 1999).

gitimation within an intensely competitive democracy. What was wrong with the feedback loops that should have given the system self-knowledge? Here the absence of validated growth theory stressed earlier restricts the strategic capacity of major actors.

Cybernetic loops were certainly operating; few nations spend more effort in self-evaluation. Various commissions were duly appointed over the years and identified reasons for state-induced failures in industrial policy—from delays to corruption.[38] Recognizing failures, one could logically conclude that the answer was better administration, more and tighter regulation, or retreat from intervention: laissez-faire or a stronger state.

The operative answer to this question came through the political process. The open split in the Congress Party in 1969 engineered by Indira Gandhi was the culmination of the drawn-out succession crisis after Nehru's death. After electoral defeats in 1967 for the Congress Party, Mrs. Gandhi could have moved in either direction: toward a stronger state or toward laissez-faire. She chose intervention, presented politically as "left," symbolized by nationalization of banks, an attack on feudal remnants (abolition of "privy purses"), and a policy to "abolish poverty" (*garibi hatao*).[39] Indira Gandhi's engineered split of the Congress marked the real beginning of praetorian populism, the decline of party organization, and the growth of symbolic appeals around control of the economy to appease the electorate. Nationalization of the banks was done not from a position of strength or economic strategy but from a position of desperation after a major electoral reversal for the Congress Party.

Indira Gandhi's new populism and statism were both supported by the work of cybernetic committees. It was becoming clear that the actual operation of licensing policy and lending policies of financial institutions in the public sector were contrary to planned goals; both functioned to strengthen the large business houses they were meant to control. Licensing policy had been one mechanism to balance the economic growth pattern and to keep the wolf of the market from the door of the weak by preventing the entry of powerful actors into spheres "reserved" for the small-scale sector. The Monopoly and Restrictive Practice Act was intended to prevent the big from growing too much or at the expense of

38. For an early academic treatment, see Michael Lipton and Paul Streeten, "Two Types of Planning," in Lipton and Streeten, eds., *The Crisis of Indian Planning* (London: Oxford University Press, 1968); for an overview, see I. J. Ahluwalia, *Industrial Growth in India: Stagnation since the Mid-Sixties* (Delhi: Oxford University Press, 1989); Frankel, *India's Political Economy*, chap. 7, passim; Shastri, "Political Economy of Policy Formation in India," pp. 106–9; Sukhamoy Chakravarty, *Development Planning: The Indian Experience* (New Delhi: Oxford University Press, 1987), pp. 40–42 and passim.

39. On politics of the period, see Frankel, *India's Political Economy*, p. 338 ff; Herring, *Land to the Tiller*, chap 5.

normatively valued sections of the economy (small-scale, traditional, and so on).[40] But big firms found ways to work the system to their advantage; their "industrial embassies" were successful in getting permission to move into new areas at the expense of protected sectors. The energy of big investors was thus directed toward circumventing the rules, and their planning efforts were diverted to circumventing the planners; capital was slowed in its investment efforts without being prevented from following its interest.

Pluralism—or horizontal disarticulation—of the Indian state was crucial in this successful strategy; the MRP act was to slow the conglomerate Birlas, but their contacts in the Directorate General of Technical Development were able to exempt and thus clear their projects anyway, though with delay.[41] Thus the creation of "closed industries" was only partially effective in equity terms but did deflect the planning and entrepreneurial energies of the largest capitalists: embedded particularism at work. The contrast with the developmental state is not that capital did not get what it wanted but that to get what it wanted it had to be inefficient.

Unintended outcomes were evident in other regulatory regimes as well. The Foreign Exchange and Regulation Act of 1973, meant to protect foreign reserves—essentially a defensive reaction vis-à-vis the international financial system and foreign capital—resulted in a net outflow of direct foreign investment as it forced investors to reduce the level of investment to 40 percent or less.[42] Controls on foreign capital and those who deal with it made political sense in Indira Gandhi's populist period precisely because of the structural context of foreign exchange crises that were chronic if not critical. Whatever the truth of commissions of inquiry into regulation, deregulation in a time of populist symbolism and widespread economic misery would not have been politically rational.

Weakening of the electoral hegemony of the Congress Party thus did not translate automatically into political support for dismantling the "Nehruvian consensus." The victory of the Janata coalition in 1977 and the growing strength of the traditionalist Hindu right—*Bharat* politics in opposition to India—reinvigorated the notion of propping up village industries, handicrafts, and any traditional, small-scale sector activity. Resistance to reforming industrial controls was not all irrationality, inertia, and statism but was rooted as well in contestatory democratic politics. Liberal-

40. Ahluwalia stresses the gaps between goals and effects, particularly in the case of the Industries Development and Regulation Act (1951); see *Industrial Growth in India*, pp. 147–65. See also Shastri's conclusion ("Political Economy of Policy Formation in India," p. 112). Datta-Chaudhuri counts the program to provide externalities for the small-scale sector a great success in India, comparing it to a similar role for trading associations in South Korea ("Market Failure and Government Failure," p. 32).

41. Shastri, "Political Economy of Policy Formation in India," p. 114.

42. Ibid., p. 119.

izing ideas were predicated on the failure of the agenda for *India*—slow industrialization, inferior consumer durables, outdated technology, and lack of international competitiveness. Failures in trickle-down results from this modernizing project in turn added weight to the culturally attractive movement to protect Bharat—culturally an attack on Michael Lipton's "urban bias" in development policy. The Janata government's Industrial Policy of 1977, for example, tried to decentralize industrial development, arguing that existing policy had concentrated industry in the metropoles.[43]

After Indira Gandhi returned from electoral exile in 1980, she evinced concern for growing evidence of India's failures in international and comparative perspective. She also recognized that entrepreneurs were trading licenses rather than producing anything. The large and affluent expatriate community was critical to the feedback loop as well. Their perspective was comparative, finding India a bad place in which to do business in comparison with the rest of the world. Mrs. Gandhi showed clear inclinations to reform in the composition of committees she set up but was assassinated before these could bear fruit. Serious consideration of liberalization began with her son, Rajiv Gandhi. His attacks on the Congress Party and on the Indian state were scathing. In his famous "Bombay Speech" to the Congress Party he said: "And what of the iron frame of the system . . . the myriad functionaries of the state? They have done so much and can do so much more, but as the proverb says there can be no protection if the fence starts eating the crop. This is what has happened. The fence has started eating the crop . . . We have government servants who do not serve but oppress . . . [T]hey have no work ethic, . . . no comprehension of the values of modern India. They have only a grasping, mercenary outlook, devoid of competence, integrity and commitment."[44]

Like his mother, Rajiv Gandhi was assassinated before his liberalization initiatives bore fruit, but retreat was forced in any event by the vigorous reaction of popular political forces, particularly labor.[45] In the debates around liberalization, the widespread ideology of preventing accumulation was pervasive: reforms would strengthen the rich and hurt the poor.

43. On Janata's policy, see ibid., p. 146. The distinction pits a Westernized "India" (the word itself seen as alien import) against an indigenous Bharat. India makes cricket bats for export to England, wears blue jeans, and watches Sky Network on cable; Bharat symbolically lives in villages and small towns, observes religious practice, wears non-Western dress. This profound divide has increasingly found political expression in the wavering support for a nationalist response to liberalization by the Bharatiya Janata Party, which formed a government in March 1998.

44. Inaugural Speech at Congress Centenary Session, Indian National Congress, Bombay, December 28, 1985, p. 13. See also the discussion in Shastri, "Political Economy of Policy Formation in India," pp. 168 ff.

45. Atul Kohli, "Politics of Economic Liberalization in India," *World Development* 17, no. 3 (1989): 305–28.

The rich had, of course, done well under a regulatory regime, and the absolute numbers of poor continued to increase, but discourse nevertheless focused on social justice as though the ideological praxis of the developmental state presaged its future.

Much as the reformist regime of Narasimha Rao (1991–95) desired to project continuity with the legacy of Nehru and the Congress founders for reasons of partisan identification, the period after 1991 witnessed fundamental shifts at the cognitive-normative level and to a lesser extent in policy. Rather than seeing the government as the solution to problems, the government has come to be seen as the source of problems, even some it did not cause. The finance minister of a Congress government took to calling the Nehru edifice "functionless capitalism" rather than a "socialistic pattern of society." The "Washington consensus" was presented as "adjustment with a human face" in Delhi, and there are indeed remnants of the political forces that impinged on the license raj.[46] A unitary state commitment to accumulation as the objective of state policy continues to meet resistance from potential losers. Thus privatization of public sector enterprises has largely remained only a promise, budget deficits are high, and there is still no "exit policy" (that is, firing workers is virtually impossible). The discipline of the market is resisted even as its superiority is celebrated.

Liberalization is supposed to be a cure for embedded particularism; markets work by universalistic criteria. To the extent that particularism resulted in decisions other than those the perfectly informed entrepreneur of theory would have made, India's developmentalism incurred an embeddedness penalty, which is in principle separable from the democracy penalty. The constraining effect of democracy is put into sharp relief when Atul Kohli writes of the Rajiv Gandhi initiatives as moments when "the state suddenly stood quite autonomous, seemingly free of societal constraints, ready to be used as a tool for imposing economic rationality on society."[47] In a classic case of Polanyi's "defensive reaction" against the market, society reared its ugly head and Kohli's sudden autonomy disappeared with Rajiv Gandhi's modernization mandate. But the opposition between state autonomy and democracy and liberalization is well taken given the long operations of the developmental state at the normative

46. John Williamson, "What Washington Means by Policy Reform," in Williamson, ed., *Latin American Adjustment* (Washington, D.C.: Institute for International Economics, 1990); Thomas Biersteker, "The 'Triumph' of Liberal Economic Ideas in the Developing World," in Barbara Stallings, ed., *Global Change, Regional Response: The New International Context of Development* (Cambridge: Cambridge University Press, 1995). On the neoliberal orthodoxy more generally, see Walton and Seddon, eds., *Free Markets and Food Riots*, chap. 1, 2.

47. Kohli, "Politics of Economic Liberalization in India," p. 312.

and political levels in Indian society; regulatory structures breed clienteles with interests.

The momentary autonomy that really enabled liberalization came later, provided by the external payments crisis of 1991, not electoral redistributions of power. The financial crisis reflected the conjunctural effects of the Gulf War, its $3.3 billion shock, increased debt servicing from the expansionary 1980, and erosion of confidence of international bankers—which together left India with enough hard currency for thirteen days of imports officially (compared with 5.2 months a decade earlier, in 1980–81)—and less unofficially. The balance of payments deficit as a percentage of Gross Domestic Product increased from 1.7 in 1980–81 to 3.5 percent in 1990–91 and in dollar amount from $2.1 billion to an official $8 billion (the reality being closer to $10 billion). Perceptually, there were no options beyond the controversial sale of gold and meeting the conditions of the IMF. What else could a developmental state—a state self-legitimated for control of economic processes, responsible for progress—do?

The external nature of the payments crisis that brought India to structural adjustment and the external source of the model both served to give international ideas, actors, and forces primacy in explaining reform in a failed developmental state. To both politicians and bureaucrats, international comparisons, particularly to South Korea, provided legitimation for reform. India had once exported machine tools and steel to South Korea but by the 1980s found itself importing the same items from South Korea. South Korea had become a major force in markets in the United States, whereas India remained marginal.[18] Simultaneously, the rise of perestroika in the Soviet Union removed one of the early models of forced-pace industrialization, autarky and planning. Probably as important, the decline, desertion, and eventual demise of the Soviet Union removed an external market and a source of imports that were sustained not by competitiveness but by geopolitical alliance.[19] The global shift in world view was supported by structural logic in the periphery.

48. More generally in comparative terms, India's share of world trade declined from around 2 percent in 1950 to 0.52 percent in 1989; Korea's share of world trade rose to 2.1 percent; China likewise surpassed India in terms of share of world trade. Expensive items in India are advertised as "export quality," implying that the rest of the world would not buy what Indian citizens are expected to buy. That only extraordinary products from India meet standards of global trade is the clear implication. On the Korean comparisons, see Datta-Chaudhuri, "Market Failure and Government Failure."

49. The trilateral conference on trade and development held in Delhi in 1989 was confirmation of this point for me personally, as well as for the Indian delegation. Abid Hussein and Manmohan Singh were both present. The German delegation described a future in which there would be two important blocs: "Japan-China, Inc." and "Fortress Europe." The German ambassador headed a faction in their delegation that openly called an Asian strat-

India's failed developmental state—like many in the poor world—was driven and sustained by a powerful understanding of history: planning for development seemed natural. Critiques of the interventionist state assumed a similar hegemonic position in the 1980s. But as Mrinal Datta-Chaudhuri reminds us, the origins of public economic policy are rooted in the failure of markets to solve all problems, including growth, even in theory: "The analytical results on 'market failure' do not disappear in the face of the evidence that most governments (or for that matter most economies of less developed countries with or without state intervention)have performed rather badly."[50]

State failure in particular instances cannot then serve as a real legitimation of laissez-faire policy. That states fail does not remove the historic understanding that market failure requires state solutions. We have come full circle; politicians seeking to maximize growth really do not know where to turn. Having tried a developmental state that failed, elites in the Indian political system turned to the magic of the market. At a bare minimum, this turn buys some legitimacy and time until the next economic crisis. It is important for states to reassure mass publics that they know what to do and are doing it.

STATES AND GROWTH: MARX AND LINDBLOM WERE PROBABLY RIGHT

India's attempts to create and operate a developmental state were not entirely counterproductive but miss Charles Lindblom's point that states have strong thumbs but clumsy fingers.[51] The implication is a staging theory of the developmental state across historical time: strong thumbs mobilize capital and effect structural transformations, but once these historic tasks are completed, interventionist states slow economic growth by trying to fine-tune that which is too complicated to micromanage. The successful developmental state is then one that knows when to quit. India's developmental state for the first fifteen years or so used strong thumbs effectively; major growth-generating advances, both in industry

egy centered on India as an "export platform" to counterbalance Japanese influence in the region. The other faction in the German delegation favored a pullback from Asia to Eastern Europe, where there were advantages of "geography and history." In neither scenario did India figure as anything but a location for strategic moves of others' capital. The Indian delegation made the now familiar pitch that India's middle class is in marketing terms the size of several large European nations and deserves to be taken seriously by international capital. On the Soviet connection, see Shastri, "Political Economy of Policy Formation in India," p. 247.

50. Datta-Chaudhuri, "Market Failure and Government Failure," p. 25.

51. Charles Lindblom, *Politics and Markets* (New York: Basic Books, 1978).

and agriculture, were the result of high levels of state investment, involvement, and planning.

For Lindblom to be right, we must assume that the sheer size and complexity of interventionist tasks inevitably become overwhelming at some point; in cognitive terms, the developmental state is one that recognizes limits of developmental statism. Sufficient political autonomy to act on that knowledge is the second necessary condition. Because all states meddle but some do well, it is difficult to know exactly how much meddling, of what kind, is necessary or sufficient for anomalously high or low growth. Not only the developmental state literature but also the European experience historically and the contemporary crisis among the Asian "tigers" suggest caution about the currently hegemonic neoliberal dispensation.[52]

It often seems to outsiders that the genius of the Japanese developmental state was that it let business tell it what to do and then did it fairly efficiently. The state in India, at least in its "iron-frame" incarnation, was unable to play the kind of facilitative embedded role that Peter Evans believes is crucial for developmental statism to succeed;[53] embeddedness came through processes that sapped authority and wasted resources.

For Marx, autonomy from the industrial class was neither necessary nor possible for the state. The capitalist state is by necessity developmental; it must simultaneously understand the needs of capital—not fractions of capital, but capital as a whole—and be able to act against particular capitals in the interest of capital as a whole. The successful developmental state, with historical irony, is one able to function as if it were the executive committee of the bourgeoisie. The question then may be more under what conditions we get a developmental *business class* than why we get a developmental state that will give capital its head—the original Marxist formula for success.

For the Japanese model to have worked in India, then, one unmet condition was a business class for itself. That historically there has not been such a class is a function of the socially differentiated and embedded character of the big business "houses," the diversity and size of the continental-scope economy, and the reservation of the "commanding heights" of the economy for the state. In contrast, the South Korean state as drawn by Jung-en Woo (Meredith Woo-Cumings) was effective in using its strategic position astride international capital flows to create a strong capitalist class.[54] The Indian state in its preliberalization incarnation was involved over the same period in an antagonistic relation to a fragmented capital-

52. Senghaas, *European Experience.*
53. Evans, *Embedded Autonomy.*
54. Jung-en Woo [Meredith Woo-Cumings], *Race to the Swift: State and Finance in Korean Industrialization* (New York: Columbia University Press, 1991).

ist class. It created a regulatory regime that divided capital by its discretionary authority (which, incidentally, generated bureaucratic rents), thus fostering embedded particularism rather than class power and cohesion.

The contrast with the archetypal developmental state is not that Indian capital did not get what it wanted but that to get what it wanted it had to be inefficient. Particular capitalists got what they wanted, certainly in contrast to peasants and workers. But money lying idle is the bane of capitalist development; India's failed developmental state slowed capital and restricted its circuit—radically, in the case of external capital—but the social purposes that legitimated this cost were largely unrealized. Inequalities persisted, and poverty deepened in terms of absolute numbers. Leviathan looked strong in its regulatory and commanding guise, but the astute knew how to make the membranes permeable—to take advantage of the selectively "soft state." The state's permeability engendered particularistic relations of capitalists to the state and to rent seeking just as the hard-looking regulatory/redistributive face led money to the black market and evasions. Labor aggravated this inefficiency; fragmented and dominated by adversarial political parties, labor has had the power to bend and block policy—and to thwart capital selectively—but not the cohesion or independence to pursue corporatist strategies or enforce social compacts.[55]

At a more macrolevel, overdeveloped democracy is always a prime suspect in the mystery of what causes states to fail economically.[56] The very partial nature of India's democracy reinforced the demand group formation process of the Rudolphs as well as the spoils-and-patronage nature of the political process.[57] Bardhan's view is that the state was not so much democratic as captured by the three elite propertied groups who contested among themselves for the spoils of governing; as a consequence, regimes necessarily tried to buy off discontent with bread, circuses, and subsidies.[58] What becomes important, then, is not the state's share of social surplus but whether it is consumed or invested.

If land reforms were crucial components of the East Asian success stories, the implication is that the Indian state intervened in property relations not too much but too little.[59] If India's decline from respectable growth in industry was caused by the decline in public investment, as

55. Vibha Pingle, "State-Labor Relations in India: Implications for Economic Liberalization and Comparative Institutional Arguments," paper for Association for Asian Studies, Annual Meeting, Washington, D.C., April 1995.

56. Mancur Olson, *The Rise and Decline of Nations: Economic Growth, Stagflation, and Social Rigidities* (New Haven: Yale University Press, 1982).

57. Rudolph and Rudolph, *In Pursuit of Laksmi.*

58. Bardhan, *Political Economy of Development in India.*

59. Herring, *Land to the Tiller*, chap. 8.

Bardhan persuasively argues, the problem is not too much developmental state but too little. Nevertheless, both outcomes were products of political process, not development logic. Failures in land reform reflected not just the social power of propertied classes but also the structural disarticulation of the Indian state that permitted the particular interests of landlords to overcome a developmental objective planned in Delhi. The decline in public investment was a political product of a failed developmental state seeking legitimation. Regimes at the Centre clung to threads of centrism and party hegemony in a system in which democracy was taking roots too deeply, in too many places, for a highly centralized Congress Party to respond in any way other than populism. Whatever autonomy the developmental state had at independence dissipated as political populism spread with democratization. Democracy creates embedded particularism on a larger scale but with the same idiosyncratic principles; if the local state is trying to enforce regulations local politicians dislike, local power will have the official in charge transferred somewhere else.

Good bureaucracy, if that is not a contradiction in terms, is necessary to exercise state power. Bureaucratic pathologies are a favorite target of journalists and neoclassical economists; India has its share. But it is unclear that India suffers comparatively more from bureaucratic pathologies; the methodological problems in making this common claim seriously are insuperable. To take one commonly used example, some level of corruption must be compatible with developmental statehood; spectacular corruption scandals in Japan are astonishing to the student of India more used to petty crimes. Probably more serious than corruption is rigidity, conservatism, and lack of accountability—the power and inclination to slow and block. The incentives and capacities engendered by the pretense of developmental statism render these pathologies more serious.

Finally, the structure of the developmental state makes a difference. In a federal system, the disarticulation of the state is matched by the incoherence of capital and labor. Even if there had been an effective developmental state in Delhi, it would have been in contest with State governments that did not share its very Western rationalist/socialist planning model. The autonomy of the States vis-à-vis the state increased over time through a political dynamic: the decline of Congress hegemony and spreading mass consciousness of democracy. In the States, populist, confessional, and primordial-loyalty parties eroded Congress's power, leaving Delhi's hold on the States even more tenuous. A tenuous hold from the Centre meant more perversion of central policy in the periphery—dragging capital accumulation, financial laxity, opportunistic start-ups of new public enterprises for patronage, and unproductive bribes from the Centre to hold the polity together and regimes in power.

The rigidities in Indian developmentalism were then not entirely cognitive—an irrational commitment to planning—but were rooted in practice, in routines; people adapt to policy regimes and develop interests in the interstices. In India, state routines of legitimation and discretionary regulation coincided with the needs of politicians: poverty abolition as slogan kept the poor at bay for a time, capital funded the Congress Party, and the big business houses got rich in protected markets collecting rents on subcompetitive quality at supracompetitive prices. The developmental state was politically rational but became economically dubious overtime.

Despite the inherent difficulty of parsing causality in economic performance, it seems that India's developmental state was hamstrung as a narrowly constituted *growth* state for a number of reasons. It viewed development as being more than mere growth and in this had no choice given the character of its highly mobilized democracy and constitutional commitments. It restricted external capital—and thus accumulation processes—for reasonable fear of neocolonial reabsorption in an unfriendly world system, absent the sweet deals more pliable clients of richer global powers obtained. Internally, the state's relations to capital were hostile yet incapable of discipline—in part because of embedded particularism, in part because of the fragmented state of capital, in part because of the structural power of capital in a poor society. More important, India's state took on a more difficult task than had other developmental states:organizing a continental political economy, more empire than nation. And it did this with one arm tied behind its back by commitment to liberal democracy.

A developmental state is clearly not a necessary condition for growth; it may however be a sufficient condition. A failed developmental state is likewise not a necessary condition for slow growth, but the Indian case suggests the ways in which it may contribute. Because we are on shaky epistemological grounds in determining the effects of developmental states on growth, perhaps the most sound conclusion is political. In the instrumental uses of developmental models for pursuing interests, developmental statism and its neoliberal antagonist serve as modern instruments in a very old struggle—the making and remaking of market society.

Index

Abe Shintaro, 45
Abramovitz, Moses, 193
Adas, Michael, 67n22
Africa: agricultural revolution in, 114–15; bureaucracy in, 220; colonialism's legacy in, 136; industrialization in, 164; predatory states in, 201, 220, 234, 303; state instability in, 146n27; U.S. aid for, 154n49. *See also specific countries*
agrarian sector: bureaucracy and, 97–100; colonialism and, 108, 111–15, 124–25; development and, 114–17, 248; emphasis on, 322; land reforms and, 162, 164, 180, 318, 332–33; as natural resource base, 308n4. *See also* propertied groups
Ahluwalia, I. J., 326n40
aircraft industry, 30, 260, 271n58, 272
Alder, Ken, 257n39
Alemán, Miguel, 286
Allinson, Gary, 43
Amsden, Alice: on bureaucracy, 219; on South Korean state, 26–27, 35, 94n2, 163, 225–26; on state planning, 222; on Taiwanese exports, 164n78; on Taiwanese industrialization, 226; on world system, 142
Anderson, Benedict, 168
Anderson, Perry, 5
Aoki, Masahiko, 16
Aoki Shūzō, 87–88n76
Applebaum, Richard P., 141
Arellano, David, 297n78
Argentina: economy of, 148, 305; political system in, 289, 302; social relations in, 155

Asia. *See* East Asia; Northeast Asia; Southeast Asia; *specific countries*
Aubry, Martine, 240
Austria: bureaucracy of, 220, 232–33; characteristics of, 218–19; comparative perspective on, 23; economy of, 203, 231–33; external challenge to, 223, 231; industrialization in, 230, 231; nationalization in, 223, 232; political system in, 222; trade relations of, 178n116
authoritarianism: under colonialism, 105–7, 108; development and, 19–20, 51–52, 68–70; industrialization and, 298–99; liberalization and, 191; maintenance of, 53; political exclusion in, 288–89
automobile industry, 243, 245, 249
autonomy: of bureaucracy, 322–23; embedded, 132, 133n115, 304; liberalization and, 328–29, 330
Azariadis, Costas, 206n11

Balladur, Édouard, 239, 240
banking institutions: deregulation and, 269; industrialization's link to, 175, 250; investment by and through, 248, 261, 281–82; nationalization and, 243, 245–46, 287, 300n89, 325; privatization of, 267; savings in, 111, 113, 311; state control of, 119, 120, 121, 149–50, 152, 176, 229. *See also* credit rationing; interest rates
Baran, Paul, 5, 182, 320
Bardhan, Pranab, 314, 332–33
Barshay, Andrew, 74n39
Barshefsky, Charlene, 30

Cornell Studies in Political Economy

A SERIES EDITED BY
PETER J. KATZENSTEIN